An Introduction
to the Italian Economy

An Introduction
to the Italian Economy

Kevin Allen & Andrew Stevenson

GLASGOW SOCIAL & ECONOMIC RESEARCH STUDIES 1

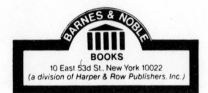

BOOKS
10 East 53d St., New York 10022
(a division of Harper & Row Publishers, Inc.)

First published in the U.K. 1974 by Martin Robertson & Co. Ltd., London.

Published in the U.S.A. 1975 by Harper & Row Publishers, Inc., Barnes & Noble Import Division.

ISBN   06   490156   4

Printed in Britain at The Pitman Press, Bath

Contents

Preface   ix

Authors' Notes   x

CHAPTER 1 **An Introduction and Overview**   1
1.1 Take-off; 1.2 War, Fascism and war again; 1.3 The
postwar recovery; 1.4 Recovered but still poor; 1.5 Economic success and structural change; 1.6 Italy: a case of
easy growth? 1.7 Rapid economic growth in spite of . . .
1.8 In spite of rapid economic growth . . . 1.9 The future

CHAPTER 2 **Economic Growth**   48
2.1 1950–1963; 2.2 1964–1972

CHAPTER 3 **The Balance of Payments**   72
3.1 Early postwar developments; 3.2 The current account;
3.3 The capital account; 3.4 Conclusions

CHAPTER 4 **Labour Markets, Labour Costs and Industrial Relations**   104
4.1 The changing employment structure; 4.2 The tightening
labour markets; 4.3 Wages, earnings and labour costs;
4.4 Labour market dualism; 4.5 Industrial relations and
collective bargaining

CHAPTER 5 **The Short-Term Management of the Economy**   145
5.1 The budgetary system and fiscal policy; 5.2 The financial
system and monetary policy; 5.3 Conclusions

CHAPTER 6 **The South: Problems and Policies**   176
6.1 The nature of the problem; 6.2 The causes of the
problem; 6.3 Southern development policy; 6.4 The results
of southern policy; 6.5 Conclusions

CHAPTER 7 **The State Holding Sector and its Role in Italian
Development**   217
7.1 IRI; 7.2 ENI; 7.3 Organisational structure and control;
7.4 Finance; 7.5 Efficiency and performance; 7.6 Southern
development and other roles

Appendix: Postwar Political Developments   267

A Postscript   284

Index   289

v

Tables

1.1   Italian development, 1861–1913.
1.2   The Italian economy, 1938–1950.
1.3   Major indicators of Italian economic growth, 1951–1971.
1.4   Italian standard of living relative to other countries, 1971.
1.5   Average numbers employed per industrial establishment in Italy.
2.1   Annual average growth rates of real GDP, 1950–1970.
2.2   Standard deviation and co-efficient of variation of growth rates, 1951–1968.
2.3   Italian economic growth, 1951–1972: main indicators.
2.4   Structure of aggregate demand in Italy.
2.5   Growth of exports and gross domestic product in ten countries.
2.6   Exports, value-added and productivity in Italian manufacturing industries, 1951–1963.
2.7   Gross profits in 134 Italian manufacturing firms, 1963–1972.
3.1   Intra-European trade liberalisation, 1956.
3.2   Italian balance of payments on current account and basic balance, 1950–1972.
3.3   Export growth in volume terms in ten countries, 1950–1972.
3.4   Changing composition of Italian exports, 1952–1971.
3.5   Geographic distribution of Italian exports, 1951–1970.
3.6   Average annual percentage change in unit values of manufactured exports: an international comparison.
3.7   Analysis of changes in Italy's exports, 1955–1964.
3.8   Commodity composition of Italian foreign trade, 1951–1972.
3.9   Average annual balance on current items in the Italian balance of payments, 1950–1972.
3.10   Italian earnings from tourism, emigrants' remittances, and workers' earnings abroad, 1950–1972.
3.11   Italian balance of payments on capital account, 1950–1972.
4.1   Employment in Italy by sector, 1951–1971.
4.2   The composition of Italian total employment, 1951–1971.
4.3   Italian unemployment, 1954–1971.
4.4   Italian net emigration, 1871–1971.
4.5   Italian strike activity, 1951–1971.
4.6   Days lost through strikes per 1000 people employed: an international comparison.
4.7   Annual percentage changes in Italian minimum contractual wages, cost of living and labour productivity.
4.8   Hourly and monthly manufacturing earnings in Italy, 1970.
4.9   Italian labour costs and productivity: annual growth per employee unit, 1951–1971.
4.10   Italian manufacturing work force by size of establishment.
5.1   Individual taxes as a percentage of total taxation in fourteen countries, 1968–1972.
5.2   Principal categories of public administration expenditure in Italy, 1951–1969.
5.3   Time profile of selected central government expenditure.
5.4   Burden on state budget of interest subsidies.
5.5   Sources of finance for gross investment of 376 Italian companies in the private sector, 1964–1971.
5.6   Creation of monetary base in Italy, 1958–1971.
6.1   Indicators of the southern problem.
6.2   Trends in activity rates: North and South.
6.3   Net emigration: North and South, 1871–1971.

6.4 Economic structure in South and North, 1969.
6.5 Value-added per labour unit employed in manufacturing: North and South, 1969.
6.6 Rates of natural population change: North and South.
6.7 Employment trends in North and South.
6.8 Gross regional expenditure: North and South.
7.1 State holding sector: sources of finance, 1956–1970.
7.2 Value-added per employee: state holding sector v. Italian manufacturing in general, 1967.
7.3 IRI and ENI: financial position and performance: annual averages, 1968–1970.
7.4 Financial position and performance: ENI group v. other Italian companies.

Preface

The principal objective of this book is to describe and analyse the main features and issues of the Italian economy and its development over the postwar period. Apart from one or two notable exceptions, very few up-to-date economic studies of Italy exist in English. And yet the Italian economy is interesting, not only in its own right or because it is an important member of the EEC, but also because it still remains a cross between a developed and an undeveloped country. In consequence, Italian development in the postwar period has lessons for nations at all stages of development. For underdeveloped countries, its rapid growth and the results of not catering for its consequences, and particularly the problems of evolving appropriate legislative and executive systems, are instructive, as are the difficulties of eradicating dualism at late stages of development. But Italy has also introduced systems and policies that are relevant to developed countries – its uses of the state holding sector and its measures for regional development are striking examples.

Wherever possible the book relates Italian problems and policies to those in other countries, and particularly the United Kingdom. At the same time we have tried continually to caution the reader against the pitfalls of 'blind' international comparisons. Italian statistics are frequently collected on a different basis from other countries and, even when standardised, can be interpreted meaningfully only when set in a broader economic context. The relative success of southern development policy cannot, for example, be understood without a knowledge of the state holding sector, while the relatively low levels of unemployment can be appreciated only with a knowledge of the unemployment benefit system and other features of the labour market. Without doubt, following Britain's entry into the EEC, attempts at inter-European comparisons will become more common. If this book does little more than provide an Italian economic context for more meaningful international comparisons it will have fulfilled a useful role.

The book is in seven chapters. Chapter 1 is an overview, introducing the key features and issues of the economy covered in subsequent chapters, and is aimed at setting a broader economic and historical context. Chapter 2 analyses the process of economic growth in postwar Italy and the explanations for its pace and stability, as well as assessing future prospects. Chapter 3 examines Italy's postwar success in respect of the balance of payments, the factors on which this success has been based and the consequences for overall Italian growth and development. Chapter 4 is concerned with postwar changes in respect of labour markets and employment structure, and how these have affected labour costs and dualism, as well as providing an analysis of the changing pattern of industrial relations. Chapter 5 examines in detail Italian monetary and fiscal policy, drawing out how shortcomings in this field have affected overall economic performance. Chapter 6 is devoted to one of Italy's most serious and long-standing problems – the South. It provides an analysis of the nature and causes of the problem and a critique of southern policy. Chapter 7 is a detailed survey of the state holding sector, with an assessment of its contribution to Italian development. Chapter 7 is followed by a brief appendix on postwar political developments. This has no pretentions of being comprehensive but is aimed primarily at providing a political context for the economic issues discussed in the preceding chapters. The greater part of the book was completed in late 1973. During 1973 and 1974 a number of major changes took place in the Italian economy. We have therefore provided a brief postscript to the book outlining the main economic events of 1973 and the first half of 1974 and assessing their significance for the future.

It is said that an economics book was once reviewed with the words, 'There is much in this book which is true, there is much in this book which is new, the unfortunate thing is that that which is new is not true and that which is true is not new'. In writing this book we have been fortunate in having the co-operation of a large number of people. Without their help, advice and interest the contents of this book would undoubtedly have been less true and substantially less new. Many of these people have not only been unstinting with their time and in providing material; a number have also been kind enough to read and comment on earlier drafts. We would like in particular to thank Dr Marsan, Dr Brunelli and Dr del Canuto of IRI; Dr Colitti of ENI; Dr Ganella and Dr Frassenetti of the Ministry of State Holdings; Dr Prisinzano of the Cassa per il Mezzogiorno; Dr Majnoni of INEA; Dr Russolillo of ISPE; Professor Lafranconi and Dr Grossetti of INPS; Professor dell'Angelo, Dr Cafiero, Dr Busca and Dr and Mrs Cagliozzi of Svimez; Dr Ciampi, Dr Ciampicalli, Dr Tresoldi, Dr Santini, Dr Morcaldo and Dr Fazio of the research department at the Bank of Italy; and Dr Russo of the University of Rome. We are indebted to Mr Paul Littlewood of Glasgow University for his collaboration in the preparation of the political appendix. We should also like to thank Professor Hunter and Professor Wilson of the University of Glasgow for their constant encouragement and support.

The book is aimed primarily at economists with no special knowledge of the Italian economy. We are, therefore, especially grateful to Mr Douglas Yuill of the University of Glasgow who, being in this position, kindly read and commented upon all the chapters when they were in draft. Others, similarly placed, read individual chapters and we would particularly like to thank Dr Sirc, Mr Skinner, Mr Moody and Mr Smith, all of the University of Glasgow, and Mr Upson of the Department of Trade and Industry in Glasgow. Although the book has been written primarily for economists we have tried to make it intelligible for non-economists, and would like to thank Mr Spooner of the Department of Geography at the University of Hull for reading a number of the chapters with this criterion in mind.

The greater part of the typing for the book was done by Miss Christine Kerr and Miss Frances Stevenson. Only those familiar with our hand-writing will appreciate the enormity of their task.

We want also to thank our publishers, and especially David Martin, who has shown enormous patience and understanding.

Finally, but most important, we want to thank the 3 K's who have had to tolerate a lot during the writing of this book.

Because many of the people whose help we have acknowledged work for government or semi-government bodies, it is especially important to stress that errors of fact or judgement that remain in this book are entirely our responsibility.

K.J.A.
A.A.S.

Authors' Notes

Milliard: the term milliard means one thousand million.

Footnotes: in the interests of economy these have been placed at the end of chapters rather than at the base of the page. We have tried to reduce the inconvenience of this for the reader by keeping textual notes to a minimum. Any such notes are marked with an asterisk after the footnote number.

Labour units: a continuing problem in Italian labour market analysis is the large number of marginal units – people working for less than thirty-three hours per week. For a number of purposes it is advisable to reduce these to labour units. The standard Italian practice, and one that we have followed, is to do this by assuming that they represent one-third of a full-time worker. Thus, labour units are full-time workers plus one-third of the marginal workers.

Abbreviations: the titles of most Italian institutions are virtually descriptions of their functions and roles. Inevitably these titles get abbreviated. In this book, the first time an abbreviation is used, its full title is given. All abbreviations are listed in the index.

Exchange rates: unless otherwise stated, the exchange rate used is that which was current during the particular period under discussion. In round terms, the lira/sterling exchange rate from 1950 to 1967 was 1750, and 1500 from then onwards.

Population: census population figures used in this book are generally for 'resident' population, i.e. resident at the time of the census. Where 'present' population figures are supplied a note is made to this effect.

CHAPTER 1

An Introduction
and Overview

*Well, this bit which I am writing, called Introduction, is really
the er-h'r'm of the book, and I have put it in, partly so as not to
take you by surprise, and partly because I can't do without it
now. There are some very clever writers who say that it is quite
easy not have an er-h'r'm, but I don't agree with them. I think
it is much easier not to have all the rest of the book. (A. A.
Milne, Now We Are Six)*

THE purpose of this chapter is basically threefold. First, it is designed to
set Italy's postwar economic development within an historical perspective,
by means of a brief survey of Italian economic history since unification.
Secondly, it is aimed at underlining the basic theme of the book as a
whole – that Italy's rapid postwar growth has not been accompanied by
'economic development', and that in terms of economic structure and
social infrastructure, Italy is still largely 'underdeveloped'. The chapters
that follow this introduction deal with specific key features and issues of
the Italian economy. A third purpose of this chapter is, therefore, to
introduce these topics, show how they are interrelated and set them in a
broader context. Since the structure of the chapter is broadly chrono-
logical, we start with a brief summary of Italian economic development
from unification to the First World War, a period during which Italy
'took-off', in Rostovian terms.

1.1   Take-off

Italian take-off, which occurred between the mid-1890s and 1913, was
late by European standards and followed a period since unification during
which economic growth had been pitifully slow. National income at
constant prices grew by slightly less than one per cent per annum between
1861–65 and 1891–95.[1] The economy was characterised in this period by
a low rate of investment and a virtually stagnant level of international
trade. The vicious circle of low income and low levels of investment is a

1

general feature of the pre-take-off period, making it a slow and often long drawn out process. But there can be little doubt that in Italy's case the process was even more lengthy and slow as a consequence of European and world economic conditions in the last three decades of the nineteenth century. This was the so-called great world depression, which lasted from the early 1870s to the mid-1880s, when industrialised countries had excess productive capacity combined with slowly growing markets, leading in some instances to state-subsidised 'dumping' abroad. Moreover, it was also a period when great amounts of wheat from the United States and Russia were reaching western Europe and forcing prices down. A common response by a number of European countries was to seek new markets through colonial expansion, but Italy's few attempts at colonialism were not highly successful, and market outlets in this direction were consequently limited. In these generally depressed and highly competitive conditions it was difficult for any country to secure rapid growth, and particularly so for a relatively underdeveloped country like Italy, with low levels of industrialisation, much of which was of a poorly capitalised and inefficient artisan character, and with an agriculture that, especially in the South, was over-populated and had suffered from centuries of neglect.

Italy's economic performance between unification and the last decade of the century was not improved by government economic policy. At unification the new state adopted the very low Sardinian tariff and this laid the economy wide open to the harsh international competition mentioned above; and when in 1888 (after mild tariff increases in 1878) tariffs were raised, the increases were so great, especially for iron, steel and textiles, that they provoked retaliation from a number of other countries, France in particular. Indeed, between 1888 and 1898 there was a 'tariff war' between France and Italy. This had particularly damaging results for Italian agricultural exports, especially those from the South. Through its effects on agriculture the tariff war reduced the credit activities of the major banks, who were heavily dependent on agriculture, and this in turn had deleterious effects on industrial expansion. Apart from these schizophrenic and disastrous tariff policies, the only other major government intervention aimed at economic development were subsidies, given from the mid-1880s for steel and shipbuilding, as well as other sectors more directly tied to military expansion.[2]

Although Italian growth was slow between unification and the 1890s a number of changes were taking place in the economic structure which provided a basis for take-off. By 1890 the transport system was well developed and the rail network was virtually complete, while the protectionist policies of the 1880s had encouraged the growth of a number of basic industries (though often to the detriment of other, dependent, industries, and engineering in particular). However, although the foundations for take-off had been laid, a catalyst was needed if these were to be exploited. To a large extent this was provided by the ending of the great world depression at the turn of the century and the subsequent upsurge in economic activity both in Europe and the United States, giving encour- aging foreign market opportunities for Italy. In addition, rapid industrial expansion was both allowed and stimulated by the development in Italy of German banking techniques during the early 1890s. 'It is possible to surmise that the upsurge of 1896–1908 was largely rendered possible by the importation of the great economic innovation of German banking in its most developed and mature form. As in Germany, not only capital but a great deal of entrepreneural guidance was channelled to the nascent and expanding industrial enterprises'.[3]

Protected to some degree at home, with rapidly growing markets abroad, and with the development of a sophisticated and promotional banking system, the Italians enjoyed a period of very rapid industrial growth, starting in the mid-1890s and accelerating after the turn of the century. This great expansion, relative to the first three decades after unification, is shown in table 1.1.

Table 1.1   Italian Development, 1861 – 1913
(milliard lire at 1938 prices, annual averages)

	Gross domestic product	Exports	Imports	Gross invest- ment	Gross product at factor cost		Popu- lation
					Agri- culture	Manu- facturing	
							('000)
1861–65	54.3	4.3	5.8	4.1	23.3	8.0	26,125
1891–95	66.9	7.6	7.1	5.7	26.5	10.9	31,995
1896–1900	70.2	9.1	8.4	6.7	27.1	12.1	32,989
1901–05	80.0	11.4	11.0	11.8	31.4	14.9	34,059
1906–13	94.8	13.9	16.8	15.7	34.5	20.6	35,708

Source: Calculated from data in P. Ercolani 'Documentazione Statistica di Base' in G. Fuà (ed.) *Lo Sviluppo Economico in Italia* vol. III Milan: Franco Angeli (1969).

Gross investment, which averaged some 8.8 per cent of gross domestic product (GDP) over the period 1861–95, rose to 14.5 per cent in 1896– 1913; exports grew from 10.7 per cent of GDP to 14.3 per cent, while GDP itself rose by 45.0 per cent between 1896 and 1913. In absolute terms, over the seventeen years 1896–1913 GDP increased by nearly twice as much as during the previous three and a half decades. Manufac- turing output, as table 1.1 shows, expanded at an enormous rate, and particularly after 1905.

However, although the years between 1896 and 1913 were years of rapid growth for Italy, and represent to most observers her take-off period, and although the growth rate was high by earlier standards, it was somewhat disappointing by international standards. Industrial growth, for example, between 1885–94 and 1906–13 was below that of Germany, Russia and Sweden. Although slightly faster than France and about double that of the United Kingdom, the latter had long since enjoyed her take-off.[4]

One might, perhaps, have expected that a late-comer to industrialisation would enjoy very rapid growth. It is not in fact clear why Italy's was relatively low. The eminent economic historian, Gerschenkron, suggests three possible explanations. First, unlike in Germany and Russia, government assistance and subsidisation was very limited and primarily involved tariff protection for the basic sectors, and particularly iron and steel – policies that were 'likely to retard rather than promote [industrial] development'.[5] Secondly, the railway system was virtually complete by the time of take-off. 'The failure of the industrial "push" to coincide with a period of "railway fever" with its specific stimulation to industrial activity may well have kept the rate of industrial growth below what it would have been, had the Russian situation reproduced itself in Italy'.[6] Thirdly, the political situation 'was not propitious to quiet economic growth. The disastrous harvest of 1897, coupled with the government's prolonged hesitation to suspend or to reduce the wheat duties, led in the course of the *anno terribile* – 1898 – to unrest and disorders in several regions followed by two years of repressive policies . . .'[7] The years 1901–13 were characterised by more liberal policies and, not unrelated, by large numbers of strikes.

Thus, Italian take-off was late by most standards, and less powerful. It was also timed such that events both in Europe and Italy did not allow its full exploitation until after the Second World War.

1.2 War, Fascism and war again

The period 1914–45 was a political and economic disaster for Italy. It represented, lying as it did between take-off and the rapid economic growth of the 1950s and 1960s, 'a great temporal parenthesis'.[8]

The First World War inflicted great costs on Italy, with resources that could have been devoted to economic growth being wasted in the war effort. It would, of course, be wrong to suggest that all the effects of the war were negative. Industry, at least for the first two years, benefited from the rapid growth in demand and high profits, features that allowed and encouraged technical innovation, economies of scale and the development of new products. A number of new sectors, such as chemicals, grew rapidly and many firms which were later to become Italian industrial

giants, e.g. Fiat, owe their early development to the pressures and opportunities of First World War.

The immediate postwar period saw Italy in considerable turmoil. A
number of firms that had benefited from the war found themselves unable
to convert to peacetime products and consequently collapsed, threatening
the banking system, which held substantial industrial investments, in the
process. The failure of large armament firms such as Ilva and Ansaldo,
which brought down the Banca Italiana di Sconto, is an example of this
point. In general, industry found conversion difficult and manufacturing
output did not get back to prewar levels until 1922. Unemployment was
high, and the economy was unable to absorb the demobilised troops; land
reforms promised during the war to urge on a tired population came to
little; and inflation was rife. The costs and consequences of the war were
serious and 'the fruits of victory paid for by the lives of 600,000 soldiers
were few'.[9] Most sections of the population were disillusioned and bitter,
and the situation was an ideal breeding ground for extremists, not least
because the political system was weak with governments being formed
and disbanded at a bewildering rate. Strike activity, much of it politically
motivated, was widespread while a number of factories and estates were
occupied by workers. Certainly during the late summer of 1920 a left-
wing revolution seemed distinctly possible and, in the context of the
period, such an event would not have been remarkable. The left-wing
leaders were, however, ill-prepared, being 'more at home in the cafés
and in the parliamentary halls than in the firing line'.[10]

The chaos of the immediate postwar period almost inevitably brought
forth a demand for strong government, a demand that the existing
political parties were unable to meet. No party had an absolute majority
in Parliament, while a coalition between the newly created Catholic
Partito Populare (later Christian Democrats) and the Socialists appeared
impossible, the former being uncertain about the objectives and morality
of the latter, who in turn were unclear about their proper goals and way
to power – revolution or democracy. For their part, the right-wing, conservative parties were unsure of the seemingly reformist *Partito Populare*.
Conditions were ideal for the Fascists who, in the immediate postwar
period, had rapidly expanded their following, initially making their plat-
form Italy's poor returns at the peace conference table but soon, seeing
the opportunities, fighting on the basis of the need to save Italy from
communism. The first Fascist government, following the 'March on
Rome', was formed in late 1922, by which time the economy had recovered its prewar level and was, indeed, buoyant. This benefited the
Fascists who, despite belated attempts by the *Partito Populare* and the
Socialists to unite, got 65 per cent of the vote in the 1924 elections. These
were to be the last democratic elections in interwar Italy. Non-Fascist
parties were soon to be suppressed and/or forced into exile. Slowly, but

purposefully, Italy became a one-party state, as the trade unions and other potential opposition were emasculated.

Between 1922 and 1925 the economy showed signs of recovering its prewar dynamism. However, the second half of the 1920s saw the beginnings of radical Fascist policies which, combined later with the world depression, put a stop to these promising trends. The 'Battle for Grain' (to secure self-sufficiency) was announced in 1925 and, in an attempt to create a strong currency, the lira was upvalued in 1926. From then until 1938 a series of measures and policies based more on the pillars of autarky and nationalism than economics, and encouraged by international economic difficulties, were introduced. Substantial tariffs and quotas were levied to protect industry and agriculture, and to secure independence in key sectors. The Fascists, trapped by their mania for a strong lira, held off an economically desirable devaluation until 1936. The desire for a self-sufficient agriculture saw measures introduced to hold the agricultural population in the rural areas and to stop migration into the towns through a stringent permit system. State expenditure rose rapidly during the 1930s but was primarily (more than 50 per cent) on defence and colonial development.[11] Given the autarkic features of the regime, overseas trade inevitably became a less important component of the economy, less important in the 1930s than at any time since unification.[12] Moreover, the balance of payments ran serious deficits and gold reserves fell substantially – by some 74 per cent between 1927 and 1939.[13] In 1936 the balance of trade, largely because of poor wheat and olive harvests, suffered a deficit that was greater than total visible exports. In October 1936 the 'strong lira' policy was dropped and the lira devalued, but the situation in 1937 was hardly less desperate, and indeed had the impression of near collapse when the government started to sell arms – 'selling them to any country, friendly or otherwise, that could pay for them in hard currency'.[14]

Many of the Fascist policies not only damaged the economy during the interwar period itself but also gave rise to deleterious consequences in the long term. Although the battle for grain, 'to free the Italian people from the slavery of foreign bread', involved some policies that were laudable, such as the development of selected seeds, increased use of tractors and other machinery (and in some areas there was indeed a rapid rise in the productivity of cereal production), in the South it resulted in more land, often afforested, being given to grain. The destruction of the forests worsened the South's long-standing erosion problem. The Fascist policies to halt rural depopulation merely aggravated the over-population of southern agriculture, a problem which was further exacerbated by the 'battle of births', aimed at correcting the falling birth rate and founded on the belief that 'the indispensable basis for political power is a numerous, healthy and virile population'.[15] The difficulties of resolving the southern problem after the Second World War were made all the greater by these policies.

It would be wrong to paint a completely negative picture of Fascist economic and development policy. Motorways were built and the transport system was generally improved, social services were extended, while land reclamation, accompanied by massive publicity, was pursued in a big way. 'At constant prices, the expenditure for reclamation works have been over three times as large as those sustained by all the previous administrations since 1870.'[16] In some respects, Mussolini's aim 'to translate other people's pious and worthy intentions into concrete achievement'[17] was secured.

The overall performance of the economy during the Fascist period was, however, poor, with *per capita* national income growing by only 1.5 per cent per annum.[18] Even these slight gains were swept away by war – war to Mussolini was not only inevitable but necessary. 'Before everything, Fascism believes neither in the possibility nor in the utility of perpetual peace . . . Only war brings all human energies to a maximum tension and imprints a mark of nobility upon the people who have the virtue to face it.'[19] In part, such sentiments were a reflection of Mussolini as a man, 'an impressionable second rate journalist of superficial brilliance',[20] supported by the comic-sounding, though powerful, Ministry of Propaganda (Minculpop), rather than a clear statement of objectives. By the second half of the 1930s, however, objectives and ambitions were becoming dangerously confused. Mussolini's infatuation with Germany, combined with greed and confusion, finally led Italy into a war for which she was woefully ill-prepared. The eight million bayonets which could, it was claimed, be mustered turned out to be 1.6 million at mobilisation in 1940, and not even all these men could be equipped. The army was one-third of a million rifles short and only 20 per cent of divisions could be put in uniforms. The equipment available was poor and inappropriate for the type of war that was to be waged. The infantry rifle was an 1891 model, the tanks were light, and tracked vehicles generally were in short supply.[21]

Even as early as 1941, Mussolini was disenchanted and depressed. Military defeat followed military defeat. On the home front foodstuffs were rationed and in short supply. The calorific content of Italian food rations was about the same as in Poland, and about half the German level. Price controls slowly started to break down, and collapsed in 1943 when the Allies invaded Italy and began to move north. Inflation reached serious proportions after 1943, fuelled by widespread hoarding and speculation, high government expenditure (five times receipts by 1944)[22] and the Allied injection of money into the system. The retail price index stood at 273 in 1943 (as against 100 in 1938) and rose to 1215 in 1944 and 2392 in 1945.

Italy was a major battleground throughout the war with the Allies wreaking havoc as they moved up the peninsula and the Germans destroying materials and property as they retreated. Often, what was not lost in this fashion was sabotaged by partisans, 'evacuated' to Germany or requisitioned by the Allies. Agricultural livestock was reduced to 75 per cent of the prewar level, much agricultural equipment was destroyed, and agricultural productive capacity as a whole was cut by 40 per cent.[23] Even though the damage to industrial plant was far less serious than initially feared and as we shall see in chapter 6 largely concentrated in the South, over all some 20 per cent was destroyed or lost while much of what survived was suffering from heavy wear and tear and/or was obsolete. As a result of these factors, combined with grave shortages of materials and semi-finished inputs, industrial output in 1945 was some 25 per cent of the 1941 level, and just about equal to that of 1884.[24] The transport system was also very badly damaged by the war. On the railways one-quarter of track had been destroyed, one-third of the bridges and 60 per cent of wagons and trucks. Merchant shipping capacity was reduced to one-sixth of its wartime peak and port facilities were almost decimated. Some 35 per cent of national roads and 90 per cent of lorries were destroyed or damaged.

The destruction and disruption of war had wiped out all the economic gains secured during the Fascist period and indeed for many years prior to that. In 1945 real income per head was equal to some 49 per cent of the 1938 level and below that at unification.[25] Moreover, large-scale demobilisation, the inflow of refugees from lost Italian territories and the virtually complete curb on emigration resulted in large-scale unemployment (over two million). At the end of 1945 Italy was close to starvation with a daily consumption of calories per head of 1737 as against 2652 in 1936–40.[26] The situation in 1945 was indeed desperate, 'with nine million inhabitants on the verge of starvation, with an income per head below that of 1914, with a vast building of moral and physical goods to accomplish patiently, with an industrial skeleton built up in the deceptive hot house of autarky, with international relations to relink in uncompetitive conditions, with gigantic unresolved problems of poverty'.[27]

1.3 The postwar recovery

The general economic and political conditions of Italy in the immediate postwar period were not conducive to a rapid recovery.[28] The wartime inflation continued and indeed intensified, becoming particularly acute in 1947, and was only brought under control in 1948 (largely through monetary policy as we shall see in chapter 5), by which time the index of retail prices, taking 1938 as 100, was at 4844. Raw materials such as coal, as well as vital inputs like iron and steel, were in desperately short supply and represented a further impediment to industrial recovery, while shortages of foreign currency curtailed resort to imports. On the agricultural front the recovery of output was set back by bad weather and poor harvests, particularly in 1947. The political situation was confused and unstable.

In spite of these problems, and estimates by some observers that recovery would take a decade or so,[29] the economy had regained its prewar strength by the late 1940s. Manufacturing industry was virtually back to 1938 levels of output by 1948, agriculture by 1950, and *per capita* income by the same year. Various indicators of this economic revival are shown in table 1.2.

Table 1.2   The Italian economy, 1938–1950
(milliard lire, 1938 prices)

	Cost of living (1938 = 100)	GDP per head (1938 = 100)	Gross product at factor cost		Gross investment	Exports	Imports
			Agriculture	Manufacturing			
1938	100.0	100.0	40.1	37.4	28.7	11.6	12.3
1939	104.4	104.8	42.1	40.8	34.1	10.6	10.9
1940	121.9	99.1	39.7	41.2	25.9	8.8	10.9
1941	141.0	96.6	38.3	38.5	23.5	0.2	8.2
1942	163.0	94.9	34.1	33.3	18.2	8.0	7.9
1943	273.3	90.0	29.6	25.8	11.2	7.8	8.9
1944	1214.5	70.5	28.6	15.7	8.0	1.6	6.8
1945	2392.0	52.9	27.0	10.9	6.1	0.5	7.2
1946	2823.0	76.5	33.5	26.6	24.7	5.3	10.3
1947	4575.0	85.2	35.1	34.0	37.1	9.4	21.6
1948	4844.0	89.1	36.4	36.3	26.1	14.9	19.2
1949	4915.0	92.3	38.4	40.0	27.9	16.3	19.6
1950	4849.0	97.7	39.8	46.0	31.9	18.4	21.2

Sources: P. Ercolani 'Documentazione Statistica di Base' in G. Fuà (ed.) *Lo Sviluppo Economico in Italia* vol. III Milan: Franco Angeli (1969). The cost of living figures are from ISTAT *Sommario di Statistiche Storiche dell' Italia 1861–1965* (Rome, 1968).

In order to understand the speed with which the economy recovered from the disastrous situation of 1945, it is important to appreciate that the abysmally low level of economic activity and standard of living at that time was partly a consequence simply of the disorganisation that inevitably accompanied the ending of hostilities, combined with the fact that key sections of the infrastructure system had been destroyed or were inoperative. This was particularly true of the transport system where, for example, a vital bridge destroyed during the fighting could cause enormous disruption. Often this type of impediment could be corrected with relatively little effort and investment. But in addition the recovery was assisted, and some would argue made possible, by generous aid from the Allies, various international bodies, and the United States in particular. Aid had been given to Italy by these groups since 1943 by way of grants, loans at favourable interest and, during the war itself, foodstuffs and materials. Between 1943 and April 1948 Italy received outside aid to the value of 2230 million dollars, of which some 70 per cent was in the form of non-repayable grants.[30] The greater part of this aid (some two-thirds) was spent on imported food and fuel. The former was vital to feed a near-starving population until Italian agriculture could recover its prewar strength; the latter was an important component of industrial recovery. Industrial output soon after the end of the war was, in fact, well below what could be explained by the destruction of industrial plant, and much of this disparity was a consequence of the shortage of vital materials, fuel in particular. Foreign aid allowed fuel to be imported at a time when Italy's own balance of payments situation, exports being understandably low, was not sufficiently strong to allow such imports on a large scale. American aid to Italy continued after 1948, and indeed intensified when the first payments under the Marshall Plan were made in April 1948. Few would dispute that, without Marshall Aid, the Italian recovery (and indeed European recovery in general) would have been much more protracted. In the three years to 1951 Europe received 11,314 million dollars, of which Italy got 11.4 per cent – 1310 million dollars in total, and mostly in the form of grants. This aid was crucial to the Italian recovery, particularly in allowing essential commodities to be purchased abroad. In the first year, Italy's receipts under the Marshall Plan were equal to some 35 per cent of her total imports, in the second year 29 per cent and in the third 13.3 per cent.

By 1950, then, the Italian economy had recovered its prewar position. Not only had the prewar levels of income per head, industrial and agricultural output been attained, but plans and policies aimed at structural change in agriculture and industry, southern development and the revitalisation of basic industries like steel were being introduced. Within the space of five years Italy had come through a period of desperate economic conditions; amazingly, and in spite of political instability and turmoil, without a revolution. It is a moot point whether this was primarily a result of government policy, the inadequacies of the revolutionary forces, or the fact that 'Italy is a good country for revolutionaries but a poor one for revolutions'.[31]

1.4 Recovered but still poor

Although Italy had largely recovered from the war by 1950, it was still
a very poor and backward country. Some 44 per cent of the labour force ✓
was employed in agriculture, much of which was on an uneconomic scale,
with the average size of farm in 1951 being very small and often fragmented in non-contiguous pieces. Large proportions of agricultural land
were in mountain or hill areas, poorly irrigated and often suffering from
serious erosion. Inevitably, the sector was characterised by substantial
amounts of underemployment – as high as 34 per cent.[32] Agriculture
was, in many ways, 'a refuge sector for that part of the population which
could not find other outlets'.[33] In this environment modern agricultural
techniques were neither financially nor technically feasible, and agricultural productivity was consequently low. Despite the fact that it held
44 per cent of the labour force, agriculture accounted for a mere 23 per
cent of GNP.

But much of industry was also backward and on a small scale. In 1951
the average manufacturing establishment employed fewer than six people,
27 per cent of the manufacturing labour force was in establishments employing five or fewer people, and over 90 per cent of establishments had a
work force of fewer than five.[34] The steel industry was technologically
backward while industries such as chemicals and vehicles were of an
inadequate size relative to their counterparts in more advanced countries.
Although no accurate estimates are available, unemployment in Italy
was very high – certainly well above 10 per cent.

High unemployment and a predominance of inefficient and low-
productivity agriculture and industry in the economic structure inevitably
meant a low level of income per head – some 290 dollars in 1950, and not
much above the 200 dollars by which, 'according to a United Nations
convention, a country was considered as underdeveloped'.[35] A number of
other features of the Italian economy reflected its low income. Infant
mortality, for example, (excluding still births) in 1950 was 63.8 per
thousand live births, as against 31.4 in the United Kingdom and 29.2 in
the United States.[36] Illiteracy, using as a measure that part of the population which could not read and was aged more than six years, was in
1951 some 12.9 per cent.[37] Although concentrated in the higher age
groups (a rate of 35 per cent was recorded for those aged 65 and above),
the illiteracy rate was nevertheless as high as 7.6 per cent in the 18-25
age group, a reflection of poor and inadequate schooling. In 1951 the
school leaving age was 13; being raised only in 1963 to the current
level of 14. Teaching was poor, schools were overcrowded and absenteeism rife. In 1952–53, only about three-quarters of 11-year-olds attended
school, half the 12-year-olds and a third of the 13-year-olds.[38] Housing
conditions were also very poor. The 1951 census showed that of Italy's

10.8 million houses, only 1.2 million had a bath, 4.1 million had running drinking water within the house and 4.7 million had an internal lavatory.[39] A parliamentary inquiry into poverty and unemployment in 1952–53 revealed that some '232,000 families lived in cellars, attics or warehouses; 92,000 in caves or shacks; and that the major part of the homes declared habitable were devoid of a minimum of hygienic installations'.[40] In the same report, '11.7 per cent of Italian families were declared to be in a condition of utter destitution and almost as many to be needy, while 65.7 per cent were living in "modest" conditions'.[41]

But in the early 1950s Italy was not only very poor by European standards; it was also a spatially dualistic economy, with conditions in the South being substantially inferior to those in the North. As we shall see in detail in chapter 6, the South is a long-standing problem, but at the start of the 1950s the North–South differential was wider than it had ever been – a consequence of continuingly inadequate regional policies and the autarkism and nationalism of Fascism, as well as the Second World War, during which enormous damage was inflicted on the South. The southern economic structure was much more heavily weighted with agriculture – 57 per cent of the labour force in 1951 was employed in this sector as against 38 per cent in the North. Southern farms were smaller and the land was intrinsically poorer. Moreover, erosion was a major problem and water was in scarce supply. Agricultural underemployment in 1951 was about 43 per cent, as against 28 per cent in the North.[42] Agricultural value-added per person employed was some 75 per cent of the northern level. Only 20 per cent of the southern labour force was employed in industry and a mere 13 per cent in manufacturing, as against 34 and 27 per cent respectively in the North. The South, with some 33 per cent of the national labour force, had only 22.5 and 19.5 per cent of the national industrial and manufacturing labour force respectively. More so than in the North, the industrial sector, was characterised by small, almost artisan, units and value-added per person employed was some 65 per cent of the northern level. Southern unemployment and underemployment was higher than in the North, and activity rates lower.

Given such conditions it was inevitable that southern expenditure per head was low – some 62 per cent of the northern level. Those features of Italian backwardness mentioned above such as illiteracy and housing showed themselves in a particularly acute form in the South. Around 20 per cent of southern males were illiterate as against less than 2 per cent in the north. Only 28 per cent of southern houses had internal running drinking water, 45 per cent had an internal lavatory and 4 per cent had a bath. The comparable figures for the North were 44, 43 and 15 per cent respectively. In all this comparison of the South with the North, it needs to be kept in mind that the north itself was poor by European standards.

1.5 Economic success and structural change

Over the period 1951–71 Italy experienced a very rapid rate of economic growth. If the term was not so abused one could say that she underwent an economic revolution. Some indicators of this growth are shown in table 1.3. The major and predominant feature of the economy over this period was the rapid growth of national income. This, as we shall see in detail in chapter 2, was very high as well as being stable, both by international and by prewar standards. A good indication of the rapidity of this growth is that income per head at constant prices increased more between 1951 and 1971 than over the whole period 1861–1950.

Table 1.3 Major indicators of Italian economic growth, 1951–71
(milliard lire, constant prices)

	1951	1971	1971 index (1951 = 100)
Gross national product (market prices)	15,816	45,094	285.1
Gross national product per head ('000 lire)	333.5	836.6	250.9
Exports (market prices)	1012	11,455	1131.5
Gross investment (market prices)	2649	8721	329.2
Value-added at factor cost:			
Agriculture	2892	4581	158.4
Industry (including construction)	4146	16,168	390.0
Manufacturing	2952	12,145	411.4
Value-added per labour unit* ('000 lire)			
Agriculture	433.2	1461.4	337.4
Industry (including construction)	942.7	2077.0	220.3
Manufacturing	709.2	2098.6	295.9

*For a definition of labour units see p. xii above.
Sources: ISTAT *Annuario di Contabilità Nazionale 1971* (Rome, 1972); ISTAT *Occupati Presenti in Italia 1951–1970* (Rome, 1971); ISTAT *Annuario Statistico Italiano 1972* (Rome, 1973).

The high rate of postwar growth has been associated with a number of other features and changes in the economy. Three are of particular importance: first, a generally high rate of investment; secondly, an impressive growth of exports; and thirdly, a substantial drop in the numbers unemployed and a great change in the employment structure.

Table 1.3 shows gross investment rising faster than GNP – from the internationally high level of 16.7 per cent of GNP in 1951 to 19.3 per cent in 1971. Even this understates the growth in that 1971, when the economy was depressed, was a year of low investment. Over the whole period 1951–71 gross investment averaged some 20 per cent of GNP. This high percentage reflected a number of factors, but of prime importance was the high level of reinvestment or self-financing, allowed in turn, particularly up to the mid-1960s, by weak unions and wage increases below those of productivity. As we shall see in chapter 2 the high level of investment, particularly since much of it was in productive plant and equipment, made a substantial contribution to Italian growth in the postwar period.

But conditions on the wages front not only allowed high levels of self-financed investment; they are also an important explanation of the competitiveness of Italian exports and their rapid growth, at a rate indeed which, as can be seen from table 1.3, was faster than GNP. The considerable liberalisation of world trade over the postwar period, of which Italy was in the forefront, and the creation of the EEC in 1958 (followed by the very swift dismantling of tariff barriers between the member countries) enabled this competitiveness to be exploited. The rapid growth of visible exports, combined with a strongly positive 'invisible' balance (in particular, high earnings from tourism and emigrants' remittances), generally gave Italy a surplus on the balance of payments on current account – in fifteen years over the twenty-one year period 1951–71. The balance on capital account was much more erratic, and particularly in the late 1960s, but over the period as a whole a surplus was achieved – a result of favourable foreign investment conditions in Italy, plus a rather poor Italian performance in terms of aid to underdeveloped countries.[43]* Overall, Italy's balance of payments performance was such as to allow her to build up substantial gold and foreign currency reserves. By 1971 these were worth 5700 million European units of account – slightly more than the UK reserves, and the fourth highest in Western Europe.[44] These reserves have enabled Italy to weather temporary fluctuations in the balance of payments without frequent need to resort to the stop–go policies (and consequences) that have bedevilled the United Kingdom economy. But the contribution of Italy's foreign trade performance to the country's rapid postwar growth has not only been permissive. For many observers this performance has been a major propulsive element; and, as we shall see in chapter 2, in many ways Italy is a good example of export-led growth.

A third major factor associated with Italy's rapid postwar growth was the absorption of large amounts of underemployed and unemployed labour in the first ten or fifteen years after the war, and the continuing and large-scale sectoral switching of labour – features that are covered in detail in chapter 4. The main form of the switching has been out of agriculture and, up to the mid-1960s, 'through the filter of construction',[45] into industry. In 1951 agriculture accounted for 43.9 per cent of the total labour force; this had fallen to 18.9 per cent by 1970 – an absolute decline of five million. This exodus tended to speed up during the 1960s when Italian labour markets in general tightened, with a quarter of a million people per annum leaving the sector.

The great movement of labour out of agriculture has been both a consequence and cause of the rapid economic growth. The presence of non-
agricultural job opportunities represented an encouragement for people
to leave the sector (though there have also been other, less economic,
factors at work) while, as we shall see in detail in chapter 2, the movement out of agriculture has itself contributed to overall national growth.
It has done this first because it involved a shift of labour from low to
higher productivity sectors, agricultural productivity being about a half
of that in industry. Secondly, it rid the sector of much of its marginal,
low-productivity labour and went some way towards enabling larger and
more viable farms to be created. Few would doubt that the massive postwar agricultural exodus has been an important factor in the very rapid
rise in agricultural productivity – at a rate which, as table 1.3 shows, has
been greater than for industry. But not all the results of this exodus have
been favourable for agriculture. 'On the one hand it has given rise to an
increase in productivity per worker in as far as it has liberated . . . the
notable surpluses of labour. On the other hand, however, it has created
a deterioration in the agricultural labour force, above all through the
ageing of it'[46] – the great majority of those leaving the sector were under
thirty years of age.[47] Moreover, the opportunities for the restructuring
of holdings which the exodus gave have been barely exploited – a consequence of the peasant instinct to hold on to his land, plus the lack of
appropriate government policies. Thirdly, the movement out of agriculture has contributed to national growth in so far as the sector has
acted as a labour reservoir, such as generally to ensure slack labour
markets. This in turn weakened the trade unions and kept down wage
demands, increased profits and allowed high levels of self-financed
investment.

So far in this section, we have given little more than a global and
general view of the major changes in the Italian economy over the postwar period and have paid little attention to the accompanying and
underlying changes in the major economic sectors. In both industry and
agriculture these have been substantial.

We have already made the point that in the early 1950s Italian industry was characterised by small units, operating on a scale that was
inadequate by international standards and using relatively backward
technologies. At the same time, a number of larger firms in basic or key
industries, and often under the state holding sector (discussed in detail
in chapter 7), were grossly overmanned, technologically backward and in
need of radical reorganisation. The shortcomings in these key sectors
inevitably placed other industries, using their products as inputs, at a
disadvantage. Over the postwar period many of these deficiencies were
corrected – albeit sometimes belatedly, as in shipbuilding where corrective
measures involved substantial cuts in the labour force and could only be

undertaken in the tighter labour market conditions of the 1960s. But in general, Italian industry saw rapid and favourable changes in output, scale and technology – trends that were aided and encouraged by the continuingly heavy overseas and domestic demand, high and rising profits allowing substantial levels of investment, the availability of new techniques and technologies abroad which could be easily applied, the relative lack of controls on business initiative (including, as we shall see, the absence of controls on monopolies and restrictive practices), generous credit facilities for small and medium firms and very generous tax concessions for the bigger firms. By the end of the 1960s major industries such as steel, chemicals and vehicles were operating on European scales and using the most advanced technologies. This was particularly true of the state holding sector, heavily concentrated in vital areas of iron and steel, cement, oil, chemicals and energy. It is unlikely that private enterprise, particularly since it lacked the easy access to very cheap and generous finance which the state holding sector enjoyed, could have developed these industries with anything like the same speed or on the same scale. The state holding intervention therefore ensured the avoidance of bottlenecks, heavy imports or higher prices in key areas of economic activity.

Agriculture over the postwar period has experienced a structural change that has been no less dramatic than that in industry. We have already seen that Italian agriculture was, in the early 1950s, characterised by very small, fragmented farms making little use of modern techniques. Since then considerable changes have taken place. Not only did the average size of farm increase between 1951 and 1970, but also, over the same period, there has been a substantial growth in the degree of mechanisation and use of modern methods and inputs. Overall, a good measure of the technical advances in Italian agriculture is the fact that while in 1951 the value of agricultural inputs, other than labour, was 13.4 per cent of gross saleable output, this had risen to 22.2 per cent by 1970. Large areas of land have been irrigated and drained, while anti-erosion schemes have been developed on a grand scale. In terms of products, there has been a switch away from low-productivity cereal and vine cultivation into the more profitable fruit, meat and horticultural products. As we have already pointed out, these structural changes, combined with the (associated) exodus of surplus labour, gave a growth of productivity in agriculture that was in fact faster than that in industry.

The great postwar restructuring and development of Italian agriculture has involved comprehensive policies and substantial funds. These policies, heavily directed towards the South where agriculture was particularly backward, have had four main components.[48] First, irrigation, land reclamation and land improvement schemes have been initiated. Secondly, a great range of incentives, including grants and cheap loans, have been introduced with the objective of encouraging the use of modern agricultural techniques. Thirdly, though primarily in the South, very large and poorly managed farms have been expropriated and then redistributed to peasant owners. Finally, and less clear cut, agricultural development has been aided by the EEC's Agricultural Guidance and Guarantee Fund.[49] Between 1962–63 and 1968–69, for example, Italy got more from the Guidance (restructuring) section than she paid in, which placed her in a fairly unique position. On the other hand, however, and in common with all other EEC countries except France, Italy lost out in respect of the Guarantee section, paying in some 228 milliard lire more than she got out of it. This negative balance was some four times as large as her positive balance in respect of the Guidance section. Yet, perhaps more than the fact that Italy has not profited in money terms from the EEC's agricultural policies, the Italian authorities have been bitter in their complaints that the EEC's pricing policies have detracted from their attempts to shift Italian agriculture towards meat, fruit and horticulture and away from cereals and wine.[50]

1.6 Italy: a case of easy growth?

In many ways it is possible to argue that Italy's postwar economic performance has been 'easy' because of the existence of conditions (sometimes fortuitous) that were highly favourable to rapid growth. Prime among these, and already mentioned, was the ability to profit from the large numbers of geographically mobile unemployed and underemployed workers. As we shall see in chapter 2, the employment of these resources made a substantial contribution to economic growth. Secondly, because of Italy's continuing slack labour markets, the trade union movement was weak over much of the postwar period. This, as we have said, allowed high profits and high levels of self-financed investment, as well as ensuring the continuing international price competitiveness of Italian goods. This competitiveness in respect of visible exports, combined with the large invisible earnings mentioned earlier, gave rise generally to an overall balance of payments surplus which, in conjunction with normally slack labour markets, made few calls on the authorities to adopt short-run demand management measures. The need for stop–go policies was entirely absent during the 1950s and occurred only twice during the 1960s.

A third favourable factor has been the benefits to the postwar economy from its inheritance of IRI and the other state-controlled industries that make up the state holding sector. Already mentioned briefly above, and discussed in detail in chapter 7, the state holding sector has played a variety of roles in the economy, ranging from regional development to the strengthening of basic or key industries, from the rescuing of sick firms to the creation of infrastructure. It has been a means of circumventing the inadequacies of the Italian capital market and the government expenditure system (see chapter 5). In a country with no monopolies and restrictive practices legislation, it has played a role, even if of doubtful value, in ensuring higher levels of competition. In industrial relations it has been a model employer, while its industrial training schemes, if nothing else, have highlighted the abysmal systems existing outside the sector.

Two final factors that have been conducive to easy growth were the finding of indigenous gas and oil and the benefits that Italy secured by starting from a low technological base in the early postwar years. The gas and oil finds were a cheap form of energy in a country with no coal deposits of any importance and with limited prospects for further development of hydro-electric power. The gas finds in particular were extremely important and indeed Italy is now virtually self-sufficient in this fuel. Although the oil finds were useful in the early postwar years, they never accounted for a substantial proportion of Italy's needs, and by 1971 all but about one per cent of oil used in Italy was imported. Turning to the benefits that Italy enjoyed by starting from a low technological base in the immediate postwar years, these were substantial. Advanced foreign technology had been little applied in the autarkic economic conditions of the interwar years, or during the war. Big returns could, therefore, be secured merely by the application of these new technologies, and without the need for expensive research investments. 'The Italian economic miracle can be explained to some degree as the making up for lost time by a system which was technologically backward with the respect to the levels reached in other parts of the world.'[51]

1.7 Rapid economy growth in spite of . . .

On the other side of the coin to the factors and features favourable to rapid postwar growth listed above were a number of others which were distinctly unfavourable.

First, Italian capital markets have a number of shortcomings. The share market is particularly underdeveloped, and equity is a relatively unimportant source of company finance. The continuing fall in share prices since the early 1960s has diminished still further the possibilities of floating equity for the normal firm.[52]* This state of affairs, combined with an almost complete lack of a merchant banking system, makes outside risk capital very difficult to obtain. Although fixed interest capital is an easier source of finance (through, as we shall see in chapter 5, a plethora of special credit institutes), this source of capital does result in high gearing – no problem in an expanding economy but imposing great difficulties during any economic downturn. The severity of the recent, 1970–73, Italian depression can be attributed in part to the problems arising from high gearing. Nevertheless, it needs to be said that over much of the postwar period the deficiences in the capital markets have not represented a major problem, in that self-finance has been by far the major source of investment funds while stable and rapid national growth has both allowed and encouraged high gearing. In view of Italy's less favourable prospects for growth in the 1970s, discussed in chapter 2, one suspects that the inadequacy of the market for risk capital is likely to inflict more serious problems in the future.

Secondly, the impressive postwar economic performance of the economy has been in spite of the inadequacy of short-term demand management techniques. As chapter 5 will show, fiscal policy can only be described as almost inoperative. The great majority of government expenditure requires legislation – making for great inflexibility in the Italian political context. In addition, as we shall see, the administrative system in Italy is such that rapid changes in expenditure are not at all easy to effect. On the government revenue side, the fact that changes of most tax rates must go through the cumbersome parliamentary procedure (and then be implemented by the inefficient administrative system) make any alterations in government revenue similarly difficult. Moreover, the Italians have a long tradition of fiscal evasion.[53]* This makes for problems in collecting the taxes and, in as far as evasion is particularly rife with respect to direct taxes, has resulted in a system of taxation which, more than most other ECC countries, is oriented heavily towards indirect taxes. However, the use of indirect taxes for aggregate demand management often causes deleterious side effects when used for deflationary purposes. Monetary policy has, therefore, taken the major brunt of counter-cyclical policy and, as we shall see in chapter 5, the Italians have developed a system of monetary control that is as sophisticated as any in Europe. Monetary policy in any country does, however, have substantial limitations, particularly when used for reflationary purposes. The slowness of the economy's recovery from the crises of 1963–64 and 1969–70 can in part be attributed to the poverty of monetary policy in a situation requiring substantial reflation. In addition one might add that, in the Italian context, monetary policy, when used as a deflationary measure, has had undesirably harsh results. In 1963–64 and again in 1969–70 the government, in an attempt to curb inflation and safeguard the balance of payments, restricted credit and raised interest rates. Highly geared firms consequently found finance more expensive and in short supply at a time when markets were turning down. At the same time, firms that had previously relied heavily on self-finance were experiencing low profits (as a result of the inflationary wage awards of 1963 and 1969 and depressed labour market conditions), with the result that self-finance was also low. But yet, resort by these firms to the market for finance was difficult and costly because of the government's monetary policies. Monetary policy, when used for deflationary purposes, is of course expected to restrain aggregate demand. In the Italian context it has often resulted in the collapse of a large number of firms.

The shortcomings of both monetary and fiscal policy have been recognised by the authorities. As we shall see in chapter 5, recent tax reforms have been aimed at correcting the worst deficiencies of the Italian tax system. The impact of these reforms however remains to be seen. In the past the shortcomings of fiscal policy have encouraged the authorities to consider and to use supplementary counter-cyclical policies. The investment decisions of the state holding sector, for example, have in part been geared to this end. Also, the method whereby the social security system is financed (largely, as we shall see in chapter 4, through employer contributions and accounting from some fifty per cent of wages) has given scope for its use as a counter-cyclical weapon. However, like indirect taxes, the manipulation of these contributions, particularly for deflationary purposes, carries serious disadvantages. Social security contributions by employers have risen rapidly over the postwar period to finance a system that has become more generous and of wider coverage, thereby forcing up the cost of labour and diminishing industrial competitiveness abroad. The use of higher contributions to deflate the economy adds further to this problem, often coming at a time when the balance of payments requires a lowering rather than a raising of costs.

Thirdly, Italy's rapid growth over the postwar period has been in spite of poor educational and industrial training systems. The school-leaving age (fourteen) is low by European standards, and many schools are desperately overcrowded – a result of the rapid growth of population in the major towns combined with legislative delays in allocating funds for the school-building programme after the raising of the school-leaving age (from thirteen) in 1963. In many city schools shift systems are operating. The standard of teaching is viewed by most observers as being poor, discipline is lax and absenteeism remains high. (The high levels of absenteeism at the start of the 1950s have already been noted, but the situation was still serious in the late 1960s. In 1966–67, for example, only 72 per cent of thirteen-year-olds and 85 per cent of twelve-year-olds actually attended school.) The universities have expanded rapidly in terms of student numbers over the postwar period and particularly in recent years, when entry was made possible for all school-leavers having the basic entrance qualifications; but the funds available for the universities have not kept pace with the number of students. A substantial proportion of students hardly attend classes, and indeed space is not available for all those enrolled. The numbers in some faculties have reached nonsense levels – 13,000 in the Faculty of Medicine at Rome University for example.[54] University professors, paternal if not feudal, and intent on maintaining their substantial privileges, often seem more interested in extra-mural consultancy than teaching.[55] There still remains a serious shortage of university places and facilities in engineering and science while, particularly in the South, excessive numbers of students are taking degrees in the arts, law and medicine. Turning finally to industrial training, this is very poor both at the level of the firm (with the marked exception of the state holding firms) and in the government training centres. The great majority of firms either run no training courses for their workers or run short, almost derisory, courses. The public or state training centres (of which there are a large number) are poorly co-ordinated and short of funds (and, as with other public bodies in Italy, administratively incapable of spending the funds allocated), with poor-quality teaching and low-quality courses. The participants are paid little or nothing during their period of training.[56] In the context of the great occupational switching from agriculture to industry and of Italy's poor school education system, the lack of adequate worker education and training systems is particularly serious. The point can hardly be overstressed that the great majority of Italian workers have had little or no formal schooling. In 1969, 18 per cent of industrial workers had no school-leaving certificate and 70 per cent only had at most the (very) elementary certificate. It is not putting the point too strongly to say that – the majority of the Italian population is only semi-literate.

Two final factors, in spite of which the Italian economy has grown, need to be discussed. They have already been mentioned in this section but deserve to be treated in more detail. The first is the inefficint public administration and civil service, and the second is the political system.

The civil service is a source of fun and ridicule in most countries. Italy is no exception but, considering the inadequacies of the public administration, it is often more justifiable (and also, from a legal standpoint, more dangerous[57*]). The civil service is inflexible, overstaffed and poorly trained, with promotion resting heavily on seniority. Starting pay is low, often resulting in poor-quality recruits, though in many other respects the civil servants are in a privileged position. Compared with their counterparts in private industry, civil servants enjoy far better pension arrangements, are almost impossible to dismiss, receive remark-

able 'golden handshakes' when leaving the service and have better family
allowance systems, longer holidays and shorter hours.[58] At the top,
appointments are largely political. At all levels, the service is heavily, and
increasingly, staffed by southerners, with all their associated traditions.
'Italy is a country with a European majority governed by a Mediterranean minority. The South dominates the administration and imprints
on it two traditionally Mediterranean habits of mind: a profound sus-
picion of the public and a belief that public office is a benefice rather
than a public service'.[59] Co-operation with the public is indeed very poor,
as is inter-ministerial and inter-departmental co-operation – common in
many countries but carried to extreme, and often superficially amusing,
degrees in Italy.[60]* Bribery and corruption are present in the service,
though some of it, especially at the lower levels, is merely an attempt to
speed up a decision. There is little evidence that this particular problem
has become less widespread in recent years.[61]*

It would be completely wrong, however, to see the inefficiency of the
Italian public administration as being solely, or even primarily, a consequence of the civil servants *per se*. A major problem is the *system* of
public administration, whereby even minor decisions need to go through
vast, laborious and highly legal systems of checks and counter-checks –
not only within a department or ministry but also outside it, primarily
through the Court of Accounts. Proposals and decisions must comply
perfectly with the spirit and letter of the law governing that particular
decision or operation; and yet many of the laws are archaic or contra-
dictory. It is hardly surprising that the civil service is heavily staffed, if
not dominated, by lawyers. The system is such that, first, it is never clear
who has responsibility for a decision. Secondly, the process of decision-
making is so difficult and lengthy that many ministries are unable to
spend the funds allocated to them – a point to which we return shortly.
Thirdly, the system is so legal that economics seems an almost incidental
component of policies and decisions.[62] We shall see later that a major
feature of Italy in the postwar period has been the failure of social
investment to keep pace with economic growth. The public administration system must bear much of the responsibility for this. It was largely
the public administration system which effectively 'disarmed' the 1966–70
national plan, impeded the achievement of almost every one of its social
investment targets, and confirmed it as a 'book of dreams'. But the
problem goes beyond social investment. As we shall see in chapter 5,
there is hardly a ministry or department in Italy which, through administrative problems, does not have substantial *residui passivi*. These are
funds, often enormous, voted to departments and not spent. They 'demonstrate clearly how political wishes to spend have not been followed by
expenditure and reflect the inability of the administration to implement
the wishes of the government'.[63] These deficiencies not only have impli-

cations for long-term Italian development but also, as we shall see in chapter 5, have impeded the use of fiscal policy for the purposes of short-term economic stabilisation.

There is an acute awareness of the public administration's faults and the extent to which they have impeded development. A long series of commissions has investigated the problem and few postwar governments have been without a minister having special responsibility for civil service reform. But there has been little, if any, success. Reform is difficult, not only because of the extent of the problem (and one which piecemeal measures could not resolve and indeed would probably aggravate), but also because it is impeded by the bureaucrats themselves – a not inconsiderable electoral force. The attractions of the present system with the diffused nature of responsibility are anyway, for them, considerable. Certainly no major reform will be possible unless the top of the service can be cleared of its dead wood – an enormously difficult task. 'Under the old civil service legislation it is practically impossible to sack a state employee. Someone once said that a civil servant who shot his minister would probably have to go so long as he could also be shown to be a Fascist'.[64]

The inefficiencies of the public administration in Italy are complemented by the inadequacies and failings of government and the political system. Only rarely has any single political party had a parliamentary majority and almost all postwar governments have been coalitions. More often than not, as we shall see in the appendix, these coalitions have been uneasy alliances, often characterised by bickering, squabbling and frequent attempts to rearrange under new leadership. In all, since 1945 there have been thirty or so governments. But the problems of governing through a coalition in Italy are not simply a consequence of inter-party differences. Perhaps more important are the differences within the individual parties, and particularly the Christian Democrat party which holds an amazingly wide range of political ideas and has been the centre-pin of all postwar governments.

Weak coalitions and attempts to hold these and the component parties together have had serious and deleterious effects on growth and development, as well as on other aspects of Italian life. On occasion, political uncertainty has directly impeded economic growth. There is, for example, little doubt that the recovery of the economy from the 1970–73 recession was delayed by political problems, which adversely affected business confidence as well as impeding the introduction of relevant economic control packages. On a different tack, the rivalries between parties in the coalitions have been an obstacle to the creation of a single economics ministry to replace the current three (Treasury, Budget and Finance), which, though giving a party political balance in economic affairs, makes for enormous difficulties of co-ordination.[65]* Additionally, the continued weakness of government inevitably raises questions about who is in command. The seemingly perpetual discussion, for example, about whether the state holding sector is under the control of the government or vice versa is not academic. But yet the state holding sector is only one of many tails which often appear to be wagging the dog – the Church, farmers, trade unions and private industry are only a few of an almost endless list of pressure groups.[66] These types of pressure groups exist in other countries, of course, and are not *a priori* an undesirable part of a political system. They do however require a strong government to withstand their more pernicious traits, and in particular their general tendency towards conservatism. In Italy weak and fragile governments have often found themselves forced to adopt policies which, as a result of the pressures of vested interests, are tempered more towards the *status quo* than in the direction of radical change. The recent (1971) law for the reform of the retail and wholesale trade is a good example of this point. Earlier legislation had heavily protected existing enterprises by allowing new businesses to be set up only under quite exceptional circumstances. The result was a sector characterised by tiny units, the very slow development of large-scale units, and considerable underemployment. Major reform was necessary, in particular to allow greater ease of access for the larger units. In the context of weak government the political power of the sector was, however, such that the new law was able to make little leeway in curbing the degree of protection enjoyed by the existing units.

But, at least, a new law was introduced, no matter how weak. There remain other areas in which inter- and intra-party strife have resulted in legislation that is either totally inadequate or non-existent. Italy's anti-pollution legislation is, by European standards, pitiful. In a country undergoing an urban revolution, the long promised law to reform the system of urban development and control is still awaited. Moreover, Italy remains almost unique in Western Europe in having virtually no monopolies and restrictive practices policy. This is in spite of a very high degree of industrial concentration. Bain, in his study of industrial concentration, noted that of the nineteen Italian industries covered, '14 are significantly more concentrated than their counterparts in the United States, 4 are slightly more or less concentrated or have about the same concentration, and only one (flour) is significantly less concentrated'.[67] In recent years, through mergers and the rapid growth of big firms, the degree of concentration has increased.[68] Through a Fascist law of 1942 monopolies can be disallowed, and since the mid-1960s mergers between firms having a turnover of more than one milliard lire may not qualify for the fiscal benefits of merging if an unfavourable ministerial decision is taken. Monopoly power will be considered in this decision. What is lacking for this to be effective, however, are clear criteria, and these could only be evolved through specific monopolies and restrictive practices legislation and an appropriate body to administer it. Although a number of bills have been drafted and discussed in Parliament and in spite of a major parliamentary inquiry during the early 1960s, legislation has still not been passed – a result of inter-party differences about what is needed and, perhaps even more serious, disagreement within the parties. The financial ties between big business and the Liberal and Christian Democrat parties do not make radical legislation in this field any easier to introduce.

There is hardly an area of Italian life that has not suffered from the shortcomings of the political system, and few aspects of the economy or economic policy can be understood without some political context. The slight use of fiscal policy in demand management control, as mentioned above, is in no small way a consequence of political factors – a result of 'the slowness of the decision-making process both at the level of government and parliament, a slowness caused by the ministerial fragmentation of government economic policy and by the lengthiness of parliamentary procedure, aggravated by political instability'.[69] At a broader level the dreadful overcrowding in the schools, reported earlier, largely results from a laudable government decision to raise the school-leaving age and its inability rapidly to push through legislation to expand the school-building programme. The overcrowding in the universities reflects a politically expedient decision to ease student entry and the collapse of the university reform bill (with the premature elections of 1972), which contained provisions for increasing university finance. But the universities and schools are not the only socio-economic areas where political weakness has impeded radical, or even relevant, reforms. Others are health, social security, housing, transport and penal reform, with essential legislation frequently being long delayed (often lasting through several governments) and, when finally passed, through inter- and intra-party compromise often being only a shadow of the original proposal and almost totally inadequate.

Regional devolution has for a long time been seen by many, and particularly the Socialists, as one way round the inadequacies of central government and administration. It may perhaps seem ironic that only a century after unification proposals were being put forward for regionalisation. But, except during periods of extreme nationalistic fervour, there has always been a distrust of the central government. For many regions the government appointed prefect was merely a successor to a long line of foreign representatives. It is therefore not very surprising that, following on the highly centralised Fascist experiment, the 1948 Constitution recognised regions as well as provinces and municipalities.[70] Statutes were rapidly (by the end of 1948) approved for Sicily, Sardinia, the frontier regions of Aosta and Trentino, Alto Adige and, in 1963, Friuli–Venetia Julia. Historical and political factors dominated the decision to create these so-called 'special' regions – all of which were given considerable autonomy. They have powers which, in many respects, are 'as full as the State's, so that the regions can modify or repeal laws issued by the State on the same matter and pass their own thereon'.[71]

No move was made, however, with respect to the other fifteen so-called ordinary regions until the late 1960s – not least because the Christian Democrats and right-wing parties were afraid of the possibility of Communist–Socialist dominated regions in the Centre and North. It was only with the move of the Socialists away from the Communists in the 1960s, and with their participation in a centre–left coalition (see appendix), that proposals for the creation of the ordinary regions were reactivated. The Socialists had long claimed that regional government was the only way to mitigate the bureaucratic and political sterility that seemed to dominate postwar Italy; indeed, one of their conditions for taking part in the centre–left government was that positive steps should be taken towards the activation of the ordinary regions. Between 1968 and 1971 a number of relevant laws for the regions were passed, covering in particular the electoral system and methods of finance. By mid-1971 regional councils had been elected, a system of finance evolved and regional statutes approved by Parliament. By 1973 the regions were in operation and a number of previously central functions and personnel had already been transferred.

It is necessary to be careful not to overstate the powers of the new regions. The Constitution limits their influence to three main areas – health and public welfare; regional transport and other infrastructure; and a group of economic activities including agriculture, tourism and 'fishing in inland waters, mineral and thermal water, quarries and peatbogs, fairs and markets'.[72] The key areas of industry and education are excluded, even though the special regions have a considerable degree of control over these sectors. Some of the ordinary regions, however, have tried to secure more power than was foreseen by the Constitution and many, principally the left-wing regions, have managed to incorporate quite broad (and vague) objectives in their statutes. Nevertheless, two important points need to be kept in mind when viewing the power of the regions and the possible control by the State. First, all regional laws must be approved by a centrally appointed regional commissioner – a kind of regional prefect. Secondly, the financing of the regions will, to a considerable extent, be through state funds. The regions have limited scope for imposing their own taxes and the main source of finance is expected to be specified proportions of national taxes and special discretionary grants. It is not unlikely that these grants, envisaged initially as being largely for the southern regions, will form a growing item of revenue for all the regions – again giving power of control to the State. 'He who pays the piper calls the tune'.

Our own view concerning Italian regionalism is one of pessimism.[73] Already political problems are impeding action in some regions. Bureaucracy has neither diminished nor notably improved, while the problems of co-ordination (difficult even in the three-tier system of state, provinces and municipalities) have been exacerbated. The lack of a national plan, which would have formed the basis of co-ordination, means that this task now rests substantially with the regional commissioners; with no framework on which to operate, and with some heavily politically inspired regions, his task cannot be easy. At a more basic level, our fear is that the new regions will at least perpetuate, and probably exacerbate, the regional differences already existing in Italy. The North, with a higher tax base, efficient government and a better bureaucracy, will undoubtedly do better than the South.

1.8 In spite of rapid economic growth . . .

So far we have documented Italy's postwar economic success – her rapid and stable rate of growth, her impressive export performance and buildup of gold and foreign currency reserves, and the great changes in economic structure. All this has been in the face of a number of unfavourable factors, and especially a political system which has often been deficient in legislating for essential reforms and a system of public administration incapable of implementing legislation even when passed. However, in spite of Italy's impressive economic performance, she remains a poor – country by EEC standards. Secondly, she continues as a labour surplus economy. Thirdly, in spite of the vast agricultural exodus, agriculture remains a major sector and is for the most part extremely backward. Fourthly, the industrial structure is still dominated by small, often inefficient, firms. Fifthly, the problem of the South remains, in some ways no less serious than it was at the end of the war. Finally, and perhaps most important, the level of social investment has not kept pace with economic growth, and to a large extent Italy must be viewed as being a country that has enjoyed growth without development. We intend now (briefly, since many of these issues are covered in succeeding chapters) to discuss each of these topics in turn.

. . . a poor country still

There is no wholly satisfactory method of making international comparisons of standards of living. Two approaches are normal, the first using income per head and the second using physical measures of consumption as proxies for income. The results from either method must be treated with caution. Income per head comparisons take no account of income distribution and, perhaps more important, involve exchange rates to convert into a common currency. These exchange rates are, however, determined largely by balance of payments performance and do not fully reflect domestic price levels. Changes in exchange rates, as we shall see in chapter 4, can often make nonsense of international income comparisons. Physical consumption indicators also have disadvantages – they take no account of qualitative differences or the fact that a particular indicator reflects social, historical, political and even climatic factors as well as economic. One example that can be used to illustrate this point concerns television ownership – a common physical consumption measure. The extent of television ownership is a function of many factors – price of televisions, licence charges (and evasion), renting and hire purchase systems, quality of programmes and alternative forms of amusement, to name but a few. Standard of living, which it is hoped to reflect, is therefore only one of many factors involved and can quite easily be overshadowed by the others.

Nevertheless, although both income per head and physical indicators have their faults, they can give rough indications of a nation's standard of living, and table 1.4 provides a number of comparisons between Italy and some other EEC countries. The bracketed figures show these measures as an index, taking Italy as 100.

Table 1.4 Italian standard of living relative to other countries, 1971

	Italy	UK	West Germany	France
GNP at market prices per head (European units of account)	1,867 [100]	2,420 [129.6]	3,387 [181.4]	3,177 [170.2]
GNP at market prices per member of the labour force (European units of account)	5,208 [100]	5,377 [103.2]	7,729 [148.4]	7,737 [148.6]
Calories per head per day, 1970	3,020 [100]	3,190 [105.6]	3,170 [105.0]	3,270 [108.3]
Proteins (grammes) per head per day, 1970	88 [100]	90 [102.3]	83 [94.3]	102 [115.9]
Passenger cars per '000 population	187 [100]	213 [113.9]	237 [126.7]	245 [131.0]
Television receivers per '000 population	180 [100]	293 [162.8]	272 [151.1]	214 [118.9]
Telephones per '000 population	174 [100]	269 [154.6]	226 [129.9]	171 [98.3]

Source: Statistical Office of the European Communities *Basic Statistics of the Community 1972* (Luxembourg).

The picture resulting from table 1.4 is by no means clear but, in general terms, Italian income per head is relatively low and, as one would expect, this is reflected in the other measures of consumption. It will be noted that Italian income per member of the labour force is higher relative to the other countries than the income per head figures – a reflection of Italy's low activity rates and a topic to which, among others, we now turn.

. . . a continuing labour surplus economy

In spite of rapid economic growth over the postwar period this growth has not been adequate to absorb the labour supply and remains characterised by labour surpluses. Although, as we shall see in detail in chapter 4, unemployment had fallen to 'European levels' by the 1960s, activity rates have declined and overseas migration has continued at a high level.

Migration has been a long-standing feature of the Italian economy. Although the rate of net emigration in the postwar years has been below the massive pre-First World War movements, the numbers are still impressive. Net emigration from Italy involved 1.2 million people between 1951 and 1961 and a similar number between 1961 and 1971. The downward trend in activity rates, like migration, is a long-standing phenomenon, but it has tended to speed up in the postwar period. Italian activity rates are now among the lowest in Europe. In 1970 the male rate for the age group 14–65 was 80.8 per cent as against the EEC (the six) rate of 81.8 per cent in the same year, while female rates were 29.3 and 37.8 per cent respectively.[74] The reasons for the low and declining activity rates are, as we shall see in chapter 4, still open to dispute, though few would doubt that the lack of job opportunities is of paramount importance.

The inability of the economy to absorb the labour supply in spite of its rapid rate of growth reflects a number of factors. The first is the substantial increase of population, from 47.5 million in 1951 to 54 million in 1971 – a population growth incidentally that has been more a consequence of a low and generally falling death rate than a particularly high birth rate. In 1971 the Italian birth rate was 17.4 per thousand population as against the EEC (the six) average of 15.8, and 16.3 in the UK. Death rates were 9.6, 10.7 and 11.6 respectively.[75] Secondly, particularly during the 1960s, industrial labour costs increased rapidly, as we shall see in chapter 4, with an inevitable reduction in the ability of this part of the economy to absorb the agricultural exodus. Thirdly, and very important, this exodus has, as we have seen, been on a massive scale, and is by no means wholly related to the presence of job opportunities in the rest of the economy. The outcome has consequently been increased emigration abroad and a fall in activity rates.

The seeming inability of the economy adequately to expand employment opportunities is well illustrated by the results of the 1966–70 national plan, when employment targets were not met in spite of an economic growth rate of 6 per cent per annum as against a target rate of 5 per cent.[76] It was hoped that the 5 per cent target would give a net employment expansion of 800,000. In fact, employment fell slightly. This was a result of two factors. First, there was higher than anticipated productivity growth in industry (7.8 per cent per annum as against the planned rate of 7 per cent) and in services (7.0 per cent as against 4.2 per cent). The major reasons for these higher productivity growth rates would appear to have been reorganisation and better working methods rather than higher levels of investment, this latter being virtually in line with the plan.[77] Nevertheless, the overall result was that non-agricultural employment grew by only 1.1 million as against the planned increase of 1.4 million. Secondly, and more serious, the exodus from agriculture at 1.3 million was much more acute than expected – about double the plan figure.

In spite, therefore, of rapid economic growth, and largely reflecting the mechanisms involved, employment has expanded over the whole of the postwar period at a disappointing rate. The exodus from agriculture has to a large degree been 'accommodated' by overseas emigration and falling activity rates. Unless there is a substantial cutback in the outflow of labour from agriculture (and, as we shall see, this is not anticipated), these trends are likely to continue, at least over the next decade.

. . . a continuingly backward agriculture

Agriculture still represents a major component of the Italian economy, some 18.8 per cent of the total labour force being employed in the sector in 1971 – much lower than the 1951 level of 43.9 but still high by EEC standards. In 1971 Germany, for example, had 8.3 per cent of its labour force in agriculture, France 13.2 and Belgium 4.4. At the same date the UK level was 2.7 per cent.[78] However, not only is agriculture still a major sector in Italy but, in spite of improvements over the postwar period, it remains very backward.

The prime source of this backwardness is the continuing small size of farms. Although the average size of farm has grown over the postwar period, the increase has been slight – rising from 6.2 hectares in 1961 to 7.0 in 1970 (and only marginally above the average of 6.3 hectares in 1930).[79] Italian farms remain 'small with respect to the needs of modern agriculture and the size of farm in the other member countries of the EEC'[80] – being some 60 per cent of the EEC average.[81] The inability to make any substantial increase in the size of farm, in spite of the vast postwar exodus of labour from the sector, reflects a number of factors, including the peasant tradition of holding on to land, the lack of a satisfactory EEC restructuring policy and the failure of Italian governments to introduce relevant policies. Indeed, in this latter context, policies have until recently often tended to exacerbate the problem. For political reasons, the agricultural incentives have been indiscriminate and have tended to maintain the existing farm structure, while the early land reform schemes involved the creation of units that were too small to be economically viable. It is never easy to give an indication of what is economically viable. Some would claim that only a figure as high as 50 hectares is 'adequate for the new technological needs of modern agriculture'.[82] The EEC, through the Mansholt Plan, is thinking of 15 hectares as being a minimum size, below which policy would try to encourage abandonment and merger. Even a level of 15 hectares, however, has enormous implications for Italian agriculture. In 1970 some 76 per cent of Italian farms were of 5 hectares and below, and 95 per cent were under 20 hectares. At the same date 18 per cent of agricultural land was being cultivated by farms of 5 hectares or less, and 45 per cent by farms of 20 hectares or less. The attempt to rid EEC agriculture of the smaller farms will have a much more marked effect in Italy than the other member countries.[83]*

The small size of Italian farms, combined with a considerable degree of fragmentation, is a substantial deterrent to the use of modern farming methods. The inevitable result is a level of productivity well below other sectors and, associated, low levels of income.[84]* In 1970 agricultural value-added at constant prices per person employed was some 54.6 per cent of that in the non-agricultural sector – a rise over the 1951 proportion of 32.0 per cent, though this reflects more the improvement in agriculture relative to services (another problem sector as we shall see) rather than a marked improvement *vis à vis* industry. While in 1951 agricultural value-added per person employed, again at constant prices, was 46.9 per cent of that in industry (including construction), it had risen to only 53.0 per cent by 1970.

. . . *the continuing predominance of the small firm*

It is not only agriculture that is characterised by small units. Although there has been a tendency for the average size of industrial establishments to rise over the postwar period it is still small by European standards.

Table 1.5 shows the average size of establishment by industrial sector, measured in terms of labour force, as revealed by the three postwar industrial censuses. The most important figures are those for manufacturing and construction, which in 1971 employed 5.3 and 1.0 million people respectively out of a total industrial labour force of 6.5 million. The marked fall between 1951 and 1971 in the average size of construc-

Table 1.5 Average numbers employed per industrial establishment in Italy

	1951	1961	1971
Extractive	14.3	14.2	12.2
Manufacturing	5.5	7.4	8.4
Construction	12.3	13.3	6.2
Gas, electricity and water	11.8	13.3	17.5

Source: ISTAT *Annuario Statistico Italiano* (Rome, various issues).

tion establishment was largely a result of a very rapid growth in their numbers – from 67,500 establishments in 1961 to 160,800 in 1971. Obviously, many of these new units were very small. However, although there was during the 1960s a general tendency for small construction establishments to be created, these figures may exaggerate this trend, since 1971 was a year of depression and many construction workers tried to set up on their own account.

It can be seen from table 1.5 that the average size of manufacturing unit has tended to increase slightly over the postwar period, though more slowly during the 1960s than the 1950s. Even so, the average size is low by European standards and distinctly small by UK standards, where in 1963 the average size of manufacturing establishment was around 88 workers.

An important feature of the Italian economy is not only that the *average* size of industrial establishment is small but, and more critical, that a substantial proportion of the industrial labour force works in very small establishments, a very high percentage of which are tiny. In manufacturing, for example, around 88 per cent of establishments in 1971 had a work force of less than 10, and some 23 per cent of the manufacturing work force were in establishments below this size. Many of these small establishments will have very low levels of productivity, will often pay low wages to what would be predominantly non-unionised (and often under-age) labour, and will evade many of their social security responsibilities. Relative to their counterparts in the bigger establishments, these workers are in a substantially inferior position and in this sense the labour market is 'dualistic' – a topic to which we return in detail in chapter 4. Similar points apply with even greater force to the construction industry, where 84 per cent of establishments employed less than 10 people and 37 per cent of the work force were in this size of establishment, and to large parts of the service industry, especially retailing and catering, where low productivity, underemployment and extremely poor conditions of employment are widespread.[85]

It is important to stress that the industrial size distribution figures mentioned above do not include outworkers (cottage industry workers).

These are not covered by official statistics and little concrete information is available about their numbers, though 1½ – 2 million is the generally accepted figure. Most observers agree that their conditions of employment are pitiful. Predominantly composed of women, generally working part-time, having an hourly income around 60 per cent of that in industry and rarely covered for social security, these workers are without doubt underprivileged even if one is reluctant to use the term exploited. In recent years their numbers have increased substantially, with employers discovering the profitability of a group that does not strike, accepts low pay and low social security coverage and can be sacked without the costs and problems accompanying the dismissal of factory workers. We return to the plight of the Italian outworker in chapter 4.

. . . the continuing problem of the South

The South represents one of Italy's major problems – and certainly one of the most long-standing. Chapter 6 is devoted to the southern problem and traces its origins (going back before unification), the widening of the North–South gap during Italian take-off and the damage inflicted by the autarkic and nationalistic interwar policies, culminating in a war that had more disastrous consequences for the South than the North. By 1950 the disparities between North and South were more serious than they had ever been.

Since then, as we shall see in chapter 6, successive governments have introduced radical policies backed by substantial funds to help the South. Through the *Cassa per il Mezzogiorno* (created in 1950) and other government bodies, basic infrastructure has been improved, major land reform schemes have been set in motion and, from the late 1950s, adventurous policies have been adopted to encourage the movement of industry into the area. In this latter respect generous incentives have been made available; the state holding sector has been obliged to locate high proportions of its new investment in the South and, through growth area policy, an attempt has been made to remodel the settlement structure and to provide a more attractive environment for industry. Moreover, southern industry has been given favourable conditions with respect to government contracts, while the public administration has been required to place in the area a high proportion of their investment and expenditure. Overall, there has been a substantial transfer of resources into the South – equal, in fact, to some three-quarters of gross southern investment.

In retrospect, it is not difficult to be critical of postwar southern policy. The industrialisation programme was only introduced belatedly (in 1957); much of the early expenditure on infrastructure was of a public works rather than development character; while the farms created in the land reform schemes were often too small to be viable. Not only were many of the southern policies deficient but, as with much else in Italy, there was often a 'slip twixt cup and lip' – between ambition and practice. In particular, the funds available for industrial incentives were inadequate, while the impact of the Cassa's expenditure was reduced by the inability (both in organisational and financial terms) of the public administration and local authorities to exploit the Cassa's investments. In many ways the South was fortunate that there was general agreement between the political parties that substantial development efforts and reforms were necessary, though there was often strong disagreement about the relevant components. But beyond this, southern policy has been a microcosm of so many other Italian programmes – short of funds and let down by an inefficient public administration.

As we shall see in detail in chapter 6, the results of southern policies have been mixed. On the one hand, unemployment and underemployment have been reduced substantially, as has the importance of agriculture. In 1951 agriculture accounted for 56.7 per cent of southern employment, and this was down to 30.7 per cent by 1970. Industry in 1970 employed 32.0 per cent of the labour force as against 20.1 per cent in 1951. In both agriculture and industry productivity has risen rapidly, reflecting in the case of agriculture the exodus of surplus labour and the use of more advanced agricultural techniques. In industry, new firms have come into the area and indigenous firms have grown. On the other hand, non-agricultural employment growth has not been adequate to absorb the agricultural exodus and the growth of population. Indeed, total employment in the South declined between 1951 and 1971, from 6.5 million to 6.0 million, with the resultant surplus labour being accommodated by a fall in activity rates and continuingly heavy out-migration. Between 1951 and 1961 net emigration from the South was 1.8 million; it rose to 2.3 million between 1961 and 1971. It is little consolation that migration has increasingly been to the North rather than abroad.

Although the South has seen a substantial change in employment structure over the postwar period, the structure is still heavily weighted towards agriculture (30.7 per cent against 13.7 per cent in the North) – an agriculture which, more than in the North, is dominated by small, fragmented, low-productivity farms. Agricultural productivity (value-added per person employed) in 1970 was 72.5 per cent of that in the North. Industry still has a low weighting in the southern employment structure (accounting for 32.0 per cent of the labour force as against 46.7 per cent in the North), while the industry that does exist is largely composed of small, undercapitalised, low-productivity units. Industrial value-added per person employed in 1970 was some 69 per cent of the northern level.

With an employment structure still heavily weighted by agriculture, and with both southern agriculture and industry having lower levels of productivity than in the North, it is hardly surprising that the standard of living is low – gross southern expenditure (at constant prices) in 1970 was some 70 per cent of the comparable northern figure. (In 1951 the proportion was 62 per cent.) Other measures of standard of living changes over the postwar period give a less favourable picture, sometimes showing the South losing out relative to the North. In some ways one can be depressed that, even on the more favourable figures, the disparity between North and South has narrowed only slightly over a period of two decades. On the other hand, it is over-optimistic to think that there is any swift solution to regional problems. To change the economic structure and mental attitudes, which lie at the base of the problem, is a slow process. Resolution is likely to take many decades rather than years. Moreover, it is dangerous and misleading to be over-concerned about differentials *per se*. The conditions in the South are now much better than they were twenty years or so ago. One can in fact argue that it is surprising that the South has managed broadly to keep pace with the more advanced and very rapidly growing North, and surely absolute levels of material well-being are more important than disparities.

Three final points deserve to be made about the southern problem. These are developed in chapter 6 but at least warrant mention here. First, we have so far concentrated on the economic features of the South. However, the social conditions associated with these are moving – the frustration and degradation of unemployment and underemployment, of living in an area with few job opportunities and the social problems of migration both for those who go and for those who remain. Secondly, we have concentrated largely on average figures for the South. But Italy is a country where averages are particularly meaningless, and it is important to stress that serious disparities also exist within the South, with some areas where the standard of living is well below the southern average and where migration has reached a scale tantamount to abandonment, leaving villages composed almost wholly of women and the elderly. For many areas, often the inland, so called *osso,* or bone, there has been a virtual *desertificazione.* Thirdly, and a point encouraging optimism, there has in the past decade been a considerable change in attitude on the part of the authorities towards the southern problem. *Meridionalismo,* for so long based on sentiment, equality, national pride and humanity, has recently had strong economic support; it is being increasingly recognised that the relatively uncontrolled and concentrated development in the North, fed by southern immigrants, has inflicted serious national costs, particularly in the provision of infrastructure.[86] Additionally, and more important perhaps, there is a growing view that the two inflations, 1962–63 and 1969–70, which prefaced the depressions of the succeeding years and slowed down the overall rate of postwar growth, were in no small part a consequence of worker discontent with the inadequacies of social infrastructure in the major urban centres of the North, and that the failure to develop the South and the concomitant migration to the North had exacerbated these difficulties.[87] 'To have a good salary meant nothing for the worker if he had to use much of it to pay for inhospitable and often unhealthy lodgings and far from his work, if he had to incur notable expenditure for transport, if hospitals, doctors and medicines were in short supply and expensive, if schools for his children were inadequate, if the cost of living was higher than that to which he was used in his area of origin'.[88] The violence that accompanied the wage negotiations of 1969–70 was also in part a consequence of these conditions, combined with the sense of alienation felt by the southern immigrants. The growing recognition that southern development can have national benefits, or at least alleviate national problems, can but represent an impetus for future southern development policy.

. . . inadequate social investment

A great shortcoming of the Italian economy over the postwar period, and not unassociated with the continuance of the southern problem, has been the inability of the authorities to cope with the consequences of growth, and in particular the failure of the public sector to provide those social conditions which a more prosperous and rapidly growing urban population requires. Housing in many urban areas is poor, scarce and expensive.[89]* In 1965 some 50 per cent of Italian houses were without an internal lavatory, two-thirds were without a bath, and half were without running water. Housing shortages have become particularly acute in the north. In spite of repeated attempts to evolve meaningful policies to increase the supply of cheap public housing the results have not been impressive.[90]* The social security system, discussed in chapter 4, is similarly open to serious criticism. Although both coverage and benefits have increased in recent years, many recipients are left in very needy conditions. In the early 1970s some 80 per cent of Italian pensioners were having to exist on a pension of 25,000 lire per month or less. The basic unemployment pay is meagre (400 lire per day), while the health system pays benefits that do not fully cover the costs of medical attention. Hospitals are overcrowded and often have poor facilities. The family allowance system is inferior to all others in the EEC, the sums involved in 1972 (5720 lire per month for each child and 4160 lire for the spouse) being between four and six per cent of average industrial earnings. Even these allowances are not dynamised with respect to the cost of living and are not stepped, as in most European countries, to give proportionately more to the worker with a large family. Away from social security, the school-building programme has not kept pace with demand, nor has teacher training. As we have already seen, the conditions in many city schools are little short of chaotic. The quality of education is poor and the majority of the population remain only semi-literate. Although inter-urban transport is of high quality, with good *autostrade,* air and rail networks, the urban transport systems are very poor. The roads in most cities are simply unable to take the traffic, while public transport is inefficient and inadequate. Streets are dirty and ill-kept with piles of unswept rubbish not uncommon in the suburbs of many cities. 'Without indulging in *catastrafismo,* one cannot but fail to note the fact that social conditions in Italy are not worthy of a modern society, which aspires to a place among the most advanced countries of the world'.[91]

There are a number of factors responsible for these social inadequacies. First, many of the deficiencies are of an urban character and reflect the great urban explosion that Italy has experienced over the postwar period, combined with a local authority system that is poorly admini-stered, short of funds and with low standards of urban planning (and almost non-existent urban planning legislation). The point can hardly be overstressed that Italy is currently undergoing a great urban revolution, an almost inevitable result of the vast exodus from agriculture – a sector in which occupational mobility involves spatial mobility and a movement into towns and cities. The rapid urbanisation process is found in both North and South but the problem has been exacerbated in the former by immigration from the latter. Between 1951 and 1966 the proportion of the Italian population living in urban areas having a population of more than 110,000 in 1961 rose from 34.5 to 41.8 per cent – an absolute increase of 5.5 million.[92] All the signs are that these urban areas will, in the future, take an increasing share of national population, a reliable estimate being that they will hold 49.1 per cent of the Italian population in 1981 as against 41.8 per cent in 1966 – a rise of 6.7 million people. A second factor explaining the inadequacy of social investment and the backwardness of Italian social conditions is that the trade unions took little interest in social issues until very recently. Indeed, only in the late 1960s did they recognise that successes on the wage bargaining front had been 'for the most part compromised by economic and social disequilibria existing outside the factories'.[93] However, having recognised this fact, they were prepared to use industrial action to secure social reform. As we shall see in chapter 4, the great pension reforms of the late 1960s, for example, are not unrelated to trade union pressures. Thirdly, there is little doubt that during the 1950s social investment and expenditure was purposefully neglected by government, economic growth being the prime objective. 'Productive' investment in industry and agriculture was given priority over 'unproductive' social investment. The shortsightedness of this policy was, however, being recognised in the early 1960s, and was set out in 1962 by La Malfa in his *Nota Aggiuntiva,* which clearly pointed to the serious inadequacies in the fields of education, social security, health, housing, public transport and urban services in general. Planning was seen as the vehicle for the resolution of these problems.

A key element of the 1966–70 national plan was, therefore, to make headway in overcoming social investment deficiencies. The objective was that 22.5 per cent of the increase in national income would be devoted to these ends – primarily education, health, housing, transport and communications. In the event this objective was almost attained, a figure of 21.8 per cent being secured. However, this was very largely a result of higher-than-planned (some 30 per cent higher) investment in housing, an increase that hid shortfalls in almost every other sector. Education investment was only 35 per cent of the plan figure, health 35 per cent, urban transport 34 per cent, and public works 58 per cent.[94] Moreover, the success in respect of housing needs to be treated with caution since much of this investment did not involve an increase in low-cost public housing but rather 'the expansion of traditional housing at inaccessible prices for the greater part of the population'.[95]

In a remarkably frank document, the authors of the 1971–75 plan set out the reasons why the 1966–70 plan targets with respect to social investment were not met.[96] Some of the reasons were peculiar to the period 1966–70; the economic difficulties at the start and end of the plan period, and rapid cost rises in the construction industry (often forcing contract renegotiations). But others were more long-standing and would equally apply to the whole postwar period. Singled out for particularly strong criticism was the slowness of the administrative procedures, the problems of inter-departmental co-ordination and the 'complexity of the formal controls with which the expenditure of the public administration is subjected by law (often half a century old)'[97] – deficiencies that have already been discussed above. It is relevant to note that those areas of social investment that are the responsibility of groups not subject to the limitations of the public administration proper (the state holding sector, for example) have not suffered from these problems, and have generally met or superseded their targets. Interestingly, since the early 1970s the state holding sector, and IRI in particular, has been encouraged by government to expand its construction activities, often taking over programmes that would normally be done by the State or local authorities, in an attempt to get round the problem of operating through the public administration system.

In brief, administrative inadequacies, combined with a political system that is far from ideally suited to introduce reforms, have meant that social investment has not kept pace with economic growth. Inevitably a vast backlog now exists. The problem of resolving this will be made more difficult by the continuing inflow of population into the major towns. The situation has already resulted in (belated) industrial action by the trade unions to try to force the government to effect more active measures. We have already seen that the shortages of social investment have to some extent been responsible for two economic crises in the past decade, but the consequences could in the long run be much more serious if radical action is delayed much longer. Most industrialised countries were allowed decades to resolve the urban and social chaos and other shortcomings of their industrial or economic revolutions. Faced with various pressure groups, many of which are capable of exploiting the deteriorating situation for their own ends, and in a society of excellent communications, the Italians cannot enjoy such luxury.

1.9 The future

Italy is now at a fascinating and difficult stage of development. A key question is how her future rate of growth is likely to compare with that of the past. The question is important not only because Italy is still a relatively poor country, but also because rapid growth, among other things, is required if the substantial backlog of social investment is to be rectified. Moreover, rapid growth is also the necessary medium for the eradication of spatial and industrial dualism and the absorption of labour surpluses.

Few would doubt that the potential for rapid growth still exists in Italy, particularly through the switching of resources from low-productivity sectors. We have already made the point that agricultural employment (much of it low-productivity) is, relative to other European countries, still a major feature of the economy, and that a large proportion of the non-agricultural labour force is employed in very small scale, and generally low-productivity, units. To the potential for growth from switching can be added that of the continuing slack labour markets. Although unemployment is (officially) low, migration remains high and activity rates are among the lowest in Europe. The absorption of these resources into the economy could aid growth substantially. However, the important question is whether the potential for growth can be exploited on anything like the previous scale.

In many ways the favourable conditions of the 1950s and 1960s, particularly those of the 1950s, now no longer exist or have been seriously eroded. A particularly important change has concerned industrial relations. The weak trade union system, which earlier allowed wages to rise at a much slower pace than productivity, and which in turn stimulated exports and allowed high levels of self-financed investment, has been radically altered. Since the mid-1960s, as we shall see in chapter 4, a strong and militant union system has been making wage demands well in excess of productivity growth. This has implications for overall economic growth on a number of counts. First, it diminishes Italy's competitiveness in foreign markets. Secondly, it reduces the possibilities of self-financed investment, forcing industry to go to the capital market for funds – a market which in Italy, as we have seen, is very poorly developed. Thirdly, the high wage demands have primarily concerned the advanced sector of the economy and the large, unionised firms. This not only preserves, or even increases, labour market dualism, but it also reduces the prospects of labour switching from low- to high-productivity activities – an important component, as we have seen, of past Italian growth.

A further factor that does not augur well for the future concerns the balance of payments. As we shall see in chapter 3, net earnings from tourism and emigrants' remittances, which have been important components of Italy's postwar balance of payments success, have tended in recent years to decline. One can anticipate in the future a continuing, if slow, whittling away of the surpluses on both these items. However, more important than the trends in respect of these items, the balance of payments has in recent years been bedevilled by enormous and adverse capital movements. Finally, although the inflationary wage settlements of the late 1960s and early 1970 do not appear to have affected visible exports, it is a moot question as to whether this situation will continue for long into the future. It is important to stress that these potentially unfavourable trends in respect of the various balance of payment items have implications beyond the balance of payments *per se* and, on two counts, could have serious repercussions for the overall rate of national growth. First, as we have seen, the surpluses on the balance of payments, which Italy has generally enjoyed over the postwar period, have freed the authorities from a constraint that has strangled many other countries, including the United Kingdom. If Italy in the future needs to resort to deflationary policies in order to protect herself from intermittent balance of payments problems, this can but slow down the long-term rate of economic growth. Secondly, for many observers, as we shall see in chapter 3, Italy is a clear case of export-led growth. In so far as this is still a valid interpretation of Italian growth, any cutback in the rate of growth of visible exports will have serious repercussions for overall economic growth. In many ways, however, the degree to which balance of payments difficulties affect the economy will depend upon Italian attitudes towards exchange rates, and the hope must be that there will be no zealous adherence to an unsuitable rate. In this context the EEC's ambitions for economic and monetary union are very worrying – not only because of the possible effects on national growth, but because this growth is the major means whereby Italian dualism can be eradicated.

For Italy, the complete exchange rate rigidity which economic and monetary union implies could be quite disastrous.

Given these changes in labour market and balance of payments conditions, one can expect the future growth process to be less stable – and certainly less stable than during the 1950s. As we shall see in detail in chapter 2, there are a number of possible theoretical interpretations of Italian growth in the 1950s, but all rest heavily on the contribution of excess labour supplies. In the context of that period, when neither the balance of payments nor trade union pressures acted as constraints, these interpretations explain well the pace and stability of Italian growth. Since the early 1960s, however, Italian growth has been less stable, as the balance of payments became erratic and the trade unions pushed for inflationary wage awards. But our view is that this instability was exacerbated, and overall growth consequently restrained, by the poverty of demand management techniques (which were barely needed during the 1950s). For administrative and political reasons, fiscal policy is almost inoperative while monetary policy, because of the nature of Italian capital markets, has an over-severe impact when applied to deflate the economy. In a reflationary context monetary policy in Italy, as in other countries, is slow to effect a response. The savage consequences of deflationary measures in 1963–64 and the very slow recovery of the economy from these measures were to a large degree a result of inadequate demand management techniques.

However, the 1969–73 crisis gave more dramatic expression to these shortcomings and the new problems of the Italian economy. This was a period characterised by substantial inflation and a very marked monetary policy-induced downturn, followed by a prolonged recession. Political instability and premature elections stymied an early recovery, as did overseas market conditions, but the inadequacies of monetary policy and the total absence of effective fiscal policies were important factors which converted the downswing in 1970 into a three-year recession of great severity. Without an improvement in Italy's demand management techniques, the prospects for rapid and stable future growth are not good.

Few would doubt that the period 1969–73 represented lost years for Italy in terms of economic growth, but they may also be viewed by historians as vital years – years that taught many lessons and forced major reappraisals. Some of the results in this respect are already being seen. For example, the great expansion of southern policy in 1971 (detailed in chapter 6) reflected to a large extent the recognition that the inflationary and violent wage demands of 1969–70 were, in part at least, a result of the great migratory inflows into the major northern cities, in turn a consequence of the inadequacies of earlier southern policies. The recent impetus to the reform of the tax system is not un-related to the recognised need to develop a stronger fiscal policy and reduce the earlier over-reliance on monetary policy. Moreover, by mid-1973 the trade unions were taking a more constructive and less militant line – in part a result of their recognition that the move to the right in Italian politics during the early 1970s was not entirely unrelated to their militant and extreme actions at the end of the 1960s (though whether the unions will be able to make their members adhere to the new line, particularly in an economy suffering serious inflation, is a moot point).

One would hope, however, that a prime lesson of 1969–73 will be a recognition by government that social investment and social expenditure need to be increased substantially. We have already made the point that, in many ways, Italy in the postwar period has been a country that has had economic growth without development. Years of political and administrative ineptitude have resulted in a sadly unbalanced country in the economic sense, and a socially backward one. Although in narrow economic terms Italy is now among the top ten industrialised countries of the world, she remains in other ways very backward. The director-general of Italian planning recently wrote of Italy's 'insufficiency of education and training; of the shortage of housing; of the bad state of basic social and public services, from the administration of justice to the schools, from sewerage to the national public transport system; the degradation of the national environment and historic and artistic heritage; the continuance of corporative and parasitic bodies, of property income, of *mafiose* intermediaries, of fiscal evasion, of protected niches of inefficient bureaucracy'.[98] The problems are not new, nor is the admission that they exist. The major hope must be, however, that the economic and political events of 1969–73, which these conditions largely spawned, will encourage action. Without it, the future is bleak.

Italy is currently in a difficult position. She needs continuing rapid growth if the problem of dualism is to be resolved, and if the backlog of social investment is to be reduced. 'The truth is that when the economy does not move, nothing moves'.[99] On the other hand, without action in respect of social investment and dualism, economic growth could be imperilled. Yet growth may well exacerbate the inadequacies of social infrastructure in that it will probably be associated with a further and rapid expansion of the major towns. But even without growth the movement of population into these towns will continue, the evidence being that job opportunities are not the sole explanation for the inflows into the urban centres. To a large extent, Italy is now in a cleft stick, and a dangerous one. Shortages of social infrastructure can imperil growth and have already led to frustration and violence. But if to these shortages was added the problem of serious unemployment and underemployment, as there would be if economic growth slows down substantially, then the situation could be extremely delicate.

Notes to chapter 1

1. This and other figures used below for Italian development up to the First World War are calculated from data in P. Ercolani 'Documentazione Statistica di base' in G. Fuà (ed.) *Lo Sviluppo Economico in Italia* vol. III, Milan: Franco Angeli (1969). Other statistical sources and analysis do exist and are sometimes at odds with the Ercolani figures. For a very good article with an excellent bibliography and indicating well the various sources of data and the differing interpretations of Italian economic development up to the First World War see L. de Rosa 'La Rivoluzione Industriale in Italia' *Rassegna Economica* (1971) pp. 43–90.

2. For a discussion of military expenditure in Italian economic development before the First World War, see L. de Rosa 'Difesa Militare e Sviluppo Economico in Italia (1861–1914)' *Rassegna Economica* (1969) pp. 287–318.

3. A. Gerschenkron 'Notes on the Rate of Industrial Growth in Italy' *Journal of Economic History* (December 1955) pp. 374–5.

4. A good source for historical international comparisons is B. Mitchell *The Fontana Economic History of Europe, Statistical Appendix 1700–1914* London: Fontana (1971).

5. Gerschenkron, op. cit., p. 370.

6. ibid., p. 372.

7. ibid.

8. R. Tremelloni *L'Italia in una Economia Aperta* Milan: Garzanti (1963) p. 5.

9. W. Welk *Fascist Economic Policy* Cambridge, Mass.: Harvard University Press (1938).

10. M. Einaudi and F. Goguel *Christian Democracy in Italy and France* Indiana: University of Notre Dame Press (1952) p. 15.

11. Tremelloni, op. cit., p. 13.

12. Ercolani, op. cit.

13. L. Matassi 'The Great Depression and the New Recovery of Italian Industry' in Banco di Roma *Review of Economic Conditions in Italy* (July 1969) p. 309.

14. ibid., p. 309.

15. Welk, op. cit., p. 180.

16. ibid., pp. 191–3.

17. Quoted in C. Seton-Watson *Italy from Liberalism to Fascism 1870–1925* London: Methuen (1967) p. 706.

18. From data in Ercolani, op. cit.

19. Quoted in E. Wiskemann *Fascism in Italy: its Development and Influence* London: Macmillan (1970) p. 35.

20. ibid., p. 120.

21. For a good description of Italy's lack of preparedness for war, and the consequences, see S. Clough *The Economic History of Modern Italy* New York: Columbia University Press (1964) pp. 260–87.

22. N. Negro *L'Italia Economica* Milan: Etas Kompass (1969), pp. 7–8.

23. The details of war losses given below, unless otherwise stated, have been taken from various articles in Banco di Roma, *Ten Years of Italian Economy 1947–56;* Clough, op. cit.; and CIR, *Lo Sviluppo dell'Economia Italiana nel Quadro della Ricostruzione e della Cooperazione Europea* (Rome, 1952).

24. 'La Rivoluzione Industriale in Italia', op. cit., p. 81.

25. From data in Ercolani, op. cit.

26. CIR, op. cit., p. 8.

27. Tremelloni, op. cit., pp. 20–1.

28. For an excellent survey of the immediate postwar problems and policies in Italy see CIR, op. cit.

29. Negro, op. cit., pp. 9–10.

30. For an excellent discussion and analysis of foreign aid to Italy during these years and during the later Marshall Aid period, see CIR, op. cit. Most of the figures in the text below are taken from this source.

31. D. Horowitz *The Italian Labor Movement* Cambridge, Mass.: Harvard

University Press (1963) p. 1.

32. Svimez *Notizie sull'Economia del Mezzogiorno* (Rome, 1956).

33. A. Servidio *Il nodo Meridionale* Naples: Edizioni Scientifiche Italiane (1972) p. 141.

34. Svimez *Un Secolo di Statistiche Italiane: Nord e Sud* (Rome, 1961).

35. M. Finoia 'Aspetti e Problemi dello Sviluppo Economico Italiano dal 1951 al 1968' *Rassegna Economica* (1970) p. 622.

36. United Nations *Statistical Yearbook 1954* New York: United Nations Organisation (1954).

37. *Un Secolo di Statistiche*, op. cit.

38. *La Formazione Professionale in Italia* Bologna: Il Mulino (1972) vol. II, p. 102.

39. *Un Secolo di Statistiche*, op. cit.

40. G. Mammarella *Italy after Fascism: a Political History 1943–1965* Indiana: University of Notre Dame Press (1966) p. 242.

41. ibid.

42. *Notizie sull'Economia del Mezzogiorno*, op. cit., p. 19.

43. Between 1956 and 1967 Italy gave 278 million dollars per annum in private and public aid to the underdeveloped countries. Italy has frequently been criticised both for the low amount of aid given relative to her income and for the 'ungenerous' composition of that aid. For a very good article on Italian aid to underdeveloped countries, see P. Logli 'L'Assistenza Economica Fornita dall'Italia ai Paesi in Via di Sviluppo' *Rassegna Economica* (1970) pp. 373–414.

44. Statistical Office of the European Communities *Basic Statistics of the Community 1972* Luxembourg: EEC (1973).

45. R. Pasca di Magliano 'L'Agricoltura nel Processo di Trasformazione del Mezzogiorno: Considerazioni in Margine al Modello di Ranis-Fei' *Rassegna Economica* (1972) p. 1036.

46. G. Ruffolo *Rapporto sulla Programmazione* Rome/Bari: (1973) p. 51.

47. L. de Rosa 'Italia Squilibrata' *Rassegna Economica* (1972) pp. 715–45.

48. For a very good discussion of Italian agriculture and agricultural policies see Servidio, op. cit., and D. Prinzi *L'Agricoltura Italiana Oggi* Rome: Edizione Radiotelevisione Italiana (1970).

49. For a good description and analysis of Italy's profits and losses from the Agricultural Guidance and Guarantee Fund, see 'Italia Squilibrata', op. cit.

50. See Ministero del Bilancio a della Programmazione Economica *Programma Economico Nazionale 1971–75*, Allegato Secondo *Programma 1966–70: Obiettivi e Risultati* (Rome, 1972).

51. Negro, op. cit., p. 12.

52. One consequence of the substantial fall in share prices (from 100 in 1961 to 48 in spring 1972), and one which has only recently provoked comment, has been the purchase of many Italian companies by foreigners. In 1971 foreigners held 20 per cent of Italian share capital, as against 15.3 per cent in 1965. Some of this will be held by Italians through illegally exported capital in an attempt at tax evasion. Even so the proportions are impressive. For a discussion of foreign control in Italy see L. Preti *Italia Malata* Milan: Mursia (1973), who cynically comments on Italy becoming 'a colonial republic founded on our work for the profit of others' (p. 121) — a play on article 1 of the Italian Constitution.

53. Fiscal evasion is generally acknowledged to be rife in Italy. There are probably three major reasons for this state of affairs, and two of them reflect on the inefficiency of the public administration. First, most Italians can remember a time when the state did not give them their due, with tax evasion being seen as a way of recouping these monies. Secondly, the administrative system is such that evasion is easy (and the law such that the penalties are not heavy). Thirdly, as we shall see in chapter 5, many of the direct taxes are extremely complicated, with concessions and allowances in abundance. A number of direct taxes also, ambitiously, try to measure wealth and figurative income – laudable in principle, but giving enormous scope for evasion.

54. Preti, op. cit., p. 61.
55. For a good brief critique of Italian universities, and particularly in respect of the staff, see J. Meynaud *Rapporto sulla Classe Dirigente Italiana* Milan: Giuffrè (1966) pp. 155–8.
56. A telling and comprehensive indictment of the Italian industrial training system can be found in the recently published *La Formazione Professionale in Italia,* op. cit.
57. Ridicule or disrespect towards public figures or the public administration can result in prosecution. For a discussion of this point (the crime of *Vilipendio*) see J. Adams and P. Barile *The Government of Republican Italy* London: Allen and Unwin (1961); and Meynaud, op. cit. This latter reference (pp. 43–64) has an excellent discussion of the Italian civil service.
58. For a very stimulating discussion of state and para-state employees, including the civil service, see E. Gorrieri *La Giungla Retributiva* Rome: Il Mulino (1973).
59. Adams and Barile, op. cit., p. 218.
60. 'Thus, for example, the Ministry of the Treasury has been trying for years to get back millions of acres of good land that the Ministry of Defence took over for cavalry horses during the war.' Ibid., p. 219.
61. In 1959 it was reported that 'the question of bribery of public servants has reached such proportions that the Roman Catholic Church has come out with advice for priests who hear confessions, suggesting that it is not a sin to offer or pay a bribe to a public servant when it appears to be the only way a citizen can get a service to which he has a right, and it is not a sin to accept payment for assistance to the public that goes beyond the call of duty'. Ibid., p. 220.
62. The dominance of legal aspects in public administration decisions, at the expense of economic and other criteria, is stressed by Ruffolo, op. cit.
63. F. Ventriglia 'L'Economia Italiana Oggi' *Rassegna Economica* (1969) p. 1336. This interesting article gives some good examples of *residui passivi.*
64. *Economist* (28 March 1964) p. 1251.
65. In addition to the three main economics ministries there are also various economic sector ministries (transport and communications, South, state holding, industry and labour), which add to the problems of co-ordination. In theory, co-ordination should come through the Interministerial Economic Planning Committee (CIPE), but this is understaffed and overburdened with an enormous list of tasks – the co-ordination of public administration and public bodies to the national plan, the approval of ENEL and state holding sector programmes, credit policy and criteria for the South policy, to name but a few. For a good discussion of the problem of economic co-ordination in Italy and the roles of CIPE, see Ruffolo, op. cit., pp. 71–5.
66. See J. La Palombara *Interest Groups in Italian Politics* Princeton: Princeton University Press (1964).
67. J. Bain *International Differences in Industrial Structure* New Haven, Conn.: Yale University Press (1966) p. 96.
68. For a good discussion of recent trends in industrial concentration in Italy and the various attempts to introduce monopoly and restrictive practices policies, see F. Forte *La Strategia delle Reforme* Milan: Etas Kompass (1968) chapter II. See also G. Amato (ed.) *Il Governo dell'Industria in Italia* Bologna: Il Mulino (1972) pp. 259–63.
69. Ruffolo, op. cit., p. 27.
70. For a very good discussion of the evolution and powers of the system of regional government in Italy, see M. Semprini 'Actuation of the Regional System in Italy: First Experiences and Prospects' in Banco di Roma *Review of the Economic Conditions in Italy* (May 1971); and, by the same author, 'Considerations on the First Period of Activity of the Regions with Ordinary Statutes' in Banco di Roma *Review of the Economic Conditions in Italy* (May 1972). Much of the information below has been taken from these sources.
71. Semprini (1971) op. cit., p. 185.
72. ibid., p. 192.

73. For a similarly pessimistic view see Preti, op. cit., pp. 55–60.
74. *Basic Statistics of the Community*, op. cit.
75. ibid.
76. See *Obiettivi e Risultati*, op cit.
77. See Finoia, op. cit., p. 655.
78. *Basic Statistics 1972*, op. cit.
79. *Un Secolo di Statistiche*, op. cit.
80. G. d'Aragona 'La Bonifica negli Anni '70' *Rassegna Economica* (1971) p. 328.
81. *Basic Statistics of the Community*, op. cit.
82. V. de Falco 'Nuovo Occasioni di Sviluppo per l'Agricoltura' *Rassegna Economica* (1972) p. 778.
83. The following figures from *Basic Statistics of the Community 1972*, op. cit., illustrate this point and are for 1970. It should be noted that the size groupings are not strictly comparable with those given for Italy in the text.

	Italy	Germany	France
Farms of between 1 and 5 hectares (%)	68.4	37.5	22.9
Land cultivated by farms of between 1 and 5 hectares (%)	21.8	8.4	2.9
Farms of between 1 and 20 hectares (%)	94.6	83.7	65.5
Land cultivated by farms of between 1 and 20 hectares (%)	53.1	52.2	26.4

84. For Gorrieri, op. cit., agricultural workers and farmers were a distinctly underprivileged or exploited group (together with pensioners, workers with large families and outworkers). While a manual worker in industry or construction earned some 125,000 lire per month, the agricultural worker received around 98,000 lire. More desperate was the position of farmers who, by Gorrieri's estimates (based admittedly on a very small 'sample'), had an income for their labour of 57,000 lire – 89,000 lire per month. This was on farms which, in terms of size, were well above average. The majority of Italian farmers would be in a yet more pitiful situation. It should be added that farmers are also underprivileged in other respects relative to the industrial workers. They do not receive the golden handshake paid to most Italians on leaving their employer; they enjoy no paid holidays, receive no sickness benefit, have themselves to pay for drugs supplied under the health service, enjoy much lower pensions and retire five years later than their counterparts in industry.
85. For a good article on the Italian retail sector see C. Salviuolo 'La Distribuzione al Dettaglio in Italia e nel Mezzogiorno' *Rassegna Economica* (1971) pp. 1505–27.
86. See S. Cafiero and A. Busca *Lo Sviluppo Metropolitano in Italia* Rome: Giuffrè (1970).
87. Two very good articles covering the two crises of the 1960s, which lay heavy stress on the contribution of southern migration, are F. Ventriglia 'Mezzi e Modalità della Ripresa dopo Due Crisi Congiunturali' *Rassegna Economica* (1972) pp. 927–55; and 'Italia Squilibrata', op. cit., pp. 725–6.
88. 'Italia Squilibrata', op. cit., pp. 725–6.
89. And yet Italy also has an enormous number of uninhabited houses. Of the 17.5 million houses in existence in 1971, only 15.4 million were occupied – a reflection of the enormous rural exodus of the postwar period and the degree to which industrial development has been concentrated in the urban areas.
90. Between 1961 and 1965 only 6.5 per cent of houses constructed in Italy were public houses, and this proportion fell even lower during the second half of the 1960s. The problem of increasing the number of public houses is a good example of the Italian public sector in action. Substantial funds do exist for public house building (contributed by employers and employees), but they have not been spent by the main agency involved, GESCAL. The failure to spend has been a consequence of many factors – frequent changes of president (with associated reorganisation), political conflict between at least one of the presidents and the Minister of Public Works, the lack of relevant legislation and the long drawn out process of introducing

it, the difficulties of operating within the extremely legal public administration framework, and particularly in respect of expropriation. In the early 1970s a new president was appointed to GESCAL who has been prepared to cut corners and take risks, with a resulting dramatic increase of expenditure. It is perhaps ironic that this comes at a time when GESCAL is due to be disbanded and its powers allocated to the regions. Indeed, its recent successes could perhaps be explained to some degree by the fact that it is no longer seen as a political force.

91. Ruffolo, op. cit., p. 179.
92. For more details of urban population changes and forecasts discussed below, see Cafiero and Busca, op. cit.
93. E. Guidi *et al. Movimento Sindacale e Contrattazione Collettiva 1945–1970* Milan: Franco Angeli (1971) p. 28.
94. See *Obietivi e Risultati,* op. cit.
95. ibid., p. 38.
96. ibid.
97. ibid., p. 40.
98. Ruffolo, op. cit., p. 150.
99. Preti, op. cit., p. 195.

CHAPTER 2

Economic Growth

*This time it vanished quite slowly, beginning with the end of the
tail, and ending with the grin, which remained some time after
the rest of it had gone* (Alice in Wonderland)

A 'SATISFACTORY' rate of growth is usually listed in modern economics
textbooks as one of the prime goals of government policy, together with
price stability, low levels of unemployment and a sound balance of payments. While other parts of this book cover prices, unemployment and
the balance of payments, it is the task of this chapter to outline, analyse
and try to explain Italy's postwar economic growth.

Economic growth can be narrowly defined as an increase in Gross
National Income, or synonomously Gross National Product (GNP),
usually measured over a year. Insofar as we can use national income
figures to measure the economic welfare of a country in any one year,
we can measure its rate of economic advance by calculating the percentage increase of national income over a given period. To avoid any
distortion by inflation, it is customary to measure this at constant prices.
Moreover, economists are usually concerned with economic growth as a
sustained process over a considerable period of time, and although a ten
per cent increase in GNP in one year would represent, by our strict
definition above, a considerable rate of economic growth, this could be
of a type not sustainable over a longer period. It might, for example,
represent the taking into employment of previously unemployed resources
(either labour or capital) and therefore reflect only the absorption of slack
within the economy. In normal circumstances this would be a short-run
phenomenon and would not generate steady growth. Theories and studies
of economic growth are generally concerned with increases in national
income that are backed up by increases in productive capacity, and therefore capable of being sustained over a considerable period of time.

However, the distinction between increases in GNP through the absorption of slack and increases in productive capacity is not at all clear cut
in the Italian context where slack, in the form of unemployment and
underemployment, is also regarded as a source of long-run growth.
Indeed, as we shall see, some of the most influential interpretations of

Italian growth stress the role of excess supplies of labour.

A familiar exercise in assessing a country's economic performance is to compare its average annual growth rate with that of other countries. Table 2.1 presents such a comparison for the period 1950–70. It will be noted that the table refers to Gross Domestic Product (GDP) rather than

Table 2.1 Annual average growth rates of real GDP, 1950–1970

Country	1950–1960		1960–1970	
	Total	*Per capita*	Total	*Per capita*
	(%)	(%)	(%)	(%)
Japan*	8.0	6.8	10.6	9.4
USA	2.9	1.2	4.6	3.2
UK	2.7	2.3	2.8	2.1
West Germany	7.7	6.6	4.6	3.6
France	4.4	3.5	5.7	4.6
Belgium**	2.7	2.0	4.5	3.9
Netherlands	4.6	3.3	5.3	4.0
Sweden	3.6	2.9	4.3	3.5
Italy†	5.5	4.9	5.2	4.4

```
        *   1952–1960, 1960–1969
       **   1953–1960, 1960–1969
        †   1951–1960, 1960–1969
```
Source: United Nations *Yearbook of National Accounts Statistics* (New York, various issues).

GNP, the former being the most reliable data available for the period covered. The only difference between GNP and GDP is net property income from abroad, and although there can occasionally be considerable differences between *levels* of GDP and GNP, it is likely to be a sufficiently stable difference as to leave their *growth rates* virtually identical.

Japan's phenomenal postwar boom makes her the undisputed leader of the countries listed in the table, but Italy emerges as one of Europe's most rapidly growing economies, in absolute and *per capita* terms, over both the 1950s and the 1960s.

However, the figures presented in table 2.1 are annual averages and give no indication of the stability and pattern of Italian growth over time. In fact, by international standards the *stability* of Italian growth has been as notable as its rapidity.

There are two ways in which we can measure stability.[1] The first is to calculate the standard deviation of annual growth rates from their geometric mean, thereby indicating the extent to which actual growth rates diverge from their overall average. The objection to this method is, however, that it will tend to reflect the absolute value of growth rates, so that a country with rapid growth will tend to have a high standard deviation for that very reason. The second method, which avoids this

criticism, is to divide the standard deviation by the geometric mean to
give the co-efficient of variation. From table 2.2 it can be seen that by
either method Italy exhibits the most stable growth, measured in terms
of GDP, of the countries listed.

**Table 2.2   Standard deviation and co-efficient of variation of growth
rates, 1951–1968**

Country	Standard deviation	Co-efficient of variation
Japan	3.92	0.42
USA	2.58	0.69
UK	1.51	0.59
West Germany	2.81	0.59
France	1.43	0.31
Belgium	1.84	0.53
Netherlands	2.52	0.51
Sweden	1.63	0.42
Italy	1.36	0.26

Source: Calculated from United Nations *Yearbook of National Accounts Statistics*
(New York, various years).

Although stable by international standards, this is not to say that the
Italian growth rate has not shown substantial variations over the postwar
period. Indeed, growth rates for individual years have ranged from
1.6 per cent in 1971 to 7.8 per cent in 1961. Annual Italian growth rates,
together with other national accounts data which we shall have occasion
to use later, are provided in table 2.3. Even from a casual inspection of
the table it can be seen that during the 1960s and early 1970s Italian
growth became slower and less stable, in sharp contrast to the 1950s.

As we have noted in chapter 1, the early 1950s saw Italy consolidating
her recovery from the wartime destruction of capital equipment and
infrastructure, interrupted only slightly by the impact of the Korean War
on the balance of payments. From the mid-1950s onwards, however, there
was a clear accelerating trend of growth (with a slight dip in 1958),
reaching a peak in 1961 and then slowing down in 1962 and again in 1963,
the year when the economy ran into its first serious postwar balance of
payments crisis and when stringent monetary measures were applied in
an attempt to deflate the economy. Nevertheless, between 1950 and 1963
the growth rate had been a substantial 5.5 per cent per annum. In many
respects, the 1963 crisis marked the end of Italy's years of 'easy' growth,
and we shall later argue that since then the growth process has fundamentally altered, in a way that has been masked by the relatively high
average growth rate (4.1 per cent) registered between 1964 and 1972.

Table 2.3 Italian economic growth, 1951–1972: main indicators at constant prices (milliard lire)

	Gross national product		Value-added by sector				Aggregate expenditure				Wholesale prices (1966=100)
	Absolute terms	Growth rate	Agriculture	Industry	Services	Public administration	Consumption	Industrial investment	Total investment	Exports	
1951	14,473	(N.A.)	2892	4146	5254	2168	13,296	900	2649	1012	92.9
1952	15,022	3.8	2845	4426	5524	2227	14,107	970	2685	1190	87.8
1953	16,073	7.0	3159	4828	5803	2283	14,870	1047	3117	1385	87.4
1954	16,609	3.3	2987	5300	6005	2317	15,174	1126	3391	1502	86.5
1955	17,711	6.6	3141	5794	6366	2410	15,747	1255	4038	1695	87.4
1956	18,479	4.3	3146	6186	6681	2466	16,452	1354	4238	1982	88.9
1957	19,429	5.1	3194	6644	7038	2553	17,056	1446	4567	2415	89.8
1958	20,377	4.9	3553	6909	7269	2646	17,783	1450	4703	2475	88.2
1959	21,729	6.6	3675	7599	7694	2761	18,649	1527	5154	2749	85.5
1960	23,036	6.0	3499	8452	8232	2853	19,722	1766	5967	3354	86.3
1961	24,843	7.8	3794	9260	8826	2963	21,033	2100	6739	3838	86.5
1962	26,316	5.9	3758	10,109	9410	3039	22,352	2355	7308	4308	89.3
1963	27,679	5.2	3840	10,757	9944	3138	24,170	2561	7778	4753	93.8
1964	28,482	2.9	3999	10,938	10,293	3252	24,909	2045	7111	5486	96.9
1965	29,487	3.5	4115	11,297	10,718	3357	25,647	1621	6576	6599	98.5
1966	31,193	5.8	4249	12,131	11,323	3490	27,223	1789	6852	7394	100.0
1967	33,324	6.8	4566	13,191	11,997	3570	29,039	2030	7740	7965	99.8
1968	35,435	6.3	4431	14,430	12,900	3674	30,417	2248	8097	9119	100.2
1969	37,424	5.6	4563	15,422	13,693	3746	32,115	2496	8987	10,545	104.1
1970	39,309	5.0	4547	16,392	14,527	3843	34,322	2826	9725	11,790	111.7
1971	39,953	1.6	4620	16,302	15,082	3949	35,411	2824	8853	13,245	115.5
1972	41,240	3.2	4394	16,935	15,850	4061	36,773	2790	9031	14,938	120.2

Sources: Banca d'Italia *Relazione Annuale* (Rome: various issues) and ISAT *Annuario Statistico Italiano* (Rome: various issues).

In fact, as we shall see, since 1964 the overall development of the economy has been characterised by two prolonged recessions, separated by a brief and unsustained recovery between 1966 and 1969. The first of these recessions set in when the monetary measures adopted in 1963 had an over-severe impact on the domestic economy, pushing the growth rate down to under 3 per cent in 1964. Gross industrial fixed investment fell by over 20 per cent in real terms in both 1964 and 1965 and, indeed, as can be seen in table 2.3, it was not until 1970 that it reattained the 1963 level.

However, the growth rate of GNP recovered more swiftly, rising to 3.5 per cent in 1965 and 5.8 per cent in 1966, to reach a post-1963 peak in 1967 of 6.8 per cent. But this trend was not sustained, and the growth rate thereafter fell every year without exception until 1971 when a mere 1.6 per cent was secured – the poorest single year of the entire postwar period. By this time Italy was in the throes of its second major recession – one that lasted from 1970 to 1973. Even from this cursory survey, it is clear that the pattern of Italian development changed dramatically after 1963 and it is one of the central tasks of this chapter to analyse in detail the reasons for this.

The chapter is in two parts. Section 2.1 examines the period 1950–63, hailed by domestic and foreign observers alike as an 'economic miracle'. In particular, we shall assess the extent to which the growth process in this period is adequately explained by the commonly cited interpretations of Italian growth, which emphasise the role of excess labour supplies on the one hand and a propulsive export sector on the other. Section 2.2 examines why these same mechanisms were not at work after 1963 and the extent to which economic theory can explain the loss of dynamism in these years, and ends with an assessment of Italy's future prospects for growth and the factors on which these depend.

2.1 Italian economic growth 1950–1963

As we have seen, the years 1950–63 represent the most successful period of economic development in Italy's history and, as such, they have attracted considerable analysis and interpretation. It is the task of this section to examine the economic theory underlying these interpretations and at the same time to test their validity in the light of empirical evidence.

We take as our starting point the Kindleberger interpretation of Italian growth, which is based on the application of one particular development theory, or model, to Italy's postwar experience.[2] This, the so-called Lewis model,[3] highlights the role of an elastic labour supply in economic development; it is used by Kindleberger to explain the rapid growth of West Germany, Italy, Switzerland and the Netherlands, as well as the slow growth of the Scandinavian countries, Belgium and the UK. Kindleberger's study is a particularly appropriate starting point for our argument since it represents a formal connection between a theory of economic development and the recent growth experience of industrialised countries; and in that one of the central features of Italy's economic structure is, as we have seen in chapter 1, the availability of large surpluses of labour, any theory seeking to explain Italy's postwar growth must ascribe some role to these substantial reserves.

The Lewis model of economic development, as adopted by Kindleberger, involves a 'dualistic' economy. On the one hand, there is a 'capitalist' industrial sector employing modern production techniques, while on the other there is a depressed or backward sector consisting of agriculture and small-scale, low-productivity industrial and tertiary activities. It is from this backward sector that the elastic supply of labour comes. The wage rate in the backward sector is extremely low relative to the modern advanced sector and this differential is sufficient to attract labour out of the backward sector when it is required, and to 'compensate for the higher cost of town over rural life'.[4]

In these conditions the process of economic growth is as follows. Given capital accumulation in the capitalist sector, the level of productivity in that sector is raised and, with a constant wage rate, so are profits. These profits are then reinvested, resulting in an increased demand for labour. However, the important point is that this demand does not lead to a rise in the wage rate, because of the elastic supply of labour available from the backward sector. Thus, the new investment, pushing up the level of productivity, generates yet more profits, which are, again, reinvested. So the process continues. The motive force of growth is capital accumulation in the advanced sector, but the self-sustaining nature of the process is due to the continuance of low wages, which allow profits to increase, which in turn induces and finances further investment. However, this process will continue only as long as the labour supply remains perfectly elastic. As soon as the excess supplies of labour are diminished, such that an increase in employment in the advanced sector can only be brought about by an increase in the wage rate, then the process will begin to run down as profits are squeezed by rising wages, and investment tails off.

Given the central role attributed to the shift of labour from low- to high-productivity sectors, the Lewis model involves three possible sources of productivity growth in the economy as a whole. First, labour productivity in the advanced industrial sector could be raised by increased investment. Secondly, the movement of underemployed labour out of the backward sector will result in higher output per person employed, since the Lewis hypothesis is that the marginal product of labour employed there is equal to zero, so that any reduction in employment will leave total product unchanged and therefore raises output per person employed. These two points relate to productivity within each sector. A third source of productivity growth concerns the economy as a whole. The movement of labour out of the backward sector into modern industry means a shift of resources from low- to high-productivity employment, and this change in the structure of resource allocation raises overall productivity in the economy. For these three reasons, as long as the economy has under-employed labour to absorb, it can enjoy what Kindleberger called 'super-growth'.

The key element in Kindleberger's approach is the elastic supplies of labour afforded by the existence of a backward sector alongside an advanced sector. This economic dualism is vital to Kindleberger's explan-ation of how a country can sustain a process of super-growth. Other writers, however, have devoted more attention to the sources and causes of dualism as the central problem of the Italian economy.[5] This is not to say that they divorce dualism from growth; indeed, the most prominent of these writers, Vera Lutz, regarded economic growth as the only feasible route towards the eradication of Italy's dualism. Of course, the growth process envisaged by Kindleberger would also involve the gradual disappearance of dualism in that as the advanced sector absorbed more and more labour, productivity in the backward sector would increase and eventually wages would rise, partly as a reflection of the higher produc-tivity in that sector, but primarily because of tighter labour markets. The eventual exhaustion of the excess labour supplies, in Kindleberger's thesis, would not only bring to a close a period of sustained and rapid economic growth, it would also see an end to dualism. For Kindleberger, however, this seems almost incidental, and the key point about dualism, in the context of his analysis, is the opportunity it affords for economic growth. For Lutz it represents one of Italy's fundamental economic problems.

As we shall see in chapter 4, the main source of economic dualism, according to Lutz, is imperfections in the labour market. 'The primary characteristic of the dual system is that labour doing (or capable of doing) the same kind of work, and often working in the same branch of economic activity, is remunerated at two different rates of pay'.[6] The high wages (and better conditions of employment) in the advanced sector are considered to be due to the existence and power of organised labour and, in this sense, those employed in this sector are 'protected'. On the other hand, the backward sector is characterised by a much lower wage level since labour is not organised into unions, and is therefore 'unprotected.'

A critical point in Lutz's argument is the close connection between the size of the firm or plant and the degree of unionisation. Firms employing more than ten workers will not be able to avoid hiring unionised labour, and will therefore have to pay wages higher than those in the corresponding industry in the backward sector. The degree of unionisation is, however, only one factor in this dualism. Another is the different levels of productivity – the larger firms are able to pay higher wages because of economies of scale and the use of advanced production methods. The small firms exhibit low productivity and therefore low wages, due to poor entrepreneurship and the restricted possibilities for employing more capital intensive techniques. The reason why, in general, such firms are able to co-exist with the large-scale firms is, of course, the wage differential between the two sectors.

This wage differential determines the structure of employment insofar as the numbers employed in large-scale firms are inversely related to the wage level in that sector, while the wage in the backward sector performs the function of clearing the labour market of those unable to secure high-wage employment. This is not to say that Lutz envisages wages in small-scale firms falling far enough to secure full employment in the economy as a whole, such a possibility being 'barred by the lack in many cases of the minimum amount of property and entrepreneurial capacity necessary to set up the extra, small production – or commercial – unit'. [7]

Given this economic structure, the propulsive element of Lutz's economic growth is basically the same as that of Kindleberger's – investment in the advanced industrial sector. However, the emphasis in Lutz's analysis is on the factors that could impede the absorption of labour from the low-wage sector, and therefore delay the attainment of a unified, non-dualistic, economic system. In particular, she examines the consequences of (a) different types of wage behaviour in the advanced sector, and (b) the changing degree of capital intensity in that sector. Under (b) the greater the extent to which capital accumulation serves only to increase the capital–labour ratio in the high-wage sector, the smaller will be the increase in employment in that sector. Points (a) and (b) are not, of course, unconnected in that the behaviour of wages could affect the capital–labour ratio. For example, if wages are forced up by trade union pressure, then investment will be directed towards raising the capital–labour ratio. It is, indeed, possible for wages to rise sufficiently to channel all investment into raising this ratio, thereby choking off employment effects which might have eased the pressure of excess labour in the low-wage sector.

Thus, the autonomous (trade-union-determined) behaviour of wages in the large-scale sector is a significant aspect of Lutz's model. The central point in Kindleberger's thesis is that the availability of excess labour supplies keeps the wage rate down and preserves profit margins to finance new investment. However, if wages can be pushed up in the advanced sector by trade union pressure, then profit margins will be squeezed long before the excess labour supplies are totally absorbed, and any new capital accumulation will be directed towards raising the capital–labour ratio. Nevertheless, in terms of the mechanism whereby excess labour supplies can 'feed' economic growth, Lutz and Kindleberger are in broad agreement. The question that now arises is whether the empirical evidence of Italian growth up to 1963 supports such an interpretation.

At its simplest level, the excess labour interpretation of growth has considerable evidence to support it. Italian growth up to 1963 was indeed characterised by a considerable absorption of unemployed and under-employed labour and a vast movement out of the backward, low-productivity agricultural sector into higher-productivity non-agricultural employment. As we shall see in detail in chapter 4, the agricultural labour force fell by 3.3 million between 1951 and 1963: accounting for 44 per cent of the labour force in 1951, it was down to 27 per cent by 1963. On the other hand, the construction industry's employment grew by almost a million, and manufacturing by 1.2 million. This sectoral switching was in addition to a substantial drop in the numbers unemployed – from 1.6 million in 1954 to 500,000 in 1963. Moreover, there was a fall in the number of underemployed, some indication of which is given by the fact that the number of marginal workers declined from 4.1 million in 1951 to 1.9 million in 1963.

The dividing line between the advanced and the backward sector is not simply that between industry and agriculture, since economic dualism also exists within industry. It is of course possible that the movement of labour out of agriculture was not into the advanced industrial sector but into the backward sector, and if this was the case the contribution to economic growth made by this switching would be much diminished. Lutz, in contrast to Kindleberger, considered that the greater part of the movement out of agriculture was indeed into the backward sector. There is, however, evidence, albeit limited, that this was not the case. It will be recalled that Lutz viewed the backward industrial sector as being made up of small establishments, employing a work force of ten or less. Although between the census years 1951 and 1961 the numbers employed in manufacturing units of this size increased slightly, by far the greater part of the overall increase in manufacturing employment (some 85 per cent) was accounted for by the growth of employment in units employing a work force of more than 10. Inevitably, the proportion of the manu-facturing work force in the smaller establishments employing less than 10 declined – from 32 per cent in 1951 to 28 per cent in 1961. In this sense the economic growth of the 1950s diminished the scope for econ-omic dualism, even if doubts remain about its intensity – a subject discussed in more detail in chapter 4.

In brief, there seems to be adequate statistical evidence to justify the excess labour theory in general and the view that Italy's growth, up to 1963 at least, was fed by the absorption of surplus labour and by the switching of labour from low- to high-productivity sectors and activities. Such a view, particularly with regard to the importance of switching, would also be in line with the empirical findings of a number of more detailed studies of the economy over this period – especially that of Denison, with his attempt to identify and measure the 'sources of growth' in a number of Western countries, including Italy.[8]

Denison was exclusively concerned with the supply side of economic growth, and his sources of growth fall under two general headings – total input, and output per unit of input. Within these categories the various sources were disaggregated and estimated. His most important result, in the context of our argument, is the large role attributable to 'improved allocation of resources' (which he estimated to account for 24 per cent of Italian national income growth in the period 1950–62), and in partic- ular through the contraction of agricultural inputs, which he estimated to contribute 17 per cent of Italy's growth. According to Denison, improved allocation of resources was the most important single source of Italian growth,[9] and indeed contributed more in Italy than in any of the countries studied. Such a reallocation of resources must, of course, be reflected in the composition of Italian GDP. Details of this have already been given in table 2.3, but in brief, there was a substantial fall in the importance of agriculture from 20.0 per cent of GDP in 1951 to 13.9 per cent in 1963, offset by the increasing importance of industry, and in particular manufacturing which accounted for 27.6 per cent of GDP in 1963 compared with 20.4 per cent in 1951.

Thus far, then, we have seen that the excess labour supply theory of growth provides a reasonably accurate picture of Italian development in the period up to 1963. There is however one further point, which we mentioned earlier but have since tended to ignore. This is that the existence of excess labour will only regenerate growth if it is associated with relatively stable wage levels, or at least wage levels that rise less rapidly than productivity, and thus allow increasing profits. As we shall see in detail in chapter 4, between 1951 and 1961 industrial wages did rise slower than industrial productivity, the former growing at an average rate of 4.1 per cent and the latter at 5.0 per cent, although this advantage was eroded in the inflationary years of 1962 and 1963 when industrial wages increased by 26 per cent and industrial productivity rose by only 8 per cent. Even so, for much of the period the wage aspect of the excess labour interpretation holds.

The interpretations of Italian growth presented so far have one element in common. They are all essentially concerned with the supply side. In a sense, the theories of Kindleberger and Lutz are in the spirit of most classical models insofar as problems of deficient demand are not really confronted. The propulsive element in both models is capital accumulation in the advanced sector, and the problem of what initially induces the investment is not of central concern.[10]* Yet the availability of excess supplies of labour does not, of itself, provide a stimulus to investment. The advanced sector must experience favourable demand conditions before the absorption of underemployed labour, and the process of growth, can get off the ground.

As can be seen in table 2.4, the two most important sources of growth in demand in the Italian economy up to 1963 were investment and exports.

Table 2.4   Structure of aggregate demand in Italy at 1963 prices

| | Composition of expenditure | | Average annual growth rate |
	1951	1963	1952–1963
Consumption,	78.4	65.8	4.9
of which: Public	15.3	11.1	3.8
Private	63.1	54.7	5.4
Gross investment,	15.6	21.2	9.4
of which: Gross fixed			
investment	13.9	20.1	9.3
Exports	6.0	13.0	13.8
TOTAL	100.0	100.0	

Source: ISTAT *Annuario di Contabilità Nazionale 1971* (Rome, 1972).

A major feature to emerge from table 2.4 is the declining share of consumption (caused by the relative fall in private consumption), offset by the increasing importance of gross fixed investment and exports. The same information is given alternative expression in the final column, which shows the average annual growth rates of the components of aggregate demand. These show exports clearly to be the most dynamic element in Italian growth, rising at an average annual rate of 13.8 per cent, while gross fixed investment grew by 9.3 per cent per annum. In other words, the declining share of consumption in aggregate expenditure allowed more resources to be devoted to exports and investment, obviously via a high savings ratio. But why should a low-consumption, high-savings economy necessarily be a rapidly growing economy?

Without needing to construct a formal growth model, we can point to obvious reasons why one would expect a high investment ratio to lead to a high rate of economic growth. Fixed investment (net, of course, of replacement) increases the capital stock, which thereby increases the productive capacity of the economy. Moreover, the newer the capital stock, the greater will be so-called embodied technical progress; and the more rapid the growth of the capital stock, the younger will be its age distribution. Thus, investment is not only a category of expenditure on the demand side; more important, it is a source of increased productive capacity, and therefore growth potential, on the supply side.[11]*

If one accepts that a high investment ratio is generally associated with a rapid growth of productive capacity and national income, Italy's impressive growth record can be partly viewed as a function of the maintenance of high profit levels up to 1963, which provided both the inducement and the finance for this investment. But this cannot be the whole story for, as we have seen, an even more dynamic element of aggregate demand in this period was exports, and we must now examine how these could induce rapid and sustained economic growth.

The main line of argument suggesting that an export-oriented economy will enjoy rapid economic growth is based on the inter-relationships between exports, investment and industrial productivity. These have been formally set out in models of export-led growth, and the importance of foreign trade in Italy's postwar development has led many economists to believe that such models best explain her economic performance. There are a number of reasons why one would expect a high growth rate of exports to be associated with a high overall growth rate of GNP, and a considerable literature on the subject has emerged.[12] The essence of export-led growth models is the circularity of the process involved. Economies that experience rapid growth together with a strong expansion of exports are said to be in a 'virtuous circle', while those with sluggish exports and slow growth are caught in a 'vicious circle'. What are the causal links within the virtuous circle? Rapidly rising exports are held to induce an increase in domestic productivity, through economies of scale resulting from production for larger (foreign) markets and increased investment due to favourable demand expectations. Irrespective of source, increases in productivity afford a competitive advantage abroad, giving a further boost to exports, and so the process is regenerated. It is the circularity of the process that ensures that export-led growth will be self-sustained growth.

The structure, stability and pace of Italian growth suggests that such a model may have relevance. At a general level one can see the relative importance of Italy's exports as a component of GDP levels and growth from table 2.5. The table shows that the share of exports in Italian GDP rose from 9.8 per cent in 1953 to 18.9 per cent in 1963, the largest proportionate increase of all the countries listed. When one measures the increase in exports as a percentage of the increase in GDP over the period, Italy falls into the middle of the league table, but this is partly explained by the higher share of exports in national income in some of the smaller European countries such as Belgium, the Netherlands and Switzerland.

Thus, exports were clearly an important component of Italy's growth up to 1963, but this says nothing about the dynamics of the growth

Table 2.5   Growth of exports and gross domestic product in ten countries
(constant prices)

Country	Exports as a percentage of GDP		Increase in exports (1953–63) as a percentage of increase of GDP
	1953	*1963*	
Belgium	25.4	38.2	68.6
France	13.3	15.6	19.2
West Germany	16.8	23.7	31.1
Japan	10.8	12.9	14.3
Netherlands	40.0	53.9	79.6
Sweden	22.3	28.3	40.1
Switzerland	25.6	30.5	38.8
UK	19.3	20.3	23.5
USA	3.8	5.0	8.4
Italy	9.8	18.9	30.2

Source: United Nations *Yearbook of National Accounts and Statistics* (New York, various years).

process. A key element in export-led growth models is that the growth of major export industries is associated with their productivity performance, and that industries with rapid export growth will also enjoy a high growth of productivity. Table 2.6 highlights this relationship for Italian manufacturing.

Table 2.6   Exports, value-added and productivity in Italian manufacturing industries, 1951–1963
(current prices)

	Average annual growth of exports	Average annual growth of value-added	Average annual growth of productivity*	Share of exports in total output**
Food, drink and tobacco	5.3	6.6	5.6	2.9
Textiles	2.7	4.2	7.6	29.8
Clothing and footwear	15.3	6.4	0.9	12.1
Leather, furs, etc.	16.1	6.8	9.1	12.1
Wood and furniture	9.2	9.6	5.3	5.8
Metallurgy	11.3	8.4	9.1	18.0
Mechanical engineering	16.4	10.9	4.0	27.8
Vehicles	15.4	11.6	9.9	27.3
Non-metallic minerals	10.3	11.3	6.3	8.9
Chemicals	14.2	10.4	10.1	17.2
Paper	0.4	12.8	9.2	6.9
Rubber	10.0	6.4	6.8	13.6
TOTAL MANUFACTURING	10.3	8.7	6.0	18.1

    * Productivity is measured by value-added per labour unit (see page xii). above for a definition of labour unit).
    ** These figures refer to exports and gross output in 1965.
Sources: ISTAT *Annuario di Statistico Italiano* (Rome, various issues); and ISTAT *Tavola Intersettoriale dell'Economia Italiana per l'Anno 1965* (Rome).

From table 2.6 one can assess the productivity, export and growth performance of the main Italian manufacturing industries. It is clear that, in general, the most rapidly growing industries, in terms of value-added, are also those that have exhibited a good export performance – the important examples being vehicles, chemicals, metallurgy, non-metallic minerals and mechanical engineering. However, according to the export-led growth models, these industries should also lead the table in terms of productivity growth. Again this is indeed largely the case, although a notable exception is engineering, perhaps explicable in terms of both the size and the heterogeneity of the industry, which exhibits a dualism almost all of its own, insofar as it includes both technologically advanced products such as domestic electrical equipment and precision instruments, and low-productivity activities such as small repair workshops. In very general terms, however, the table substantiates the basic export-led growth argument, which links productivity growth to output and export growth.

Indicative though these figures might be, they do of course in no way represent a *formal* application of an export-led growth model to the Italian case. The only study of this type yet published is that of Stern,[13] which covers the period 1951–63. His results at an aggregate level were not encouraging, but he did find that at an industry level those industries that were Italy's most important exporters also recorded the most rapid increases in total output. Moreover, he found a significant relationship between gross output and gross fixed investment in these industries – a crucial link in the export-led growth process. However, the final link in the virtuous circle is that increasing productivity should be translated into competitiveness, and thence into a further increase in exports. Thus, for export-led growth models to be meaningful, export growth must be seen to be primarily a function of increasing competitiveness. As we shall see in chapter 3, this is precisely the result obtained by Stern in a constant market share analysis of Italian manufacturing exports in the period 1955–63, when over 60 per cent of export growth was attributable to increased competitiveness.

So far, we have discussed the standard export-led growth approach, which concentrates on the virtuous circle created through visible exports. However, it is possible to develop the virtuous circle concept to envelop overall balance of payments performance. The argument in this case would be that a consistently favourable balance of payments is conducive to rapid economic growth because it removes an important constraint from the actions of policymakers. Any sustained growth process needs balance of payments success insofar as a weak balance of payments will require some form of deflationary policy from the authorities or a devaluation, most probably supported by a deflationary package. A sound balance of payments is therefore a *permissive* factor which allows economic growth to proceed free from periodic restrictions. Moreover, one could go further and claim that the absence of a balance of payments constraint is a *causal* factor which raises the rate of growth in that investment is primarily determined by expectations concerning future demand, and the uncertainty of such prospects in a 'stop–go' economy where short-run growth is interrupted by periodic balance of payments difficulties tends to lower the level of investment. If demand prospects remain free from these threats of deflationary measures, then the investment ratio, and thus the rate of growth, may be correspondingly higher. Such an argument has nothing directly to do with export growth, except in the case where rapidly rising exports are such as to ensure a regular balance of payments surplus, so that domestic entrepreneurs judge future balance of payments, and therefore demand, prospects by current export trends. As we shall see in chapter 3, Italy, at least up to the early 1960s, enjoyed a consistent surplus on her overall balance of payments – not, however, solely due to the performance of her manufacturing industries. Indeed, the balance of visible trade was in continuous, and sometimes substantial, deficit in these years, and the security of the overall balance of payments was largely attributable to the surplus on invisibles (particularly tourism) and emigrants' remittances, and to substantial foreign investment in Italy. Irrespective of source, however, the overall surplus freed the authorities from a constraint which has bedevilled many other countries.

Whichever virtuous circle argument one adopts, the foreign sector played a vital role *on the demand side* in Italy's postwar growth (at least up to 1963), and theories of export-led growth appear to provide at least a partial explanation of the inducement to invest – a factor that is largely neglected in the labour surplus models, which concentrate on *the supply side* of the development process. Taken together, these two sets of theories would seem to provide an adequate explanation of the process of Italian growth up to 1963. Even so, a major question which still remains is that of how this process got started in the 1950s. Excess labour supply theories explain how the growth process can be *sustained* by the availability of an elastic supply of labour, *given capital accumulation in the advanced sector,* while export-led growth models explain the inducement to invest, *given an increase in exports* (and/or a favourable balance of payments); but yet the theory of export-led growth essentially describes the operation of a circular process without providing any indication of how an economy may enter the virtuous circle.

Our view would be that it was only after the setting up of the EEC in 1958 that exports became the leading propulsive element in Italian growth. This is not to say that they were not important earlier in the 1950s, when the lira was slightly undervalued after the adjustments of 1947–49 and the general liberalisation of European trade was well under way (see chapter 3). Before the EEC's impetus to Italian exports, however, the major stimulus to aggregate demand, and investment in particular, came from the government rather than from foreign trade. Government expenditure programmes in transport, communications, agriculture and the South all combined to provide a considerable catalyst for private investment, and our view is that in the years 1950–58 Italy's growth process is explained by the excess labour supply theory, with public investment projects providing the crucial inducement to invest in the advanced sector. After 1958 the demand side of the growth process was provided by exports, and it was during the 'economic miracle' years 1958–62 that the growth of the Italian economy can be described as truly 'export-led'.

However, by the end of 1963, as we have already seen, the economic miracle was clearly at an end, and an inevitable question is what brought this about. The simplest explanation, and one that fits very neatly into the interpretations outlined so far, is that Italy encountered some form of full employment constraint. In the context of the excess labour supply theory, of course, this would herald the end of super-growth. Moreover, labour shortages can equally well explain how a country could be forced out of the virtuous circle. The final link in the export-led growth argument is that increases in domestic productivity are translated into increasing international competitiveness, thus giving a further boost to exports. However, this would be the case only if wages rose less quickly than productivity, and to this extent the maintenance of the export-led growth process depends on an elastic supply of labour. Within this theoretical framework the tightening of certain key labour markets (particularly for skilled and semi-skilled workers) in 1963 provides a neat explanation, whereby inflationary wage increases rendered exports uncompetitive and cut off the inducement to invest.

While this rather simple analysis provides part of the explanation for the 1963 crisis, it is by no means the whole story, and needs to be modified in two major respects. First, the wage inflation of 1963 is not explicable solely in terms of tightening labour markets, but is also reflected in the increasing aggressiveness of trade union bargaining in the early 1960s, when union leaders pushed hard for wage increases which, they felt, would regain some of the ground lost during the 1950s, when such aggressive wage bargaining had been conspicuous only by its absence (see chapter 4). This, in part, represented the realisation of Lutz's fears that monopolistic trade unions in the advanced sector could impede the growth process long before the excess supplies of labour were absorbed and dualism eradicated.

Secondly, it is an over-simplification to suggest that the post-1963 recession was solely a result of a slump in exports owing to domestic inflation. In fact, although the growth of exports did slacken off slightly in 1963, to 6.9 per cent, the subsequent fall in investment is better explained by a combination of a number of factors that were operative in 1963–64 and in particular by the psychological impact of the labour unrest of 1963 and the very real impact of the restrictive monetary policy adopted by the authorities. The balance of payments deficit of 1963, which arose out of a large increase in visible imports and a marked deterioration on capital account, induced this policy of severe monetary restraint from the authorities, which in turn depressed industrial investment. Thus, the virtuous circle, which had been based upon a secure balance of payments, was now broken.

The 1963 crisis, therefore, was compounded of a number of different elements which combined to make that year something of a turning point in Italian postwar development. From then on, despite the continued existence of considerable supplies of underemployed labour, the problem of inflation, particularly wage inflation, was never really absent. Exports no longer consistently 'led' growth. The balance of payments was placed in constant jeopardy by a volatile capital account. The whole economic environment in Italy changed, and consequently the nature of the growth process after 1963 was fundamentally different from that enjoyed up to that year. It is the task of the next section to describe and analyse Italian growth since 1963, and to assess the prospects for the future.

2.2 Italian economic growth 1964–1972

After 1963 the annual rate of Italian growth slowed down and became more unstable. As we have seen, the economy recovered only slowly from the 1963 crisis and its associated deflationary policies, with growth rates of 2.9 and 3.5 per cent in 1964 and 1965 respectively, as against an annual average of 5.5 per cent between 1952 and 1963. In 1966 and 1967 there were signs of recovery when the economy grew at 5.8 and 6.8 per cent respectively. However, from then onwards the growth rate fell in every year without exception, to a postwar low of 1.6 per cent in 1971. Although this rose to 3.2 per cent in 1972, few would disagree that the economy was, in 1970–72, locked in deep recession. The whole period between 1963 and 1972, when the average annual growth rate was 4.1 per cent, bears little resemblance to Kindleberger's 'super-growth', or a sustained 'virtuous circle' in the manner of export-led growth theories.

The overall lower rate of growth between 1964 and 1972 can be attributed to a number of factors, but of prime importance was the failure of industrial investment to recover from the severe recession of 1964–65. Over the period 1964–72 gross industrial fixed investment grew in real terms at an annual rate of 1.0 per cent compared with 9.1 per cent for the period 1952–63. An alternative expression of this investment slump is that, while industrial investment rose, as a proportion of GNP, from 6.2 per cent in 1951 to 9.2 per cent in 1963, the proportion in 1972 was only 6.8 per cent. Annual figures for industrial investment can be found in table 2.3 at the start of this chapter. From that table it can be seen that such was the fall in industrial investment in 1964 and 1965 that it was not until 1970 that the 1963 level was recovered in real terms.

Thus, although since 1963 the economy has achieved an overall growth rate that has been at least respectable by international standards, in many ways it has been 'false' growth in so far as it has not been associated with comparable increases in industrial investment. Instead, it was gained by attempts (following upon the inflationary wage awards of 1963) to rationalise production methods, to increase working hours, and in general to work existing productive capacity much harder. While these changes succeeded in raising output in the short run, the process was inevitably a temporary phenomenon and it reaped its full return in 1969, when the labour disputes of that year were undoubtedly fired with increased bitterness and violence owing to the deterioration in working conditions which had been suffered after 1963.

The fall in the investment rate cannot be divorced from another fundamental change in the Italian economy after 1963 – the new relationship between wages and productivity. As we have already seen, the excess labour supply theory postulates a rate of growth of wages below that of productivity, and indeed, export-led growth models depend on it. These conditions were certainly fulfilled before 1963, but since then wages, and certainly labour costs in total (including the important employers' social security contributions), have regularly outstripped productivity by a substantial margin. Over the period 1964–71 industrial wages rose by 77 per cent, while industrial productivity grew by a mere 42 per cent, and because of the dramatic rise in social security contributions labour costs in general rose by a massive 90 per cent. It is questionable, however, whether the rapid rise in wages and labour costs was a consequence of tighter labour markets rather than autonomous trade union pressures. Certainly, as we shall see in chapter 4, by European standards Italian labour markets remained slack throughout most of the 1960s, with continuingly high levels of emigration, low and falling activity rates and substantial amounts of underemployment, as well as an exodus out of agriculture which was even greater in the 1960s than during the 1950s. Our view would be that trade union pressures have been the major factor explaining the rapid growth of wages and labour costs.

The change in the relationship between labour costs and productivity growth has been reflected in the declining profitability of Italian industry in general. An indication of this has been the higher proportion of value-added taken by labour costs after 1963 (and conversely the smaller proportion available to finance investment). Between 1951 and 1962 labour costs averaged some 55.8 per cent of total value-added in industry (including construction), rising to 64.1 per cent for the years 1963–71. By 1971 labour costs had risen to some 70.9 per cent of industrial value-added. Inevitably, profitability declined drastically after 1963, and this is illustrated in table 2.7. When it is borne in mind that the figures in this table are in current prices, and cover a period characterised by continuing and serious inflation, the overall decline in profitability is remarkable. Given weak Italian capital markets and the importance of self-finance, this decline inevitably had an impact on investment, and indeed the investment trends outlined earlier are largely explicable in terms of the profitability of Italian industry. Certainly the pattern of low profits in 1963–64 and 1971–72 coincides with the slump in investment in those years.

Table 2.7 Gross profits in 134 Italian manufacturing firms, 1963–1972
(milliard lire)

1963	1964	1965	1966	1967	1968	1969	1970	1971	1972
504.5	506.8	560.4	620.8	632.2	709.6	738.6	731.7	492.4	568.4

Source: Banca d'Italia, *Relazione Annuale, 1972* (Rome, 1973).

The fall in profits and investment after 1963 and the factors that brought this about should have implications for the export-led growth argument. In export-led growth models inflationary wage awards and escalating labour costs can break the 'virtuous circle' in that exports are restrained by a fall in international competitiveness. However, this in fact has not come about, since exports have continued to grow at relatively spectacular rates throughout the 1960s, and even into the recession of the early 1970s. Indeed, Italian exports seem to respond well to depressed domestic conditions, rising by 15.4 and 20.3 per cent in 1964 and 1965 respectively, and by 12.3 and 12.8 per cent in 1971 and 1972 respectively. Over the whole period 1964–72, exports rose by 13.5 per cent per annum – only slightly down on the annual figure of 13.8 per cent recorded between 1950 and 1963. What we have to explain, therefore, is first, why, by and large, export growth persisted after 1963 and secondly, why it did not induce growth in the rest of the economy, as export-led growth models would suggest.

The persistently rapid growth of exports is not easy to explain. However, one possible reason is that the export sector was able to absorb the labour cost increases of the 1960s and maintain price competitiveness. Between 1962 and 1964, for example, when labour costs per employee unit rose by 33.1 per cent, export prices rose by a mere 2 per cent; similarly in 1960–71, when labour costs per employee unit rose by 31.4 per cent export prices increased by only 11.6 per cent. Certainly, between 1961 and 1971 the exporting industries did better than the domestic industries. Thus the export sector has been able to absorb labour cost increases better than the more backward, domestic sector, and this has been primarily a result of its greater productivity growth. In the non-export sector rising labour costs have squeezed profits with the result that investment has been choked off, whereas in the export sector increased labour costs have been absorbed by increased productivity, reflected in the continuing growth of exports. In short, the 'virtuous circle' argument now applies to the export sector alone, rather than to the economy as a whole.

This point not only has implications for the national rate of growth but also casts doubt on whether economic growth will tend to eradicate dualism. Indeed, in these circumstances dualism will become worse as the advanced export sector grows and the backward domestic sector struggles in its wake. Few would doubt that this is what happened after 1963, though some observers would claim that this process was in operation even during the 1950s, arguing that, at a theoretical level, there is a possible incompatability between the maintenance of an export-led growth process (as set out in the theory of export-led growth) and the absorption of underemployed labour into the advanced (export) sector, as envisaged in the Lutz–Kindleberger model. The point of contrast between the two sets of theories concerns the nature of investment in the advanced sector. In the supply side theories investment is basically capital-widening, insofar as it gives rise directly to an increase in employment. In the export-led growth models investment must be capital-deepening, because it is an essential part of the argument that investment should lead to an increase in the productivity of labour, and this would require an increase in the capital–labour ratio. The more that investment in the advanced sector is devoted to raising the capital–labour ratio in that sector, the less will economic growth eradicate dualism.

The inter-relationships between economic dualism and foreign trade have been formally worked out by Graziani[14] in a study, the main purpose of which was to examine the hypothesis that Italy's economic dualism was attributable to her over-dependence on foreign trade. Italy, according to Graziani, had to develop as an open economy because of the lack of domestic supplies of many raw materials. Because these had to be imported, she was forced to evolve an economic structure in which exports would play a dynamic role, and thus pay for imports; and she had to switch resources from labour-intensive industries like textiles to capital-intensive ones such as chemicals, metallurgy and electronics. Thus, the advanced sector in Graziani's model is also the export sector and, for

Graziani, it is the reliance of this sector on international demand that creates the dual economic structure.

The advanced sector must be competitive in international markets and this, in conjunction with the technological characteristics of the industries involved, dictates the production technique and therefore the capital–labour ratio which, in most cases, Graziani argues, is very high. This has two important implications. First, it means that the purpose of most investment in the export sector is to raise productivity and not employment. Secondly, given the higher level of productivity, and most probably profits, wages in this sector will tend to be higher than in the stagnant or backward sector, which exhibits entirely different characteristics because of the fact that it is producing for the domestic market and does not require the advanced technology demanded by the rigours of international competition.

The characteristics of Graziani's dualism then are more or less the same as those of Lutz, the advanced sector being a high-productivity, large-scale, capital-intensive, high-wage sector, at least relative to the backward or stagnant sector. The key difference between the two analyses lies, however, in the *source* of economic dualism. Lutz, as we have seen, stressed the importance of imperfections in the labour market, whereas it is the existence of a large export sector with employment and investment behaviour dictated by the necessities of international competition that characterises Graziani's dualism.[15*]

Whichever view one adopts about the source of Italy's dualism, there must be some doubt as to whether economic growth of itself is sufficient to resolve the problem. Certainly, many of the institutional factors that created Lutz's labour market dualism still exist today, though, as we shall see in chapter 4, in rather different forms. Although wages have increased substantially this has not reflected the total absorption of excess labour supplies, but rather trade union militancy, and occasional bottlenecks in the supply of skilled and semi-skilled labour. This has hindered the movement of labour out of agriculture into the advanced sector; and, indeed, much of the agricultural exodus in the 1960s has been into services – a large proportion of which belongs unambiguously to the backward, small-scale sector.

Aside from the problem of economic dualism, can we now write off the rapid growth experience of the 1950s as economic history? It seems reasonable to suggest that Italian growth in the future will never again match the outstanding performance of these early years. First, trade union militancy, supported by some labour market tightening, has on two occasions, 1963 and 1969, been a factor allowing considerable wage increases. These increases caused considerable inflation, a shrinking of profit margins and a fall in investment rates. Moreover, in industry as a whole, entrepreneurial confidence was slow to recover from the traumatic industrial relations and political events of 1969–72, even though monetary policy was, after 1970, broadly expansionary. Of course, there is plentiful evidence to show that there are still substantial under-utilised resources to be switched out of low-productivity sectors, particularly agriculture. Moreover, emigration is still high and activity rates are low. Thus, there remains considerable potential for further rapid economic growth in the long run. Whether or not this can be exploited depends upon whether the industrial sector is able to recover its former dynamism, and particularly whether the economy can remain free of the periodic inflationary crises that characterised the 1960s. Whether or not this is the case depends to a large degree on future developments in industrial relations.

A second source of pessimism surrounding future Italian growth prospects concerns the fact that the economy has lost the security afforded by a safe balance of payments. Although the current account is still solidly in surplus, the susceptibility of the economy to severe capital flights now regularly places the balance of payments as a whole in jeopardy (see chapter 3). This relatively recent development means that the authorities face a further constraint in the formulation of their overall economic policy. This would hinder growth, however, only if the typical policy response to a capital flight was to deflate the economy. With the emergence of more flexible attitudes to changing exchange rates, following upon the dollar crises of 1971 and 1973, it is possible that the solution to Italy's capital account problems may not be completely incompatible with expansionary policies at home; though this remains to be seen, especially as the EEC moves towards its objective of economic and monetary union.

In the event of Italy's not being able to rely on flexible exchange rates, all the more weight will be placed on short-term demand management techniques. In the past, as we shall see in chapter 5, these have been extremely deficient. Since 1963 they have been largely responsible for a cyclical pattern characterised by savage downswings and prolonged recessions – with an inevitable decline in the trend rate of growth. Without any improvements in these techniques, future growth cannot but be slower and less stable.

In conclusion, Italian growth is at the cross-roads. It is not impossible that a recovery from the current malaise may push development along the same export-led lines that were evident before the late 1960s. The success of such a process would depend largely upon how fast the underemployed resources of the economy can be switched to industrial employment, and how trade unions respond to this. On the other hand, there are signs that the authorities are now disenchanted with export-led growth as a means of solving Italy's central economic problem – dualism. The lack of domestic feedback from recent export growth does much to strengthen the arguments of Graziani. However, any alternative to export-led growth must involve the stimulus of domestic demand, and this poses two problems. First, if domestic demand is increased, this may divert productive capacity away from exports and increase the demand for imports, placing further strain on a balance of payments position, which already exhibits considerable weaknesses on capital account. Secondly, there is plentiful evidence to suggest that the government could not inject sufficient domestic demand to generate a growth process that did not rely on exports. The painfully slow recoveries from the 1964–65 and 1970–73 recessions reflect the poverty of expansionary demand management policies at the disposal of the government. Monetary policy seems effective only in a deflationary direction, while fiscal policy is virtually useless in any context. The most conspicuous policy failure of recent years has been the inability of government to implement major public investment programmes, largely, as we have already seen in chapter 1, because of the inefficiencies of the public administration. Now that exports no longer appear to generate sufficient investment in the economy as a whole, the government must play the leading role; and yet hopes in this direction are slight in the absence of some radical reforms in the system of public administration. Without such reforms there could be tragic consequences, not only for overall growth but also for Italy's already slow progress towards a unified economic system.

Notes to chapter 2

1. See T. Wilson 'Instability and the Rate of Growth' *Lloyds Bank Review* (July 1966).
2. C. Kindleberger *Europe's Postwar Growth: The Role of Labour Supply* Cambridge, Mass.: Harvard University Press (1967).
3. See W. Lewis 'Development with Unlimited Supplies of Labour' *The Manchester School* (May 1954).
4. Kindleberger, op. cit., p. 6.
5. See P. Rosenstein-Rodan 'Rapporto fra Fattori Produttivi nell'Economia Italiana' *L'Industria* (No. 4, 1954); R. Eckhaus 'Factor Proportions in Under-developed Areas' *American Economic Review* (September 1955); V. Lutz *Italy: A Study in Economic Development* Oxford: Oxford University Press (1962).
6. Lutz, op. cit., p. 17.
7. Ibid., p. 29.
8. E. Denison *Why Growth Rates Differ* Washington: The Brookings Institution (1967).
9. See also Comitato Nazionale per la Produttività *Misure della Produttività in Italia* (Rome, 1967).
10. This is not to say that Kindleberger's work as a whole neglects the demand side. The importance of the export sector is discussed in his *Europe's Postwar Growth,* op. cit.; and indeed, Kindleberger was responsible for much of the early work on models of export-led growth.
11. Not all investment is, of course, geared to increasing productive capacity. In Italy's case between one-fifth and one-third of gross fixed investment in the period

1951–63 was in housing, the most rapidly growing type of investment, with the remainder in the more growth-oriented categories of non-residential construction, vehicles, plant and machinery.

12. See Kindleberger, op. cit.; W. Beckerman 'Projecting Europe's Growth' *Economic Journal* (December 1962); and W. Beckerman and Associates *The British Economy in 1975* London: National Institute for Social and Economic Research (1965); A. Lamfalussy *The UK and the Six: an Essay in Economic Growth in Western Europe* Homewood, Ill.: The Free Press (1966), and 'Contribution à un Theorie de la Croissance en Economie Ouverte' *Recherches Economiques de Louvain* (1963); N. Kaldor *Causes of the Slow Rate of Economic Growth in the United Kingdom* Cambridge: University Press (1966) and 'Conflicts in National Economic Objectives' *Economic Journal* (March 1971). For a formal application of export-led growth models to the Italian case see R. Stern *Foreign Trade and Economic Growth in Italy* New York: Praeger (1967).

13. Stern, op. cit.

14. See A. Graziani *Lo Sviluppo di un'Economia Aperta* Naples: Edizioni Scientifiche Italiane (1969).

15. It might be added that Graziani's dualism has a further side effect, which Lutz fails to develop – the distortion of domestic consumption. Because of the higher productivity of the advanced sector, prices rise more slowly than those of the backward sector, with the result that domestic consumption becomes biased towards the products of the advanced sector and against the products of the backward sector. Graziani refers to this as 'distortion' because it results in a higher consumption of luxury consumer durables at the expense of the more basic needs of society in a country where average income levels would not suggest such a consumption pattern.

CHAPTER 3

The Balance of Payments

'Write that down,' the King said to the jury, and the jury eagerly wrote down all three dates on their slates and then added them up and reduced the answer to shillings and pence. (Alice in Wonderland)

A key feature of Italian postwar economic development has been her highly successful balance of payments and foreign trade performance. Between 1947 and 1972 the balance of payments was in deficit on only eight occasions, and five of these occurred before 1955. The predominance of balance of payments surpluses, associated with a rapid growth of exports and the build-up of substantial foreign exchange reserves, has had important implications for the structure and pace of economic development, as we have already seen in chapter 2. The basic aim of this chapter is to examine in greater detail Italy's postwar balance of payments and foreign trade performance.

The chapter is in four parts. Section 3.1 traces early postwar experience and assesses the extent to which this laid the foundations for subsequent foreign trade and general economic success, while sections 3.2 and 3.3 outline and analyse the major items of current and capital account respectively in the period since 1950. Since the late 1960s there has been a considerable deterioration in Italy's balance of payments performance, and it is the aim of section 3.4 to analyse these recent problems and to assess future prospects.

3.1 Early postwar developments

The immediate postwar years were highly significant for Italy's later development as they witnessed a major change of economic strategy and the implementation of policies that laid the foundations of an economy in which foreign trade was to occupy a key position.

At the end of hostilities Italy faced the choice of either continuing the rigid exchange controls and protectionist tariffs and quotas introduced

72

during the Fascist period, or pursuing open development with foreign trade playing a propulsive and leading role. Given her dependence on foreign supplies of raw materials and semi-finished goods, free trade was vital for Italy's economic recovery; and the open economy strategy, though inevitably giving rise to short-run problems as the domestic sector after years of protection was exposed to foreign competition, was the more promising from a long-run viewpoint and consequently was adopted. The implementation of this strategy involved a number of complementary policies and three in particular – the stabilisation of the lira, the liberalisation of trade and the accumulation of an adequate stock of foreign exchange reserves. We shall now examine these in turn.

Chapter 1 has already made passing reference to the chronic inflationary problems of 1944–47, and the moderate but highly successful monetary measures taken by the government to stabilise domestic prices. Having protected the domestic value of their currency, the authorities turned to the problem of re-establishing its international value. To a certain extent the distinction between internal and external monetary stabilisation is a false one, since rapid domestic inflation will have a detrimental effect on the external value of any currency. Thus, the stemming of inflation at home contributed significantly to the stabilisation of the lira abroad. However, this did not solve the problem of how to find a new equilibrium exchange rate, since the old rate had been rendered meaningless by the wartime and postwar inflation. The successful way in which the authorities tackled this problem is important in explaining the stimulus given to foreign trade in the early postwar years.[1]

The first step was to establish a 'free' foreign exchange market, in which the lira could be 'floated' with respect to certain 'hard' currencies, and principally the US dollar. This free market was created by the so-called 'fifty per cent rule', whereby exporters could sell up to fifty per cent of their export proceeds at the free rate of exchange – which could, of course, diverge from the official rate. Throughout 1946 and early 1947 the lira was progressively devalued in the free market and reached a low point of 905 lire to the dollar in May 1947 with the official rate, fixed since May 1946, at 225 lire. Largely through the successful application of monetary policy, domestic inflation abated in the latter half of 1947, and the free lira rate stabilised at 575 early in 1948. This lira–dollar rate was then used to fix the cross-rates of the other major currencies, and the setting of a new rate with sterling in December 1948 completed this realignment.

The method by which the external value of the lira was stabilised is significant in so far as there is reason to suppose that the adjustments of 1948 left it undervalued overall. Although the lira might have been at an equilibrium rate *vis à vis* the dollar, the fixing of the lira with respect to other currencies through the lira–dollar rate would only leave the lira 'right' with respect to these currencies if they, in turn, were 'right' with respect to the dollar. However, in the early postwar years most European currencies were overvalued with respect to the dollar, and consequently this left the lira undervalued in relation to the currencies of Italy's European trading partners. If one couples this argument with the fact that the wholesale price index actually fell, from 5443 in 1948 to 4897 in 1950 (1938=100), then there is an *a priori* case for supposing that the measures of internal and external monetary stabilisation in the immediate postwar years improved Italy's international competitiveness, at least in the short run, and this at a time when the reconstruction of productive capacity was beginning to increase the supply of exports. In spite of unfavourable exchange rate adjustments following the devaluation of sterling in 1949,[2]* Italy retained an exchange rate advantage, encouraging a rapid growth of exports and the development of industries capable of producing import substitutes.

The second feature of Italian balance of payments policy listed above was a determined commitment to free trade. This must be seen in the context of the more general European desire to create a more liberalised climate for international trade and to escape from the restrictions and bilateralism of the prewar years. Any attempt to make this a reality had two basic requirements. First, the prewar and wartime protectionist devices of quotas, licences and tariff barriers needed to be reduced. Secondly, facilities for international payments had to be created to replace the prewar system of bilateral trade agreements. This second requirement was finally met by the establishment of the European Payments Union in 1950 which facilitated a multilateral pattern of European trade by creating a financial clearing arrangement for the participating countries. The problem of protectionist commercial policies by European countries was tackled partly by the Organisation for European Economic Co-operation, whose objectives included the removal of quantitative trade restrictions. Italy's actions in respect of these restrictions were more rapid than those of most of her European trading partners, reflecting the importance attached by the Italians to foreign trade in their country's postwar recovery and laying the basis for long-term development. Whereas in 1946 only 4.7 per cent of Italian imports were free from quantitative restriction, the figure was nearly 70 per cent by 1953.[3] More detailed comparative information is given in table 3.1.

The percentages in table 3.1 do not refer to actual imports in 1956, but to the percentages which would have been free given the various agreements on liberalisation up to that date and the 1948 *structure* of imports. In other words, it provides a good measure, and one not distorted by the changing composition of imports, of the extent of trade liberalisation by 1956. It shows clearly how Italy, relative to other European countries, led the way in the removal of quantitative restrictions on trade.

Table 3.1 Intra-European trade liberalisation, 1956
(Free imports as a percentage of total imports in the reference year 1948)

	Foodstuffs	Raw materials	Manufactured Goods	Total
Benelux	69.0	98.6	91.8	91.1
Denmark	80.6	98.2	77.5	85.5
France	72.9	96.3	71.6	82.3
Germany*	81.3	98.0	96.2	91.5
Italy	97.5	100.0	99.2	99.1
Norway	81.3	90.9	73.2	78.2
Sweden	79.6	100.0	90.6	92.6
Switzerland	67.8	100.0	94.1	91.3
UK	90.3	99.0	90.2	93.7

* The figures for Germany use 1949 as the base year.
Source: European Payments Union *Sixth Annual Report of the Managing Board* (Paris, 1955–56).

The reduction of tariff barriers was however a slower process, and Italian manufacturers did enjoy a considerable measure of protection in the early 1950s. Nevertheless, the direction of Italian commercial policy was towards lowering the general level of tariffs. Although it is difficult to compare the overall level of tariffs over time because of changes in the structure of imports, it has been estimated that whereas the average effective rate of customs duties in 1938 stood at 13.8 per cent by 1952 it was only 6.5 per cent, to fall still further from then on.[4]

By the mid-1950s, then, and ahead of most other countries, Italy had thrown off the greater part of her earlier protectionist policies. This was in spite of events in 1952 and 1953 when the balance of trade ran into serious difficulties, largely because of a deterioration in the terms of trade associated with the Korean War and the resumption of trade restrictions by France and Britain.[5] These restrictions adversely affected Italian exports of textiles, which had been the major element in her export growth after 1948.[6] Even so, the authorities were not inclined to reverse the free trade policy (which some commentators blamed for the crisis), and this decision was to be vindicated by Italy's subsequent development.

Perhaps one of the most remarkable features of Italy's postwar economic recovery was the speed with which she was able to build up adequate foreign exchange reserves from a chronically weak balance of payments position immediately after 1945. In 1946 and 1947 conditions were particularly acute, with current account deficits of 438 million dollars and 679 million dollars respectively, while total exports of goods and services in the same two years were a mere 465 million dollars and 878 million dollars. These deficits were largely financed by foreign aid, particularly from the United States. As we have seen in chapter 1, with-

Table 3.2 Italian balance of payments on current account and basic balance, 1950–1972
(million dollars)

Item	1950	1951	1952	1953	1954	1955	1956	1957	1958	1959	1960	1961
Visible exports	1203	1642	1382	1470	1578	1775	2082	2478	2520	2856	3570	4101
Visible imports	1366	1921	2129	2217	2222	2454	2820	3246	2898	2994	4216	4679
Balance of visible trade	−163	−279	−747	−746	−643	−678	−739	−768	−378	−139	−646	−573
Freight and insurance (balance)	−48	−96	−42	−18	−15	−10	−6	−48	−40	−99	−164	−186
Other transport (balance)	−14	−8	−15	−23	−0	−5	−4	−7	+8	+35	+60	+62
Tourism (balance)	+67	+72	+75	+131	+138	+190	+215	+323	+411	+448	+548	+647
Income from capital (balance)	−17	−7	−13	−7	−12	−18	−27	−25	−34	−5	−30	−51
Services and Govt transactions (balance)	+25	+25	+52	+117	+167	+168	+122	−1148	+94	+93	+66	+49
Other services (balance)	+57	+55	+93	+110	+131	+117	+143	+179	+190	+167	+186	+199
Total goods and services (balance)	−93	−239	−597	−437	−236	−236	−297	−198	+250	+501	+19	+141
Private transfers (balance)	+59	+71	+86	+111	+112	+127	+169	+199	+269	+251	+129	+339
Public transfers (balance)	+212	+224	+168	+109	+48	+33	+33	+35	+36	−7	−27	−7
TOTAL CURRENT ACCOUNT BALANCE	+178	+55	−343	−217	−76	−76	−95	+36	+955	+759	+283	+474
CAPITAL ACCOUNT BALANCE	−168	+53	+197	+123	+107	+167	+223	+216	+170	+199	+76	−170
BASIC BALANCE	−40	+122	−134	−79	−7	+72	+86	+206	+793	+850	+438	+574

Item	1962	1963	1964	1965	1966	1967	1968	1969	1970	1971	1972*
Visible exports	4590	4973	5863	7104	7929	8605	10,095	11,642	11,642	14,828	17,261
Visible imports	5503	6877	6508	6458	7595	8626	9044	11,100	13,498	14,500	17,259
Balance of visible trade	−915	−1903	−645	+646	+334	−21	+1051	+542	−381	+382	+2
Freight and insurance (balance)	−195	−284	−262	−343	−350	−399	−353	−399	−462	−404	−421
Other transport (balance)	+96	+112	+113	+142	+166	+167	+157	+185	+222	+206	+204
Tourism (balance)	+724	+749	+827	+1062	+1199	+1126	+1112	+1139	+912	+1045	+1055
Income from capital (balance)	−91	−114	−98	−88	−40	−14	+33	+105	−23	−31	−82
Services and Govt transactions (balance)	+47	+27	+37	+46	+33	+19	+8	+27	+9	+47	+48
Other services (balance)	+236	+319	+337	+403	+385	+328	+296	+328	+298	+343	+154
Total goods and services (balance)	−99	−1904	+308	+1867	+1728	+1236	+2305	+1928	+575	+1534	+960
Private transfers (balance)	+383	+355	+345	+408	+1438	+427	+488	+508	+506	+550	+567
Public transfers (balance)	−49	−6	−34	−65	−48	−64	−149	−95	−320	−237	−167
TOTAL CURRENT ACCOUNT BALANCE	+235	−745	+620	+2209	+2217	+1599	+2644	+2340	+761	+1846	+1358
CAPITAL ACCOUNT BALANCE	−309	−485	+110	−455	−1277	−1023	−1691	−3624	−237	−1150	−2166
BASIC BALANCE	−50	−1252	+774	+1594	+696	+324	+627	−1391	+356	+783	−1203

* The figures for 1972 in this table and in all subsequent tables in this chapter have been computed from lira figures, using the 1971 dollar exchange rate, thus abstracting from the distortions caused by the exchange rate adjustments of 1972.

Sources: Banca d'Italia *Relazione Annuale* (Rome, various years); and
Banca d'Italia *Bilancia dei Pagamenti dell'Italia 1947–67* (Rome).

out this assistance Italy's foreign payments position would have been critical and her overall economic recovery much retarded.

However, in 1948 the current account moved into a small surplus of 37 million dollars, largely due to an extraordinary 60 per cent increase in exports, and it remained in surplus until 1952. Over the same period, the traditional source of 'invisible' earnings, tourism, was recovering and yielding a surplus of 72 million dollars in 1951. While the current account position steadily improved, the influx of dollars continued, now through Marshall Aid, and amounted to 1030 million dollars in the four years 1948–51. The conjuncture of this foreign aid with Italy's improving current account allowed her to build up substantial holdings of gold and foreign exchange reserves, from 248 million dollars in 1948 to 1003 million dollars in 1951. It was the accumulation of these reserves that enabled the economy to weather the balance of payments difficulties of the early 1950s, mentioned above, without serious deflation or any change in Italy's liberal commercial policies.

The priority given by the authorities to the immediate postwar policies of currency stabilisation, trade liberalisation and the accumulation of reserves was a deliberate and conscious choice. This concern with what was essentially a long-run development strategy was especially courage-ous given Italy's urgent short-run problems, particularly the large surplus of labour, and the eagerness of the government's opponents to exploit these difficulties. Abroad, Italy was sharply criticised by a number of international organisations for adopting an over-cautious monetary policy in the face of chronic unemployment, many feeling that more govern-ment action should have been directed towards stimulating domestic demand and thereby reducing unemployment. By contrast, the Italian authorities were more concerned with the longer-term benefits of a sound currency and a line of economic development firmly based on foreign trade. Friedrich Lutz, in a letter to the *New York Times* in 1949, wrote: 'If those responsible for Italy's economic policy had been less conscient-ious – if, for example, Italy had embarked upon a heavy investment programme in order to absorb at least part of the unemployed, they would have produced a balance of payments situation just as critical as that of Great Britain.' In the light of Italy's subsequent economic development these priorities would appear to have been soundly justified.

3.2 The current account

This section is concerned with the major items in Italy's balance of payments on current account. It can be seen from table 3.2 that, although the current account has been in overall surplus throughout almost the whole period 1950–72, there are substantial differences between the individual component items. It is our aim to deal with these items under three headings, starting first with visible exports (i.e. exports of physical goods), whose growth has perhaps been the most spectacular single element in the balance of payments. Secondly, we shall examine the structure and growth of visible imports – of crucial importance to the Italian economy because of its heavy dependence on foreign supplies of material inputs. Finally, we turn to the remaining items of current account, 'invisibles' and emigrants' remittances, whose position in the balance of payments is particularly vital since, as we shall see, it is here rather than in visible trade that the source of Italy's almost continual current account surplus lies.

Visible exports

The rapid growth of visible exports is one of the most important features of the postwar Italian economy. Table 3.3 shows the visible export performance of Italy and other major industrial countries over the period 1950–72.

Table 3.3   Export growth in volume terms in ten countries, 1950–1972

Country	Average annual growth	
	1950–61	*1962–72*
	%	%
Italy	10.7	12.1
West Germany	12.7	8.8
France	7.5	7.9
Belgium–Luxembourg	7.2	10.1
Netherlands	8.7	10.0
UK	1.9	4.7
Sweden	5.4	7.2
USA	4.2	5.9
Canada	5.7	8.3
Japan	13.6	16.5

Source: United Nations *Monthly Bulletin of Statistics* (New York, various issues).

From the table, it is clear that Italy's export growth ranks high by international standards. Over the period 1950–61, only the celebrated export growth records of Japan and West Germany surpassed that of Italy, while since 1962 only Japan performed better. Associated with Italy's rapid export growth have been two important structural changes. The first concerns commodity composition, the second geographic distribution. These are now discussed in turn.

As is clear from table 3.4, Italian exports have become increasingly concentrated in manufactured goods while primary industries (including extractive) have seen their share diminish substantially, falling from

15.6 per cent of total exports in 1952 to 4.9 per cent in 1971. More interesting, however, than the increasing share of manufacturing as a whole is the changing composition *within* manufactured exports. From

Table 3.4   Changing composition of Italian exports, 1952–1971

Commodity	1952	1961	1971
Primary and extractive	15.6	11.0	4.9
Manufactures	84.4	89.0	95.1
Food and tobacco	11.1	6.3	4.6
Leather	0.5	0.7	0.9
Textiles	19.7	14.5	11.1
Clothing	3.6	5.9	7.6
Wood and paper	2.1	1.7	2.4
Metallurgy	4.8	4.9	6.1
Mechanical engineering, *of which*:			
Machinery	11.3	14.6	20.0
Precision instruments	1.7	3.7	3.4
Vehicles	7.8	12.1	12.1
Other	2.2	3.3	4.5
Non-metallic minerals	2.7	2.3	3.4
Chemicals	13.4	14.4	13.3
Rubber	1.1	1.4	1.5
Other	2.4	3.2	4.3
TOTAL	100.0	100.0	100.0

Source: ISTAT *Annuario Statistico Italiano* (Rome, various years).

the table, it is clear that exports of textiles and food have greatly diminished in importance, and that vehicles, machinery, metallurgy and clothing have been the most dynamic export industries. To a very large extent Italy's export success has been based on a relatively narrow range of industries. One indication of this is the fact that 63 per cent of the increase in total exports over the period 1952–71 was accounted for by the engineering, chemicals and clothing industries alone.

The growing export industries have been those facing a rapid increase in international demand. At a general level, world trade in manufactures has been rising much more rapidly than in primary products and raw materials. Over the period 1955–70 world imports of food and drink, for example, grew by 143 per cent, while imports of raw materials, oils, fats and fuels increased by 146 per cent. On the other hand, world imports of chemicals grew by 387 per cent, machinery and vehicles by 506 per cent and other manufactures by 303 per cent. Although these figures are not sufficiently disaggregated to match our Italian data, it is clear that, in general, Italian export growth has been heavily concentrated in commodities for which world demand has been rising most rapidly. We come back later to the significance of this point.

Turning now to the geographic distribution of exports, the greater part of Italian export growth has been in the buoyant EEC market. This is shown in table 3.5. Up to 1958 (i.e. before the setting up of the EEC) West Germany, France, Belgium, Luxembourg and the Netherlands absorbed little more than one-fifth of Italy's exports; by 1970 they accounted for more than 42 per cent. This was partly offset by the declining importance of EFTA markets, but even so the proportion of Italy's exports going to the rapidly growing[7]* Western European markets as a whole rose from 54 per cent in 1954 to 63 per cent in 1970.

Within the EEC West Germany has always been the largest market for Italian exports, but in recent years, as table 3.5 shows, an increasing proportion has been directed towards France, largely reflecting the new buoyancy of the French economy in the 1960s. The UK's share of Italian exports has fallen steadily, from 13.5 per cent in 1951 to 3.8 per cent in 1970, a trend that may be reversed with the entry of the UK into the EEC. Outside Europe, Italy's most important market is the USA, taking on average a little under 10 per cent of her exports. The other major markets of the early postwar period (principally Latin America and the Middle East) have declined in importance.

So far we have shown how Italian exports have become increasingly concentrated, with regard to destination and commodity structure, in rapidly growing markets. However, this cannot be regarded as the sole explanation of her rapid export growth over the period, since we have till now ignored the question of international competitiveness, i.e. Italy's

Table 3.5 Geographic distribution of Italian exports, 1951–1970

	1951	*1954*	*1958*	*1962*	*1965*	*1968*	*1970*
Western Europe, *of which*:	54.5	54.9	52.7	61.2	65.3	62.7	63.7
EEC	—	—	24.0	33.7	40.2	40.1	42.9
West Germany	7.7	11.3	14.3	18.2	21.2	18.7	21.6
France	9.0	5.9	5.3	9.2	10.3	12.6	12.9
Belgium–Luxembourg	2.4	2.4	2.3	2.9	4.0	4.2	3.8
Netherlands	2.0	2.2	2.1	3.4	4.7	4.6	4.7
EFTA	—	—	—	21.0	17.2	14.7	14.2
UK	13.5	7.9	6.8	6.0	4.7	4.4	3.8
Switzerland	5.6	7.2	7.0	7.1	5.4	4.5	4.7
Eastern Europe	4.0	3.5	3.5	5.2	4.6	5.4	5.4
USA	6.9	7.9	9.7	9.5	8.6	10.7	10.2
Canada and Japan	0.9	1.5	1.5	1.5	1.5	1.7	1.9
Middle East	(N.A.)	7.1	7.0	5.5	5.9	5.8	2.9
Latin America	(N.A.)	9.6	10.7	6.6	4.4	4.4	4.2
Other	(N.A.)	22.6	15.9	8.5	9.7	9.3	11.7
TOTAL		100.0	100.0	100.0	100.0	100.0	100.0

Source: United Nations *Commodity Trade Statistics; Series D* (New York, various issues).

ability to undercut competitors within the growing markets mentioned above.

To define, and consequently measure, international competitiveness is extremely difficult. However, if one temporarily adopts the simple approach that the main determinant is export price differentials, then some conclusions can be drawn by looking at the export price indices of Italy and her major competitors. Since Italy's export growth has been concentrated in manufactures, an index of export prices (or unit values) of manufactures is most appropriate.

Table 3.6 shows the average annual percentage change in unit value of manufactured exports for a number of countries. The figures should be taken as being only a general indication of export price competitiveness since they are not adjusted for changes in export commodity structure. Even so the results are interesting, clearly showing that the rate of increase of Italian export prices has been less than that of most of her trading competitors.

Table 3.6   Average annual percentage change in unit values of manufactured exports (export price index): an international comparison

Country	1950–60	1961–70
USA	+2.9	+2.3
Canada	+3.1	+2.2
Japan	+0.3	+0.7
West Germany	+2.0	+1.9
France	+2.3	+1.4
Belgium–Luxembourg	+0.4	+1.3
Netherlands	+0.5	+0.5
UK	+2.8	+2.0
Sweden	+4.1	+2.7
Switzerland	−0.1	+3.5
Italy	−0.5	+1.1

Source: United Nations *Monthly Bulletin of Statistics* (New York, various issues).

In the 1950s Italian export prices actually fell while those of her competitors were rising by some two or three per cent per annum, with the notable exceptions of Japan and Switzerland. In the 1960s Italy's performance was slightly less impressive, but she was still the third most competitive exporter of the countries listed, in terms of the rate of export price increase. One must remember, however, that the table shows only the change in *relative* competitiveness and says nothing about actual price levels, comparisons of which are made virtually impossible by the usual problem of how to select an appropriate exchange rate. Nevertheless, the evidence from price movements does suggest that Italy became increasingly 'price-competitive' over the 1950s and 1960s, and this, as we have seen, from a position in the late 1940s when Italian exports were already favoured by an undervalued lira.

However, competitiveness involves more than price differentials alone. Non-price elements, though difficult to quantify, are important components of international competitiveness. Among these non-price elements are the ability to meet delivery dates, efficient foreign market research and the availability of after-sales services such as maintenance and spare parts – particularly important in the export of consumer durables or capital equipment which, as we have seen, make up a sizeable proportion of Italian exports. Even more difficult to measure are the competitive effects of fashion and styling – especially relevant for clothing, footwear and motor cars. The international appeal of these and many other products is not readily explicable merely in terms of price.

So far we have outlined three essential characteristics of Italy's export growth – a commodity structure concentrated in a range of goods for which demand is growing rapidly, a geographic distribution concentrated in markets with rapidly growing import demand, and international competitiveness. A technique is available whereby one can estimate the contribution of these factors to export growth, and this is known as 'constant market share analysis'.[8] By calculating the extent to which a country increases its share of export markets, and after taking account of the structural factors of commodity composition and geographic distribution, constant market share analysis tells us the percentage of a country's export growth that is attributable to four separate factors: the increase in total world imports, the commodity structure of its exports, the geographic distribution of these exports, and increased competitiveness. It is important to note that, since this last factor is measured by the extent to which the exporting country increases its share of world markets, it involves a much wider concept of international competitiveness than one resting solely on export price differentials.

A constant market share analysis of postwar Italian export growth has been carried out by R. Stern,[9] and his general results are summarised in table 3.7.

The table shows that in the period 1955-64 almost 60 per cent of Italian export growth was attributable to increased competitiveness, and only in the inflationary years 1962-63 does this proportion fall below 50 per cent. Thus, by this analysis, the competitive element is of paramount importance while the structural factors are much less significant.[10*]

Although constant market share analysis is a useful analytical tool, the results need to be evaluated with caution. First, any increase in world market share (adjusted for structural factors) is identified as an increase in competitiveness, yet total world demand is measured by import growth and therefore ignores import substitution, so that the country is assumed

to be competing only with other exporters and not with domestic producers.[11] Secondly, the level of commodity disaggregation in Stern's study,
in common with most others, is less than might be desired. Finally, constant
market share analysis is exclusively concerned with the demand side of
export growth. There are, however, a number of factors on the supply
side which could also affect a country's ability to produce for export at
competitive prices. A high level of domestic demand, for example, could
be a constraint to export growth, and vice versa.[12]* Nevertheless, in spite
of these qualifications, the evidence does strongly suggest that competitiveness has been the major element in Italy's remarkable export
performance.

Table 3.7   Analysis of changes in Italy's exports, 1955–1964

	1955–59 %	1959–62 %	1962–63 %	1963–64 %	1955–64 %
1. Owing to increase in value of world trade	41.9	26.7	60.6	41.2	36.8
2. Owing to commodity composition of increase in world trade	5.0	3.6	−2.1	—	2.7
3. Owing to market distribution of increase in world trade	−5.2	3.0	3.2	2.0	0.7
4. Owing to increased competitiveness of Italy's exports	58.3	66.7	38.3	56.8	59.9

Source: R. Stern *Foreign Trade and Economic Growth in Italy* (New York:
Praeger, 1967).

Before concluding our discussion of visible exports we must mention
the promotional role of the State. There are two main ways in which
the State can promote exports – by granting export subsidies, or by
extending export credit guarantee facilities. Officially, Italy, as a signatory
of the EEC and other agreements, is not permitted to subsidise exports.
However, until recently there did exist an important method whereby a
hidden export subsidy could be granted. Before the introduction of a
value-added tax (IVA) in January 1973, the major form of indirect
taxation in Italy was a 'cascade tax' (IGE), which was similar to IVA
insofar as it was levied at each stage of production, but different inas-
much as it was applied to gross rather than net output. This meant that
the tax on a given commodity accumulated through its different stages
of production and, at the end of the day, it was very difficult to assess
exactly how much tax had actually been levied. This was important for
the exporter because, when the commodity was sold abroad, the domestic
tax was reimbursed. Because of the difficulties in assessing precisely the
tax paid there was scope for the exporter to be over-reimbursed and
therefore subsidised. There is, of course, no way of telling the extent to

which this kind of hidden export subsidy was given. It could however be one possible reason for the Italian reluctance to change over to the value-added system, where the same opportunities for export subsidisation do not exist.

Another, and more internationally acceptable, method by which the government can promote exports is through the provision of export credit guarantee facilities, i.e. by undertaking to reimburse exporters in the event of non-repayment of trade credit by foreign importers. Italian export credit guarantee facilities have been gradually improved in a number of respects over the postwar period.[13] First, the range of exporting activities covered by guarantees has been progressively widened, as has the variety of insurable risks. In 1953 the facilities covered a limited range of goods and applied only to 'special risks' such as political events, national disasters and currency restrictions. In 1961, they were extended to all exports of goods and services as well as Italian projects carried out abroad, while in 1967 the cover of special risks was increased to include commercial insolvency. Secondly, the maximum proportion of risk covered has been raised. Originally set at 70 per cent in 1953, it was increased to 85 per cent in 1957 and to 90 per cent in 1967. The export credit guarantee system in Italy is now fairly flexible and discretionary. The authorities determine coverage, the time to elapse before non-payment constitutes a claimable loss, and the limits within which cost variations (another of the 'special risks') are subject to compensation. This flexibility, valuable in itself, gives scope for the use of these guarantees to subsidise exports.

The current system of guarantees represents a considerable advance on what was available to exporters in the 1950s. However, whether or not these have given a competitive edge to Italian exports must, for the most part, remain an open question since similar improvements have been made in other countries. The whole subject of export guarantees, together with other potential non-tariff barriers to trade, is currently being investigated by GATT.

In conclusion, Italy's rapid growth of visible exports has been a function of several factors, of which competitiveness appears to be the most important. She has firmly established herself in a number of markets, taking a share of world trade which few would have anticipated in 1950. By 1972 Italy accounted for 7.4 per cent of manufactured exports by the industrialised countries of the world – a substantial rise over the 1950 level of 3 per cent. This rapid growth has been important not only for the balance of payments but also for the domestic economy as a whole, to the extent that many observers see Italy as a clear case of export-led growth – a topic already discussed in chapter 2.

However, even though a nation may enjoy rapid export growth, or spectacular growth as in Italy's case, this does not necessarily ensure a favourable balance of payments. Impressive though Italy's export performance may be, her visible trade balance has been in persistent deficit throughout the postwar period. To understand why this should be so, we must examine visible imports.

Visible imports

Reference has already been made to Italy's relative lack of natural resources, and this partly explains the quite substantial growth of imports (see table 3.2 above) – comparable with that of exports, and much greater than that of national income. But the lack of indigenous raw materials is not the sole explanation. Although primary imports have risen considerably, they have declined as a proportion of the total import bill, and there has been a very rapid growth of semi-finished and finished manufactured imports such that they now represent a significant proportion of the total. The change in the commodity composition of Italian imports (in current prices) is shown in table 3.8, together with comparable export data. The table shows that less than 50 per cent of imports in 1972

Table 3.8   Commodity composition of Italian foreign trade, 1951–1972

Commodity Group	Imports		Exports	
	1951–55	*1972*	*1951–55*	*1972*
Raw materials	24.5	9.0	5.2	0.7
Auxiliary materials	23.2	22.7	13.0	9.0
Fuel	19.2	14.9	7.7	4.2
Other	4.0	7.8	5.3	4.8
Semi-finished manufactures	15.8	15.1	13.2	12.2
Final consumption goods	24.4	35.7	51.7	48.0
Food	18.1	20.5	22.7	8.8
Other non-durable	3.1	5.4	19.5	21.3
Durable	3.2	9.8	9.5	17.9
Final investment goods	12.1	17.5	16.9	30.1
Plant, machinery and equipment	9.5	13.7	11.9	23.9
Industrial vehicles	1.8	2.6	3.8	4.4
Other	0.8	1.2	1.2	1.8
TOTAL	100.0	100.0	100.0	100.0

Source: Banca d'Italia *Relazione Annuale, 1972* (Rome, 1973).

consisted of primary products (raw materials, fuel and food) compared with an average of 65 per cent for the period 1951–55. Imports of final consumption goods (excluding food) and final investment goods have leapt from 18.4 per cent to 32.7 per cent over the same period. The reasons for these changes are not clear but two possible explanations are, first, the rapid growth of wages during the 1960s and, secondly, the fact that domestic productive capacity was often fully stretched and could not meet the growth in demand, particularly for consumer goods. Nevertheless, Italy remains predominantly an importer of raw materials and semi-finished products and an exporter of final goods. In 1972, manufactured goods (including semi-finished) accounted for some 50 per cent of imports and over 80 per cent of exports. To put the matter in rather a different way, in 1972 Italy showed a visible trade surplus on manufactures and semi-manufactures of 5551 million dollars, and a visible trade deficit on food and raw materials of 6242 million dollars. The deficit on food alone was 2182 million dollars – a remarkable position for an economy that still supports a substantial agricultural sector, and reflecting well the inefficiency of Italian agriculture.

A large and growing proportion of Italian imports is from the EEC – 41.2 per cent in 1971 (of which just under a half were from West Germany) as against 21.8 per cent in 1958. Over the period 1950–58 Italian imports from the EEC countries expanded at an annual rate of 14.4 per cent while exports to these countries grew at only 11.6 per cent per annum, whereas between 1958 and 1970 exports to, and imports from, the EEC have both grown at the annual rate of 20.6 per cent.[41] Italy's visible trade balance with the EEC was in deficit until 1963, since when the trend has become erratic. Non-EEC Western European countries supplied 11.2 per cent of Italian import needs in 1970 while 26.7 per cent were from developing countries; the latter reflects Italy's dependence on foreign supplies of raw materials and primary products, a dependence such that her trade deficit with the underdeveloped world has grown steadily throughout the 1960s.

Despite their rapid growth, then, Italian exports have not been sufficient to match imports, and between 1947 and 1964 Italy ran an uninterrupted deficit on visible trade. Some of these deficits, as can be seen from table 3.2 above, have been dramatic, 1963 being particularly notable when imports exceeded exports by 1903 million dollars compared with an average deficit of 570 million dollars between 1950 and 1962. The 1963 trade deficit was such as to create a deficit on total current account (the first since 1956) and the first overall balance of payments deficit since 1954. In the years after 1963 visible exports have occasionally more than paid for visible imports, usually when the domestic economy was relatively depressed, but it remains to be seen whether these trends represent a permanent change in the structure of Italy's foreign trade.

Invisible trade and remittances

In contrast to the visible trade balance, Italy's current account as a whole has predominantly been in surplus since the war. The major surplus items between 1950 and 1972 can be identified from table 3.9.

Table 3.9   Average annual balance on current items in the Italian balance of payments, 1950–1972

Item	Average balance	No. of surplus years	No. of deficit years
Visible trade	− 322	6	17
Invisible trade			
Freight and insurance	− 202	0	23
Other transport	+ 80	15	8
Tourism	+ 618	23	0
Income from capital	− 30	2	21
Government services and transactions	+ 64	23	0
Other services	+ 220	23	0
Total goods and services	+ 427	13	10
Private transfers	+ 343	23	0
Public transfers	− 16	10	13
TOTAL CURRENT ACCOUNT	+ 740	17	6

Sources: Banca d'Italia *Relazione Annuale* (Rome, various years); and Banca d'Italia *Bilancia dei Pagamenti dell'Italia* 1947–67 (Rome).

This table shows that the majority of current items have been in surplus since 1950, the largest single deficit being on visible trade, for reasons we have already outlined. The two deficit invisible items are freight and insurance, and income from capital. The latter in particular is at first sight puzzling because, since the 1960s, Italy has been a heavy exporter of capital, and one would expect that the resultant income would yield a surplus under current account. However, as we shall see, much of the capital outflow involves the illegal export of Italian banknotes to Switzerland, some of which are then invested abroad while the rest are reinvested in Italy. In the case of the former, the income from capital will accrue to the smuggler of the banknotes who is now formally a non-resident, while in the latter case the income from 'fictitious' foreign capital invested in Italy flows abroad to the 'non-resident'.

Turning to the surplus items on current account, table 3.9 shows tourism, private transfers and other services (principally earnings from Italian labour abroad) to be Italy's richest sources of foreign exchange:[15] As can be seen, 'other transport' and 'government services and transactions' are the more minor items. The former, chiefly made up of passenger services, has become increasingly important in recent years with the success of Italian airlines in international markets and particularly on the transatlantic routes, while the latter includes a wide range of items, the most important of which is United States military expenditure in Italy, amounting to 87 million dollars in 1972. However, although these items generate useful surpluses, they pale into insignificance compared with the earnings from tourism and remittances.

The importance of tourism is well illustrated in table 3.10, showing it to be in massive and continuing surplus over the entire postwar period. It can be argued that if Italy's balance of payments strength is to be judged by her ability to produce an overall surplus in all but the most critically inflationary circumstances (e.g. 1963), then the key to this success lies not in the rapid growth and competitiveness of her manufacturing export industries, but rather in the long-established and continuing attractions of her most valuable natural resources – areas of outstanding natural beauty, plentiful beaches, and a climate that appears to be attractive to many foreigners. Over ten million tourists visited Italy in 1972, the majority (four million) coming from the other Common Market countries, and just over two and a quarter million from the United States.

Tourism has always been a major Italian industry. In the postwar period, however, its importance has grown considerably, particularly between 1950 and 1965, although in recent years, as can be seen from table 3.10, there has been a tendency for foreign exchange earnings from tourism to level off. The problems appear to have originated in 1962–63 when the industry's growth was curbed by the inflationary problems of these years, though with a recovery in 1965 and 1966. This was, however, cut short by a number of factors in 1967–68, especially the recession in West Germany and the currency restrictions placed on foreign travel by other countries, notably the UK. Indeed, in 1967 gross foreign earnings from tourism fell for the first time since the war and, although these recovered in the years that followed, the long-run trend appears to show a levelling off. There is increasingly a wider selection of countries which provide the basic 'infrastructure' to attract foreign tourists. Moreover, since 1968 Italy has suffered considerable domestic inflation, coupled with industrial, political and social unrest, and this has undoubtedly harmed her tourist industry.

An additional threat to Italy's net tourist position is the increasing tendency for Italians to take their holidays abroad. Although only some twenty-five per cent of Italians currently take holidays,[16] with rising income levels it can be expected that this percentage will increase rapidly and that growing numbers will take foreign holidays. Although it is difficult to imagine tourism as a deficit item in the foreseeable future, it seems likely that the surplus will be consistently whittled down. It can be seen from table 3.10 that the surplus tended to stagnate in the late 1960s and fell substantially in 1970, when Italian tourist expenditure abroad rose enormously. A considerable part of this rise was however a result of the illegal smuggling of currency out of Italy for investment purposes rather than a reflection of genuine tourist expenditure.[17*]

Table 3.10 Italian earnings from tourism, emigrants' remittances and earnings abroad, 1950–1972 (*million dollars*)

	1950	1951	1952	1953	1954	1955	1956	1957	1958	1959	1960	1961
Tourism												
Inflow	83	89	91	147	156	211	257	381	492	530	643	755
Outflow	16	17	16	17	18	21	42	58	80	82	94	108
Balance	+67	+72	+75	+130	+138	+190	+215	+323	+412	+448	+549	+647
Emigrants' remittances												
Inflow	45	44	64	74	74	80	101	115	188	170	214	261
Outflow	—	—	—	—	—	—	—	—	—	—	—	—
Balance	+45	+44	+64	+74	+74	+80	+101	+115	+188	+170	+214	+261
Workers' earnings abroad												
Inflow	29	36	51	60	53	53	89	127	148	158	183	230
Outflow	—	2	5	2	5	7	8	11	15	19	30	34
Balance	+29	+34	+46	+58	+48	+46	+81	+116	+133	+139	+155	+196

	1962	1963	1964	1965	1966	1967	1968	1969	1970	1971	1972
Tourism											
Inflow	847	932	1035	1288	1460	1424	1476	1632	1639	1882	2039
Outflow	124	183	209	226	261	298	363	493	727	837	985
Balance	+723	+749	+826	+1062	+1199	+1196	+1113	+1140	+912	+1045	+1054
Emigrants' remittances											
Inflow	298	283	280	326	353	348	401	426	446	514	522
Outflow	—	—	—	—	—	—	—	—	—	—	—
Balance	+298	+283	+280	+326	+353	+348	+401	+426	+446	+514	+522
Workers' earnings abroad											
Inflow	300	355	397	491	551	502	520	+579	604	643	677
Outflow	38	48	54	70	78	90	72	+60	69	70	74
Balance	+262	+307	+343	+421	+473	+412	+448	+519	+535	+573	+603

Sources: Banca d'Italia *Bilancia dei Pagamenti dell'Italia 1947–67* (Rome); and *Relazione Annuale* (Rome, various issues).

Italy's other major sources of foreign exchange on current account, as we have seen, are emigrants' remittances and workers' earnings abroad. Table 3.10 above provides details of these. Formally, the distinction between the two depends on the period spent abroad by the worker, and the regularity of the remittances – regular remittances from a worker abroad over a period longer than one year are classified as emigrants' remittances. It is somewhat ironic that Italy's most intractable problem, the South, has contributed, through migration, to her strong balance of payments position. In 1972 gross earnings from emigrants' remittances amounted to 522 million dollars, of which 336 million dollars came from EEC countries and the United States. Workers' earnings abroad amounted to 677 million dollars with just over half coming from Common Market countries. It is obvious from table 3.10 that the corresponding outflow has been negligible.

As with net tourist receipts, there is some evidence that emigrants' remittances and workers' earnings abroad are beginning to level off, and this has been a result of a number of factors. The German recession of the mid-1960s, for example, reduced employment opportunities abroad for Italians, as have the Swiss immigration restrictions, while the less settled economic climate in Italy in recent years has dissuaded emigrants from holding their wealth at home. Moreover, the discount on lire held abroad after June 1972 has encouraged remittances in lire rather than foreign currency. In the long run, as domestic employment opportunities expand and migration rates fall, emigrants' remittances will inevitably decline.

For a number of reasons, then, there is evidence to suggest that the traditional sources of strength of Italy's invisible earnings, remittances and tourism, are being eroded. The authorities are acutely aware of the long-term significance of this trend. Of course, there can be no overt official concern about the levelling off of remittances since this reflects, at least in part, the expansion of employment opportunities at home. On the other hand, the Italians can be more openly concerned about foreign earnings from tourism, and there is evidence of determined attempts to boost the now flagging tourist industry in particular through financial incentives and pressures to hold prices at competitive levels.

Our discussion of the Italian current account can be summarised briefly. First, visible trade is a continuing deficit item despite the rapid and sustained growth of visible exports. Secondly, receipts from tourism, workers' earnings abroad and emigrants' remittances have been consistently large enough to give a current account surplus in seventeen years over the twenty-six-year period 1947–72. Recently, however, invisibles and remittances have levelled off, and although these, unlike visible exports, are of little direct importance for the growth of the domestic economy as a whole, they are crucial to the maintenance of external current balance which has important indirect implications for domestic growth. These relatively recent trends with respect to invisibles and remittances must therefore be regarded with some concern.

3.3 The capital account

This section is concerned with the remaining part of the balance of payments, the capital account, which covers all external movements of capital. We must at the outset distinguish between 'autonomous' and 'induced' capital movements, both of which are contained in capital account. Induced capital movements, comprising changes in the domestic country's gold and foreign currency reserves and its account at the IMF, reflect the overall balance of payments position. Although we shall have something to say about Italy's stock of foreign exchange reserves at the end of this chapter, we are more centrally concerned in this section with the autonomous capital movements. In the Italian case these can be divided into four categories: private capital movements; remittances of lira banknotes from abroad; local authority lending and borrowing abroad; and central government capital movements.[18] The balance for each of these four categories and the total balance of autonomous capital movements are shown in table 3.11.

From 1950 to 1961 the capital account as a whole was almost continuously in surplus, averaging a net inflow of 127 million dollars a year. From 1962 onwards, however, a surplus has been recorded on only one occasion (1964), and over the period 1962–72 there has been a massive annual average deficit of 1119 million dollars. In the early 1960s, then, there occurred a dramatic change in both the nature and size of capital movements. It is fairly clear from the table that this is largely explained by the behaviour of two capital account items in particular – private capital movements and banknote remittances.[19*] We now intend to examine these in turn.

Throughout the 1950s (with the exception of 1950 itself), Italy enjoyed a considerable surplus in respect of private capital movements, foreign capital being attracted by the plentiful supplies of labour, the low level of wage costs and the stability and pace of Italian growth. At the same time, there was little investment abroad by Italians, there being sufficient opportunities at home for those with capital to invest. However, while the private capital inflow continued during the 1960s, the outflow increased dramatically. This was a result of three main factors. First, private individuals were exporting capital, pulled by the prospects of a higher return overseas and, more often, pushed by the confused economic and political conditions in Italy. Secondly, direct investment abroad –

Table 3.11 Italian balance of payments on capital account, 1950–1972
(*million dollars*)

	1950	1951	1952	1953	1954	1955	1956	1957	1958	1959	1960	1961
Private capital movements												
Inflow	87	162	222	165	101	181	363	222	327	467	689	1009
Outflow	245	62	2	4	51	89	131	93	141	207	459	538
Balance	−158	+100	+220	+160	+50	+92	+22	+129	+186	+239	+220	+471
Italian banknote remittances (balance)	—	—	—	—	—	—	—	—	—	—	−185	−330
Local authority transactions	—	—	—	—	—	—	—	—	—	−63	—	—
Central government transactions	−10	−47	−26	−37	+57	+80	−8	+87	−16	−23	+31	+29
Total capital movements												
Inflow	129	167	257	181	196	293	407	387	471	561	791	1113
Outflow	297	114	59	58	89	126	183	171	301	361	715	944
Balance	−168	+53	+197	+123	+107	+167	+223	+216	+170	+199	+76	+170

	1962	1963	1964	1965	1966	1967	1968	1969	1970	1971	1972
Private capital movements											
Inflow	1302	2054	1774	1191	1412	2230	2603	2507	4477	4519	5297
Outflow	850	1065	1103	1398	2046	2350	4293	6392	4701	4757	6404
Balance	+452	+989	+671	−207	−634	−120	−1690	−3634	−226	239	−1107
Italian banknote remittances (balance)	−766	−1470	−577	−314	−589	−801	−1127	−2256	−951	−892	−889
Local authority transactions	—	+19	+23	—	−9	−3	—	−5	+1	+52	−3
Central government transactions	+5	+23	−8	+67	−75	−100	−64	−25	+718	−70	−166
Total capital movements											
Inflow	1395	2161	1902	1384	1487	2326	2603	2768	4477	4993	5762
Outflow	1704	2646	1791	1839	2763	3350	4294	6392	4701	6142	7928
Balance	−309	−485	+110	−455	−1276	−1023	−1691	−3624	−237	−1150	−2166

Sources: Banca d'Italia *Relazione Annuale* (Rome, various issues); and Banca d'Italia *Bilancia dei Pagamenti dell'Italia 1947–67* (Rome).

largely by big Italian companies setting up branches or carrying out projects overseas – increased substantially. During the 1950s such direct investment had been severely restricted by the authorities, but as these controls were lifted in the 1960s the foreign operations of Italian industry became increasingly important. Olivetti's new branches in Spain and Argentina, Fiat's investments in Argentina, large construction work abroad by Montecatini and ENI's extensive searches for oil fields in the Middle East and North Africa are but a few examples. Overall, direct investment abroad doubled between 1962 and 1972, rising from 250 to 500 million dollars.[20] The third major source of the increased private capital outflow in the 1960s has been the rapid development of export credit. Though relatively unimportant in the 1950s, this expanded considerably during the 1960s, from 165 million dollars in 1962 to around 1300 million dollars in 1972.[21]

However, the *legal* private capital movements discussed above are only one of the explanations for the major change in capital account during the 1960s. As can be seen from table 3.11, the other concerns banknote remittances, which have increased dramatically since the early 1960s.[22] These flows largely represent the *illegal* export of Italian capital. 'By the term remittances is meant those dispatches of Italian banknotes made by foreign banks to Italian banks for conversion into foreign exchange or for crediting to a non-resident's capital account.'[23] In theory, these remittances could reflect spending by Italian tourists abroad or smuggled imports. However, a number of factors indicate that, in practice, this cannot be the whole explanation. First, Italy runs a regular surplus on tourism, and this suggests that withdrawals of banknotes by Italians travelling abroad should be more than offset by foreigners visiting Italy. Secondly, the sums involved in Italian tourist expenditure abroad are negligible relative to the capital outflow associated with banknote remittances. Thirdly, some ninety per cent of Italian banknotes abroad are remitted from Switzerland, which suggests causes other than tourism. Finally, the volume of remittances exhibits violent fluctuations from year to year. For these reasons it is more than permissible to suppose that banknote remittances represent the illegal export of Italian funds for investment purposes.

The motives for the illegal smuggling of banknotes abroad depend on whether the smuggler is intending to invest his funds back in Italy, ostensibly as a non-resident, or whether he intends to invest in another country. In the latter case, the reason might simply be to avoid the legal restrictions on investment abroad. However, these have been progressively removed, especially with respect to long-term capital movements. Why, then, should Italians wish to invest abroad illegally by first smuggling lire abroad? The answer lies in the Italian system of dividend taxation. All shares in Italy bear the name of the buyer (so the tax on dividends cannot be avoided) and when an Italian resident legally buys foreign shares these must be lodged with an Italian bank authorised to deal in such business. The only way in which an Italian resident can escape the tax on dividends is by smuggling banknotes abroad, usually into Switzerland, and anonymously investing from there. However, and this is important, not all illegally exported Italian capital is invested abroad. Some returns to Italy as so-called 'fictitious' foreign investment. The reasons for these 'fictitious' capital movements are purely fiscal.

Whereas illegal investment abroad avoids the tax on dividends, 'non-resident' Italians making 'fictitious' foreign investments in Italy incur a lower level of dividend taxation than if they obeyed the law and invested as residents. Since a withholding tax was first introduced in 1962, there has always been some degree of discrimination between the taxation of domestic and foreign investors, offering 'a striking prize to any resident who succeeded in becoming a non-resident'.[24] Initially, residents were taxed at the domestic income tax rate (which was progressive), and non-residents at a flat rate of 15 per cent. This provided a distinct incentive to Italian residents with high dividend income to smuggle their funds abroad in order to invest from there as non-residents, and this was reflected in the illegal capital outflow at that time.[25]

Between January 1963 and March 1964, 1713 million dollars left Italy in the form of illegally exported banknotes of which, it has been estimated, 1060 million dollars returned in the form of 'fictitious' investment. The rest of this illegal outflow was probably part of a general outflow of capital associated with speculation against the lira – speculation that was prevalent over the winter of 1963–64. In February 1964 the system of dividend taxation was changed to give residents the choice of a flat rate tax of 30 per cent or a tax 'on account' of 5 per cent, while non-residents were subjected to a flat rate of 30 per cent. These new arrangements appeared largely to remove the incentive to invest in Italy as a non-resident since for the next three years the average monthly outflow of banknotes fell to 34 million dollars, compared with a figure of 114 million dollars for the period January 1963 – March 1964. However, in February 1967 the system was again changed, when the option of a 30 per cent flat rate for residents was removed. The 'prize' for becoming a non-resident was thus restored, but at a lower value than in 1962 when the tax differential was much greater. In 1967 the outflow of Italian banknotes rose to 801 million dollars, of which 43 per cent returned as 'fictitious' investment, and in 1968 the outflow was 1127 million dollars, 34 per cent of which returned.

The situation reached critical proportions in 1969 when, exacerbated by interest rate differentials and political and economic instability, the outflow increased to 2256 million dollars. In February 1970 the Bank of Italy took direct action to curb the outflow, centralising all the crediting procedures of remitted banknotes with the deliberate aim of delaying the process of crediting and increasing the costs involved, so that remitted banknotes were now, in fact, at a discount.[26] These moves had the effect of reducing the illegal capital outflow in 1970 to 951 million dollars. This respite was, however, only temporary and in 1972 the lira again came under severe speculative pressure, to which the Bank of Italy responded dramatically. In June 1972 it refused to convert remitted banknotes into foreign currencies, thus restricting the opportunities for domestic residents to get rid of banknotes they had smuggled abroad. It is too soon to say whether this measure will completely resolve the problem of illegal capital exports. It will certainly make 'fictitious' foreign investment much more difficult. Nevertheless, we must emphasise that the dangers of *legal* capital flight remain as long as the general political and economic climate in Italy continues to be unsettled.

In conclusion, Italy's capital account has exhibited two distinct phases in the postwar period. During the sustained and rapid growth of the 1950s Italy attracted considerable foreign investment to hasten her development. In this respect, the capital account of the 1950s had significant implications for the growth of the domestic economy. In the 1960s the whole trend of capital movements changed dramatically for the reasons mentioned earlier. This gave the capital account a new significance for the economy and, for the first time since the war, Italy was in almost continual danger of running a balance of payments deficit, not because of any marked deterioration on current account, but rather as a result of huge capital outflows. Insofar as the capital account problems of the 1960s eroded the security of the Italian balance of payments, traditionally based on a current account surplus, they have introduced a new constraint into the formulation of general economic policy.

3.4 Conclusions

Over the postwar period as a whole, Italy's balance of payments has been one of the most successful features of her development, an overall surplus of some 200 million dollars per annum being achieved between 1947 and 1972 (see table 3.2). This success has been reflected in the rapid growth of her gold and foreign exchange reserves, from 774 million dollars in 1951 to 3799 million dollars in 1961 and 6787 million dollars in 1972. By the latter year these reserves, in relation to the volume of trade, were among the largest in Europe.

Italy's strong balance of payments has had considerable implications for the economy as a whole. First, her export performance (both visibles and invisibles) has enabled her to pay for imports, and particularly the vital imports of raw materials and fuel. Secondly, the rapid growth of visible exports has built up the industries involved into leading sectors of the economy. Italy has often been cited as a clear example of export-led growth – a view that has ben examined in detail in chapter 2. Thirdly, the accumulation of substantial foreign exchange reserves, as a result of overall balance of payments success, has for much of the post-war period freed the authorities from the necessity to deflate the economy in response to balance of payments problems, and has afforded more leeway in short-term economic policy. The policy-induced 'stop–go' pattern of development, arising largely from balance of payments weakness, which has characterised the postwar growth of the UK economy, has certainly been much less important in the Italian case, and the relative stability of Italian growth over the postwar period is to a certain extent attributable to her balance of payments success. However, this is not to say that problems and crises have not been encountered. On three occasions in particular the balance of payments has run into severe difficulties, and it is worth examining these in some detail, not least because they cast doubt on future prospects.

The first crisis came in 1963, and followed eight years of steady balance of payments success. Before 1955 Italy's external balance had been somewhat unsettled and, as mentioned above, the severe deterioration in the visible trade balance in 1952 and 1953 caused some concern. But as invisible earnings grew and visible exports recovered, the current account moved into steady surplus in 1957, as had the overall balance of payments two years earlier. From 1957 to 1962 the balance of payments continued in steady surplus as the export boom reached its peak and foreign capital flowed into the country. However, this success was brought to an end in 1963, and with it the relative immunity of Italian policy-makers to balance of payments problems.

The 1963 crisis represented a considerable interruption to Italy's postwar boom, coming at the end of four years of remarkably rapid growth. In that year, the combined effects of strike activity and wage inflation brought about a marked deterioration in the visible trade balance which showed a deficit of 1903 million dollars. However, this was more a product of a leap in imports than a slump in exports. Indeed, as can be seen from table 3.2, exports did rise between 1962 and 1963 from 4590 to 4973 million dollars, but at the same time imports grew by 1374 million dollars, and, with no substantial offsetting movement in other current items, the current account showed a deficit of 745 million dollars. Moreover, these problems on current account were compounded by a net capital outflow of 485 million dollars, owing to a number of factors – the political situation after the 1963 elections, uncertainty on the part of foreign investors following the nationalisation of the electricity industry, and the implementation of the new withholding tax on dividends.

Coupled with social unrest and the worsening of the general economic climate, these developments initiated a capital flight which reached a peak in the winter of 1963–64 and, to prevent the widespread fear of a lira devaluation being realised, a massive international financial support operation had to be put into effect.

The 1963 crisis is significant for a number of reasons. First, and most important, it marked the end of the 'easy' years for Italian balance of payments policy. Although the balance of payments did not re-enter deficit until 1969, the whole climate of economic policy had changed. The capital flight of 1963–64 was the first hint of what was to become a most pressing problem for the Italian authorities. The instability of the capital account, where domestic labour problems and political instability were to find most dramatic expression, had effectively removed the cushion of security against external deficit traditionally afforded by the steady surplus on invisibles. Secondly, the authorities' reaction to the 1963 crisis produced a textbook example of domestic deflationary policies implemented to cure a balance of payments deficit.[27] The result was that it was late 1965 before the economy began to recover from its policy-induced depression. Italy was no longer a stranger to 'stop–go'. Finally, the 1963 crisis was in many respects similar to the troubles that exploded in 1969–70.

The 1969 crisis came at the end of five years of relatively satisfactory balance of payments performance. Between 1964 and 1968 the balance of payments remained in comfortable surplus, with 1965 witnessing an impressive recovery of visible exports, to produce the first visible trade surplus since before the war. Visible exports continued to expand rapidly until the final quarter of 1969. Meanwhile, current account as a whole remained in solid surplus, to more than offset the increasing outflow of private capital. These overall favourable conditions were, however, terminated in 1969 which, like 1963, was characterised by widespread industrial action followed by inflationary wage settlements.

The impact of these events on the balance of payments was, however, in some senses different from 1963. The deficit in 1969 was entirely due to a capital flight which, as we have seen, was largely a result of the export of capital by Italian residents. Despite a current account surplus of 2340 million dollars the overall balance of payments ran a deficit of 1391 million dollars.

In 1970, however, the pattern changed markedly, with visible trade re-entering a deficit as the impact of the 'hot autumn' registered, shrinking the current account surplus to 761 million dollars. But the astounding development of 1970 was the dramatic fall in the capital account deficit, from 3624 million dollars in 1969 to 237 million dollars in 1970. This was due to two main factors – heavy borrowing in Euro-currency markets by Italian financial institutions, particularly the 'special credit institutes' (see chapter 5), at the request of the Italian authorities, and a substantial increase in Italian interest rates as the government ended its policy of 'pegging' bond prices. However, this improvement was not sustained, and in 1972 the balance of payments again ran into difficulties. Although the current account remained in surplus, there was a severe capital account deficit of 2166 million dollars, reflecting renewed speculation against the lira in the context of general international currency disorders.

The authorities' response to this new crisis was a significant departure. Whereas in 1963 and 1969 the Italian policy had been one of general monetary restraint (even though much of the problem had lain in capital rather than current account), early in 1973 the lira was floated, first on capital account in January, and then also on current account in February of that year. In a sense, this is a more logical response to capital account problems in so far as it did not entail any great restraint on the (very slow) recovery of the domestic economy from the post-1969 depression, but it can only be regarded as a temporary policy instrument in so far as the EEC commitment to monetary union removes the possibility of a floating lira in the future.

In conclusion, although Italy's balance of payments performance over the postwar period as a whole has been impressive in terms of overall surplus, the external account lost much of its security in the later 1960s. Italy's capital account problems arrived at precisely the wrong moment, insofar as the continuance of economic growth in the 1960s required more positive government action than in the 1950s, and the authorities were diverted from expansionary policies both in 1963–64 and in 1969–70 when the balance of payments ran into deficit. Over the years 1963–72 the instability and relative weakness of the balance of payments has imposed a substantial cost on the economy as a whole. Prospects for the immediate future are a little brighter insofar as the floating of the lira has allowed the economy to weather the recent capital account problems. In the longer term, with visible exports giving no indication of slackening off and invisibles, despite some shrinkage, continuing in steady surplus, it is not unreasonable to predict a continuing surplus on current account. However, with the very recent deterioration in Italy's terms of trade, a soaring import bill could represent a threat in the future. More serious, perhaps, is the capital account which shows few signs of greater stability, and it is here that future problems will probably lie.

Notes to chapter 3

1. For a more comprehensive discussion of the points covered below, see F. and V. Lutz *Monetary and Foreign Exchange Policy in Italy* Princeton: Princeton University Press (1950).

2. Sterling was devalued by 30.5 per cent against the dollar in September 1949. Many other countries followed suit, the Scandinavian countries and the Netherlands by an identical amount, and others by less: West Germany devalued by 20.6 per cent, France by 21.8 per cent, Portugal by 13.0 per cent, and Belgium and Luxembourg by 12.3 per cent. Italy, reflecting the authorities' acceptance that the lira had been substantially undervalued in 1947, devalued by only 8.3 per cent.

3. S. Clough *The Economic History of Modern Italy* New York: Columbia University Press (1964) p. 103.

4. See C. Zacchia 'Features of the Present Italian Customs Tariff' *Banca Nazionale del Lavoro Quarterly Review* (July-September 1953).

5. See G. Pietranera 'The Crisis in the Italian Balance of Trade' *Banca Nazionale del Lavoro Quarterly Review* (January 1953); and G. Carli 'The Italian Balance of Payments Problem' *Banca Nazionale del Lavoro Quarterly Review* (July-September 1953).

6. For details of these and other factors, see P. Baffi 'Monetary Developments in Italy from the War Economy to Limited Convertibility (1938–1958)' *Banca Nazionale del Lavoro Quarterly Review* (December 1958).

7. Over the period 1958–70, total EEC imports rose by 272 per cent and EFTA imports by 162 per cent. Non-European import growth was much lower – 76 per cent for the USA and Canada, and 47 per cent for Latin America.

8. An exhaustive bibliography of the methodological issues involved in constant market share analysis is to be found in E. Leamer and R. Stern *Quantitative International Economics* Boston: Allyn and Bacon (1970) chapter 7.

9. R. Stern *Foreign Trade and Economic Growth in Italy* New York: Praeger (1967) pp. 33-42.

10. An extension to constant market share analysis makes it possible to assess the impact of the Common Market on Italy's export growth by distinguishing between intra-Community trade and trade with the rest of the world, so that one can estimate the growth of exports due to competitiveness within the EEC market and that due to the increase in trade brought about by the setting up of the EEC. It has been estimated that over the period 1958–70, both in the case of total and manufactured exports from Italy to the EEC, the competitive element has been more important than the growth in demand generated by the market. See F. Masera 'Italy in Ten Years of the Common Market' *Review of Economic Conditions in Italy* Rome: Banco di Roma (September 1967); and by the same author *The Italian Experience in the Common Market* published by the Italian Chamber of Commerce for Great Britain.

11. For an approach which incorporates domestic competition, see R. Gross and M. Keating 'Analysis of Competition in Export and Domestic Markets' *Occasional Studies, OECD Economic Outlook* (December 1970).

12. At least one recent study, using multiple regression analysis as an alternative to constant market share analysis, has highlighted the importance of domestic demand in determining Italy's manufacturing export performance during the 1960s, concluding that an increase in domestic demand sufficient to increase the degree of capacity utilisation restrained export growth despite favourable demand and price conditions abroad. See M. Roccas 'Funzioni di esportazione e importazione dell'Italia: alcuni aggiornamenti' *Contributi Alla Ricerca Economica* Rome: Banca d'Italia (1972).

13. See F. Masera *I Movimenti di Capitali nel Quadro Istituzionale Italiano e Internazionale* Rome: Banca d'Italia (January 1970) pp. 39–50.

14. *The Italian Experience in the Common Market,* op. cit., p.4.

15. For a full discussion and quantitative analysis of Italy's earnings from services, see P. Miurin 'Struttura e Analisi Quantitative del Settore dei Servizi della Bilancia dei Pagamenti Italiana' *Contributi alla Ricerca Economica* Rome: Banca d'Italia (1971).

16. ISTAT *Indagine Speciale sulle Vacanze degli Italiani nel 1968* (Rome, 1969).

17. Italian tourist expenditure rose by almost 50 per cent in 1970, and yet the number of Italian tourists travelling abroad increased by a mere 10 per cent. The illegal smuggling of currency out of Italy, disguised as holiday money, was obviously

carried out on a substantial scale, largely in response to the confused economic and political circumstances of the period. Earnings from tourism were again distorted in 1972 when, in June, the Bank of Italy suspended the crediting of banknotes remitted from foreign banks in an attempt to discourage the illegal export of Italian capital. This had the side effect of placing all lire held abroad at a discount, so that when Italians travelled abroad they exchanged their lire for foreign currency in Italy, while foreign tourists converted their currencies into lire before they entered Italy. Because of the method by which the figures for tourist expenditures are collected, this had the effect of swelling Italian tourist expenditure abroad and diminishing foreign tourist expenditure in Italy.

18. For a detailed discussion of the institutional framework of Italian capital movements, see *I Movimenti di Capitali nel Quadro Istituzionale Italiano e Internazionale,* op. cit.

19. The other two categories, local authority and central government transactions, have been much less important over the period, except in 1970, when the Italian government borrowed heavily abroad, giving rise to a net inflow of central government capital movements of 718 million dollars.

20. Banca d'Italia *Relazione Annuale* (various years).

21. ibid.

22. For fuller discussion of this phenomenon, see *I Movimenti di Capitali nel Quadro Istituzionale Italiano e Internazionale,* op. cit., pp. 54–62; V. Mesalles 'Banknote Remmittances: Italy's Recent Experience' *Banca Nazionale del Lavoro Quarterly Review* (March 1968); F. Vicarelli 'L'Esportazione di Banconote nell'Esperienza Italiana dell'Ultimo Decennio: Una Analisi Quantitativa' *Studi Economici* (Naples).

23. Mesalles, op. cit., p. 75

24. ibid., p. 86.

25. The figures which follow are taken from *I Movimenti di Capitali nel Quadro Istituzionale Italiano e Internazionale,* op. cit.

26. Banca d'Italia *Relazione Annuale, 1972* (Rome, 1973).

27. See F. Modigliani and G. La Malfa 'Inflation Balance of Payments Deficit and their Cure through Monetary Policy: The Italian Example' *Banca Nazionale del Lavoro Quarterly Review* (March 1967).

CHAPTER 4

Labour Markets, Labour Costs and Industrial Relations

L'Italia e una Repubblica democratica fondata sul lavoro
(Article 1 of the Italian Constitution)

ITALY's rapid economic growth in the post-war period has been associated with quite fundamental changes in the field of Italian labour and labour markets. The employment structure has undergone a radical transformation, labour markets have tended to tighten, strikes have become more common and altered their character, wages and earnings have risen rapidly and, associated, so too have labour costs, while collective bargaining has changed in scope and nature. Labour market dualism, for which Italy is frequently cited as a case study, has been substantially modified – in form if not in degree. Not only are these features related to economic growth and economic development in the broader sense, but they are also themselves closely inter-related. The tightening of the labour markets encouraged and gave new possibilities for collective bargaining; the rapid rise in wages and earnings reflects the tighter labour markets and the growing strength of the trade unions; while the changes in employment structure cannot be divorced from collective bargaining or the increasing tightness of the labour markets

This chapter is aimed at gauging and analysing these various features of the labour market and how they have developed over the postwar period. It is in five parts. Section 4.1 is concerned with the changes in employment structure. Section 4.2 discusses the tightening labour markets and the great increase in strike activity. Section 4.3 looks at wages, earnings and labour costs and how these have changed over the period. Section 4.4 analyses the nature and intensity of labour market dualism, while section 4.5 examines the changing forms of collective bargaining and trade unionism. We have tried throughout to stress the inter-relationships between these various features.

4.1 The changing employment structure

A major characteristic of the Italian economy over the postwar period, and one that has been both a cause and consequence of the rapid economic growth and great spatial reorganisation of the population, has been the radical change in employment structure. An indication of the extent of this is given in table 4.1, which shows employment in the major economic sectors between 1951 and 1971. The table covers all employment and includes the self-employed and marginal workers as well as full-time employees. The marginal workers consist of people in employment but working less than thirty-three hours per week.

Table 4.1   Employment in Italy by sector, 1951–1971

	1951 ('000)	Propor- tions	1961 ('000)	Propor- tions	1971 ('000)	Propor- tions
Agriculture	8640.0	43.9	6207.0	30.4	3652.0	18.9
Extractive	145.4	0.7	149.7	0.7	116.1	0.6
Manufacturing	4455.9	22.6	5485.0	26.9	6011.3	31.0
Electricity, gas and water	93.0	0.5	115.1	0.6	160.8	0.8
Construction	1108.7	5.6	1896.2	9.3	1873.8	9.7
Trade and public services	1874.2	9.5	2492.3	12.2	2744.5	14.2
Transport and communications	611.4	3.1	860.2	4.2	1041.0	5.4
Banking and insurance	180.3	0.9	246.1	1.2	310.0	1.6
Various services	1446.3	7.3	1564.1	7.7	1680.5	8.7
Public administration	1137.7	5.8	1414.7	6.9	1805.0	9.3
Total	19,692.9	100.0	20,430.4	100.0	19,395.0	100.0

Sources: ISTAT *Occupati Presenti in Italia, 1951–1970* (Rome, 1971); and ISTAT *Annuario Statistico Italiano 1971* (Rome, 1972).

A number of points arise out of this table but the most impressive is the enormous fall in agricultural employment. While in 1951 agriculture accounted for 43.9 per cent of total employment, this was down to 18.9 per cent by 1971 – a reduction in absolute terms of almost 5 million. The enormity of this change can perhaps be judged by the fact that in the ninety years between 1861 and 1951 agricultural employment fell by only 2.6 million.[1] The decline of agricultural employment during the 1960s when, as we shall see, the Italian labour market was often tight, was greater than during the 1950s. Between 1961 and 1971 more than a quarter of a million people were leaving the sector every year. It can be seen from table 4.1 that manufacturing employment has not increased spectacularly – some 1.5 million between 1951 and 1971 – and certainly not enough to absorb the outflow from agriculture.[2]* Although some of the exodus was absorbed by industry, often 'through the filter of construction',[3] substantial proportions either stayed in the construction industry, went into the service sector or, particularly true of females, left the labour force altogether. A point worth noting from the table is that total employment fell slightly between 1951 and 1971, and this over a period when the Italian population increased from 47.5 million to 54.0 million. Inevitably, there has been a fall in activity rates and we discuss these shortly.

Of the five million workers who left agriculture between 1951 and 1971, the vast majority were either marginal workers or self-employed. The former group made up some 44 per cent of the decline while the latter accounted for a further 50 per cent. Many of these workers, either because of age or sex, would not take other jobs on leaving the land. The decline in the numbers of full-time self-employed agricultural workers sometimes carried the advantage that it allowed an increase in the average size of farm. The point should not however be exaggerated, for many of these people, as we have seen in chapter 1, continued to hold on to their land even when they left their areas.

Table 4.2   The composition of Italian total employment, 1951–1971

	1951				1971			
	Full-time employ-ees	Full-time self-em-ployed workers	Mar-ginal work-ers	Total*	Full-time employ-ees	Full-time self-em-ployed workers	Mar-ginal work-ers	Total*
Agriculture	14.9	51.0	34.1	100.0	26.2	52.6	21.2	100.0
Extractive	89.5	7.8	2.8	100.0	84.2	7.8	7.9	100.0
Manufacturing	68.8	21.4	9.9	100.0	79.6	14.8	5.6	100.0
Electricity, gas and water	96.5	3.6	—	100.0	98.3	0.7	—	100.0
Construction	84.7	10.3	5.0	100.0	78.3	9.9	11.8	100.0
Trade and public services	22.5	59.3	18.2	100.0	35.7	59.2	5.2	100.0
Transport and communications	76.6	16.1	7.3	100.0	71.6	26.9	1.5	100.0
Banking and insurance	91.1	5.6	3.3	100.0	93.8	3.6	2.7	100.0
Various services	65.6	14.6	19.8	100.0	72.3	22.0	5.7	100.0
Public administration	100.0	—	—	100.0	100.0	—	—	100.0
TOTAL*	43.9	35.1	20.9	100.0	64.5	27.3	8.3	100.0
TOTAL* ('000)	8653.5	6915.9	4915.5	20,484.9	12,499.2	5292.3	1603.5	19,395.0

* Totals may not add due to rounding.

Sources: ISTAT *Occupati Presenti in Italia, 1951–1970* (Rome, 1971); and ISTAT *Annuario Statistico Italiano 1971* (Rome, 1972).

The decline in the number of marginal and self-employed workers in agriculture, largely reflecting the improved prospects of obtaining better and more secure alternative employment, is found also in most other sectors. Table 4.2 shows the proportion of the labour force, by sector, made up of full-time employees, full-time self-employed workers and marginal workers in 1951 and 1971.

The most interesting point to emerge from table 4.2 is the considerable decline in the importance of marginal workers – they fell from 20.9 per cent of the total work force in 1951 to 8.3 per cent in 1971. In absolute numbers this was a reduction of 2.5 million from the level of 4.1 million in 1951. The fall in the number of marginal agricultural workers was particularly dramatic – from 2.9 million in 1951 to 0.8 million in 1971. It will be noted that the only major sector in which the weighting of marginal workers has grown substantially is construction where, in absolute terms, they increased from 55,000 in 1951 to 221,000 in 1971. In part this was a reflection of the depressed state of the construction industry in 1971, marked by a considerable amount of short-time working, but it is not the whole explanation. Construction has been plagued throughout the postwar period by a rapid growth of small firms whose labour force is underemployed.

The importance of the self-employed in the Italian employment structure, like the marginal workers, has fallen, though not nearly so spectacularly. In absolute terms, however, the decline has been substantial, with a fall of some 1.3 million between 1951 and 1971 from the 1951 level of 6.9 million. The sector particularly affected by this decline was agriculture, though this is not immediately apparent from table 4.2. The rise in the percentage of agricultural self-employed registered in the table is a direct result of the great reduction of marginal agricultural workers and certainly does not imply an increase in the self-employed. In fact, within agriculture, the number of self-employed fell from 4.4 million in 1951 to 1.9 million in 1971.

The general movement out of agriculture and the overall decline in the number of self-employed and marginal workers have had two important consequences. First, they have contributed substantially to Italy's rapid rate of growth in that labour has been switched from what is generally low-productivity employment to jobs having a higher productivity. According to Denison, some 24 per cent of the growth of Italian national income between 1950 and 1962 was explained by 'improved allocation of resources', i.e. switching[4] – a point already discussed in chapter 2. Secondly, the decline in the numbers employed in agriculture has been an important explanatory factor in the great spatial restructuring of the Italian population, with quite dramatic movements out of the rural areas and small towns and into the major centres. In 1951 some 34.5 per cent of the population was living in metropolitan areas of more than 110,000 population. This had risen to 39.2 per cent by 1961 and to 41.8 per cent by 1966, with an estimate that in 1981 the proportion would reach 49.1 per cent.[5] The change between 1951 and 1966 resulted in a net increase of 5.5 million people in these larger centres and the forecasted change between 1966 and 1981 will involve a further 6.7 million.

This urbanisation must to a large extent be seen as a consequence of the declining job opportunities in agriculture and/or the presence of better jobs in the towns. Certainly the decline in agricultural employment is closely associated with national economic conditions, being high during periods of economic boom and low during recessions. (It dropped, for example, to almost zero in 1965 when national unemployment rose and the economy was depressed.) At the same time, the point should not be exaggerated. There is evidence that a not inconsiderable proportion of the migration is simply an attempt to escape from rural living which, particularly in the South, can be a very restrictive (and unhealthy) existence. The consumer society, so attractive to the young, and made evident through television, is very much an urban society. In the South, as we shall see in chapter 6, the escape from the rural areas often involves inter-regional migration, and frequently a move to the North or abroad. Net migration from the South was 1.8 million between 1951 and 1961 and a further 2.3 million between 1961 and 1971, out of a population that has averaged some 18 million over the postwar period.

The postwar urbanisation of the Italian population has been on such a scale that it would have created problems for almost any country. The added problem of inter-regional migration and the concentration of the migrants in a limited number of northern cities, principally Milan and Turin, has exacerbated these difficulties. Moreover, most Italian cities are simply incapable of planning for, and financing, the accommodation of this great influx. As we have seen in chapter 1, conditions in many towns are both chaotic and pitiful, with transport systems, hospitals, schools and other elements of the urban infrastructure being quite inadequate. The continued growth of the urban population in the future will inevitably result in a further deterioration unless there is some major local authority and public administration reform.

4.2 The tightening labour markets

The Republic recognises the right of all citizens to work.
(Article 4 of the Italian Constitition).

This section looks at three aspects of Italian labour markets and the extent to which these indicate a tightening. The three aspects covered are unemployment and underemployment, emigration, and activity rates. The section ends with a discussion of the not-unrelated topic of strikes.

Unemployment and underemployment

The postwar growth of the Italian economy has been such that not only
has it been largely able to absorb the structural changes that have taken
place, but labour markets, on at least one measure – unemployment –
have also substantially tightened.

Table 4.3 shows male and female unemployment rates between 1954
and 1971. A number of points need to be made immediately about these
figures. First, the unemployment percentages have been calculated by
expressing the unemployed as a percentage of the labour force, i.e.
employed plus unemployed. Secondly, up to 1960 the employed include
those temporarily working abroad. From 1961 onwards this practice is
dropped. In that this diminishes the denominator (by something like
500,000 out of a 'home' labour force of some 20 million), it increases the
unemployment percentages slightly. Thirdly, and largely in an attempt
to improve comparability over the period, we have included marginal
workers as being part of the labour force. Finally, the figures in the table
are based on a sample survey. Since 1959 the sample has been taken four
times per annum as against once or twice a year between 1954 and 1958.
Inevitably, because of seasonal factors, the annual figures for these early
years are not strictly comparable with those for later years.

Table 4.3   Italian unemployment, 1954–1971

	Males		Females	
	Number unemployed ('000)	Percentage unemployed	Number unemployed ('000)	Percentage unemployed
1954	1168	8.0	501	7.9
1955	1051	7.0	440	6.7
1956	1318	8.7	549	8.6
1957	1075	7.0	460	6.8
1958	935	6.1	405	5.8
1959	826	5.4	402	4.5
1960	601	4.0	229	3.6
1961	488	3.4	220	3.5
1962	410	2.8	201	3.3
1963	348	2.4	156	2.6
1964	376	2.6	173	3.0
1965	518	3.5	203	3.5
1966	558	3.8	211	3.9
1967	487	3.3	202	3.8
1968	475	3.3	219	4.0
1969	439	3.1	224	4.1
1970	407	2.9	208	3.9
1971	405	2.9	208	3.9

Sources: ISTAT *Bolletino Mensile di Statistica* (Rome, various issues); and ISTAT
          Annuario Statistico Italiano (Rome, various issues).

These shortcomings and qualifications are however unlikely to change the basic trend shown in the table – a fairly steady fall in the unemployment rate to a level that is reasonable by European standards. However, in a number of ways the unemployment figures exaggerate the tightness of the Italian labour market, and one would certainly need to be very cautious in making international comparisons.[6] As mentioned earlier, the unemployment figures are gathered on a sample survey basis, with the unemployed being classified as those people aged fourteen or above who were looking for their first job or had lost their previous job and who, in the reference week of the sample, were both actively searching for a job and in a position to accept one if it was offered. The resultant unemployment therefore excludes those people who, though not looking for a job in the reference week, had looked in the past. These are the so-called 'discouraged unemployed'. In February 1971, 104,000 of the population classified as not part of the labour force (and not unemployed) said they would like a job and, though not looking for work in the reference week, had done so in the past.[7] At that time there were some 676,000 unemployed in Italy as a whole, so the proportion in the discouraged unemployed category is not insubstantial.

In addition to the obviously discouraged unemployed there is a group in the non-labour force who would like a job but who were not actively searching because they thought they were too old, too young, not sufficiently experienced or qualified, or would have difficulty in getting to work because of transport problems. Interpretation of whether this group should be classified as unemployed is obviously difficult. Many would, however, register and be classified as unemployed in the United Kingdom and probably should, in reality, be considered as such. In 1971 the number in this category who said they would like a job was 128,000.[8]

With these points in mind, it becomes readily apparent why the straight unemployment figures should be viewed with caution as a measure of labour market tightness. But a further reason that could be added is that the heavy weighting of agriculture and the self-employed in the Italian economy, together with the very low basic unemployment benefits (discussed later), encourage underemployment rather than unemployment.

It is not easy to design a simple but effective measure of underemployment. One that is common in Italy classifies the underemployed as those working for between 1 and 32 hours per week for economic reasons – that is, because of a lack of job opportunities. It thus excludes those working a short week because of illness, poor weather, holidays or where such a short week is part of the labour contract. On this basis the male underemployed in 1970 numbered 123,000 and females 127,000 – equal to some 30.2 per cent and 61.1 per cent of the male and female unemployed respectively. Though difficult to devise an alternative, most observers would agree that hours worked is no satisfactory measure of underemployment and involves a considerable amount of understatement. In the service trades in particular, where underemployment according to the hours worked criterion is slight, large numbers of people are working very long hours even though obviously underemployed.

In brief, although the trend given by the official unemployment and underemployment figures is probably realistic, at any particular point in time they understate to a considerable degree the seriousness of the problem. In other words, ordinally they can be accepted with reasonable confidence, but cardinally they must be treated with great caution.

Emigration

In spite of the unemployment trends outlined above, Italy still remains a distinctly labour-surplus economy, not only because 'true' unemployment and underemployment remain high, but also because large numbers of the population need to go to other countries to find work. Net overseas emigration is an important and historical feature of the Italian economy, as well as one which, through remittances, has made a substantial contribution to the balance of payments – a point discussed in detail in chapter 3. Table 4.4 provides figures for net overseas emigration between census years since 1871.

Table 4.4   Italian net emigration, 1871–1971

	Population ('000)	Net emigration ('000)	per '000 population (annual rates)
1871–1881	26,839	− 361	1.3
1881–1901	28,954	−2180	3.8
1901–1911	32,966	−1646	5.0
1911–1921	35,845	− 404	1.1
1921–1931	39,944	− 977	2.4
1931–1936	41,652	− 319	1.5
1936–1951	42,994	−1010	1.6
1951–1961	47,516	−1194	2.5
1961–1971	50,624	−1157	2.3

Note: The population figures are for the initial years and measures 'resident' population (except for 1871, when these figures were not collected and 'present' population has been used). The rate of emigration is calculated on the basis of population in the initial year.

Sources: Svimez *Un Secolo di Statistiche Italiane: Nord e Sud 1861–1961* (Rome, 1961); and the census results of 1961 and the provisional results of 1971.

The table shows well the long-standing nature of overseas migration. The low levels recorded between 1911 and 1921 are largely explained by the First World War, while those between 1931 and 1936 reflect the Fascist policies, described in chapter 1, aimed at curbing migration (both internal and external) and, probably more important, the lack of job opportunities in the United States and the rest of Europe.

The rate of net emigration (in relation to population) was lower during the 1950s and 1960s than the massive movements between 1881 and 1911, even though the numbers on an annual basis are fairly similar. Other changes have also taken place which distinguish postwar emigration from that of earlier years. First, a much higher proportion of the emigrants are from the South, and indeed evidence suggests that as the labour markets tightened during the 1960s the North enjoyed net immigration from abroad. Certainly there was high total net immigration (including that from the South) – equal to 573,000 between 1951 and 1961 and 1.2 million between 1961 and 1971. Secondly, growing proportions of Italian emigrants have been going to European countries as opposed to trans-oceanic destinations. In view of the labour mobility permitted within the EEC, the restrictions imposed on immigration by many of the traditional receiving countries, and the understandable preference for migrants to be close to their own country, this trend is not particularly surprising. While between 1871 and 1950 51 per cent of emigrants went to non-European countries, this was down to 27 per cent over the period 1951 to 1965 and amounted to only 10.6 per cent between 1966 and 1969.

Activity rates

An intriguing feature of the Italian labour market and one that appears, at least initially, to be at odds with the falling unemployment rates noted earlier, is the fact that activity rates (labour force, i.e. employed plus unemployed, as a percentage of total population) have been rapidly declining over the postwar period – a trend which, like migration, has been present since unification. It has however tended to speed up in the postwar period, and especially during the 1960s when male activity rates fell from 60.1 per cent in 1962 to 56.8 per cent in 1966 and 54.2 per cent in 1971. Female activity rates in the same years were 24.1, 19.9 and 19.2 per cent. The rate for males and females combined, again in the same years, were 41.6, 37.9 and 36.2 per cent.[9] Italian activity rates are now among the lowest in the world, with only Portugal being lower within Western Europe.

Opinions still differ as to the relative weighting of the various influences behind the declining activity rates in the postwar period. Most observers are agreed, however, that the reduced importance of agriculture is a key factor, particularly for female activity rates.[10] The movement out of agriculture is, however, rather a 'catch all' explanation, gathering within it a variety of factors associated with an increasingly urban, rich and industrialised society. Among these factors are, first, the growing numbers of young people attending further education institutions (though it is a moot question as to what proportion of students are studying because of the lack of job opportunities). Secondly, the pensionable age has fallen (now being generally sixty for men and fifty-five for women – five years lower than the prewar levels) and pensions have continually risen in value and coverage.[11] Thirdly, higher male incomes have reduced the need for females to work. But probably much more important in explaining the falling female activity rate has been the break up of the extended family (not unassociated with the great postwar migratory flows) and the lack of nursery systems. However, tradition has also undoubtedly played a part in some areas where, although it is acceptable for women to work in the fields, a job in the factory is viewed in quite a different light. In consequence the movement of females from agriculture has frequently been into the non-employed rather than the employed. Fourthly, and this applies to both males and females, the continuing slack labour markets, even though now tighter than earlier, would tend to depress activity rates. Finally, the Italian population has for many decades been characterised by growing proportions in the school and pensionable age groups – a result of natural population trends, the rising school-leaving age and the falling pensionable age. All these forces would tend to reduce activity rates. On the other hand, there have been factors tending to raise them – the growing income needs in an increasingly consumer society; the tendency of young women to think of a career; the greater scope for mothers to work given by family planning and smaller families. These, however, have not been sufficiently powerful to offset the activity rate 'depressants'. It is expected that the downward trend in activity rates will continue, at least to 1981 for males, though with perhaps a slight upturn for females in the late 1970s and early 1980s.[12]

Strikes

We want to end this section by discussing a feature of the Italian labour market that is not entirely unrelated to the postwar changes of employment structure and the tightening labour markets (at least measured by unemployment) – a rapid growth of strike activity. Table 4.5 provides the basic data. It shows a fairly steady rise in strike activity over the postwar period, and particularly in terms of hours lost. This has coincided with the unemployment trends discussed above and, not unassociated, the growing importance and militancy of the trade unions – the subject of a later section.

Although table 4.5 gives the impression of fairly steady growth, the point does deserve to be made that strike activity fluctuated wildly from year to year. On average, over the period 1951–71, some 83 million hours were lost each year by strike activity. However, and reflecting the

Table 4.5   Italian strike activity, 1951–1971

	Number of strikes	Workers involved ('000)	Hours lost ('000)
1951–55	1689	2389	39,795
1956–60	1994	1685	44,646
1961–65	3666	2971	12,534
1966–71	3662	4019	135,108

Sources: ISTAT *Sommario di Statistiche Storiche dell'Italia 1861–1965* (Rome, 1968); and ISTAT *Annuario Statistico Italiano* (Rome, various issues).

greatly increased strike record in the 1960s, this figure was never reached in any single year until 1962. In that year, with the economy overheating and major wage contracts about to be negotiated, 181 million hours were lost, while in 1969, concentrated largely during the so-called 'hot' autumn, a record 303 million hours were lost, more than during the whole eight-year period 1951–57.

As might be expected, most strike activity has been in industry – more than the proportions engaged in that sector would warrant. Over the whole period 1951–71 some 62.4 per cent of hours lost through strikes can be allocated to the industrial sector. The much less unionised agriculture and services have only accounted for 14.6 and 22.9 per cent of hours lost respectively. Moreover, industry has been taking an increasing share of total hours lost – rising from 60.1 per cent in the quinquennium 1951–55 to 65.3 per cent in 1966–71. Agriculture on the other hand has accounted for a falling proportion. The service sector has seen a quite strong rise, particularly among the public administration – in this case reflecting industrial action both for their own ends and to secure more general social reforms.

In a fascinating article first published in 1959 an American researcher, A. M. Ross, attempted to examine the features of strike activity over time in a number of countries, and to group these countries into strike type.[13] He placed Italy firmly in the 'Mediterranean–Asian pattern', that is with strikes characterised primarily by high worker participation and short duration. Throughout the first half of the 1950s (1951–55) Italian strikes were indeed of very limited duration, averaging 16.7 hours per annum per worker involved. This was a period when, as we shall see, the slack labour market conditions did not encourage anything other than short, almost public sympathy, strikes. The average duration has tended to rise since then – to 26.5 hours between 1956 and 1960 and 34.5 and 33.6 hours in 1961–65 and 1966–71 respectively. By international standards, however, these figures are still low. In part this results from labour market conditions, which in many senses remain slack, but also it is a consequence of four other factors.

In the first place, strikers do not normally receive strike pay from their union, a reflection of the strong political base of Italian unions and their heavy financial dependence on political parties. Money paid by the parties is to buy votes, not to finance strikes. As we shall see, in the late 1960s the unions reduced their dependence on political parties and introduced better systems for the collection of dues from members, and in consequence a number of unions are now building up their own strike funds. Secondly, strikers are not eligible for social security assistance, though they can apply for meagre *ad hoc* awards from the local author-ities in cases of serious hardship. The lack of strike pay and social security assistance are important factors explaining not only the short duration of Italian strikes but also their 'dirty' character – no-holds-barred affairs, the aim being to inflict maximum damage with the mini-mum loss of earnings. Thirdly, and particularly during the second half of the 1960s, many strikes were demonstrative (and as such were short), aimed primarily against social conditions and global government policies. The point does, perhaps, need to be added that short, sharp strikes can be just as damaging as those of a longer duration. There is little doubt that during the late 1960s and early 1970s they sapped entrepreneurial morale and confidence as well as imposing high financial costs.

Table 4.6   Days lost through strikes per 1000 people employed: an international comparison

	Annual average		
	1960–64	1965–69	1960–69
Belgium	164	156	160
Canada	460	1556	1008
France	352	243*	303*
West Germany**	34	10	22
Ireland	686	1350	1018
Italy	1220	1574	1396
Japan	302	198	250
Netherlands	62	12	37
Switzerland	10	—†	—†
United Kingdom	242	294	268
United States	722	1232	977

* The 1965–69 figures for France in fact cover 1965–67 and 1969 only, while the 1960–69 figures are for 1959–67 and 1969 only.
** The West German figures exclude West Berlin.
† Less than 5.

Source: Department of Employment *Department of Employment Gazette* London: HMSO (February 1971) p. 164.

International comparisons of strike figures are difficult since the definition of a strike differs substantially between countries; and while some exclude strikes involving less than a specified number of days or workers from their official statistics, others include them. On at least one reasonable estimate, however, Italy is unenviably at the top of the international league table for the number of days lost through strikes per 1000 people employed. Table 4.6, which covers mining, manufacturing, construction and transport, shows Italy as having lost 1396 days per annum over the ten year period 1960–69 – higher than any other major country in the world. (The United Kingdom was well down the list with 268 days.)

Although we would not want to understate the damage that strikes have caused particular firms in Italy, especially the larger ones, or the turmoil and viciousness that lie behind the figures (particularly during the second half of the 1960s), strike figures need to be kept in perspective. Even in the record strike year of 1969 the number of hours lost per worker in Italy through strikes was about 16 – some two working days. Relative to, say, absenteeism (voluntary and involuntary), this figure, though not paling into insignificance, becomes less important. In 1969, for example, the number of hours lost in Italian manufacturing through strikes has been estimated at only 23 per cent of the total hours lost through strikes and absenteeism combined; and the point has already been made that 1969 was an exceptional year for strikes. Comparable figures for 1967, 1968 and 1970 are 3.8, 4.9 and 8.4 per cent respectively.[14] At the end of the 1960s, one worker in nine was absent from work for reasons other than industrial action, primarily because of illness. It is not altogether cynical to say that 'an effective anti-influenza serum would probably be of more measurable benefit to the economy than an effective anti-strike law – and perhaps be less difficult and costly to produce.'[15] It might, furthermore, be added that many observers have noted that strikes and absenteeism are to some degree complementary, absenteeism falling when strike activity is high and rising during periods of low strike activity.

4.3   Wages, earnings and labour costs

The worker has the right to a reward proportional to the quality and quantity of his work and in any case sufficient to guarantee him and his family a free and dignified existence. (Article 36 of the Italian Constitution).

This section is in three parts. We look first at contractual wages – how they have changed over time and the factors associated with these changes. Secondly, we move on to earnings and their trends, and a brief discussion of wage drift in Italy. Thirdly, we examine movements in

labour costs defined in the broader sense to include social security contributions which, in Italy and in the EEC generally, make up a major part
of the total wages bill.

Table 4.7 is a fairly basic table for this section. It shows the percentage
changes in minimum contractual wages for workers in agriculture and
industry between 1951 and 1971 and, over the same period, the changes
in the cost of living index and labour productivity. The latter has been
measured by dividing value-added at constant prices by employee units
(full-time employees plus one-third of the marginal employees – a variant
on the standard Italian system for calculating labour units defined on
p. xii).

Table 4.7 **Annual percentage changes in Italian minimum contractual
wages, cost of living and labour productivity**

	Agricultural wages	Agricultural productivity	Industrial wages	Industrial productivity	Cost of living
1951–1952	5.3	2.7	4.1	3.1	4.2
1952–1953	5.7	16.2	2.8	4.0	1.9
1953–1954	4.2	0.3	3.7	4.0	2.7
1954–1955	4.5	8.6	4.8	7.9	2.8
1955–1956	4.4	3.0	5.8	5.7	4.9
1956–1957	3.2	2.4	4.5	5.0	2.1
1957–1958	5.1	12.3	5.2	3.6	4.7
1958–1959	2.1	2.4	1.2	8.1	−0.3
1959–1960	0.9	−9.6	4.7	5.0	2.7
1960–1961	5.0	9.4	4.2	3.3	2.8
1961–1962	15.0	−8.3	11.3	4.9	5.1
1962–1963	21.3	6.1	14.3	3.3	7.6
1963–1964	14.4	9.3	17.4	1.6	5.9
1964–1965	8.7	10.5	8.3	8.5	4.3
1965–1966	6.0	6.3	3.7	7.9	2.1
1966–1967	9.2	4.0	5.0	4.5	2.0
1967–1968	5.1	6.4	3.8	8.4	1.3
1968–1969	10.8	3.9	7.3	3.8	2.8
1969–1970	17.5	4.6	20.7	3.4	5.0
1970–1971	13.7	33.6	11.9	−0.1	5.0
Annual arithmetic average	8.1	4.7	7.2	4.8	3.5

Sources: ISTAT *Annuario di Contabilità Nazionale* (Rome, 1971); ISTAT *Occupati
Presenti in Italia 1951–70* (Rome, 1971); ISTAT *Bolletino Mensile di
Statistica* (various issues); ISTAT *Annuario Statistico Italiano 1972* (Rome,
1973).

A number of points need to be made about the data in table 4.7 before
going on to discuss their significance. First, minimum contractual wages
cover basic pay and any other payment that is general and continuous.
The figures are aimed at measuring hourly contractual wages. They

exclude family allowances – largely because the basis on which these are calculated has changed over time with inevitable problems of comparability. A second point, still concerned with the wage figures, is of a more technical nature. This is that while up to 1966 the wage index took 1938 as the base year, in 1966 a new index was compiled taking that year as 100. We have used the 1938 index up to and including 1966 and from 1967 have used the new index even though, because of changed coverage, it is not strictly comparable with the earlier index. Thirdly, the wages figures are for manual workers, and we have not given an index for white-collar workers. For the record, white-collar industrial wages have followed a similar trend to those for manual workers, though rising slightly faster up to 1968 and then, probably reflecting trade union pressure in the late 1960s for the removal of white-collar/manual worker differentials, increasing more slowly between 1969 and 1971. Fourthly, the cost of living figures for 1952 and 1953 are not fully comparable with those from 1954 onwards in that they are based on two separate series. It should also be noted that we have used the cost of living index and not the consumer prices index. The former covers the cost of living for a typical non-agricultural family whose head is a manual or white-collar worker. The latter index is not family-based. The advantage of using the cost of living index is that it is possible to take it further back in time; the disadvantage is that it does not cover agricultural families. In practice, however, the two indices give very similar results.

Having made these qualifications and addenda, let us now discuss the main points to come out of table 4.7. First, it can be seen that both agricultural and industrial wages have risen faster than the cost of living. While the latter rose by 3.5 per cent per annum between 1951 and 1971, agricultural wages increased by 8.1 per cent and industrial wages by 7.2 per cent. Obviously, in real terms, the Italian worker is now substantially better off than he was previously. Deflating for cost of living changes, real agricultural wages have increased by some 4.6 per cent per annum and real industrial wages by 3.7 per cent. Secondly, wages have increased faster than productivity, which rose by some 4.7 per cent per annum in agriculture over the period, and by 4.8 per cent in industry. Agricultural wages rose slightly faster relative to productivity than did industrial wages. Thirdly, it will be noted that agricultural wages have risen slightly faster than industrial wages. Given the low degree of unionisation in agriculture, and that productivity in both industry and agriculture has grown at a fairly similar rate, this is frankly surprising. It should, however, be said that differentials between agricultural and industrial wages remain substantial.

A point that comes out with considerable force from table 4.7 is that wages increased slowly during the 1950s relative to the 1960s. The weakness of the trade unions and, associated, the very slack labour markets of the 1950s resulted in an annual growth of agricultural wages of 3.9 per cent between 1952 and 1960 and of 4.1 per cent in industry, as against 11.5 and 9.8 per cent respectively over the period 1961–71. Moreover, between 1952 and 1960 the annual growth of wages was below the growth of productivity – 4.3 per cent in agriculture and 5.2 per cent in industry. Relative to the 1950s, the annual growth of productivity was lower in industry over the period 1961–71 (4.5 per cent) and higher in agriculture (5.1 per cent), but in both sectors wages rose much faster than productivity. The massive increases of wages in the early and late 1960s, when unemployment was low and the trade unions particularly militant, stand out clearly from the table.

So far, we have limited ourselves to a discussion of contractual wages – basic wages negotiated through collective bargaining at a national level. In most countries earnings are above wages. Earnings include not only wages but also a number of other forms of remuneration, in particular overtime pay and payments negotiated at the plant or firm level. The tendency in most Western countries has been for earnings to rise faster than wages, a phenomenon known as wage drift.

Although wage drift has been present in Italy over the postwar period in general it has not been a serious phenomenon, averaging, for industry, some 0.3 per cent per annum between 1953 and 1969.[16] It did, however, increase, though not significantly, in the latter half of this period – averaging 0.5 per cent between 1961 and 1969 as against 0.2 per cent per annum between 1953 and 1960. It is possible to rationalise the higher wage drift in the 1960s with two arguments. First, and a point to which we return later, the 1960s saw a strengthening and growing militancy of the trade unions, particularly at the plant level, a trend that would tend to push earnings above wages. Secondly, as we have seen, the 1960s were characterised by tighter labour markets, at least in terms of unemployment, and this provided conditions which the plant bargainers could exploit, as well as encouraging more overtime working.

Our concern so far has been with wages and earnings trends over time. An inevitable question concerns the absolute level of Italian earnings. Table 4.8 shows Italian monthly and hourly earnings for manufacturing employees in 1970. The figures exclude family allowances but include holiday pay and tips.

At the then current rate of exchange (1500 lire to the pound sterling), average earnings in Italian manufacturing industry were 50.5p per hour, £75.9 per month and £911 per annum. In October 1970 average hourly earnings for manual workers (male and female combined) in UK manufacturing were around 56.6p while annual earnings averaged some £1263. In brief, UK hourly and annual earnings were, respectively, some 12 and 39 per cent above those in Italy. The smaller differential in respect of hourly earnings reflects the lower levels of overtime working in Italy.

Table 4.8 Hourly and monthly manufacturing earnings in Italy, 1970

	Hourly earnings (lire)	Monthly earnings ('000 lire)*
Foodstuffs	752	116.9
Textiles	643	87.8
Engineering and vehicles	849	130.5
Chemicals	937	146.2
Various	643	94.6
Average manufacturing**	757	113.9

* Monthly earnings have been calculated using average hours worked per worker by industry and multiplying these by hourly earnings.
** The average earnings are weighted averages using total hours worked in the various industries as weights.

Source: From data in *Relazione Generale sulla Situazione Economica del Paese (1970)* Vol. II (Rome, 1971) pp. 158–60.

The Italian trade unions in the postwar period have been particularly anxious to curb overtime working in an attempt to create more jobs. Most collective contracts limit overtime to about 200 hours per annum per worker. There is also a legislative limit on overtime working going back to 1923 when a statutory maximum of forty-eight hours' work per week was set for industrial workers. At the present time, and based on legislation introduced in 1955, industrial workers are still not allowed to work for more than forty-eight hours per week, except in emergency situations and when the factory's problems cannot be resolved by taking on additional workers. Permission for this must be sought from the Labour Inspectorate of the Ministry of Labour. In addition, employers must pay 15 per cent of the wages paid for hours worked over forty-eight into the funds of the national unemployment scheme. It remains to be added, however, that both the trade union and statutory controls are evaded to a considerable degree, with the subsequent understatement of true earnings.[17]

Having presented UK–Italy earnings comparisons, we must warn the reader to be extremely cautious in using them. First, because of false earnings declarations, the Italian figures (more so than in the United Kingdom) understate earnings, and particularly annual earnings. The understatement is due to the unofficial overtime working mentioned above and also to the practice of *fuori busta* (sums paid separately from the wage packet), which is widespread in some sectors of the economy, especially in construction and small manufacturing firms. The employees benefit from the practice by paying less tax, the employers by often having to pay lower social security contributions. Secondly, and an offsetting factor, the Italian figures overstate earnings (both hourly and annual) in that the data source excludes firms employing fewer than ten.

These will often be paying earnings below the average – a point to which we return shortly. Thirdly, any international comparisons of earnings need to be treated with great caution since they generally use the official exchange rate. This is not a satisfactory measure of cost of living differences, and in consequence international earnings comparisons give a poor indication of real earnings differentials. An example of the nonsense that can arise from the use of official exchange rates for this purpose was the sterling devaluation in November 1967 which, at a stroke, increased the relative value of Italian earnings by 14.3 per cent.

The earnings discussed thus far are earnings before tax and before employee social security contributions. The UK–Italy earnings differential would be reduced if measured in terms of take-home pay. First, the Italian industrial worker would, in 1970, be paying about 7 per cent of his earnings as social security contributions against some 4–7 per cent (depending on whether or not the worker was contributing to the graduated pension scheme) in the United Kingdom. Secondly, income tax payments are lower for the Italian worker relative to his UK counterpart. Taking account of the various allowances, an Italian married male with two children receiving the manufacturing average earnings in table 4.9 would pay virtually no direct tax. In the United Kingdom a worker in a similar position would pay some 7.7 per cent of his earnings in income tax. Again, however, one needs to be very careful in interpreting these figures in order to gauge real standards of living, since tax payments do give rise to benefits, and furthermore a large portion of government revenue in Italy is raised through indirect as opposed to direct taxation (see chapter 5). These and other reasons mentioned earlier are probably sufficient to warn the reader of the problems involved in international earnings comparisons.

Although in most countries wages and earnings form the major part of labour costs, social security contributions paid by the employer on behalf of his labour force are, in many instances, becoming increasingly significant. The importance of these contributions varies from country to country, depending on the 'generosity' of the social security system and/or the extent to which social security expenditure is 'fiscalised', i.e. financed through general taxation. As a result, any international comparison of labour costs that uses wages or earnings as a proxy, or any attempt to make international comparisons of the reward to labour by concentrating exclusively on wages and earnings, would be extremely misleading.

On paper, at least, Italy's social security system is comprehensive and generous by Western European standards. The great majority of the Italian population, and virtually all industrial workers, are covered by the various social security schemes. It is worth while digressing slightly to look at the various Italian social security benefits before examining contributions.

Turning first to pensions, an industrial worker (who would usually be in the so-called general obligatory scheme) with forty years' contributions would receive an old age pension equal to 74 per cent of his best three years' earnings in his last five years of work. The great majority of pensions are, like wages, tied to the cost of living index. The Italian industrial worker has the lowest retirement age in Europe – sixty for men and fifty-five for women – with the result that more people enjoy a pension for a longer period. There is a minimum pension which, in 1972, amounted to 416,000 lire or 390,000 lire per annum, depending on age, and although in theory a minimum contribution record of fifteen years is required for this pension, in practice this condition can often be evaded by being declared disabled. About one-third of Italian pensioners are on a disability pension.[18] In the event of illness, most pensioners are covered for the main costs of medicines, doctors' fees and hospitalisation. Workers and their families are similarly covered and, in addition, workers under the main health insurance scheme (INAM) receive a cash sickness benefit equal to half their earnings for the first twenty days and two-thirds from then on, to a maximum of 180 days in any one year. Those suffering from injuries sustained at work receive 60 per cent of their previous earnings for the first ninety days and 75 per cent thereafter until recovery, or until a permanently disabled settlement is reached. Women employees in industry receive very generous maternity allowances, equal to 80 per cent of earnings for two months before the birth and three months after. Industrial workers and pensioners with a family are eligible for a family allowance which is paid for dependent children and for the spouse (subject to a means test). In 1972 family allowances were 5720 lire per month for each child and 4160 lire per month for the spouse.

At odds with this long list of generous social security benefits is unemployment pay. The basic unemployment benefit is 400 lire per day for a maximum of 180 days in any one year, though it can be substantially supplemented under certain conditions. An unemployed person with a family, for example, has his unemployment pay supplemented by the family allowances as detailed above. Industrial workers who are temporarily laid off or put on short time are eligible for payments from a special, INPS-administered, wage integration fund giving 80 per cent of weekly pay for hours not worked within the limits of the maximum hours laid down in their contract (but not to exceed forty-four). This payment can be made for three months, or even longer through a ministerial order. Industrial workers made redundant and who have been employed for more than thirteen consecutive weeks receive, again through INPS (Istituto Nazionale della Previdenza Sociale) two-thirds normal wages (less unemployment benefit) for six months. Industrial workers made redundant and aged fifty-seven (or fifty-two for women) and who have made pension contributions to INPS for fifteen years or more are eligible for the pension that would have been their due if they had been of pensionable age. Finally, all workers made redundant (or on termination of service) are eligible for severance pay; the value of this varies between industries and sectors but, generally, white-collar workers receive one month's income for every year of service, blue-collar workers receive the same except that they normally will have been expected to have completed between five and ten years of service, and manual workers get between six and fifteen days' pay for every year of service.[19]

Other than the basic unemployment scheme, the Italian social security system as described above is in theory very generous, but the point does deserve to be stressed that in practice it has many shortcomings. Even though free, hospitals are overcrowded and have long waiting lists. In spite of Italy's vast output of medical graduates, medical services within hospitals are poor. Outside the hospitals the rates paid by the health insurance scheme for a doctor's visit are rarely adequate to secure his services. The basic unemployment pay is not only meagre in amount but also an administrative nightmare. For the sums involved, many forego this benefit. Very few people are on a pension equal to 74 per cent of terminal earnings since only a minority have an adequate contribution record. Some 54 per cent of old age pensioners in the general obligatory scheme were, in 1970, on the very low minimum pension and the average pension in payment was only some 30 per cent of industrial earnings. Over 90 per cent of previously self-employed old age pensioners were on a minimum pension which, at 234,000 lire per annum in 1970, was below the general obligatory minima. A final point that needs to be made is that not all of the Italian population is insured under the various social security schemes. This is particularly true in the pensions field, where as a result of lethargy, poor enforcement and the late development of schemes for the self-employed, a considerable number of elderly people are not eligible for a pension under any of the schemes. Until 1969 they would either be a burden to their families or need to resort to erratic and *ad hoc* local authority assistance. However, in that year, a 'social pension' was introduced, aimed specifically at this group. It was set at 156,000 lire per annum and was not tied to the cost of living. In 1972 it was increased to 234,000 lire per annum and tied to the cost of living. Even so, the amount is pitiful and many social pensioners live in dire poverty. There are some three-quarters of a million social pensioners.

In spite of the shortcomings of the Italian social security system, it would be misleading to deny that it has advanced enormously over the postwar period. In health and pensions in particular, both benefits and coverage have increased rapidly. Inevitably, costs have risen and, although the State has increased its share, the main source of finance is still the employer. In 1970 employer social security contributions under the 'general schemes' (with which the average industrial worker would be insured) were 52.1 per cent of earnings, with the employee paying 6.5 per cent. Relative to her EEC partners Italy's social security contributions are the highest. In France, for example, employer social security contributions in 1970 were 32.5 per cent of earnings, in Germany 14.7 per cent, in Belgium 30.0 per cent and in the Netherlands 20.5 per cent.[20]

Italian employer social security contributions are not only the highest in the EEC but have been growing substantially, to pay for the extended coverage and generosity of the system. Since contributions have been rising faster than wages or earnings, labour costs in total have inevitably been increasing more rapidly than our earlier tables, limited to wages and earnings, would suggest. Table 4.9 is interesting in this respect. It shows the postwar growth of total labour costs (all sectors) per employee unit, broken down into earnings and employer social security contributions, again per employee unit. The growth of productivity (value-added per employee unit) is also shown.

Table 4.9   Italian labour costs and productivity: annual growth per employee unit, 1951–1971

	Earnings	Employer social security contributions	Total labour costs	Productivity
1951–1952	6.7	15.8	8.4	1.9
1952–1953	5.5	13.2	7.3	4.4
1953–1954	4.7	12.4	6.4	0.4
1954–1955	7.9	11.0	8.4	5.5
1955–1956	7.3	9.9	8.1	3.4
1956–1957	6.0	9.0	6.7	3.1
1957–1958	5.6	8.9	6.4	4.0
1958–1959	4.6	8.2	5.4	4.9
1959–1960	4.4	9.0	5.7	1.2
1960–1961	6.4	7.4	6.8	3.6
1961–1962	11.2	14.2	12.0	1.9
1962–1963	18.5	22.2	19.4	3.2
1963–1964	11.8	10.8	11.5	2.6
1964–1965	11.4	2.5	8.9	6.8
1965–1966	6.2	9.2	7.0	5.8
1966–1967	6.0	10.4	7.2	3.5
1967–1968	6.9	11.7	8.3	5.9
1968–1969	7.4	8.7	7.7	3.2
1969–1970	14.6	15.0	14.7	3.1
1970–1971	14.9	10.6	13.7	1.7

Sources: ISTAT *Annuario di Contabilità 1972* (Rome, 1973); ISTAT *Occupati Presenti in Italia 1951–1970* (Rome, 1971); ISTAT *Annuario Statistico Italiano 1972* (Rome, 1973).

A number of points arise out of table 4.9. First, earnings per employee unit have, in every year, been increasing faster than productivity: this is quite at odds with our earlier discussion of collectively bargained wages, and also suggests that there has been more wage drift in the economy as a whole than our earlier, more limited, analysis suggested. Secondly, earnings have tended to rise faster during the 1960s than in the 1950s. Between 1951 and 1960 they rose by 5.9 per cent per annum and by a massive 10.5 per cent between 1961 and 1971. This latter was a consequence of the faster growth of collectively bargained wages, the slightly faster growth of productivity (3.2 per cent per annum between 1950 and 1968 and 3.7 per cent per annum between 1960 and 1971), and more wage drift. As we have already observed, given the tighter labour markets, at least when measured in terms of unemployment, the faster growth of wages and earnings in the 1960s is not surprising. Thirdly, the table shows quite clearly the substantial postwar increase in employer social security contributions, which generally rose faster than earnings. They now, inevitably, represent a higher proportion of total labour costs than in the early 1950s, having risen in fact from 19.5 per cent in 1951 to 27.0 per cent in 1961 and 28.0 per cent in 1971. Fourthly, and stemming from these various points, total labour costs per employee unit increased faster during the 1960s than the 1950s – 7.0 per cent per annum between 1951 and 1960, and 10.6 per cent between 1961 and 1971. In the latter period they have risen faster relative to productivity than they did in the former, giving an inevitably higher rate of inflation. It has also resulted in a growing proportion of value-added being accounted for by labour costs – from 41.9 per cent in 1951 to 46.6 per cent in 1961 and 55.7 per cent in 1971.

These trends have a number of worrying implications for future Italian development. First, it is difficult to see any substantial slowdown in the growth of wages and earnings, and, given the growing importance of plant bargaining in Italian industrial relations, wage drift could become more serious. Secondly, employers' social security costs could rise substantially over the next decade in that the social security system is intended to become more generous. In addition, more people will become eligible for higher pension rights. Inevitably social security costs will rise. It remains to be seen how much of this can be fiscalised. Thirdly, in the light of these comments on labour costs, one must be worried about the future growth of productivity. The potential for rapid growth certainly exists, through labour switching from low- to high-productivity sectors, but this requires investment if it is to be exploited. Given Italy's poorly developed capital markets and the fact that much of the postwar investment has been through self-finance, the rapid growth of labour costs, especially during the early 1960s and late 1960s, has resulted in a substantial cutback in investment. These trends will inevitably affect productivity growth. Italy is running the risk of getting locked into a vicious circle of rapidly rising labour costs, low investment, low productivity growth and inflation, with inevitably deleterious consequences for overall development. To a large extent, the years 1970–73 showed Italy locked into such a vicious circle, with the situation being exacerbated by political instability. One area in which the authorities could help in securing an exit is through the fiscalisation of social security contributions. Although state finance of the social security system has been rising over the postwar period, it still accounts for only about one-fifth of total social security expenditure. This must increase if overall growth is not to be impeded.

4.4 Labour market dualism

All citizens have equal social dignity and are equal before the law. (Article 3 of the Italian Constitution)

Italy is a country in which averages are especially meaningless, disguising enormous disparities. This is particularly true in the field of labour, where there are substantial gaps in rewards and working conditions – between North and South, between white-collar and manual workers and between state and non-state employees. Relative to the manual worker the white-collar worker is in a privileged position, not only in terms of earnings but also in respect of holiday pay, sick pay and severance pay. But the privileges of the white-collar worker pale into insignificance compared with those of the state employees (both white-collar and manual), who enjoy, relative to their counterparts in industry, higher pay, better pensions, better family allowances, more holidays, better sick pay and a series of perks which often come close to corruption. A recent book by an ex-trade union leader, Gorrieri,[21] has well documented these privileges. The book is without doubt one of the most stimulating in the field of labour published in Italy for many a year. It is also a book that has had an enormous influence on the trade unions; not least because the author sees the privileges of the state employees as arising to a large extent from union action and, at the level of the union confederations, from union inaction.[22*] He also sees distinct areas of underprivilege, if not exploitation (pensioners, workers with large families, farmers and outworkers),[23*] as being in part a consequence of union lack of interest.

For most observers, however, Italy is not simply a country characterised by substantial inequality and labour market disparities; it is one of economic and labour market dualism.

For a while during the postwar period, economic dualism almost became a fad of economists (and others) and hardly a year passed without a further addition to the literature.[24] Among this literature is a major contribution by Lutz, who examined dualism within the context of Italy.[25] It is the Lutzian approach that is the main concern of this section; primarily, we want to examine the nature of labour market dualism in Italy, its changing forms and its severity. The section does not discuss the North–South dualism since this is covered in chapter 6, nor does it cover the relationship between dualism and economic growth. This latter is an important subject of chapter 2.

For Lutz, 'the primary characteristic of the dual system is that labour doing, or capable of doing, the same kind of work, and often working in the same branch of activity, is remunerated at two different rates of pay. As a first approximation we may assume that the "high"-wage group is composed of hired labour working for contractual remuneration under union protection, and the low-wage group of labour not enjoying such protection. A large part of this latter group will consist of self-employed and family labour, the remuneration of which has no contractual element at all, though we shall for convenience refer to it as a "wage". Another part will consist of hired labour working for fixed remuneration, but attached to very small concerns which fail to keep to the terms of collective contracts'.[26] The first group is assumed to be fully employed while the latter are underemployed 'in the sense that they would want to shift to the higher earnings group if employment was available there'.[27] For Lutz, dualism was closely tied to the size of the establishment. 'Differentiation in the wage system is intimately bound up with this differentiation in the size of the operating unit. For it is only by keeping small . . . that the artisan establishment, family farm or "small" business can escape the application of union rates of pay and remain in the low-wage group.'[28] It is necessary to add that Lutz saw dualism not only in the sense of wage differentials. Factors deciding whether a worker 'belongs to the more or less privileged part of the labour force, may concern one or more of three components: the rate of pay; social insurance coverage; and security of employment'.[29] In all three, size of plant is seen as being a major determining factor.

In many ways it is possible to view the dualism that Lutz observed as being directly a consequence of the law and/or its shortcomings. During the 1950s (the period to which most of Lutz's work refers) collective bargaining on wages and working conditions was only enforceable between signatories of the contract – members of the signing employers' and employees' association. Trade union membership was not large, while most of the small firms would not be members of an employers' association and would have no difficulty in finding non-union labour. Beyond wages, the small firm (and more specifically the artisan firm) often paid less in social security contributions for its workers who were, in turn, eligible for smaller benefits. Family workers were in a particularly bad position in this respect though they did not represent the extreme of the dualistic system. Outworkers were in an even more pitiful situation. These people, generally females, working part-time at home, were engaged in cottage industries, subject to no union contracts; they had little or no security of employment and were hardly covered at all by any social security schemes. Finally, at a more general level, the Italian wage system was spatially dualistic in that considerable inter-area differences were present in contractual wages, and particularly between North and South.

Moreover, the law not only allowed dualism but actually encouraged its continuation. First, small firms and artisans were given preferential credit facilities and tax concessions. This made them more viable than they otherwise would have been. Secondly, spatial mobility of labour, which would have tended to reduce inter-area wage differentials, was limited. A Fascist law, which held that no one could move to a town of more than 25,000 'unless he could demonstrate that he already had a gainful and stable occupation in the place to which he moved'[30] remained in force throughout the 1950s. (This was in spite of article 16 of the Constitution which says that 'every citizen can move and stay freely in any part of the national territory'.) Thirdly, legislation passed in 1949 further limited geographic mobility, specifying that a person could 'register only on the unemployment list of the Employment Office of the district in which he had his legal residence. And it prescribed that the local Employment Office must fill vacancies from persons registered, under the relevant job category, on its own list before it took persons from the lists of other districts'.[31] Through the same law employers could normally only hire unemployed labour through the local employment office.[32]* People did of course defy these mobility laws, but they could not then use the employment offices. Inevitably, being outside the law, they were ripe for exploitation by the small firms and would certainly find it difficult to get employment in the highly paid large firm sector.

The law thus gave ample scope for dualism in Italy. The situation was, moreover, worsened by evasion of legal responsibilities by many employers, and particularly in small firms. Such evasion was prevalent in respect of wages and even more so in respect of social security legislation. In the very slack labour market conditions of the 1950s this non-adherence to the law was perhaps inevitable.

In the late 1950s and early 1960s Lutz's dualism was largely 'abolished'. Being largely either a consequence of the law or allowed by the law, it could be overcome by the law. To this end, first, in 1961 both the Fascist legislation impeding the spatial mobility of labour and the 1949 law on unemployment registration were rescinded. Secondly, the Ergo Omnes law of 1959 (and 1960) made labour contracts enforceable on employers irrespective of whether or not they were members of the employers' association (and therefore signatories to the agreement) and/or whether or not their work force was in a union. Thirdly, a law of 1958 provided for outworkers to be paid at contractual rates (or an agreed pay approved by a provincial outworkers commission) and to receive social security and other rights similar to those enjoyed by industrial workers.[33]* Finally (but this was not to come until the early 1970s), inter-area contractual wage differentials were abolished. Thus, 'by the end of the 1950s the possibilities of hiring "cheap" labour and at the same time keeping within the law had been considerably reduced'.[34]

But this is by no means the end of the story. Few observers doubt that serious labour market dualism still exists in Italy. In part it represents a continuation of the earlier type of dualism, and in part it has reappeared in new forms. A number of points are relevant in this context. First, the Ergo Omnes law binding employers and workers to contracts operative in their sector, whether or not they were signatories, applied only to the contracts as they existed when the law was passed. The efficacy of this law could only be maintained, therefore, if similar laws had been passed in succeeding years. This was, however, not done; because of serious questions and doubts about the law's constitutionality,[35] because the trade unions had turned their interests to other matters in the 1960s, and because national collective bargaining was, anyway, going through a crisis. Moreover, even in the 1950s the unions had never been united on the need and form of the Ergo Omnes law. They were worried, in particular, about its effects on union membership.[36] The failure to update Ergo Omnes inevitably meant that the provisions of the 1959 law became obsolete through inflation and growth. Perhaps up to the mid-1960s the law was useful in setting minimum wages (though doubts about its constitutionality diminished this effect), but it certainly has no relevance today. Given the general low level of unionisation in Italy (five million members out of an employee labour force of thirteen million), particularly in the small firms, there is plentiful scope for continued wage dualism.[37]* Secondly, a source of dualism that was relatively weak during the 1950s but later grew in strength is plant bargaining. Such bargaining, as we shall see, has become particularly important since the mid-1960s, although not in small firms where it has remained a rare phenomenon. Thirdly, and very important, despite the law, evasion of contractual commitments and legal social security responsibilities is rife, and particularly the latter. We have already seen that employer social security contributions are very high, giving considerable encouragement for evasion.[38]* The employee often suffers in terms of diminished benefits. Social security and other forms of labour cost evasion are found predominantly among the small firms but are not absent even in large firms, especially in the construction industry. From

the limited information available, non-payment of social security contributions is the norm for outworkers. In the fairly rich province of
Modena, for example, one observer found that only 3 per cent of outworkers were regularly covered for social security.[39] Fourthly, and
associated with evasion, dualism continues to exist through the considerable amount of under-age working – difficult to control given the
overcrowded schools and poor inspectorate system. Again, this would be
found predominantly in the small firms and is particularly serious in the
service sector. These workers, because they are working illegally, have
little or no protection from the law. Social security contributions are not
paid on their behalf (and indeed it would be illegal to pay them), they
have no security of employment (and are often dismissed before reaching
working age), and their rate of pay is abysmal. Finally, dualism shows
itself in non-pecuniary, non-social security, benefits – safety of work,
washing, canteen and leisure facilities, as well as such perks as a free
car or subsidised housing. Again, employees in small firms are in a
relatively poor position.

A fundamental question concerns the extent of labour market dualism.
Fundamental though the question might be, it is extremely difficult to
answer. We do know that there are large numbers of very small firms in
Italy and that a large proportion of the labour force is employed in such
firms. The actual proportions always, however, come as something of a
surprise. In 1971 some 81.8 per cent of manufacturing establishments

Table 4.10   Italian manufacturing work force by size of establishment

Establishment work force size	1951	1961	1971
2 or less	17.7	11.7	9.9
3–5	9.0	9.2	7.7
6–10	5.3	7.1	5.8*
11–50	14.1	18.8	20.9**
51–100	8.0	10.1	10.2†
101–500	20.4	21.6	22.3‡
501 and above	25.4	21.5	23.2§
TOTAL	100.0	100.0	100.0
TOTAL ('000)	3449.2	4495.6	5286.7

  * Size group 6–9
 ** Size group 10–49
  † Size group 50–99
  ‡ Size group 100–499
  § Size group 500 plus.

Sources: ISTAT *Annuario Statistico Italiano* (Rome, various issues); SVIMEZ *Un
  Secolo di Statistiche: Nord e Sud 1861–1961* (Rome, 1961).

had a work force (including the self-employed) of five or less and 64.4 per cent had two or less. In the construction industry, 72.2 per cent of establishments had a work force of five or less and this size of unit dominates the service sector, as would be expected. More relevant from our viewpoint is the proportion of workers in these small establishments. The situation in respect of manufacturing is shown in table 4.10 for the three postwar census years. (The construction industry is even more dominated by small units – 25.3 per cent of the 1971 construction work force was in units employing five or less, 37 per cent employing nine or less and 73 per cent in units employing forty-nine or less.)

The most interesting point to emerge from the table is that if, as Lutz suggests, labour market dualism centres around the presence of small units, then the scope for such dualism has diminished. Lutz treated small units as those with a work force of ten or under. The proportion of the labour force in this size band has fallen from some 32 per cent in 1951 to 28 per cent in 1961 and 23 per cent in 1971. This decline should not, however, blind us to the fact that even this latter figure is high; certainly no other country in the EEC has a quarter of its manufacturing labour force in units employing ten or less people. Moreover, the official Italian figures as reported in table 4.10 understate the extent of the problem since they exclude outworkers – and these, as we have seen, have been growing rapidly in recent years.

Although the scope for labour dualism may have diminished over the postwar period (and even this is unclear), the question still remains as to the degree of dualism and how this has changed over time. Lutz, probably because of a lack of relevant data, made no attempt at a quantitative assessment of the degree of dualism. The current data situation is no more conducive to statistical analysis.[40] Indeed, given that evasion of contractual and legal responsibilities is now a major aspect of dualism, it is perhaps optimistic to think that any statistical survey will show a true picture of its intensity. We can but say that our own, admittedly non-quantitative, view is that labour market dualism remains a major Italian problem.

4.5 Industrial relations and collective bargaining

Trade Union organisation is free (Article 39 of the Italian Constitution)

Collective bargaining and industrial relations in Italy have undergone a revolution in the postwar period, particularly in the 1960s. Like any other revolution it was hazardous, often erratic, and at times seemed to be out of control. At some stages there were fears about whether the industrial relations revolution might lead to a revolution of a broader nature. The process of change is by no means complete and, as we shall see, the implications of the more recent developments are still unclear.

Trade unions in Italy have had a short, if tumultuous, history. They were heavily repressed until 1889 and striking was virtually illegal. Unions did however slowly develop, and strikes, often vicious, were not rare. It was nevertheless not until the turn of the century that any large-scale build-up of trade unions of any size and power was organised at a national level. A variety of unions were created – some as offshoots of the Socialist movement which was expanding at that time and others from less revolutionary groups. In the first decade of the twentieth century there was a large number of strikes, some of which were political in nature.

In the period immediately following the First World War the country was in disarray and the people were discontented. The Socialists and Communists, often making use of the unions and the strike weapon, pushed the country into chaos. A succession of governments, and even the return of Giolitti, were incapable of controlling the situation. The conditions were ideal for Mussolini, initially arguing that Italy had been poorly treated in the peace settlement but soon basing his policies on the shortcomings of weak government and the perils of Communism. Fascism, moving slowly at first, was to represent the end of trade unions in any meaningful sense until the last years of the Second World War. The Fascists evolved their own trade union system and made it a basis of the Corporate State. Four confederations of workers (industry, agriculture, commerce and banking) were created to head thirty-two national, industry-based federations with, under this second level, nearly six thousand local union associations. The Fascist unions were given a monopoly of worker bargaining and the earlier unions disappeared. The newly created system was under the firm control of the State and the unions could hardly be considered as free bargaining agents for the workers they represented. The strike was made virtually illegal.

The Corporate State collapsed towards the end of the war, and with it the Fascist union structure. As with many other aspects of Italian life, there was a need to rebuild institutions that had not been in operation for some twenty years and which, before then, had had a short history. In 1944, with the 'Pact of Rome', a new trade union confederation, through which the old systems were to be revised, was set up – CGIL (Confederazione Generale Italiana del Lavoro).[41] In its brief life it recreated a democratic union system, largely based on national industrial federations. The new confederation was made up of men of all political colours, though, reflecting its anti-Fascist base, dominated by the Communists.

The unity encouraged by war was not sustained in the peace. In early

1946 serious differences between the various component groups showed themselves over elections for the constituent assembly and the monarchy referendum. The rapid political polarisation of the period percolated down to the unions while the confederation's unity was not aided by radical, if not revolutionary, Communist manoeuvres or by the United States and the Vatican – the former providing financial support for the non-Communist sections.[42] The actual breakup came soon after the collapse of the early postwar all-party government coalition and the split of the Socialist party. The first group to leave the confederation, in 1948, was Catholic (Christian Democrat), setting up LCGIL (Libera Confederazione Generale Italiana dei Lavoratori). The Social Democrats and Republican groups followed in 1949 to create FIL (Federazione Italiana del Lavoro). In 1950 LCGIL and FIL amalgamated to form CISL (Confederazione Italiana Sindacati Lavoratori), though a small, anti-Catholic (Republican and right-wing Social Democrat) group from FIL refused to merge and instead created UIL (Unione Italiana del Lavoro). An unimportant neo-Fascist union, CISNAL (Confederazioni Sindacati Nazionale Lavoratori), was also formed in 1950. CGIL remained in name but was now entirely composed of Communists. These four confederations still exist, each with their own industry federation and provincial and local organisations. Negotiations are carried out with all four (or at least with three, since CISNAL is generally excluded from any inter-confederal discussions), providing imaginable problems. We shall see later that attempts to regain the earlier unity have been made in recent years.

By the early 1950s, then, the basic trade union structure had been created. Each confederation had organised below it unions for each branch of industry and below these were provincial and local unions. At this time, and indeed for much of the postwar period, wage bargaining was highly centralised with national industry unions negotiating with national employers' associations. Plant bargaining was rare and in some sectors non-existent. Indeed, unions *per se* did not operate within plants. At the plant level the workers' representatives were the works councils (*commissioni interne*).

These councils, set up in 1947 through an agreement between the employers' confederation and the then united trade unions, were elected by all employees irrespective of whether or not they were union members. Many of those serving on the councils would be union men but this was not always the case. The councils were not bargaining groups and their prime responsibility lay in the enforcement of national agreements, the settlement of disputes and the supervision of factory rules and social provisions. Employers could, and did, give better conditions than those negotiated nationally, but generally would not bargain at a local level 'and indeed the conclusion of a local agreement would have been considered an act of disloyalty towards the other members of the employers' organisation that had signed the national agreement'.[43] It must, however, be said that as the 1950s wore on, a number of works councils, frustrated by the poor results of national union bargaining, did go beyond their brief and negotiated contracts with those employers who were prepared to swallow their feelings of disloyalty.

We have already seen that the nationally negotiated wage agreements during the 1950s were not noted for their radical nature, nor, by any standard, could they be viewed as excessive. There were three main reasons for this. First, the unions were very divided, often seeming more interested in political manoeuvres and inter-union rivalry than in improving the lot of their members. The great division between East and West on a world scale found its counterpart in Italian trade unionism – between in particular CGIL, much influenced by Moscow and seeing little value in the existing political and economic system, and CISL, with its belief in operating within the system. Indeed, occasionally, CISL (perhaps in reaction to CGIL) was almost 'collaborationist'. 'At times it would seem that CISL is actually arguing the position of Confindustria, Confagricoltura, or the government against the other confederations.'[44] Perhaps the only occasion in the 1950s when a halt in the distinct antagonism between these two major confederations seemed feasible was 1956, after the invasion of Hungary; but CISL showed itself to be wholly unsympathetic to CGIL's confusion and to its proposals for unity.[45] The continuing conflict between the confederations (and it was to last for the most part until the mid-1960s) was undoubtedly a major factor in explaining the slow growth of wages during the 1950s.[46] Secondly, the employers' confederations were, for most of the 1950s, united, tough and paternalistic. 'Management's attitudes toward the workers are at best condescending; the factory is viewed as personal, inviolable property; trade unionists are considered social upstarts and dangerous revolutionaries; and rigid discipline over workers is upheld as the sanest and most efficacious means of conducting industrial enterprise.'[47] Thirdly, the unions were operating in conditions of very slack labour markets during the 1950s and this would have curbed their power even if they had been united. Strikes were 'short-term affairs aimed chiefly at enlisting the support of public opinion and the political authorities'.[48] In 1957 an Italian industrial relations expert was writing that 'a favourable public opinion and governmental goodwill [are] the only substitutes for union bargaining power in the contemporary Italian scene'.[49]

Towards the end of the 1950s the system of bureaucratic and weak national bargaining started to break down and there was a move towards local plant bargaining.[50]* The path was to be long and was not completed until the end of the 1960s. The move towards more plant bargaining came when labour markets were tightening, thereby giving more power to labour, and when a younger generation of management, less conservative and less paternalistic, was growing up. But particularly important was the break of the state holding sector from Confindustria in 1958 and the creation of independent state holding employers' associations. These were more adventurous and more amenable to change than Confindustria.[51] Finally, the spatially patchy form of Italian development also encouraged less centralised bargaining. Other than these factors, which allowed or encouraged less conservative labour relations and more plant bargaining, there was also a growing disillusionment at the rank and file level of the union movement with national, almost isolated, unions constantly involved in political squabbles. Communication with the grass roots was slight; there is little doubt that the unions had lost touch with their members, and were certainly not fully conscious of the strength of feeling which was developing.

The plant level movement initially started through the works councils. As we have noted, in the late 1950s and early 1960s a number of agreements were drawn up between management and the works councils even though these, 'like the statutory *délégués du personnel* in France, had and still have no authority to conclude agreements'.[52] In part, the later attempts of the unions to move into plant bargaining must be seen as a response to the successes of the works councils – intended to be the Cinderella of the movement, viewed by many unionists as being the stooges of management, but yet now usurping some of the unions' power.

The plant level bargaining that operated in Italy up to the early 1960s, being based on the works councils, was not formal. It was in the tighter labour market conditions of 1962 that there was a major move towards formalisation when the metalworkers' union, always the most advanced and radical in industrial relations, pushed for acceptance of the idea that national agreements should cover basic and minimum conditions and that further bargaining could take place at the local level. In other words, they were proposing a number of bargaining layers – so-called articulated bargaining. As in subsequent years the state holding sector gave way first, in November 1962.[53] Firms in the private sector held out, in spite of considerable strike activity, until February 1963 when they signed a similar agreement. Other unions and industries followed the metalworkers' example. In simple terms, the system was that the national unions would negotiate for minimum wage rates, hours of work and occupational classifications, while plant level negotiations would cover piece rates, job evaluation and productivity bonuses. Plant level negotiations were, however, to be carried out not by the works councils but by the provincial unions. Plant unions *per se* were still not recognised. Nevertheless, at long last, the unions had secured a clear *entree* into the factories, and had made a move towards displacing the threatening works councils (who were expected to resume those tasks set out in the 1947 agreement and noted above). Belatedly, the unions were also given various rights in the factories, 'notice posting, leave of absence with pay, and the deduction of union dues from wages'.[54] These were important concessions in the Italian context, not least in that they financially strengthened the unions, which had previously encountered quite considerable difficulties in collecting dues. They also gave scope for a greater degree of independence from the political parties – a freedom which, as we shall see, was later exploited.

Between 1964 and 1968 the new local bargaining powers were little used. These were years when the economy was only slowly recovering from the 1963–64 deflationary measures and for much of the period there was relative peace on the industrial relations front. The 1966 wage negotiations, especially, were quiet. But below this fairly calm surface important changes were taking place. Of prime importance was the fact that the three major union confederations began actively to talk of unity. There had been some inter-union bargaining by the metalworkers at the start of the 1960s (and this set an example), but there can be little doubt that the most significant events encouraging greater unity were Pope John's tolerance of the left, the (related) national political moves towards a centre–left government and, associated with both events, the less revolutionary stance taken by the left-wing political parties and the CGIL, particularly after Hungary. There was also a growing recognition by the unions that the workers had not secured an adequate share in Italy's postwar economic growth, that union bickering had not been unimportant in this, and that without more co-operation the rank and file members would lose faith in the movement. The recession of 1964–65 was an important event in the path towards unity, making the unions recognise the need for common action if the interests of their members were to be protected,[55] and in the spring of 1966 the three confederations met together to evolve a common approach. These meetings continued during 1967 and early 1968 though the parliamentary elections of the latter year seemed to throw back into the open the great differences between the confederations. Beyond talks of unity, other changes over the period 1964–68 included an inter-confederal agreement on the works councils, which formally diminished their role and gave the unions the exclusive right to make collective agreements and settle local disputes even though plant unions *per se* did not exist.

Towards the end of the period 1964–68, and particularly during 1968 itself, there was the start of serious trouble on the labour front (influenced to a degree by the Paris disturbances of the same year), with substantial strikes, riots and disorders in agriculture, in the universities and in the factories. These events were to be the preface to developments in 1969 – a year that was a major threshold for Italian industrial relations.

In 1969 an unusually large number of labour contracts, including that of the metalworkers, were coming up for renegotiation, and labour markets were relatively tight. Most important, there was a great growth of militancy on the shop floor, reflecting the long-standing feeling that unions were too remote, too cautious and still too tied to political parties and ideologies. The shock for the unions was, however, not so much the fact that such criticism was being levelled, but the extent to which it was supported by the rank and file, and the speed with which they organised themselves. Urged on by shop floor leaders, many of whom were from the extreme (Maoist) left, a large number of factories introduced schemes of 'factory committees', members of which (*delegati*) were elected by the factory workers. Like the works councils, the factory committees were not necessarily composed of trade unionists, and elections were by all the workers. But here the similarity ends. The election procedures were rudimentary (generally by a show of hands), the *delegati* were often selected for their radicalism, and the factory committee, through the *delegati,* were expected to keep in continuing dialogue with the workers. Although these committees often operated alongside the works councils the former were, without doubt, doing most of the running. They urged on the national unions in their negotiations and, during the autumn of 1969 (appropriately named the 'hot autumn'), affected a large number of strikes – often associated with considerable violence. For many union leaders this new animal was not desirable, and was certainly less so than the works councils, particularly as the factory committees were often as critical of the unions as they were of the employers. In a great many instances the factory committees were out of union control even though the unions were generally viewed as being responsible for their behaviour. There were fears about the ultimate objectives of the movement.

Without doubt the factory committees had a considerable influence on labour relations and union development, sometimes by giving a new direction for policy but principally by ensuring the introduction of reforms and measures that were already in the pipeline. First, the 1969–70 wage settlements were extremely generous, with substantial increases in pay and a cut in the working week. (Interestingly, the wage increases were often flat-rate rather than percentage awards, which, profiting the lower paid, reflected the newly strengthened egalitarian goals of the unions.) In general, the unions secured almost all their objectives and, as we have seen, wages and labour costs rose substantially. Secondly, the autumn troubles speeded up and influenced the parliamentary debate on a law concerned with workers' rights. This was first announced in June 1969 and became law in May 1970.[56] It has become known as the workers' charter. This *limited* the employers' rights to use audio-visual installations to control workers, to check on their physical fitness (even when absent from work) and to make personal searches. But the major advance concerned trade union activity, which was now quite firmly accepted within firms and plants. 'The right to form trade unions, to join them or to carry out trade union activities within the place of work is guaranteed to all workers.'[57] 'Upon the initiative of the workers, trade union representation may be established in each productive unit, in the ambit of: (a) associations affiliated to the confederations which are nationally most representative; (b) associations not affiliated to those confederations but who are signatories to national or provincial collective labour contracts which apply to the productive unit concerned.'[58] Workers were allowed to assemble during working hours for up to ten hours per year without loss of pay, while trade union officials were permitted ninety-six hours per annum paid leave, or more in some cases, to execute their duties. Unions were given a statutory right to fix notices concerned with trade union and labour matters and to receive dues through deductions from the salaries of consenting workers. Firms employing more than two hundred employees were obliged to provide premises for union business.

The most important point about the charter is that it was a means of strengthening the unions *per se* by giving them more facilities to carry out their duties and by recognising them at a plant level. However, although the charter recognised plant unions, it said nothing about their bargaining powers. 'The unions themselves were vigorously opposed to any definition on the ground that it would be restrictive in effect.'[59] It was, however, clear that the unions would be the main bargaining force. The increased powers given to the unions in the charter doubtless reflected fears concerning the factory committees, and came at a time when the unions' 'position appeared to be undermined from two sides – as a result of pressure from employers who were still hostile to the recognition of trade unions within the factories and pressure from spontaneous groupings and small-scale movements which questioned the whole function of a trade union',[60] principally the *delegati* movement.

A final outcome of the hot autumn was that the unions set about regaining the initiative *vis à vis* the factory committees. To do this involved setting their house in order to overcome the shortcomings which had given rise to the factory committees. In this context there were three major developments. First, the inter-confederal unity discussions mentioned earlier were pursued with more determination. The *delegati* movement had anyway 'encouraged' unity action during 1969, when much of the bargaining had been done by the unions acting together. In early 1970 the objective was set to achieve formal and complete unity, and to disband the individual confederations, by early 1973. The fall of the centre–left government and the creation of a 'rightish' government after the 1972 elections were additional factors encouraging union unity. In the event the move was frustrated by UIL and some sections of CISL who were fearful that the new confederation, as in the early postwar years, would be dominated by the Communists or other militants. Public opinion, no doubt influenced by the Italian recession after 1970, which many attributed to the events of 1969, seemed to be moving away from militancy. In these conditions, UIL (always the more moderate union) and the more conservative members of CISL felt that their views would be unheard in the new proposed confederation. The final outcome was an agreement very close to unity, involving a federation between the unions. The new federation has responsibility for wage claims and collective bargaining, social reforms and economic and social affairs in general. Membership, contact with members, training and indoctrination were, however, to remain with the individual unions. In other words, the individual confederations could still disentangle themselves if this was deemed necessary. Secondly, in an attempt to reflect the wishes of the majority of workers, the unions moved to wean themselves away from the political parties. The check-off system for collecting union dues by deductions from earnings, introduced in the workers charter, was helpful in this respect by strengthening the unions' financial position and largely freeing them of financial dependence on the political parties. But just as important was the acceptance of the principal of *incompatabilità* – that the holding of political posts was incompatible with trade union offices. A number of unionists resigned their parliamentary and local government positions and vice versa. The hope is that the unions will now be able to push for worker objectives without being hindered by party political considerations. Thirdly, the unions had to find ways of controlling the *delegati*. From the start the unions pandered to the new *delegati* force. The autumn 1969 agreements, for example, were relayed back to the *delegati* and worker meetings for final approval. The unions are now, without doubt, listening to the *delegati* and factory committees in the formulation of strategy, as well as trying to secure the appointment of their own members to the committees which have, in fact, become the basis of the now widespread plant bargaining.

It still remains uncertain as to whether the trade unions have managed to control the factory committees. The relatively peaceful bargaining autumn of 1972 (though with bitter strikes by the metalworkers from September to April) in spite of fears that this would be another hot autumn, could indicate that the factory committee system is now under union control. This might, however, be an optimistic view. The economy was in deep recession and this inevitably dampened extreme demands and actions. (In many ways 1972 resembled the wage bargaining year of 1966, but the fact that this was followed by 1969 is little consolation.) Furthermore, Confindustria took a more sensible view of industrial relations – perhaps not unrelated to the replacement of their 'old guard' president in 1970. Moreover, and most important, the unions were distinctly worried by the elections of 1972 and the creation of a centre–right government, reflecting in part a public disenchantment with the more destructive left-wing tactics of 1969–70 and, as we have noted, a belief that the subsequent recession was not unrelated. As in 1969, the final wage awards in 1972 were generally flat-rate – 16,000 – 20,000 lire per month for all categories of workers.

We have so far concentrated on the unions in their collective bargaining role. However, a refreshing aspect of Italian unionism in recent years, and many would argue belatedly,[61] has been its growing interest in social questions. This was particularly true following the union successes of 1969 when, 'for the first time in Italy since the years of the liberation, the working class became conscious of their political power'.[62] This power they used, not only on the wages front, but also to force the government to take action on the social problems of the day, reflecting a recognition that past wage successes had been 'for the most part compromised by economic and social disequilibria existing outside the factories'.[63] As unions, and not through the various political parties, they have negotiated with government over the need for educational, health and pension reforms and have been prepared to use industrial action to secure their objectives. Certainly, the great pension reforms of 1969[64] were in large measure a consequence of union-organised industrial action. Moreover, the unions have continued to press for more attention for the South. Although one may question whether the unions' actions are democratic, they are understandable in a country which, as chapter 1 has shown, is so deficient in its social capital. A social conscience, admittedly newly found, appears to be present at all union levels. An example at the firm level concerns Fiat where, following an agreement to reduce the hours of work, the workers agreed to phase these reductions over a longer period, in return for which Fiat was to agree to create more jobs in the South.[65] Many of Fiat's workers are southerners, so the agreement may reflect self-interest more than outright social conscience, but if it is anything other than this, it is impressive.

Although the great period of union involvement in government came to an end with the centre–right government in 1972, it revived yet again (and with much more constructive and conciliatory union attitudes) with the return of a centre–left government in 1973. It remains, however, to be seen how this develops.

Italian trade unions and industrial relations have reached an interesting phase. The collective bargaining system is now very decentralised – so different from the situation in the 1950s – and plant level bargaining is widespread. The unions have increasingly interested themselves in social questions and have been instrumental in forcing the introduction of socio-economic reforms. This 'new unionism' has attracted additional members, though a point which needs to be remembered is that there are still probably no more than five million trade union members out of a total employee labour force of thirteen million. Without doubt, the major current problem for the unions, and for the country, is to incorporate the *delegati* movement and plant level bargaining into the basic trade union structure. The new system is still at a very rudimentary stage and few would contend that it does not need greater formalisation (particularly in clarifying the bargaining responsibilities at the various levels), even at the risk of losing some of its dynamism. Without this there are great dangers. In some ways the current unstable system is a consequence of past union shortcomings. This may imply that it is the responsibility of the únions to control what they, even if unwittingly, have created. On the other hand, any failure to do this could have implications for much more than the Italian trade union movement.

Notes to chapter 4

1. ISTAT *Sommario di Statistiche Storiche dell'Italia 1861–1966* (Rome, 1968).
2. All the major manufacturing industries, except textiles, have grown in employment terms over the postwar period though the major part of the expansion has been concentrated in four groups – engineering, chemicals, clothing and metalworking. The first accounted for 44 per cent of the overall increase in manufacturing employment between 1951 and 1971 and all four together accounted for 78 per cent.
3. R. di Magliano 'L'Agricoltura nel Processo di Trasformazione del Mezzogiorno: Considerazioni in Margine al Modello di Ranis-Fei' *Rassegna Economica* (1972), p. 1036.
4. E. Denison *Why Growth Rates Differ* Washington DC: The Brookings Institution (1967).
5. S. Cafiero and A. Busca *Lo Sviluppo Metropolitano in Italia* Rome: Giuffrè (1970).
6. For a very good discussion of the problem of making international comparisons of unemployment figures, together with attempts at standardisation, see R. Myers and J. Chandler 'International Comparisons of Unemployment' *Monthly Labor Review* (August 1962); and 'Towards Exploring International Unemployment Rates' *Monthly Labor Review* (September 1962). For more recent attempts see *Monthly Labor Review* (September 1970).
7. ISTAT 'Indagine Speciale sulle Persone Non Appartenenti alle Forze di Lavoro' supplement to the *Bolletino Mensile di Statistica* (November 1971).
8. ibid.
9. ISTAT *Bolletino Mensile di Statistica* (August 1973).
10. For a very good discussion of the causal factors in Italian activity rates see G. de Meo *Evoluzione e Prospettive delle Forze di Lavoro in Italia* Rome: ISTAT (1970). For an excellent critique of these factors see G. La Malfa and S. Vinci 'Il Saggio di Partecipazione della Forza-lavoro in Italia' *L'Industria* No. 4 (1970).
11. For a study of Italian pensions see K. Allen 'Italy' in T. Wilson (ed.) *Pensions, Inflation and Growth: a Comparative Study of the Aged in the Welfare State* London: Heinemann (1974).
12. de Meo, op. cit.
13. A. Ross 'Changing Patterns of Industrial Conflict' in A. Flanders (ed.) *Collective Bargaining* Harmondsworth: Penguin (1969).
14. G. Bianchi, A. Dugo, U. Martinelli *Assenteismo, Orario di Lavoro e Scioperi nell'Industria Italiana* Milan: Franco Angeli (1972). This study covers the period

1967–70 and is largely limited to manufacturing. For more detailed and up-to-date figures on absenteeism, see Confindustria *L'Assenteismo dal lavoro nell'Industria Italiana* (Rome, 1973).

15. H. Turner *Is Britain Strike Prone?* Cambridge: Department of Applied Economics, University of Cambridge p. 35.

16. A. Predetti *Occupazione, Retribuzione e Reddito di Lavoro in Italia* Milan: Franco Angeli (1972).

17. See Predetti, op. cit., p. 59.

18. For more details of the Italian pension schemes see Allen, op. cit. A good general source of social security information is EEC *Comparative Tables of the Social Security Systems* seventh edition (1972). Much of the non-pension material below is from this source and is for 1972.

19. For further details on redundancy and employment termination pay see G. Ammassari 'Le Differenze di Trattamenti tra Operai e Impiegati' *La Retribuzione nell' Industria* Milan: Franco Angeli (1970), p. 109.

20. EEC *Comparative Tables of the Social Security Systems* (situation at July 1970), op. cit.

21. E. Gorrieri *La Giungla Retributiva* Bologna: Il Mulino (1973).

22. More specifically, Gorrieri sees the privileges of the state employees as arising from three main sources. First, the fact that they work for a monopoly concern, or at least one that is unlikely to go bankrupt. Secondly, the existence of a large number of unions in the state sector, the competition between these unions for members, and the fact that the big confederations are courting these smaller unions. There are, for example, thirteen school teacher unions and eight in the hospitals. Thirdly, the state employees have substantial voting power, not least because of their numbers. They are consequently pandered to by all parties, including the Communists, who would like to make inroads into this basically lower middle-class group.

23. We have already discussed the plight of the majority of pensioners in Italy. The outworker situation is treated later. Gorrieri sees the workers with large families suffering because of the paucity of children's allowances and the fact that, unlike in most other European countries, there is no positive discrimination in favour of large families (and yet the Constitution, Article 31, argues for the financial favouring of large families). The farmers he singles out as a group of distinctly under-privileged (though it must be said on the basis of a limited 'sample' of three farms), calculating their income from labour at only 70 per cent of manual workers in industry. In addition, farmers receive no severance pay on termination of service, no holiday pay, no sick pay, inferior pension arrangements, no family allowance for their wife and a lower allowance for children. One might add that the self-employed workers in other sectors are in a not-dissimilar position in terms of social security and conditions of labour. It is worth remembering that 30 per cent of the Italian labour force is self-employed.

24. For a very good bibliography and critique of economic dualism see E. Parrillo *Lo Sviluppo Economico Italiano* Milan: Giuffrè (1970).

25. V. Lutz *Italy: A Study in Economic Development* Oxford: Oxford University Press (1962).

26. ibid., p. 17.

27. ibid., p. 19.

28. ibid., p. 22.

29. ibid., p. 225.

30. ibid., p. 235.

31. ibid., p. 235.

32. Firms could, however, hire directly without using the employment office if the post was managerial or executive, if the person came direct from another job and was not unemployed or if he was a relative of a worker in the factory. These conditions still apply. It might be added that when hiring through the employment office the employer has no choice. He takes the person sent. The employment office selects labour for jobs largely by taking account of the worker's family circumstances, income and period of unemployment. Suitability for the job often comes far

down the list of criteria unless the employer has specified very clear requirements.

33.   The main law governing the employment conditions of outworkers is No. 264, 1958. This not only required employers to pay collective (or approved) rates of pay; it also gave outworkers the right to holiday pay and redundancy compensation. In terms of social security, outworkers doing non-traditional work were given the right to all the social security benefits enjoyed by factory workers. Those doing traditional outwork or employed part-time were given more limited rights – they were not covered for industrial injuries, unemployment benefits or survivor pensions.

34.   Lutz, op. cit., p. 233.

35.   For a discussion of this point see D. Napoletano 'Fine (Ingloriosa) delle Norme Delegate sui Minimi di Trattamento Economico ai Lavoratori' *Rassegna Economica* (1971), pp. 1245–57.

36.   See J. la Palombara *The Italian Labor Movement* Ithaca, N.Y.: Cornell University Press (1957), pp. 151–6.

37.   One recent survey in Modena Province, reported in Gorrieri, op. cit., found no evidence of small firms paying below contract wages. However, Modena has fairly tight labour markets, and the smallest unit in the sample employed twenty workers – large by Italian standards.

38.   It need hardly be said that the extent of this evasion is difficult to quantify. One Italian social security expert has, unofficially, suggested that perhaps as much as 20 per cent of social security contributions are evaded. INPS has now largely computerised the social security contribution system. It remains to be seen as to whether this will reduce evasion to any great extent.

39.   Gorrieri, op. cit., p. 128.

40.   The only statistical source that gets anywhere near to providing relevant information is Mediocredito *Indagine sulle Imprese Industriali* (Rome 1971). This sample survey (for 1968) examines the economic features, including labour costs, of manufacturing firms by employment size. However, the smallest firm covered employed six people.

41.   For a good discussion of early postwar unions, see La Palombara, op. cit. Even more interesting on this period with a good analysis of the personalities involved is S. Turone *Storia del Sindacato in Italia 1943–1969* Rome/Bari: Laterza (1973). A more concise and reasoned account of trade union development over the whole postwar period can be found in E. Guidi *et al. Movimento Sindacale e Contrattazione Collettiva 1945–1970* Milan: Franco Angeli (1971).

42.   See Turone, op. cit., pp. 189–93.

43.   G. Giugni 'Recent Development in Collective Bargaining in Italy' *International Labor Review* Vol. 91 (1965), p. 284.

44.   La Palombara, op. cit., p. 138–9.

45.   See Turone, op. cit., pp. 270–3.

46.   This point is stressed continually in *Movimento Sindacale,* op. cit.

47.   La Palombara, op. cit., p. 124. The reader may need reminding that this book was written as late as 1957.

48.   Giugni (1965), op. cit., p. 281.

49.   G. Giugni 'Bargaining Units and Labor Organization in Italy' *Industrial and Labor Relations Review* (1956–57), p. 439.

50.   CISL had been tentatively arguing for plant bargaining since 1951 (Turone, op. cit., p. 238), reflecting their belief in productivity as the basic criterion of wage bargaining. In 1952 Pastore (CISL leader) was arguing that 'workers in Italy must, in their own interests, restrict their requests for wage increases within the margins determined by increases in productivity' (La Palombara, op. cit., p. 86). CGIL, however, was fearful of the possible loss of membership control involved in plant bargaining and, more important, saw their job as being simply to improve the standard of living of their members, irrespective of productivity.

51.   For a good discussion of the state holding sector's break from Confindustria and its implications for collective bargaining see Turone, op. cit., pp. 278–9. See also E. Zagari 'Sul Ruolo dei Sindacati nell'Economia Italiana' *Rassegna Economica* (1972), pp. 1601–23. Chapter 7 below also covers this issue.

52.   Giugni (1965), op. cit., p. 284.
53.   For a view that this reflected the state holding sector's lack of bargaining strength rather than reasoned judgement see OECD *Recent Trends in Collective Bargaining* Supplement to the final report, Paris; OECD (1972).
54.   Giugni (1965), op. cit., p. 286.
55.   See Turone, op. cit., who lays great stress on this period as a threshold in the move towards union unity.
56.   Law No. 300 (20 May 1970).
57.   ibid., article 14.
58.   ibid., article 19.
59.   G. Giugni 'Recent Trends in Collective Bargaining in Italy' *International Labor Review* Vol. 104 (1971), p. 318.
60.   ibid., p. 318.
61.   See Gorrieri, op. cit., who argues strongly that for too long the unions were too narrow in their objectives and not sufficiently interested in non-union members or non-factory issues.
62.   Zagari, op. cit., p. 1610.
63.   *Movimento Sindacale,* op. cit., p. 28.
64.   For a discussion of these reforms, see Allen, op. cit.
65.   Giugni (1971), op. cit., p. 323.

CHAPTER 5

The Short-Term Management of the Economy

But four young Oysters hurried up,
All eager for the treat:
Their coats were brushed, their faces washed,
Their shoes were clean and neat –
And this was odd, because, you know,
They hadn't any feet. (Alice Through the Looking Glass)

OTHER chapters in this book deal with government intervention in the economy to effect structural change. Chapter 6 examines the role of the State in southern development; chapter 7 discusses the State as a quasi-entrepreneur, while other sections of the book cover the State's roles in agricultural development policy, industrial training, monopolies and restrictive practices policies, etc. This chapter, however, is concerned with the short-run management of the economy as a whole, and with the techniques available to achieve the four economic goals which most governments pursue – high levels of employment, price stability, balance of payments equilibrium and economic growth.

The techniques normally employed in Western economies to achieve these objectives – and Italy is no exception – are those of demand management. This means that the government attempts to regulate aggregate demand so as to ensure high employment and satisfactory growth without incurring an unacceptable rate of inflation which in turn could impose strains on the balance of payments. But such is the degree of incompatability between these goals, that demand management policies usually involve a 'trade-off' between them. To avoid this dilemma, most Western countries have attempted to devise policy alternatives to the orthodox demand management techniques, and three have been of particular importance. Two of these involve direct controls of one sort or another; they are, first, prices and incomes policies, to ensure price stability at full employment, and second, protective tariffs and quotas to cure a balance of payments deficit without recourse to policies of domestic deflation. The third policy, also directed towards the balance of payments, involves changing the exchange rate, whether as a once-and-for-all adjustment, or by means of 'floating'. For a variety of reasons, however, none of these policies has been used to any significant extent in Italy over the postwar period.

Direct control of incomes was never considered necessary during the 1950s, as we have seen in chapter 4, when the unions were weak and wages consistently lagged behind productivity. It was with the wage explosion of 1962–63 that the idea of a need for an incomes policy began to gain some credence, not least in the Bank of Italy. By then, however, the unions, encouraged by their new-found bargaining strength, were not over-enthusiastic. Nevertheless, the Bank of Italy and the new, more interventionist, centre–left government attempted to integrate some kind of wages policy into the first five-year plan (1966–70) – though not in any explicit or formal sense, so that in practice direct incomes control remained a dead letter. However, in the wake of the inflationary consequences of the 'hot autumn' of 1969, incomes policy proposals were again seriously put forward, notably by the Republican party.[1] Nevertheless, in common with most other Western economies the arguments about the need for an incomes policy have tended to be overshadowed by the problems of implementation, and a co-ordinated and workable incomes policy has yet to emerge in Italy. On the prices side, a number of direct controls have been operative since the war. The Inter-Ministerial Committee on Prices (CIP) was set up in 1944 to control certain key prices, especially in the service sector; but perhaps the most important single example of price regulation is the control of rents, which has been in force since the war. However, such controls never formed part of a concerted macroeconomic strategy until the summer of 1973 when, in response to serious inflationary pressures, the authorities implemented a three-month prices freeze, which was to form the first phase of a multi-phase, anti-inflationary programme. From June to October 1973, retail prices of twenty-one staple consumer items were frozen, price increases by large companies had to be sanctioned by CIP, and rents were frozen until 31 January 1974. This was very much a new departure for Italian economic policy, and while it could be regarded as merely a short-term expedient in response to balance of payments difficulties, it was also interpreted by some observers as the start of an attempt to win trade union support for a more comprehensive prices and incomes policy.

As we mentioned above, the second possible alternative to demand management policies is the use of protective tariffs and quotas in the interests of the balance of payments. Recourse to this strategy has become increasingly difficult for any one country in the postwar period, given the general movement towards trade liberalisation. However, Italy's position in this respect has been doubly difficult. Not only is she a member of the EEC, but she has also been firmly committed to development through foreign trade. Indeed, as we have seen in chapter 3, this commitment was clear even in the early postwar years. At the start of the 1950s, when the balance of payments was seriously threatened, partly due to the less enthusiastic attitude of Italy's trading partners towards liberalisation, the Italian authorities continued to abolish the wartime trade controls and to lower tariffs. Italy has adhered to this free trade philosophy throughout the whole of the postwar period.

Finally, we come to the third policy alternative to demand management – devaluation, whether by adjusting the 'peg' or by a 'downward float', to cure a balance of payments deficit. In fact, between 1950 and 1972 Italy's exchange rate remained more or less unchanged, despite pressures at various times to up-value or devalue. However, since the start of 1973, she has experimented with floating rates – an issue that has already been covered in chapter 3. The main point to note, however, is that the move towards a floating lira is a very recent phenomenon and, for almost the entire postwar period, Italy's general economic policy has been operated within the constraint of a fixed exchange rate.

Given, then, that Italy has largely rejected, for one reason or another, the use of prices and incomes policies, direct controls on foreign trade and exchange rate adjustments, the task of pursuing the four main policy objectives listed at the start of this chapter has fallen to techniques of demand management. There are two main sets of policies involved here. The government can attempt to regulate the level of demand in the domestic economy by adjusting its own revenues and expenditures, and this is referred to as *fiscal policy*; on the other hand, the level of aggregate demand can be regulated by the availability and the cost of credit, and this is the preserve of *monetary policy*. The bulk of this chapter is concerned with an analysis and critique of the use of monetary and fiscal policies in postwar Italy.

5.1 The budgetary system and fiscal policy

This section is in three parts. The first looks at the revenue side of fiscal policy by examining the Italian taxation system; the second deals with government expenditure; while the third draws general conclusions about the operation of fiscal policy in Italy since the war.

The tax system

We can obtain some idea of the general *structure* of Italian taxation by grouping taxes into six main categories and comparing their relative importance in different countries. This is done in table 5.1. It can be seen from the table that a relatively high proportion of Italy's fiscal revenue

arises from indirect taxes (i.e. taxes on goods and services) and social
security contributions [2] (largely paid by employers).

Table 5.1   Individual taxes as a percentage of total taxation in fourteen countries, 1968–1970

	Taxes on goods and services	Income and profits taxes paid by:			Social security contributions	Other taxes
		Households	Firms	Total		
Denmark	40.2	42.5	2.6	45.1	7.9	6.8
Austria	37.8	20.6	4.6	25.2	25.6	11.4
Norway	36.7	29.8	3.6	33.4	23.8	6.1
Belgium	36.5	24.6	6.6	31.2	28.9	3.4
France	35.8	11.0	5.0	16.0	40.0	8.2
Canada	33.0	29.0	13.0	43.0	7.0	17.0
Germany	30.5	25.6	6.6	32.2	31.7	5.6
Sweden	29.9	44.1	4.7	48.8	19.1	2.2
UK	29.8	31.4	7.5	38.8	13.8	17.6
Switzerland	27.2	36.6	3.5	40.1	15.0	17.7
Netherlands	26.5	26.4	7.2	33.6	35.8	4.1
Japan	24.0	21.9	20.2	42.1	18.6	15.3
USA	19.0	34.4	13.7	48.4	18.6	14.1
Italy	38.1	11.2	6.7	17.9	36.3	7.7

Source: OECD *Revenue Statistics of O.E.C.D. Member Countries 1968–1970: A Standardised Classification* (Paris, 1972).

The dominance of indirect taxes in the Italian fiscal structure does have
some advantages. In as much as they can often be changed at short notice,
they afford an element of flexibility. However, they are also regressive,
and since in the Italian case they are much more important than direct
taxes, the danger is that fiscal policy could work against a more equitable
distribution of income. Moreover, the less progressive is the tax system,
the less likely is it to operate as an 'automatic stabiliser'.

As can be seen from table 5.1, direct taxation is relatively insignificant
in the Italian fiscal system, accounting for less than one-fifth of government revenue. Nevertheless, we must examine the structure of direct
taxes in some detail since it is here that the chronic weaknesses of the
fiscal system are to be found. Direct taxation in Italy is based on four
schedular income taxes.[3] These cover income from the ownership of land
(*imposta sui terreni*), income from the ownership of buildings (*imposta sul
reddito dei fabbricati*), agrarian income (*imposta sui redditi agrari*) and
income from 'moveable wealth' (*imposta sui redditi di ricchezza mobile*),
the last tax being meant to cover income not covered in the first three
schedules, and which in fact constitutes the major source of direct tax
revenue in Italy. It is divided into four categories, dependent on the
source of income. Categories A and B refer to corporate income, while

C/1 and C/2 cover personal income. Under category A, which covers income from capital, interest on all kinds of loans and deposit accounts is taxed at source, while under category B business profits are subject to a progressive tax. As regards personal incomes, category C/1 is a tax on income from self-employment, while C/2 covers income from other employment.

Over and above these four schedular taxes, however, there are another three major direct taxes and a host of minor, sometimes *ad hoc,* taxes, which combine to make the system as a whole both cumbersome and bewildering. The three other major taxes are a corporation tax (*imposta sulle società*), which is complex in itself in so far as it covers both profits and capital; a complementary income tax (*imposta complementare progressiva sul reddito*), which is a form of surtax; and a communal family tax (*imposta di famiglia*). This latter tax is particularly unusual in so far as it is on 'well-being' rather than simply household income, so that local tax officials can adjust the individual's tax bill if, in their opinion, his income declaration does not reflect his living standard. The list of direct taxes is complete only if we add the many other minor taxes – those levied by the local chambers of commerce, industry and agriculture; the 'ECA' tax, whose receipts are distributed to communal assistance agencies (ECAs); a 'Calabria tax', with receipts to be distributed to areas with erosion problems; a withholding tax on dividends; and estate and inheritance taxes.

The system of direct taxation in Italy is, therefore, extremely complicated, not only in terms of the sheer number of taxes involved, but also because of the confusing structure of tax rates. Many of the taxes listed above are in fact additional rates levied on existing taxes. These have sometimes been applied for *ad hoc* reasons as in 1967, when a supplementary rate of ten per cent was applied to all direct taxes to establish a rehabilitation fund for the areas damaged in the 1966 floods. Moreover, an archaic and often pernicious feature of the Italian fiscal system is that many taxes are 'farmed out' to private agencies, and tax rates have to be increased by varying percentages to cover their expenses. These factors, allied to the grotesquely complicated system of exemptions and allowances, first make it difficult for the individual to calculate his tax liabilities, and secondly, make it almost impossible for the authorities to forecast the effect of a change in tax rates on government revenue, and therefore on aggregate demand. The government's problems are compounded by the widespread practice of tax evasion not unrelated to the over-complexity of the fiscal system. However, this is not the only explanation. There is something of a national psychology which suggests to Italians that the government is indebted to them from some time in the past, and tax evasion is the national reply. Evidence of this continuing habit is given by the regular and frequent amnesties granted by the government to tax evaders.

As far as indirect taxes are concerned, the picture is less complex in that, although there is a considerable number of these, the bulk of indirect tax revenue comes from a value-added tax (*imposta sul valore aggiunto* – IVA). This, covering a wide range of commodities at a basic rate of twelve per cent (adjusted to six per cent for necessities and eighteen per cent for luxury goods) was introduced only in January 1973, replacing a general sales tax or turnover tax (*imposta generale sull'entrata* – IGE). In some respects, these two taxes are similar, both being levied at each production stage of the commodity in question. The important difference between them, however, is that while IVA is based on value-added, IGE was levied on gross output at each production stage. Thus, in that the fiscal burden on a given commodity under IGE accumulated as it passed through its various production stages, IGE represented a 'cascade-tax'. One important drawback of this system was that it was virtually impossible to calculate the tax liability on any given commodity. This gave rise to three problems in particular. First, it afforded considerable scope for evasion. Secondly, it afforded an opportunity for the Italian authorities to subsidise exporters by over-reimbursing them when their goods were sold abroad – the major reason why Italy came under such pressure from her EEC partners to change over to IVA. Thirdly, there is some evidence that IGE pushed Italian industrial structure in the direction of vertical integration, and probably to the detriment of technical efficiency. The introduction of IVA largely removed these three problems.

Although IGE represented the main source of indirect tax revenue, it was supported by a plethora of minor taxes covering specific commodities, a wide range of local taxes and a miscellaneous group on various transactions, including a registration tax, a mortgage tax, an insurance tax and various kinds of stamp duty. A good example of the complications inherent in these different taxes is the tax on advertising, which was levied at different rates for different forms of advertising, from 'sandwich men' to hoisting display balloons and 'sky-writing'. These complexities were compounded by a bewildering system of exemptions owing more to history than to logic. The introduction of IVA was intended to simplify and rationalise this system, which it did to a limited degree by replacing a number of the low-yield, indirect taxes, as well as most of the local consumption taxes. Nevertheless, the structure of Italian indirect taxation remains one of the most complicated in Europe.

The changeover to IVA and the partial simplification of the indirect tax system represented the first major fiscal reform put into effect in postwar Italy, and it came after a decade of inquiry and proposals. In 1963 a tax reform commission was set up, to be succeeded in 1964 by a study group on the implementation of tax reform. This submitted a programme which was incorporated into the 1966–70 national plan, but political instability and inter-party and intra-party disagreements, combined with the complexity of the issues involved, pushed the realisation of reform further and further into the future. Indeed, it is doubtful whether IVA would have been introduced in 1973 had it not been for pressure from Italy's EEC partners. The remainder of the reform, concerned with direct taxation, is to be implemented in January 1974.

The central point of this proposed reform is the replacement of seventeen different direct taxes by four new taxes – a corporate income tax, a more progressive personal income tax, a municipal income tax and a municipal tax on 'increased value of immovable assets'. The corporate income tax (*imposta esauriale sui redditi delle persone giuridiche*) replaces the old two-part method of taxing firms' income. The personal income tax (*imposta esauriale sui redditi delle persone fisiche*) takes the place of the old schedular taxes and the complementary income tax. The municipal income tax (*imposta locale sui redditi*) is to be levied by local municipalities, covering both individuals and firms, and is seen as replacing the old family tax. The other municipal tax, (*imposta sull incremento di valore degli immobili*) is essentially a capital gains tax on property.

The main outcome of the 1973 tax reforms, and of those proposed for 1974, is a dramatic reduction in the number of taxes levied, and consequently a simplification of the system as a whole. This has three major implications. First, it will make it easier for the individual to assess his tax liabilities. Secondly, it will reduce the scope for evasion, not only as a result of the changeover to IVA, but also because the reform of direct taxation is complemented by a number of administrative measures to make evasion more difficult, including a new system of tax code numbers, increased use of computerised systems, more standardised accounting procedures and the extension of the system of collecting taxes at source. Thirdly, and from the point of view of policy most important, it could be argued that the new tax system should make it easier for government to predict the impact of tax rate changes on aggregate demand. Over the postwar period this difficulty has been a major reason why, as we shall see, fiscal policy has not played a key role in demand management. To this extent, the tax reform should improve the prospects for fiscal policy in the future. However, any such view must be tempered with healthy cynicism, since it is not only the complexity of the tax system that has impeded its use in fiscal policy, but also the inefficiencies of its administration. The simplification of the tax system could ease these problems, but it would be optimistic to hope that it will completely resolve them. Yet the administrative problems in respect of taxation pale into insignificance compared with those in respect of government expenditure – a topic to which we now turn.

The role of government expenditure in fiscal policy

It is possible to take a narrow view of government expenditure, limited to the central government, but for our purposes it is more meaningful to deal with the public administration as a whole, which includes the central government and administration, local government and administration (regions, provinces and communes), and the state insurance agencies.

Table 5.2 presents a disaggregation of public administration expenditure into current and capital account, which are further broken down to distinguish between expenditure on goods and services, and transfer payments. Over the period 1951–69 the ratio of public expenditure to GNP rose from 24.8 to 36.7 per cent, but the interesting point to note is that this was entirely attributable to the increase in current expenditure (which increased from 20.6 to 32.8 per cent of GNP), which in turn is largely explained by the very steep rise in transfers to households (from 6.3 to 15.1 per cent of GNP). These transfers to households are almost wholly made up of social security payments, and the rapid rise in this item reflects the increased coverage and 'generosity' of the social security system over the postwar period (see chapter 4). It is particularly significant that more than 80 per cent of the increase in public administration expenditure is attributable to the increase in household transfers and the labour costs of the unwieldly public administration system. The other side of the coin is, of course, the relative decline of public expenditure on capital account, from 4.1 to 3.8 per cent of GNP, and from 16.7 to 10.5 per cent of public administration expenditure.

The rather modest performance of capital expenditure represents the greatest single impediment to the use of fiscal policy in Italy as well as having profound implications for long-term development. It is an extraordinary fact of Italian life that governments find greater difficulty in spending money. The constraint lies not so much in the lack of suitable projects – as we have seen in chapter 1, there are substantial deficiencies in social investment and expenditure in Italy. The heart of the problem lies in the extremely cumbersome and inefficient bureaucracy and parliamentary system through which expenditure decisions must pass in order to be put into effect. The remainder of this section is devoted to a discussion of this problem, its sources, extent and implications.

In most Western countries the key document in any discussion of public expenditure policy is the budget. However, the Italian budget, as presented to Parliament each year, is an irrelevant document for economic analysis. There are a number of reasons for this. Of major

Table 5.2 Principal categories of public administration expenditure in Italy, 1951–1969, at current prices *(million lire)*

	Current expenditure						Capital expenditure			Total expenditure of public administration
	Public consumption			Transfers to households	Current transfers to firms	Total*	Gross investment	Transfers to firms	Total*	
	Goods and services	Labour costs	Total*							
1951	351	849	1243	678	104	2217	247	157	445	2662
1952	425	971	1413	894	102	2635	318	208	548	3184
1953	433	1038	1481	1056	138	2918	400	226	641	3559
1954	481	1119	1647	1230	133	3321	475	118	600	3921
1955	481	1254	1774	1412	161	3696	505	154	671	4367
1956	520	1361	1940	1630	211	4157	498	157	668	4826
1957	526	1483	2059	1722	224	4377	540	250	808	5186
1958	599	1612	2259	2068	213	4844	586	159	761	5605
1959	620	1740	2416	2195	255	5329	605	171	799	6128
1960	670	1880	2622	2330	328	5779	681	208	910	6690
1961	734	2058	2871	2514	264	6163	709	291	1026	7189
1962	843	2376	3348	2961	361	7237	757	282	1081	8318
1963	1032	2940	4080	3601	341	8623	837	293	1154	9777
1964	1160	3321	4593	3911	461	9598	978	313	1313	10,911
1965	1263	3780	5175	4915	500	11,304	938	557	1527	12,831
1966	1308	4064	5521	5375	596	12,318	1013	508	1562	13,880
1967	1428	4255	5861	5888	691	13,414	987	708	1752	15,166
1968	1573	4594	6363	6700	854	15,063	1207	710	1962	17,026
1969	1734	4927	6876	7777	926	16,917	1120	813	1990	18,908

* The table covers only *principal* categories of public expenditure, and therefore the 'total' columns do not exactly reflect their constituent parts

Source: G Bognetti 'Analisi Quantitativa delle Strutture e delle Tendenze del Bilancio Pubblico Italiano dal 1951 al 1969' in V. Balloni (ed.) *Lezioni sulla Politica Economica in Italia* Milan: Edizioni di Comunità (1972).

importance is the fact that the budget is a far from comprehensive document. The expenditure figures in table 5.2 refer to the public administration, which, as we have said, is what is required for a meaningful assessment of the role of the State as a 'spender' in the economy. However, the budget presented to Parliament is only that of the central government. Moreover, it is an appropriation budget (*bilancio di competenza*), setting out revenues and expenditures as are permitted by existing legislation. This is the direct result of article 81 of the Constitution, that 'with the law which approves the budget, no new tax and no new expenditure can be introduced'. This means that the budget must be accompanied by complementary legislation in the course of the year, putting forward new expenditure projects. It is to this legislation, rather than to the *bilancio di competenza,* that one must look for changes in government fiscal policy. However, projected revenues and expenditures are not always realized within the particular financial year. In consequence, each *competenza* budget is accompanied by a statement of arrears (*conto dei residui*) setting out the planned revenues and expenditures of previous *competenza* budgets that have not yet been effected, and which have therefore accumulated. It is this problem of *residui* which is the central cause for concern in Italian fiscal policy. Although these *residui* are present on the revenue side of the budget (*residui attivi*), owing mainly to inefficiencies in the system of tax collection and the problem of evasion, they are much more serious on the expenditure side (*residui passivi*), arising primarily from delays in the passing of enabling legislation, the misleading accounting treatment of multi-year expenditure programmes, and administrative inefficiency.[4] The continuing accumulation of the *residui passivi* has aroused considerable concern on the part of the fiscal authorities.[5]

An indication of the problem can be given by the following figures. In 1971 the *competenza* expenditure was 16,930 milliard lire, whereas that actually carried out (*cassa* expenditure) in 1971 amounted to 15,974 milliard lire, so that the *residui passivi* for 1971 alone was 956 milliard lire. These figures highlight the way in which the *residui passivi* increased in one particular year. However, perhaps a more meaningful measure of the extent of the problem is the total *residui passivi* outstanding at a given point in time. In fact, at the end of 1971, they stood at 8692 milliard lire. The bulk of this sum was in respect of direct investment (23.0 per cent), capital transfers (33.6 per cent), household transfers (18.8 per cent) and goods and services (12.2 per cent).[6]

However, these figures on their own tell us nothing about the causes of the problem. One must certainly be wary of regarding the continuing growth in the total stock of *residui passivi* as being a reflection of increasing 'inefficiency' on the part of the government. Recent research at the Bank of Italy[7] has suggested that this growth is due not to increasing delays in carrying out expenditure, but rather to the continuing increase in the absolute size of the budget. But this cannot be the whole explanation, since at a more disaggregated level there is evidence that different categories of expenditure are carried out with different degrees of 'efficiency'. Taking the proportion of the *competenza* effected in the first year of the expenditure programme as a measure of 'efficiency', these differences can be illustrated by setting out the typical 'time profile' of different categories of government expenditure, and this has been done in table 5.3.

Table 5.3   Time profile of selected central government expenditure

	Year 1	Year 2	Year 3	Year 4	Year 5	Year 6	Year 7	Year 8	Year 9
				(percentages)					
Current expenditure									
Wages and salaries	91.2	4.6	2.3						
Pensions	90.8	5.4	2.7						
Goods and services	54.3	28.5	10.4	0.9					
Current transfers	77.5	7.2	6.8	6.0	4.5	2.6			
Capital expenditure									
Real estate and direct investment	10.8	5.8	10.0	12.6	13.7	13.2	11.1	7.4	2.2
Capital transfers	59.6	17.1	8.5						
Subsidies etc.	97.2	2.5	1.3						

Source: S. Lo Faso and G. Morcaldo 'Analisi del Processo di Attuazione della Spesa Pubblica' in *Contributi alla Ricerca Economica* Rome: Banca d'Italia (1972).

The dominant feature to emerge from table 5.3 is the difference in performance between current and capital expenditure. For current expenditure as a whole, 80 per cent of the *competenza* is carried out in the first year, while for capital expenditure the figure is 59 per cent, the difference being largely attributable to the extremely low figure for real estate and direct investment. For the remainder of capital expenditure the rate of disbursement is quite high. Thus, the real problems under capital expenditure seem to lie in the State's direct investment projects. Indeed, the problem is more severe than it appears from the table, since the proportion of direct investment *competenza* effected in the first year has been falling over the postwar period, in contrast to all the other categories of expenditure, whose time profiles have been remarkably stable. Thus, the view that the rising overall total of *residui passivi* is due to the increasing absolute value of the *competenza* must be modified, in so far as part is also attributable to the State's increasing difficulty in carrying out direct investment projects.

The problem of the *residui passivi* can be interpreted in the context of the short run and the long run. In the short run, the difficulties which the government encounters in carrying out expenditure programmes must be seen as another weakness of fiscal policy. Although moderate short-term stabilisation measures could take account of the problem of the *residui* in so far as the relationship between *competenza* and *cassa* has in the past been reasonably stable (except for direct investment), one has doubts about whether this stability would hold in the event of any massive increase in the *competenza*. Our view is that the parliamentary and administrative procedures would not be able to cope with the disproportionately large *competenza* expenditure that a high-impact spending programme would require.

In the long run the problem is even more serious. The difficulties encountered by the State in its direct investment expenditure mean that certain projects, which are crucially important for the improvement of Italian economic and social conditions, are delayed or even cancelled. In this sense, the problem of the *residui passivi* is more important as a reflection of Italy's longer-term problems than as one source of weakness in short-term stabilisation policy.

Fiscal policy: some general conclusions

Because of the shortcomings, both on the revenue and the expenditure sides of the budget, the Italians have rarely relied upon fiscal policy to any significant extent for purposes of short-term economic stabilisation.[8*] Indeed, it was only after the crisis of 1963 that the authorities began even to regard the budget as a possible instrument of policy for demand management, rather than as something which simply had to be balanced; and before 1963, with the possible exception of 1958, the authorities relied exclusively upon monetary policy. Insofar as budget changes had any (albeit unintentional) impact on the level of aggregate demand, their effects were generally expansionary. This was appropriate in the early 1950s, when the economy was characterised by a substantial stock of underemployed resources. However, by the early 1960s, it became less appropriate as Italy approached an inflationary crisis with dramatic balance of payments consequences. It was only after this episode that the Italian authorities began to regard fiscal policy as a possible supplement to monetary policy.

The later 1960s did witness a more conscious attempt to employ fiscal policy in a counter-cyclical manner, but it is important to understand that monetary policy still remained the principle policy instrument throughout the 1960s. Indeed, the slump–boom–slump pattern which, as we have seen in chapter 2, characterised the period after 1963 is largely explicable in terms of the impact of monetary policy, and the most striking feature of the 'new' fiscal policy of this period was its conspicuous failure to act as an expansionary agent after the over-severe effects of monetary policy in 1963–64 and 1969–70 – points to which we return later.

In spite of the paucity of fiscal policy, even after 1963, the mid-1960s did witness one important development – the so-called 'fiscalisation' of social security contributions. 'Fiscalisation' in this context refers to the switching of some of the burden of social security contributions from employers, and to a lesser extent employees, to the Treasury, and the authorities attempted to manoeuvre these contributions in the interest of economic stabilisation. The basic principle is that the reduction of employers' contributions boosts profit margins, and therefore (hopefully) investment, while the reduction of employees' contributions increases consumption. The process of fiscalisation was particularly important in the years 1964–66 when the government was attempting to stimulate the economy out of slump.[9]*

The ultimate indictment of fiscal policy came during the prolonged post-1969 depression which stands as a testament to the complete failure of the authorities to implement adequate reflationary fiscal measures. This was partly attributable to political instability, particularly in 1970–71 when positive government action was most urgently required, and it was only in July 1971 that a fiscal package was approved by parliament. By that time, as we have already seen in chapter 2, the economy was locked in deep recession, and nervously watching political events. The impact of these measures was, in consequence, much reduced. In spite of subsequent attempts at fiscal expansion, the economic stagnation continued until 1973.

In conclusion, the authorities have made some attempts to move towards the use of fiscal policy in recent years, but with a singular lack of success. This is basically because the budgetary system, on both the revenue side and the expenditure side, is, as we have seen, chronically inefficient. Before the Italians can place meaningful reliance on fiscal policy as an instrument for short-term stabilisation, a number of fundamental faults need to be rectified, and the current reform of taxation is but one step in this direction.

5.2 The financial system and monetary policy

In the same way that discussion of fiscal policy requires an understanding of the fiscal system, so any treatment of monetary policy would be incomplete without an examination of the monetary and financial systems. Because monetary policy works by affecting the availability and/or the cost of credit, we must examine the institutions through which credit is channelled, since it is upon this institutional structure that monetary policy operates. This section is in three parts. The first outlines the major Italian financial institutions; the second is concerned with the techniques of monetary control available to the authorities; while the third is an analysis of the operation of monetary policy in the postwar period.

Italian financial institutions

Italian financial institutions can be divided into two main groups, one covering short-term credit, and the other involved in medium- and long-term markets. This follows the distinction made in the 1936 Banking Act. The so-called 'mixed-banking' system existing before 1936, which allowed the banks to supply to industry not only short-term working capital but also longer term investment credit, had run into severe difficulties as a result of the general economic depression of the early 1930s. One of the consequences of this crisis, as we shall see in chapter 7, was the creation of IRI (Istituto per la Ricostruzione Industriale) in 1933. IRI had two principal tasks. The first was to disengage the major banks from their long-term investments, the second was to provide new long-term credit for industry. This latter role was taken over by the special industrial credit institute IMI (Istituto Mobiliare Italiano) in 1936, when the Banking Act formally restricted commercial banks to short-term credit only, leaving the provision of longer-term credit to IMI, and later to a plethora of similar but smaller special credit institutes.

This distinction between short-term markets (the preserve of the banks) and medium- and long-term markets (the preserve of special credit agencies) is still in force today, and applies to both the lending and the borrowing sides of these institutions' business.[10*] As we shall see, however, the distinction has become slightly blurred in recent years, as certain banks have been permitted to move indirectly into the medium- and long-term credit market, but the division is still sufficiently clear to allow us to treat these two groups of institutions separately and in turn.

An outstanding feature of the Italian banking system, and in contrast to that of the United Kingdom, is the very large number of independent banks, over 1200 in 1969. These can be divided into six legal categories. The two major groups are the public-law banks (*istituti di credito di diritto pubblico*), of which there are six, and the three banks of national interest (*banche di interesse nazionale*). These two groups correspond most closely to the multi-branch UK deposit banks. The remainder consist of a large number (more than a hundred) of small, local ordinary credit banks (*banche di credito ordinario*); co-operative people's banks (*banche popolari cooperative*), essentially a by-product of the co-operative movement in Italy; the savings banks and first class pledge banks (*casse di risparmio e monti di credito di prima categoria*); and the rural and handicraft banks (*casse rurali e artigiani*). However, in spite of this very large number of banks, the system is essentially oligopolistic. At the centre stand the five largest banks (Banca Nazionale del Lavoro, Banco di Napoli, Banca Commerciale Italiana, Credito Italiano and Banco di Roma), which together account for 40 per cent of total lending.[11]

Over the postwar period, the authorities have adopted two different strategies towards the banking structure. During the early 1950s there was a discernible policy to encourage the development of the small local banks. On the one hand, the large banks were restrained from opening small local branches, while on the other the interest rate on savings accounts at the government-owned post office savings banks was reduced from 4.50 to 3.75 per cent, thus allowing local banks to compete more favourably for deposits.[12] By the early 1960s, however, it was becoming obvious that the small banks were unable to reap the substantial economies of scale available to their larger competitors and the authorities reversed their earlier strategy; they became increasingly opposed to the formation of new local banks, and now tend to encourage the takeover of existing banks by the larger banks.

Not only is the Italian banking system oligopolistic, but it is also characterised by a substantial degree of public ownership in one form or another. The six public-law banks are all public corporations, while the three banks of national interest are controlled by IRI. It is, however, worth making the point that the private sector and public sector banks are run on the same lines, and the authorities' policy of monetary control does not discriminate between the two.

Irrespective of size or ownership, the Italian banks have frequently been accused of being over-conservative in their lending policies, particularly in the recent past, when they have shown a marked tendency to channel their excess liquidity into bonds rather than advances to the private sector. Indeed, Italy has been charged with having *'troppo barcari e troppo pochi banchieri'* (too many banks and too few bankers). In their foreign business the larger Italian banks have shown considerable dynamism and enterprise, not only in terms of their substantial participation in the Eurodollar market, but also through the forging of financing links with other European banks – the collaboration between the Banco di Roma and Credit Lyonnais is a good example of this. Nevertheless, their domestic lending policies have been far from satisfactory, and especially in times of recession – symptomatic of the whole problem of monetary policy as an expansionary instrument in a depressed economy, a point to which we return later.

As we noted above, the Italian banking system operates almost exclusively in short-term markets, leaving longer-term lending to the special credit institutes, of which there are three main types – the industrial credit institutes, the institutes for mortgage credit, and a group of agencies that extend credit to the agricultural sector.[13] Of these three sets of institutions, the most interesting, and the most important, are the industrial credit institutes, the largest of which is IMI. IMI's main function,[14]* in common with the other special credit institutes, is that of a financial intermediary between lenders and borrowers, issuing its own bonds, either on domestic or foreign markets, and extending medium- and long-term loans to Italian industry. Although the other credit institutes are not nearly as large as IMI, they perform a key function in specific sectors and activities. There is, for example, a network of industrial credit institutes (ISVEIMER, CIS and IRFIS), which have played an important role in financing southern industrial development. Other institutes are active in the field of export credit – Mediocredito, Efibanca and Mediobanca are the main examples. Over the postwar years the number of special credit institutes of all kinds has risen dramatically, until in 1971 there were eighty of them with a correspond- ing increase in the volume of their lending. Between 1951 and 1971 domestic credit extended by the special credit institutes grew at a rate of 18 per cent per annum.[15]

The degree of government intervention in the operations of these special institutes is very great indeed. Although they have rarely been controlled in the interests of the overall liquidity of the economy, the government has a strong influence on their activities, with three general aims in view – the encouragement and aid of medium- and small-sized firms, the development of the South, and the fostering of exports. While their 'ordinary' lending activities are carried out at market rates, capital provided for these special activities is generally at subsidised rates of interest, with the cost of the difference between these and market rates being thrown wholly on the Treasury. The volume of subsidised credit has grown very rapidly in Italy over the postwar period and especially in the 1960s, with a corresponding increase in the financial burden placed upon the Treasury. This point is illustrated in table 5.4, which shows how

Table 5.4 Burden on state budget of interest subsidies
(*milliard lire*)

	Industry, commerce and artisans	Building	Agriculture	Total
1950	—	1.1	0.3	1.4
1960	4.9	1.1	7.4	13.4
1962	16.8	1.1	13.6	31.5
1964	39.6	1.1	21.8	62.5
1966	53.5	6.6	44.3	104.4
1968	140.0	13.5	50.6	204.1
1970	142.1	13.7	66.4	222.2

Source: V. Pontolillo 'Aspetti del Sistema di Credito Speciale con Particolare Riferimento all'Intervento dello Stato' *Bolletino* Rome: Banca d'Italia (January – February 1971).

government expenditure on subsidising interest rates has cumulated over the years.

It is clear from this table that the bulk of subsidised credit has been allocated to industry, commerce and artisans, and also that this is where the spectacular growth of such credit has been concentrated in recent years. In the early 1970s, 75 per cent of the credit extended by the special industrial credit institutes was at less than market rates of interest.

Although subsidised credit has been part of the Italian government's general effort to alleviate specific structural problems, the extent of this subsidisation is now meeting with some criticism. It is maintained that too large a section of the capital market is characterised by subsidised interest rates, and that the 'market' rate of interest no longer acts as an effective allocator of resources. In addition, the multiplicity of institutions, state aids and regional and sectoral differentials is leading to administrative inefficiency, and is obscuring the view of how further funds might be allocated.[16]

Although, through the banks, short-term lending is well covered, and although, through the special credit institutes, the longer-term credit markets are well served, in many ways the Italian capital market as a whole is underdeveloped. In particular, it suffers from two major weaknesses, both of which have important implications for short-term demand management as well as longer-term economic development. The two deficiencies are, first, an insignificant market for risk capital and, second, a poorly developed short-term money market. The former has led Italian industry to rely too heavily on fixed-interest finance rather than equity for its investment, while the latter has placed the long-term bond market in a central position in the financial structure. We shall treat these points in turn.

Table 5.5   Sources of finance for gross investment of 376 Italian companies in the private sector, 1964–1971

	Self-finance (milliard lire)	(%)	Equity (milliard lire)	(%)	Bonds (milliard lire)	(%)	Other fixed interest (milliard lire)	(%)	Total (milliard lire)	(%)
1964	426.5	45.3	258.9	27.5	51.9	5.5	203.8	21.7	941.1	100.0
1965	472.0	67.8	75.5	13.7	17.2	2.5	111.1	16.0	695.8	100.0
1966	566.5	79.3	69.8	9.8	−24.1	−3.5	102.1	14.2	714.3	100.0
1967	530.6	80.9	50.6	7.8	−26.5	−4.1	101.1	15.4	655.2	100.0
1968	640.1	88.2	29.4	4.0	−13.2	−1.8	69.6	9.6	725.9	100.0
1969	614.5	68.9	145.7	16.3	−40.4	−4.5	171.9	19.3	891.7	100.0
1970	629.9	60.0	201.0	17.4	−25.4	−2.2	286.5	24.8	1155.0	100.0
1971	508.5	43.4	204.5	17.4	−74.9	−6.4	535.4	45.6	1173.5	100.0

Source: Banca d'Italia *Relazione Annuale* (Rome, 1972).

The weakness of the equity market is well illustrated in table 5.5. From the table it is clear that self-finance is generally the major source of company finance, though it will be noted that its importance dropped dramatically in 1971, when wage inflation savagely reduced gross profits. However, the most interesting feature to emerge from table 5.5 is the composition of external finance. Bonds are of negligible and diminishing importance while 'other fixed interest' have shown a spectacular increase, particularly since 1968. This category refers primarily to loans from the special credit agencies and banks, which, as the table shows, are a much more important source of funds than equity. The Italian equity market has historically been limited and weak, and there has been no improvement over the postwar period. From the viewpoint of the individual, shares are not an attractive asset, partly because of the confused Italian accounting conventions, which often make published company returns ambiguous and unreliable. Moreover, from the firm's viewpoint, the alternative sources of finance through the special credit institutes are plentiful and cheap. The approximate rate of interest for equity finance has been estimated to be around 15 per cent, while subsidised credit could be less than 5 per cent.[17] The importance of fixed interest finance makes Italian industry dangerously vulnerable, both to an economic slump in general and to an increase in interest rates in particular; and, as we shall see, this has been put forward as one of the reasons for the harsh effects of restrictive monetary policy, especially after 1969.

The Italian bond market is of very large dimensions indeed. As a source of finance, it is of paramount importance to the State, the state holding sector and the special credit institutes. It is however of much less significance for private industry, as can be seen from table 5.5. It was during the 1960s that the bond market became especially important, particularly after the nationalisation of the electricity industry, and as the bond market grew, so too did the desire of the authorities to stabilise bond prices (and therefore long-term interest rates). There were a number of reasons for this attitude. First, as noted above, the bond market consists largely of government borrowing in one sense or another. (At the end of 1972, 40 per cent of bonds issued represented public borrowing strictly speaking, 43 per cent were floated by the special credit institutes, and 14 per cent by the state holding sector.[18]) A stable bond market makes the floating of this debt considerably easier. Secondly, because the long-term rate of interest has such a potent influence on private industrial investment, the authorities have been extremely reluctant to allow it to fluctuate. Finally, a substantial proportion of bonds is taken up by the banks, and the authorities are wary of inflicting over-severe capital losses on them through changes in bond prices, especially since from the early 1960s the banks have actually been encouraged by the authorities to hold certain bonds – in contrast to the position in the 1950s when the banks' assets were largely restricted to private sector advances and Treasury bills.

For a number of reasons, therefore, the government has tended to favour a stable bond market as part of its monetary policy. Whatever problems this might raise in itself, the authorities' position has been made doubly difficult by the lack of effective short-term money markets (such as the discount market in the United Kingdom), and thus of flexible short-term interest rates. When facing capital movements out of Italy in response to higher interest rates abroad, the authorities find themselves in a dilemma. Since there are no effective short-term markets to 'cushion' the bond market from international pressures, capital account problems in the balance of payments must be cured either at the expense of stable long-term bond prices, or by other measures – either direct controls on capital movements or, much less satisfactory, deflationary policies. The problem of how to defend the domestic bond market from external pressures in the absence of effective short-term markets lies at the heart of many of Italy's recent troubles in monetary policy.

In conclusion, the Italian financial system has some laudable features which have been of great benefit to her development. In particular, the special credit institutes have proved themselves to be excellent agencies through which industrial credit especially can be channelled, with a degree of selectivity that is crucial to an economy with structural problems such as those of Italy. On the other hand, the financial structure as a whole cannot be said to have developed in line with the productive structure of the economy, and significant weaknesses in the capital market remain, with implications not least for the practice of monetary policy. However, before we can discuss this issue we must first examine the techniques of monetary control at the disposal of the authorities.

Techniques of monetary control

In this section we examine the means at the disposal of the monetary authorities, namely the Bank of Italy, for regulating monetary aggregates in the economy. We shall first outline the main elements of control over the banking system, and then go on to show how the Bank of Italy uses its power as the central bank to regulate the liquidity of the economy as a whole, by controlling the liquidity of the banking system in particular.

The lynch-pin of the control of banking activity in all Western monetary systems is the statutory reserve requirements for the banks. There are two elements in reserve requirements – the stipulation of the types of financial assets to be eligible as bank reserves, and the proportion of assets to be held as reserves. The latter determines the extent to which the banking system can create money, while the former determines the degree of control that the authorities have over the supply of such assets, and therefore over the supply of money.

The present reserve requirements for Italian banks have their origins in the measures taken in 1947 to cure the severe inflationary problems facing Italy at that time.[19] The existing reserve regulations, laid down in 1926, stipulated that each bank should pay to the Bank of Italy, in cash and Treasury bills, any deposits in excess of twenty times the bank's own capital. Despite the raising of this latter figure after the war to thirty, the system had become nonsense by 1947. Wartime and postwar inflation had swollen the monetary value of bank deposits far beyond the value of any bank's own capital, so that the application of the 1926 reserve requirements 'would have paralysed banking activity'.[20]

In September 1947, therefore, new reserve requirements were introduced, laying down that cash, Treasury bills and government bonds were to be paid to the Bank of Italy, in amounts equal to 20 per cent of the surplus of banks' deposits over ten times their own capital, until the total sum of reserves amounted to 15 per cent of deposits.[21]* At that time the banks had deposits sufficiently well in excess of ten times their capital so that the effective reserve ratio in fact became 15 per cent of deposits. However, from October 1947, the banks had to reserve 40 per cent of any increase in deposits, until the total ratio of reserves to deposits reached 25 per cent, and in consequence the effective reserve ratio became 25 per cent.

The prime aim of the 1947 measures was to control the serious postwar inflation, and in this they were highly successful. The wholesale price index had risen from 2884 in 1946 (1938 = 100) to 5159 in 1947. It then levelled off at 5443 in 1948 and fell to 5169 in 1949 and 4897 in 1950.[22] The reasons behind the dramatic impact of seemingly moderate monetary measures by the government were largely psychological. The policy of monetary control was seen as the first determined attempt by a postwar government to tackle the problem of inflation, and two important reactions followed. First, importers and traders who had been speculatively stockpiling inventories of raw materials and finished products not only discontinued buying stocks purely to hold, but also released on to the market part of the stocks which they already held, in the belief that prices were going to fall. As a result of this, prices in fact did fall, and the speculative cycle which fed on inflationary expectations was broken. Secondly, the velocity of circulation of money fell; that is, Italians were no longer afraid to hold money, so that, although the money supply was still increasing, 'the cash balances of the public acted as a reservoir into which the additional money flowed'.[23] The important point to note is that these measures did not involve a contraction in bank credit but merely a slowing down of its rate of expansion, and they thus avoided what would have been a disastrous setback to the vital process of reconstruction.

The 1947 monetary innovations were, however, not only important in stemming inflation; by introducing meaningful reserve requirements, they also offered the postwar authorities two general methods of monetary control. The first involves changing the size of the effective reserve ratio, while the second is concerned with controlling the supply of assets eligible as reserves. We shall now discuss these in turn.

The effective reserve ratio can be changed in two different ways. On the one hand, the size of the required reserves could be manipulated by administrative fiat, an increase in the reserve ratio working towards a restriction of credit and a reduction towards an expansion of credit. On the other hand, a more subtle method of altering the effective reserve ratio is by changing the *composition* of the assets eligible as reserves. If, for example, the authorities decide to make eligible as reserves assets that the banks might in all probability have held in any case, this would have an expansionary effect on the level of bank deposits, 'freeing' for credit creation (i.e. lending) other liquid assets that previously had been held as reserves. Alternatively, the revoking of such measures has an opposite, contractionary, effect.

The change of reserve requirements by fiat has been rare in postwar Italy, the only major example being in 1962 when the ratio was reduced from 25 to 22.5 per cent as part of an expansionary monetary policy. Similarly, although there have been changes, particularly in the 1960s, in the composition of assets eligible as reserves, widening the reserve ratio to include certain medium- and long-term bonds,[24] their primary objective was not to affect the quantity of credit that the banks were able to extend: rather, it was a method whereby the Italian authorities have aided the placing of certain bonds.

Thus, changes in the size or composition of the reserve ratio have not played a major role in postwar monetary policy in Italy. Much more important has been the control of the supply of assets eligible as reserves and of those that are easily converted into reserves. The total supply of such assets is frequently referred to as the 'monetary base', and it is this that determines the maximum level of bank deposits, and therefore bank lending. The assets to be contained in an appropriate definition of the monetary base are formally described as 'those financial assets the variation of which allows a change of a multiple amount in the demand for credit and bank deposits, without changing the level of interest rates'.[25] In practice, the Italian monetary base consists of a variety of assets. Notes and coins, and deposits held at the central bank, are obviously included since these are an important part of the reserve ratio.[26] Treasury bills are also part of the monetary base, though since May 1969 the situation has been complicated by the splitting of

Treasury bills into two types, one of which is issued at a fixed price and is eligible as reserves, while the other, which is determined by the Treasury deficit and floated at market prices, is not eligible. Only the former is therefore included in the monetary base. In addition, there is a range of other assets that are included, not because they are in themselves eligible as bank reserves but because they can be converted into such reserves on demand (post office deposits, unutilised credit margins of banks with the Bank of Italy, wheat stockpiling bills and, most important, the banks' liquid foreign assets).

What the authorities can attempt to do, therefore, is to control the supply of the monetary base to the banks, and by this method affect their ability to increase their lending. The control of the supply of the monetary base is however not simply one policy; rather, it involves a whole range of policies, each one associated with a different source of monetary base. The division of monetary base by source of supply is given in table 5.6.

Table 5.6   Creation of monetary base in Italy, 1958–1971
(*milliard lire*)

	Foreign			Domestic	
	(1)	(2)	(3)	(4)	(5)
	Balance of payments	Banks' foreign business	Treasury	Banks' financing by Bank of Italy	Other
1958	509.6	70.5	482.6	−34.5	18.5
1959	536.1	93.8	216.0	−0.2	−41.3
1960	269.6	−308.0	221.0	26.6	18.6
1961	365.5	24.4	240.3	261.0	−31.9
1962	43.5	563.9	582.3	271.6	−8.4
1963	−780.6	62.6	978.7	474.7	−6.6
1964	483.9	−190.3	794.9	−164.2	6.6
1965	994.0	−367.0	932.4	−165.4	−55.1
1966	416.9	−182.2	480.5	562.3	−38.8
1967	202.4	40.5	404.6	626.6	−57.9
1968	393.3	−270.7	921.8	220.5	−23.7
1969	−869.7	221.3	1500.3	469.0	−75.6
1970	222.9	96.2	2991.0	−1276.1	119.3
1971	489.4	−11.0	2611.9	89.6	131.5

Source: Banca d'Italia, *Bolletino* (Rome, January–February, 1972).

From table 5.6 it can be seen that there are five main sources of supply of monetary base in the Italian system. The 'foreign' sources arise first from the balance of payments and secondly from the Italian banks' borrowing and lending abroad. The former involves the net inflow of foreign currency (positive when the balance of payments is in surplus), which is convertible into lire at the Italian foreign exchange office. The latter refers to the foreign business of Italian banks. In the 1960s the banks built up substantial stocks of foreign exchange through their operations on the Eurodollar market. By 'the guaranteeing or withholding of permission for the banking system to engage in borrowing or lending transactions abroad',[27] the Italian authorities have exercised a substantial degree of control over this source of monetary base. Turning to domestic sources, column 3 in table 5.6 refers to the creation of assets eligible as reserves through the budget deficit. The budget deficit must be financed by government borrowing, which can take the form either of creating assets that constitute part of the monetary base, or of creating assets that do not. In the first case, the government could obtain advances from the Bank of Italy, which would result in a direct creation of money, or could issue Treasury bills, which, as we have seen, depending on their type, may represent financial assets eligible as bank reserves. In the second case the government could issue bonds that are not eligible as bank reserves. However, the problem lies in enticing the public or the banks to take these up. The ability of the government to run a budget deficit without increasing the supply of monetary base depends on its ability to market its own gilt-edged stock, and this is one of the reasons why, as we noted in the previous section, the authorities are particularly concerned to keep the bond market stable.

The remaining sources of monetary base are relatively unimportant, and therefore less significant for policy purposes. The item in column 4 represents the central bank acting as 'lender of last resort' to the banking system. When the banks are squeezed for funds, the central bank steps in and 'lends at last resort'. Different from most other Western economies, this is not automatic and can therefore be used as a selective policy instrument for dealing with individual banks, as well as an aggregate control. The final column in table 5.6 refers to a miscellany of sources of supply of monetary base, many of them deriving from the Bank of Italy's operations with other financial institutions such as the special credit institutes. As a *source of monetary base,* these operations are not quantitatively important.[28]*

In most Western countries the control of monetary base is complemented by manipulation of Bank Rate – the rate at which funds are lent to the banking system when the central bank is operating as lender of last resort, and the rate to which most other short-term rates are linked. The Italian authorities do, of course, have the power to change Bank Rate (or re-discount rate) but in practice it has remained more or less unaltered over the postwar period – hardly surprising, perhaps, given the fact that short-term money markets are, as we have seen, relatively unimportant in Italy.

This section has been concerned with the techniques of monetary policy available to the Italian authorities, showing the major emphasis to be on control of the monetary base, and in particular through direct controls of the banks' foreign business and various methods of financing the Treasury deficit. It is the task of the next section to examine how these techniques have been employed and to assess the role of monetary policy in postwar Italian development.

Monetary policy in postwar Italy

The role of monetary policy in Italian postwar development is best examined in three main sub-periods. The years 1946–1950 posed the specific and urgent problems of reconstruction and monetary stabilisation, and details of government policy in these respects have already been outlined. The important point to note is that the task of monetary stabilisation (in terms of both the internal and external value of the lira) was successfully carried out without impairing the process of reconstruction, and in this respect the monetary measures of these early years were genuinely successful. The period 1950–62 was also one of success and achievement, but in this case the authorities were essentially building upon the foundations laid immediately after the war, for although these were years of rapid growth, increasing employment and price stability, this was due to monetary policy in only a very limited respect. In many ways, these were the 'easy' years for Italian policy-makers. The major factors explaining the 'miracle' of the 1950s were slack labour markets and weak trade unions, keeping wage increases below those of productivity, and fostering price stability and economic growth, while the resultant export growth, combined with the structural surplus in invisibles and substantial foreign investment in Italy, maintained the balance of payments in overall surplus. The role of monetary policy in this success story was essentially permissive, in that the liquidity of the economy (i.e. the supply of monetary base) was expanded in step with national income. The main contribution of monetary policy in these years was the rather negative one that it did not restrain the boom, not, however, a wholly insignificant achievement in the early 1950s, when, in spite of balance of payments problems, the authorities were not panicked into strongly deflationary monetary measures.[29] As the 1950s progressed, growth accelerated, the price level remained stable and the balance of payments improved. In these conditions there were no significant problems of short-term stabilisation, except for the mild recession of 1958, which transpired to be the prelude to four years of extremely rapid growth. In the course of the twelve years after 1950, then, discretionary policy on the part of the monetary authorities was not needed, and the supply of monetary base was not controlled in any systematic manner. However, these favourable conditions disappeared in the 1960s, and the changing economic climate was heralded by the crisis of 1963.

The background to the 1963 crisis, as we have seen in chapters 2 and 3, was the spectacular export-led expansion in the years 1958–62. Italy was, in fact, expanding into a partial full-employment ceiling, and the first sign of this appeared in 1962 as the rate of growth of real GNP decelerated and the wholesale price index began to rise after a decade of almost complete stability. The first mistake made by the authorities concerned the timing of their monetary measures. Some form of deflationary action should have been taken in 1962, but the inflationary growth continued to be fed by the injection of liquidity into the economy through a number of channels.[30] In January 1962 an estimated 200 milliard lire was pumped into the economy when the banks' compulsory reserve ratio was lowered from 25 to 22.5 per cent, while, over 1962 and 1963 as a whole, the financing of the Treasury deficit was shifted away from medium- and long-term debt towards central bank credit, resulting in a considerable increase in the supply of monetary base. A further source of increased liquidity was bank borrowing from abroad. With the development of Eurodollar markets in the late 1950s, and the authorisation of certain Italian banks to participate, these banks were able both to lend and to borrow abroad, with important implications for their liquidity. As we have seen, the use of directives from the Bank of Italy to adjust the banks' net foreign position became an important method of controlling the overall liquidity of the banking system.[31] In spite of the inflationary problems that were building up, in October 1962 the banks were granted fresh authorisation to borrow abroad, which they did, to the amount of 1082 million dollars between November 1962 and August 1963.

It was in September 1963 that the authorities belatedly changed the direction of their policy. By now it was clear that the economy could not sustain the rapid growth of the late 1950s, and, as we have seen, the continuing expansionary monetary policy of 1962–63 was being reflected not by an increase in real output, but by inflation and balance of payments difficulties. The wage and price explosion of 1962–63 not only slowed down Italy's export growth, but also induced a massive increase in imports. It was only then that the authorities reversed their expansionary policy, and a series of deflationary monetary measures were taken in late 1963. In particular, the banks were directed not to increase their foreign indebtedness. By blocking off this important source of domestic liquidity at a time of considerable inflation, the central bank had, in effect, instituted a credit squeeze. An indication of the severity of this can be given by fact that the net increase in the money supply between June 1963 and March 1964 was 533 milliard lire compared with 1319 milliard lire for the corresponding period in the previous year, while the ratio of bank loans to bank deposits fell from 78.5 per cent in December 1963 to 74.4 per cent in December 1964.[32]

The impact of these measures on the balance of payments and on the domestic economy was dramatic indeed. By 1964 the overall balance of payments showed a surplus of 773.9 million dollars compared with a deficit of 1251.8 million dollars in the previous year – largely attributable to the dramatic improvement in the balance of visible trade and the reversal of a severe capital outflow which had reflected speculation against the lira in the winter of 1963–64. However, the cost of this success in terms of domestic growth was severe. Industrial investment fell by 20.2 per cent in 1964 while real GNP rose by a mere 3.0 per cent. The domestic slump of 1964 continued through 1965 in spite of the fact that the monetary authorities were by now attempting to stimulate the economy.

Although the supply of monetary base was expanded, this did not stimulate any substantial increase in aggregate demand since the credit was not taken up by industry. Instead, the banks increased their foreign lending in the Eurodollar market, to the extent of 770 milliard lire between April 1964 and December 1965. Moreover, as we noted earlier, at this time the banks were given permission to invest in the fixed interest bonds of certain public bodies, most notably the special credit institutes, and this absorbed bank liquidity that might have been channelled directly into private sector lending. The important point to note is that the expansion of the monetary base, of itself, proved insufficient to induce economic recovery in 1964–65.

This deficiency was again emphasised in the post-1969 recession. This recession was similar to that of 1964–65 in that labour problems had led both to inflation and to balance of payments difficulties (especially on capital account). Again, monetary policy was characterised by an initial period of restriction followed by broadly expansionary measures, working through increases in the supply of monetary base in an attempt to stimulate the economy out of recession.

The most important single feature of the restrictive phase of monetary policy on this occasion was the rise in long-term interest rates which the authorities permitted on the bond market. This was largely in response to balance of payments difficulties on capital account, and marked the end of a period during which the authorities had systematically intervened in the bond market to stabilise bond prices. While this had a marked and favourable impact on capital movements, it also badly hit Italian industry, which, as we noted earlier, is particularly vulnerable to interest rate fluctuations because of its structure of external finance.

From mid-1970 onwards, the government attempted to induce a recovery through monetary expansion. By manipulating the finance of the Treasury deficit, the supply of monetary base was substantially increased, and this trend continued through 1972, accompanied by a drop of ½ per cent in the rediscount rate – a rare occurrence in Italian monetary policy. As in 1964–65, however, these measures were of themselves insufficient to stimulate recovery and private sector lending by the banks was sluggish to respond.

The experiences of 1963–65 and 1969–73 have highlighted two serious weaknesses of over-reliance on monetary policy in the Italian context. First, monetary policy has a tendency to have too severe an impact in a deflationary direction, and secondly, it appears to be inadequate as an instrument of recovery from slump, whether or not it be a policy-induced slump. Let us examine these contentions in turn.

It is certainly the case that both the 1963 and the 1969 crises were followed by periods of economic recession, and this has been blamed by many Italians on the over-severe impact of deflationary monetary policy.[33] However, it is important not to lose sight of the other adverse factors that were operating on the economy in the wake of these crises – factors that were unrelated to the authorities' restrictive monetary policies. In 1963, for example, a series of events reinforced the authorities' policy of deflation. Possibly the most important of these concerned the political developments of the early 1960s. The 'opening to the left' had provided Italy with its first centre–left government. This in itself may not have adversely affected business psychology, but the policies undertaken in 1962–63 most certainly did. The nationalisation of the electricity industry and the introduction of the new withholding tax on dividends were regarded by many in the business community as the first of a series of new, radical policies, and business expectations dropped from the high optimism of the late 1950s. Investment plans were reversed or delayed. The impact of these political developments was exacerbated by the wave of strikes in 1963 and the social unrest with which they were associated. Thus, for a number of socio-political reasons, the optimistic climate in which high investment plans had been formulated in the past was suddenly broken. Initially, at least, this had nothing to do with monetary policy.

It is also possible to regard the slump of 1964 as a natural part of the trade cycle which had reached its upper turning point at a temporary, full-employment ceiling in 1962–63, when wage inflation squeezed profits. Taking account of the importance of self-financing in Italian industrial investment, such a squeeze could only lead to a fall in investment and this, argued the Bank of Italy, was all the more likely in an open economy.

Similarly, factors other than monetary policy play some part in explaining the recession that began in 1970. As with the earlier slump, 1970–71 could be regarded as the trough of a cycle which naturally reached its peak in 1969. Moreover, the fall in industrial investment could be seen largely as a reaction to the 'hot autumn' on the part of Italian businessmen. In addition, it could be argued that the imminence of the changeover from IGE to IVA in January 1973 provided an inducement for firms to delay investment projects, because of the different fiscal treatment of stocks. Such factors undoubtedly reinforced the monetary restriction and also made recovery from recession more difficult.

In spite of the influence of such exogenous factors, our view is that much of the blame for the two recessions is attributable to the over-severe impact of the restrictive monetary policy. Even insofar as the alternative explanations for the slumps are applicable, the monetary authorities cannot be exempt from some responsibility since, if there were other factors working towards recession, then to that extent the monetary policies adopted must be regarded as inappropriate. Moreover, one can go further, and argue that Italian monetary policy, by its very nature, is too severe a policy instrument for 'fine-tuning', and because of its extremely strong effects on the financial system it is more than likely to 'overshoot' when employed in a deflationary direction. We have already mentioned the fact that the sources of finance to Italian industry are skewed away from risk capital towards fixed interest borrowing, either from the special credit institutes or from the banks. Over and above these sources of finance, and of paramount importance, are retained earnings. However, since in both crises profit margins had been squeezed, firms had to resort to other sources. The impact of monetary policy in this financial context is particularly severe. Firms that are committed to a high proportion of fixed interest debt are hit especially hard when the cycle is in the downswing. The combination of this plus the squeeze on bank (short-term) credit tends to have the effect not so much of simply reducing aggregate demand, but rather of leading to an inordinately large number of bankruptcies among smaller firms.

The severe impact of monetary policy in a deflationary direction has not been matched by equal effectiveness in recovery. In both the major recessions the authorities' attempts to stimulate economic activity by increasing the supply of monetary base have resulted only in excess liquidity in the banks, or in their increased participation in the Eurodollar market and the domestic bond market. The analogy of monetary policy as a string that is extremely effective for holding the economy back but is useless as an instrument of expansion is well borne out by the Italian experience.

5.3 Conclusions

Over the postwar period, Italian short-term stabilisation policy has been characterised by a heavy reliance on monetary policy. Yet in many ways this has not been an appropriate instrument for the new economic circumstances of the 1960s and 1970s – characterised by domestic inflation and balance of payments problems, especially on capital account. An orthodox strategy to deal with the latter is the manipulation of domestic interest rates, but this has proved difficult in the Italian case for reasons outlined earlier. Thus, the typical policy response has had to be monetary deflation. However, as we have seen, the deflationary effects of monetary policy have been undesirably harsh. Much of the sluggishness in the Italian economy after 1963 can be attributed to this, combined with the fact that monetary policy is also not an ideal reflationary weapon. This latter deficiency is, however, all the more serious in the Italian case, as fiscal policy remains largely inoperable. The lack of a viable fiscal policy has been especially important in recent years, and the prolonged nature of the current recession illustrates well the failure of the authorities either to adjust tax rates efficiently for stabilisation purposes, or to carry out expenditure programmes to induce a recovery. The 'easy years' for Italian economic policy ended in 1962, and what is even more distressing than her mixed economic fortunes since that year has been the continuing failure of the authorities to carry out the reforms, in both the financial system and the fiscal system, that are essential if more balanced and successful techniques of short-term economic management are to be instituted. The problems of the seventies require them.

Notes to chapter 5

1. See G. La Malfa *Crisi Economica e Politica dei Redditi* Rome: Edizioni della Voce (1972).
2. For a good description of Italy's changing fiscal structure over the period 1951–69 see G. Bognetti 'Analisi Quantitativa delle Strutture e delle Tendenze del Bilancio Pubblico Italiano dal 1951 al 1969' in V. Balloni (ed.) *Lezione sulla Politica Economica in Italia* Milan: Edizione di Comunità (1972). Many of the figures in this section are taken from this source.
3. Details of the Italian tax system can be found in B. Hansen *Fiscal Policy in Seven Countries 1955–1965* Paris: OECD (1969).
4. For an excellent discussion of the Italian budgetary system see C. Marzano *I Soldi di Tutti* Rome: Edindustria Editoriale (1966).
5. There is now a considerable literature dealing with this subject. The most important official documents are: Camera dei Deputati, Commissione V *Analisi dei Flussi di Cassa nel Bilancio dello Stato 1965–1970* (Rome, 1971); Ministero del Tresoro *I Residui nel Bilancio dello Stato* (May 1969). Other important publications include: S. Lo Faso and G. Morcaldo 'Analisi del Processo di Attuazione della Spesa Pubblica' *Contributi alla Ricerca Economica* Rome: Banca d'Italia (1972); G. Ruffolo *Rapporto sulla Programmazione* Rome/Bari: Laterza (1963); and L. Izzo, A. Pedore, L. Spaventa and F. Volpi *Il Controllo dell'Economia nel Breve Termine* Rome: Franco Angeli (1972) ch. 5.
6. Figures calculated from data in Banca d'Italia *Relazione Annuale 1972* (Rome, 1973).
7. See Lo Faso and Morcaldo, op. cit. Much of our discussion of the problems of *residui passivi* is based on this study.
8. This is not to say that budgetary changes have not had any significant effect

on the level of aggregate demand. Indeed, a number of studies have been carried out to estimate the impact of changes in the public administration budget on the economy, and, in particular, to discern whether fiscal policy (albeit not self-consciously *stabilisation* fiscal policy) has acted in a consistently counter-cyclical manner. See Hansen, op. cit.; G. Fua 'Influenza del Bilancio Pubblico sulla Formazione della Domanda in Italia, 1955–63' *Moneta e Credito* (March 1965); F. Romani 'Un Esame dell'Influenza del Bilancio Pubblico sulla Formazione della Domanda in Italia, 1957–67' in *Rapporto del Gruppo di Studio sui Problemi di Analisi Economica e di Politica Economica in Breve Termine* Rome: ISCO (1969); G. Campa 'Un Modello per Valutare gli Effetti Moltiplicativi della Manovra di Bilancio in Italia' in V. Balloni (ed.) *Lezioni sulla Politica Economica in Italia* Milan: Edizione di Comunità and G. Bognetti, op. cit.

9. In 1967 the policy of fiscalisation was halted, and indeed reversed, when the government, faced with the costs of rehabilitating the damage caused by the 1966 floods, raised employers' contributions and cut back on its own payments into the social security system

10. On the assets side, short-term is defined as maturities up to eighteen months, while medium-term is eighteen months to five years and long-term is over five years. For liabilities, the lines of demarcation are roughly the same, though the division between medium- and long-term is less clear-cut.

11. Figures from F. Tamagna (ed.) *Commercial Banking in a Modern Economy*, a seminar sponsored by Banca d'Italia in 1970 (Ente per gli Studi Monetari, Bancari e Finanziari).

12. For a fuller discussion of this policy, and Italian monetary policy as a whole over the postwar period, see A. Graziani 'Problemi di Politica Economica Monetaria in Italia (1945–1970)' in Balloni, op. cit.

13. For an admirable summary of the structure and functions of the special credit institutes, see V. Pontolillo 'Aspetti del Sistema di Credito Speciale con Particolare Riferimento all'Intervento dello Stato' Banca d'Italia *Bolletino* (January–February 1971).

14. IMI has also, at different periods in its history, been entrusted with 'special' operations. Before the war, it assumed responsibility for maritime credit when it took over *Istituto per il Credito Navale*. In the period of reconstruction, IMI was entrusted with the negotiation of loans from the Export-Import Bank of Washington and the management of certain Treasury funds (the fund for finance of mechanical engineering, FIM, in 1947 and the lira funds for buying machinery in 1950). It is now responsible for the administration of a Special Fund for the Finance of Small and Medium Manufacturing Industries (1965), special funds for repairing flood damage (1966), a fund for financing research and development in Italian Industry (1968), and a host of other operations.

15. See V. Pontolillo 'Medium- and Long-Term Credit in Italy' *Banca Nazionale del Lavoro Quarterly Review* (September 1972)

16. See Pontolillo (1971) op. cit.

17. See G. Ruffolo, op. cit., p. 37.

18. *The Financial Times* (30 October 1973).

19. For details of the problems facing the authorities, and the measures taken in 1947–48, see D. Menichella 'The Contribution of the Banking System to Monetary Equilibrium and Economic Stability: Italian Experience' *Banca Nazionale del Lavoro Quarterly Review* (January–June 1956); B. Foa *Monetary Reconstruction in Italy* New York: King's Crown Press (1949); P. Baffi 'Monetary Developments in Italy from the War Economy to Limited Convertibility (1935–1958)' *Banca Nazionale del Lavoro Quarterly Review* (December 1948); and 'Monetary Stability and Economic Development in Italy, 1946–1960' *Banca Nazionale del Lavoro Quarterly Review* (March 1961); A. Hirschman 'Inflation and Deflation in Italy' *American Economic Review* (September 1948); F. and V. Lutz *Monetary and Foreign Exchange Policy in Italy* Princeton: Princeton University Press (1950); E. Simpson 'Inflation, Deflation and Unemployment in Italy' *Review of Economic Studies* (1949–50); and G. Hildebrand *Growth and Structure in the Economy of Modern*

Italy Harvard: University Press (1965).

20. F. Masera *La Riserva Obbligatoria sul Sistema Istituzionale Italiano* (Ente per gli Studi Monetari Bancari e Finanziari) p. 7, n. 8.

21. In addition to the reserve requirements, a number of other monetary controls were instituted at the same time. In particular, the Bank of Italy formally became the executive monetary authority, operating through the Inter-Ministerial Committee for Credit and Saving. Furthermore, the decree laws of December 1947 and May 1948 limited the government's overdraft facilities at the central bank to 15 per cent of current account expenditure. By thus restricting the extent to which the Treasury deficit could be financed at the Bank of Italy, a significant control was placed on the increase in the money supply that directly resulted from budget deficits.

22. Figures calculated from ISTAT *Sommario di Statistiche Storiche dell'Italia 1861–1965* (Rome, 1968) table 87.

23. Lutz, op. cit., p. 14.

24. In September 1965 the banks were allowed to hold reserves in the form of real estate and land-improvement bonds. In 1967 this facility was extended to include bonds issued under the School Building Programme and bonds issued by CREDIOP; and in September 1970 the ultimate in flexibility was incorporated into the system when the Bank of Italy was empowered to allow individual banks to hold as reserves both government securities and special credit institute bonds. For further details see Masera, op. cit. and Tamagna, op. cit.

25. A. Fazio 'Monetary Base and the Control of Credit in Italy' *Banca Nazionale del Lavoro Quarterly Review* (June 1969) p. 148.

26 A minimum cash requirement of 10 per cent was stipulated in 1962.

27. Tamagna, op. cit., p. 338.

28. This is not, of course, to say that the monetary authorities do not have substantial powers of control over the special credit institutes – on their issue of bonds, for example, and on their interest rates. However, it is the case that in general the special credit institutes are not subject to the quantitative controls that characterise the control of the banking system. It is a notable feature of Italian monetary policy that medium- and long-term credit, much of it channelled to finance industrial investment, is controlled *selectively* by the authorities, while it is short-term credit that is characterised by *aggregate* control.

29. See Menichella, op. cit.

30. For a description of Italian monetary policy in this period see P. Baffi 'Monetary Developments in Italy from 1961 to 1965' *Banca Nazionale del Lavoro Quarterly Review* (March 1966).

31. For a detailed discussion of this policy see F. Masera 'International Movements of Bank Funds and Monetary Policy in Italy' *Banca Nazionale del Lavoro Quarterly Review* (December 1966). Many of the figures in the text are taken from this source.

32. Figures are taken from G. La Malfa and F. Modigliani 'Inflation, Balance of Payments Deficit and their Cure through Monetary Policy: the Italian Example' *Banca Nazionale del Lavoro Quarterly Review* (March 1967) p. 4.

33. For a severe critique of the authorities' diagnosis of the 1963 crisis and subsequent policy, see Modigliani and La Malfa, op. cit., and G. La Malfa 'Le Difficile Scelte della Banca d'Italia' *Nord e Sud* (January 1967). For a general critique of stabilisation policy over the 1960s see also A. Graziani 'Un Decennio di Attesa' *Nord e Sud* (January 1970).

CHAPTER 6

The South:
Problems and Policies

Now, here, you see, it takes all the running you can do to keep in the same place. If you want to get somewhere else, you must run at least twice as fast as that! (Alice Through the Looking Glass)

The southern problem is long-standing.[1] It certainly goes back beyond Italian unification in the mid-nineteenth century, but even at that time, relative to the North, communications were poor, illiteracy was widespread, agriculture retained a feudal or neo-feudal holding system and had a level of output per person employed that was around 20 per cent below that of the North.[2] Industry was poorly represented in the economic structure and was characterised by highly protected, small-scale, virtually artisan units.

The new State improved communications to and within the South though the effect of this was to open up the area to strong competition rather than to give it new markets. Even so, it is generally accepted that the North/South disparities in income per head and other measures of material well-being did not increase to any great degree up to the turn of the century. This was, however, as we have seen in chapter 1, a period of slow economic growth for Italy as a whole. Nevertheless, in these years, northern industry saw the start of large-scale industrial development, aided by the greater proximity to European markets, cheaper energy and, for some sectors, protective tariffs. Southern industrial employment fell by a third between 1881 and 1901, as against a rise of some 6 or 7 per cent in the North. Northern agriculture, with its more modern holding system and less harsh natural conditions, also progressed, while southern agriculture changed but little. The Italian 'take-off', during the final few years of the nineteenth century and first decade or so of the twentieth, was largely a northern phenomenon and the somewhat implicit economic and social dualism which had been present since unification became explicit.

Italian development after the turn of the century primarily involved industry, and the South, very poorly served in this respect, inevitably lost out. Moreover, in terms of employment, southern industry declined by some 10 per cent between 1901 and 1936, as against a rise of some 50 per cent in the North. During the same period southern agriculture, largely because of its holding and size structure, was incapable of exploiting new opportunities and saw virtually no rise in output, almost the whole of the national increase of around 26 per cent coming from the North. National Fascist policies which aimed at curbing migration added to the South's agricultural over-population problem, while the 'battle for grain' encouraged further encroachment into forest land with subsequent problems of erosion. During the Second World War the South was a major battlefield and suffered more damage than the North. Particularly serious was the destruction of infrastructure and industrial plant. It is estimated that while northern industrial capacity was reduced through the war by between 5 and 7 per cent, the comparable figure was 30 per cent in the Centre and South.[3] In view of these factors, it is not surprising that the disparities between North and South widened considerably between around 1900 and the end of the Second World War, when the southern problem was more serious than it had ever been.

The South still remains one of Italy's major problems. No plan or political discussion is complete without heavy reference to it. Large in size relative to the rest of Italy and with intense features of backwardness, it denies Italy's eligibility as an advanced modern economy. Although great changes have taken place during the postwar period the problem is, in many ways, no less serious today than in the early 1950s.

This chapter is in five parts. The first section looks at the nature of the southern problem, covering both the disparities between North and South as well as those within the South itself. Section 6.2 tries to go behind the various North/South disparities and examine the factors which explain them. Section 6.3 is a description and critique of southern policy over the postwar period; section 6.4 examines the results of the policy, while the final section draws general conclusions.

6.1 The nature of the problem

Defining the South as the area within which the Cassa per il Mezzogiorno (Fund for the South) operates, it is made up of the eight regions of Abruzzi, Molise, Campania, Puglia, Basilicata, Calabria, Sicily and Sardinia; the two provinces of Latina and Frosinone in the region of Lazio; the two islands of Giglio and Elba; and parts of the provinces of Rome, Ascoli, Piceno and Rieti. In broad terms the South begins about thirty kilometres south of Rome with the border then running inland to the Appenines and north-east to meet the Adriatic between Ancona and Pescara. The area involved is large, comparable in size to Greece, and holds a population of around 19 million – some 36 per cent of the Italian total.

Economists generally use four major measures to indicate the severity of a regional problem, the normal approach being to relate these to the same measures in the non-problem areas, which in Italy's case means the North. (Regional problems and policies, as we shall see, do exist in the North, though they never assume the same intensity as in the South.) The measures are the rate of unemployment, activity rates (labour force as a proportion of total population, or a specified part), income or expenditure per head and net emigration. These indicators are to a large degree inter-related. Heavy net emigration, for example, is to a great extent a consequence of a lack of job opportunities (often indicated by high unemployment and low activity rates) and low incomes. Similarly, low activity rates are generally found in areas of high unemployment while low income per head, at least in part, stems from high unemployment and low activity rates.

Using these four indicators, table 6.1 shows the intensity of the southern problem. The table illustrates well the seriousness of the southern problem – against it, regional disparities within the United

Table 6.1   Indicators of the southern problem

	South	North
Activity rates (1971)*		
Males	49.6	56.6
Females	15.0	21.3
Percentage unemployed (1971)**		
Males	4.3	2.2
Females	5.3	3.4
Net emigration (1961–71)†		
Total ('000)	−2318.0	+1161.0
Per '000 population (per annum)	−12.5	+3.6
Gross regional expenditure per head (1971)‡		
'000 lire	884.8	1294.8

 * The activity rate is the labour force (including the unemployed) as a percentage of the total population.
 ** Unemployment rates are the unemployed as a percentage of the labour force (including the unemployed).
 † Net emigration covers emigration to the North and abroad. The rate of emigration is calculated on the basis of 1961 population.
 ‡ Gross regional expenditure per head is regional consumption (public and private) plus gross investment, divided by the regional resident population.

Sources: The regional account figures are calculated from data in ISTAT *Annuario di Contabilità Nazionale* (Rome, 1972). Emigration data are from the provisional census results of 1971. All other figures are from Comitato dei Ministri per il Mezzogiorno *Studi Monografici sul Mezzogiorno* (Rome, 1972).

Kingdom, or any other Common Market country, pale into relative insignificance.[4] Indeed, rather than see the South as a regional problem it is more relevant to consider it as an element of 'dualism', reflecting the existence of two quite different economies, and societies, within the same country.

Regional expenditure per head is a key measure of a regional problem, giving a good quick indicator of the differences between North and South in terms of material standards of well-being. It is an indicator that encompasses a number of regional features – an advantage in giving an overall measure but a disadvantage in that it needs careful interpretation. The figures in table 6.1 are for *per capita* gross regional expenditure, and show that of the South to be a mere 68.3 per cent of the North. Two points about this differential are worth while making now, even though we leave the more detailed discussion until later. First, the southern expenditure figure includes quite substantial net imports from the North and abroad – equal in fact to some three-quarters of gross southern investment. Southern 'national' income (expenditure minus net imports) was in 1971 only 51.7 per cent of the comparable northern figure. Secondly, and a point upon which we lay great stress later, the North/South expenditure and income differential hides very serious disparities within the South.

Activity rates are a fairly standard regional problem indicator even though, again, their measurement and interpretation are difficult. Table 6.1 gives activity rates in North and South measured by expressing the labour force as a percentage of the total population. It shows a quite substantial differential both for males and for females, the northern rate for males being 56.6 per cent as against the southern figure of 49.6 per cent, while the rates for females are 21.3 and 15.0 per cent respectively.

Calculating activity rates on the basis of total population can give misleading results where age structure differences exist between regions. In fact, much of the North/South male activity rate differential does seem to be a consequence of age structure differences. Based on the population aged fourteen and over, the southern male activity rate in 1969 was 70.2 per cent compared with the northern rate of 73.6[5] – a much smaller differential than with the total population calculation in table 6.1 above. On the other hand, the female differences do not appear to reflect age structure. Again, using as the denominator the population aged fourteen and over, the 1969 female activity rate in the North was 27.4 per cent as against 20.5 in the South. This large disparity is in part a consequence of the serious southern decline in agricultural work for females combined with the lack of a tradition in industrial work. But, without doubt, a major part of it is 'imputable above all to the [South's] weaker economic structure',[6] and to the general lack of job opportunities. In support of this point, it is indeed interesting that Italian female emigrants, even though often not part of the labour force when in Italy, take up jobs abroad. A survey in 1969 found that while 30 per cent of Italian female expatriates had not been part of the labour force in Italy (being mainly housewives) the proportion fell to 9 per cent when abroad. 'These are data which should not be neglected when one wants to value the extent of so-called discouraged unemployment and the potential supply of the labour force in specific areas.'[7]

Even though southern activity rates are low relative to the North (and even the northern rate is one of the lowest in Europe), in both regions they have been falling fairly steadily over the postwar period – a trend for which, as we have seen in chapter 4, there is no clear explanation. Table 6.2 shows regional trends, measuring activity rates as in table 6.1, i.e. labour force as a proportion of total population.

Table 6.2   Trends in activity rates: North and South

	South		North	
	Males	Females	Males	Females
1951	59.0	16.2	66.2	22.9
1961	56.0	19.6	64.0	28.1
1965	52.2	15.9	60.8	23.6
1971	49.6	15.0	56.6	21.5

Sources: Comitato dei Ministri per il Mezzogiorno *Studi Monografici sul Mezzogiorno* (Rome, 1972); and Svimez *Statistiche sul Mezzogiorno d'Italia 1861–1953* (Rome, 1954).

The point does deserve to be made in the context of regional activity rates that even small differences can represent sizeable numbers. The current North/South activity rate differential, for example, would add 1¼ million to the southern labour force if it were ironed out. The differentials also affect regional income and expenditure. Higher southern activity rates would diminish the North/South income per head differential quite substantially. This can be illustrated by a simple calculation dividing the regional expenditure by the labour force instead of population. In 1970 southern expenditure per head was 54.4 per cent of that in the North. Dividing instead by the employed labour force gives the South a figure of some 66.3 per cent of the comparable northern level. We can see, therefore, that the activity rate differentials between North and South, with high dependency ratios in the latter, do make quite a substantial difference to the income differentials. In as far as the low activity rate reflects the lack of job opportunities in the South, as seems to be the case, then the income per head of population differential is the best measure.

The slack labour markets in the South, and the prospects of better paid employment elsewhere, are to a great degree reflected in the heavy net emigration from the South. Table 6.1 above shows net emigration over the period 1961–71 as being just slightly more than 2.3 million, and this out of a southern population of some 18 million.

Southern emigration is no new phenomenon, a point that clearly emerges from table 6.3 below, which gives net emigration figures for North and South over inter-census periods between 1871 and 1971.

Table 6.3 Net emigration: North and South, 1871–1971

	North		South	
	Population* ('000)	Net emigration** ('000)	Population* ('000)	Net emigration** ('000)
1871–1881	(N.A.)	−338	(N.A.)	−23
1881–1901	17,618	−1250	11,335	−930
1901–1911	19,961	−787	13,005	−859
1911–1921	21,982	+516	13,863	−920
1921–1931	25,111	−544	14,832	−433
1931–1936	26,954	+44	14,697	−363
1936–1951	27,708	+7	15,286	−1017
1951–1961	29,830	+573	17,685	−1767
1961–1971	32,047	+1161	18,576	−2318

* The population figures are for the initial years and measure resident population.
** Emigration covers movement to the North and abroad.

Sources: Svimez *Un Secolo di Statistiche Italiane: Nord e Sud 1861–1961* (Rome, 1961); the post-1951 figures are from the 1961 and 1971 censuses.

The table illustrates well the long history of heavy southern migration. Until recently, by far the bulk of this was abroad, rather than to the North. Indeed, one can see from the table that there was severe emigration from the North at least up to the turn of the century. It will be noted that emigration from both North and South fell considerably during the Fascist period. This was, as we have seen in chapter 1, a consequence of two factors. First, the recipient countries, and particularly the United States, were themselves in a situation of labour surplus and imposed immigration restrictions. Secondly, the Fascists developed their own controls on overseas emigration, as well as limiting migration within Italy by requiring potential migrants into the towns to secure a permit. These permits were difficult to obtain. As can be imagined, this policy of migration control had unfortunate side effects, and certainly did nothing to ease the problems of over-population in southern agriculture.

In the period after 1951 southern net emigration increased considerably. Table 6.3 shows a net loss of 1.8 million over the years 1951–61 and 2.3 million between 1961 and 1971. On the other hand, the North, particularly in the latter period, was a substantial importer of labour with net immigration of 1.2 million. Increasingly, over the postwar period, southern emigration has been towards the North rather than abroad, and particularly into the growing and prosperous areas of Lombardy and Piedmont.

Data on the direction of southern emigration abroad are unsatisfactory. The limited information that is available indicates that gross southern emigration to Europe was in 1968 about double that to non-European countries (primarily Canada, the United States and Australia), though the net figures, after taking account of return migration, show the non-European countries taking more than their European counterparts.[8] This reflects the fact that much of the migration into Europe, largely to Germany and Switzerland, is for short periods. These migrants would be taking what are tantamount to seasonal jobs in the tourist and construction industries. The nature of the migrants' jobs is one of the explanations for the temporary nature of this emigration to Europe, but another, and major, factor is the problems the migrants encounter, particularly in respect of housing and schooling. In 1967, 66 per cent of migrants returning to the South from abroad, overwhelmingly from Europe, had been out of the country for less than one year, and 47 per cent for less than nine months.[9]

A substantial proportion (68 per cent in 1967) of those emigrating abroad from the South had previously been in employment, meaning of course that the majority do not take their families with them. Most southern worker emigrants abroad are manual with, in 1967, some 23 per cent coming from agriculture and forestry and around 50 per cent from the building industry. Thus, there seems little evidence to suggest that southern emigration is draining the region of its skilled labour force. In general, it appears that most worker emigrants take the same job as they had in Italy, with the exception of agricultural workers who tend to go into industry. Particularly interesting, however, is that the repatriates take up a similar job in Italy to the one they had before their migration, rather than the type of job they had abroad – throwing doubt on the commonly accepted view that migrants enrich their country of origin when they return with skills and techniques learnt abroad.

In many ways our discussion of southern emigration, both to the North and abroad, understates the amount of migration that is taking place, for it ignores the quite considerable movement within the South, much of it to the main provincial cities such as Naples, Catania and Syracuse which have, indeed, seen sizeable inflows – not because they offer great employment opportunities but rather because they represent a stepping stone along the migratory route. 'The principal centres of his own region constitute, for the southern migrant, coming from the rural areas and the mountains, a first migratory stage while the second is normally an industrialised centre abroad or in the North.'[10]

We come now to the last of the measures presented in table 6.1 above – that of unemployment. The table showed that the unemployment rate in the South was 4.3 per cent for males and 5.3 per cent for females. The corresponding figures for the North were 2.2 per cent and 3.4 per cent respectively. These figures, using ISTAT estimates based on a quarterly sample survey of Italian families, must be treated with great caution for, as we have seen in chapter 4, they understate to a quite considerable extent the true amount of unemployment. The degree of understatement is probably greater in the very slack labour markets of the South. Even so, the figures in table 6.1 are probably considerably lower than the reader might have expected. There are two explanations for this. First, it will be obvious from our earlier discussion that the southern population is extremely mobile and there is a long tradition of migration – an alternative to unemployment. Secondly, and probably related, the Italian unemployed have a miserable existence with, as we saw in chapter 4, very low rates of basic unemployment pay. There is, therefore, real pressure for people to be employed and earning, even if this requires taking a job which involves substantial underemployment. Though difficult to quantify, underemployment is generally accepted as being a notable feature of the southern labour market.

The point needs to be kept firmly in mind that the various measures of the southern problem which we have so far been discussing are averages and have generally been related to average northern figures. Within the South, however, there are areas in which the problems are particularly acute. Activity rates in 1971, for example, (when the southern rate was 30.2 per cent and that of the North 37.3 per cent) ranged from 25.2 per cent in the province of Naples to 37.9 per cent in the province of Isernia.[11] Disparities in respect of income per head are no less serious. Calabria, for example, in 1969 had a GDP per head equal to some 79 per cent of the southern average and about a third of that in the richest northern regions of Lombardy and Liguria.[12] At a provincial level the disparities are even more startling. The province of Avellino in 1970 had a net income (net of amortisation) per head that was 67 per cent of the southern average and only 45 per cent of the Italian average.[13]

Similarly, with migration there are great provincial and intra-regional differences. Between 1951 and 1961 net emigration from the South involved 1.8 million people – equal to 10.0 per cent of the 1951 population.[14] Abruzzi/Molise, however, saw a net emigration rate equal to 19 per cent of the 1951 population, while Basilicata and Calabria suffered similar rates at 18.6 and 19.9 per cent respectively, resulting in population declines in spite of high birth rates. Breaking the migration figures down to a provincial level further emphasises the seriousness of migration in parts of the South. The province of Avellino, for example, experienced net emigration equal to 25.2 per cent of the 1951 population (reducing the population by 12.2 per cent between 1951 and 1961), while the comparable figures for Campobasso were 24.4 and 15.3 per cent, and those for Potenza 24.9 and 9.2 per cent.

As we have seen, during the 1960s migration from the South increased, and few areas escaped its consequences. Between 1962 and 1968 about 60 per cent of southern communes suffered net emigration which was above the natural population increase, with the obvious result that their population declined.[15] Migration is an emotional subject and it is necessary to be wary of declaring all migration as being undesirable or damaging. Where the line is drawn between what is an acceptable or unacceptable level is difficult to say and it will anyway depend on a variety of factors. For many southern communes, however, the outflow has been such that it has had substantial adverse affects, often involving 'almost a complete abandoning of the area'.[16]*

We have been concerned so far with the standard measures used by economists in the evaluation of regional problems. There are of course other figures and indicators, which further illustrate the seriousness of the southern problem. In 1961 16 per cent of the southern population of six years and above was illiterate as against 4.1 per cent in the North; daily newspaper circulation in 1963 was only 11 per cent of the (very low) national circulation;[17] while infant mortality in 1970 was 35 per cent above the northern rate. Compared with the other, more prosperous, countries of Europe, the problem of the South becomes yet more depressing.

But no statistics such as those we have used so far can really do justice to the human and social problems which ride in their wake – the demoralising effects of unemployment and the problems of living on the abysmally low unemployment benefit, the degradation of illiteracy, the uncertainty and poverty of the underemployed, and the corruption and paternalism associated with the lack of job opportunities. For those who escape through migration, many are forced to leave their immediate families at home, even if temporarily. Elderly members of the family rarely migrate. The migrants themselves often live in poor and difficult conditions in the area of destination. In some countries their right to work is tenuous and their other rights limited. Their departure, particularly in the numbers experienced by some areas, and noted above, causes great social problems in their area of origin, while they often exacerbate the existing problems in the receiving regions, particularly in the big cities of the North. The migrants in these cities often live in squalid housing conditions, ignored and often despised by the local population and little helped in their assimilation and 'accommodation' by the plethora of public and private groups that have been developed with this aim in mind but with inadequate funds. Inevitably, the younger age groups find it easier to assimilate, but frequently at the expense of their southern culture and attitudes, which in turn often brings inter-generational conflicts within the immigrant family. For the first generation, at least, the migrant's life is hard and miserable.[18]

6.2 The causes of the problem

The various indicators so far discussed in this chapter represent no more than the surface of the southern problem. This section is concerned with trying to look behind these indicators in an attempt to isolate some of the main causes.

As we have seen, a prime feature of the southern problem is the relatively low level of income and expenditure per head. To a large extent this reflects a low overall level of productivity, which in turn arises from two basic factors. First, the South has a higher weighting of the agricultural sector in its economic structure than the North, and secondly, in contrast to this 'structural' factor, the individual economic sectors in the South, including agriculture, have lower levels of productivity than the North.

The heavy weighting of agriculture in the southern economic structure is shown in table 6.4, which gives a sectoral division of employment (employees as well as self-employed) measured in 'labour units' (defined on p. xii above), as well as gross domestic product at factor cost.

Table 6.4 Economic structure in South and North, 1969

	Employment (labour units)		Gross domestic product at factor cost	
	South	North	South	North
Agriculture	30.5	14.3	19.6	8.4
Industry	31.6	46.3	27.6	42.8
Other activities	37.9	39.4	52.8	48.7
Total	100.0	100.0	100.0	100.0

Sources: Calculated from ISTAT *Annuario di Contabilità Nazionale 1971* (Rome, 1972); and ISTAT *Occupati Presenti in Italia 1951–1970* (Rome, 1971).

The table emphasises that the major difference in structure between North and South is the relatively low southern weighting of industry and the high weighting of agriculture – a sector which, nationally, has lower productivity than industry. Italian agricultural gross domestic product at factor cost per labour unit was, in 1969, some 62 per cent of that in industry.

But, as already mentioned, the problem of the South is not simply that it has a structure heavily weighted with the nationally low-productivity agricultural sector, but also that both its agricultural and industrial sectors have productivity levels well below those in the North. In 1969, gross domestic product at factor cost per agricultural labour unit was some 82 per cent of the comparable northern figure. An even more serious differential exists with respect to industry, where southern productivity was only 71 per cent of the North.

Overall, southern gross domestic product per labour unit in 1969 was 75.2 per cent of that in the North. It is not difficult to estimate to what extent this difference is a consequence, first, of the southern structure and secondly of productivity differentials between North and South in the same sectors. If the South, even with its existing employment structure, had had the same productivity levels as the North in each of the three main sectors, it would have had an overall gross domestic product per labour unit that was only some 7 per cent below that of the North. Conversely, if we give the South the northern employment structure and leave unchanged its actual productivity performance relative to the North, then its overall productivity would only rise from 75.2 per cent of the northern level to 79.3 per cent.

The fact that inter-regional sectoral productivity differentials rather than structure are the main cause of the large North/South overall productivity difference (and through this, the income or expenditure differences) still leaves us with the problem of explaining the differentials. This is no easy task, and certainly not one that can be done with any great degree of accuracy.

Starting, however, with the North/South agricultural productivity differential, there are a number of explanatory factors. First, a higher proportion of southern land is mountainous or hilly, and a correspondingly smaller proportion is plain. Secondly, a lower proportion of southern land is adequately drained. These two factors, beyond having a direct effect on productivity, when combined with the South's climatic conditions, give rise to serious problems of erosion. Thirdly, although Italian agriculture as a whole is characterised by small farms, the average size of farm in the South is even smaller. About 81 per cent of southern farms in 1970 were of five hectares or less and a fifth of cultivated land was farmed on holdings below this size. (These percentages are virtually identical with those for 1961, reflecting the point made earlier that the agricultural exodus has resulted in relatively little agricultural restructuring.) Fourthly, large numbers of farms are fragmented. In 1961 about 20 per cent of southern land was being cultivated in holdings composed of between five and ten non-contiguous pieces. The poor land plus small and fragmented farms are both a cause and effect of substantial agricultural underemployment (estimated at 65 per cent at the start of the

1960s),[19] and the slight use of capital inputs and modern techniques. Perhaps the best indication of this latter feature is the fact that in 1970 southern expenditure on agricultural production goods and services represented only 13.6 per cent of gross saleable agricultural output, in contrast with 27.8 per cent in the North.[20] Southern agriculture has, for a hundred years or more, been locked in a vicious circle of small and fragmented farms lacking capital and operating in unfavourable geographical and climatic conditions. As we shall see agricultural policies, particularly during the 1960s, have tended to improve the situation, but it is a slow process.

Turning now to industry, table 6.4 showed that while 46.3 per cent of northern labour units were in industry, the proportion in the South was only 31.6 per cent. And yet in a number of industries the South has a weighting similar to the North.

We can classify industry into four major groups – electricity, gas and water; mining and quarrying; construction; and manufacturing. The first two groups are not an important component of industrial or total employment in either North or South. The labour units in both these groups in 1970 amounted to slightly less than 1.5 per cent of total Italian labour units, and the southern proportion was virtually identical with that for the nation.[21] The construction industry is more important, but, in employment terms at least, there is no shortfall in the South – 13.2 per cent of total southern labour units are employed in this industry as against 10.0 per cent in the country as a whole.

It is, in fact, manufacturing where the major southern industrial shortfall is to be found. In the North (again in 1970), some 37.0 per cent of total labour units were employed in manufacturing as against a mere 17.5 per cent in the South. The South is therefore desperately short of a sector that has high levels of productivity. In addition, that which does exist has productivity levels below those in the North. Table 6.5 is interesting in this respect, showing regional value-added per manufacturing labour unit. It can be seen from the table that average southern manufacturing productivity is some 73 per cent of that in the North. In every industry except four, northern productivity is well above that of the South. The high southern productivity in iron and steel and chemicals reflects the new capital intensive plant located in the South by the state holding sector during the 1960s (see chapter 7).

The average productivity differential in manufacturing between North and South is a consequence of two factors. First, the South has a manufacturing employment structure that is heavily weighted with low-productivity industries. Secondly, the South has a lower productivity than the North in the same industries. The first we shall call the structural element and the second, non-structural. It is obviously relevant for policy to decide which is the more important. We can do

Table 6.5   Value added per labour unit employed in manufacturing: North and South, 1969

(*million lire*)

	South	North
Foodstuffs and tobacco	2.22	3.07
Textiles	0.97	1.81
Clothing, footwear, furs and leather	0.84	1.27
Wood and furniture	0.89	1.55
Iron and steel	4.00	3.52
Engineering	1.40	2.16
Vehicles	2.54	2.36
Non-metallic minerals	1.78	2.23
Chemicals and associated	5.59	4.41
Paper	3.63	3.18
Rubber	2.18	2.83
Printing and various	1.44	3.14
Total	1.69	2.32

Sources: From data in ISTAT *Occupati Presenti in Italia 1951–1970* (Rome, 1971); and ISTAT *Conti Economici Territoriali per gli Anni 1951–1969* Supplemento Straordinario al Bolletino Mensile di Statistica, No. 9 (Rome, September 1970).

this by a variant on the standard shift and share analysis, a system we used earlier in our three-sector analysis, even though we did not spell out the method.[22] The method involves applying the northern employment structure to the total number of labour units in southern manufacturing, multiplying the resultant employment distribution by actual southern value-added per labour unit for each manufacturing industry to calculate what average southern manufacturing value-added would have been if the South had had the northern employment structure and its own levels of productivity. The results show that, on this basis, in 1969 average manufacturing southern value-added per labour unit would have been 1.85 million lire as against an actual 1.69 million lire. It will be recalled from table 6.5 that the overall difference between southern and northern manufacturing was 0.63 million lire per labour unit. Our calculations, therefore, imply that some 25 per cent (1.85 million lire minus 1.69 million lire over 0.63 million lire) of the North/ South overall manufacturing productivity differential can be explained by relatively poor structure, and some 75 per cent (the remainder) by non-structural factors, i.e. a result of the fact that the same industries have lower productivity in the South than in the North. The intriguing question that remains, as in our agricultural discussion above, is why these productivity differences should exist.

There are two possible explanations. The first is that there are serious locational disadvantages in the South. If this is the case, then of course the problems and costs of trying to industrialise the South are likely to be severe. Unfortunately, there is little quantitative evidence that would enable us to indicate how far such locational disadvantages are at the root of the low southern manufacturing productivity. Our own view, and it is subjective, is that the differentials are more a reflection of a second factor – a poorer 'structure' within each of the industry groups rather than fundamental locational disadvantages. Some support for this argument is, in fact, given by table 6.5, which showed that modern industry in the South, particularly iron and steel and chemicals, has productivity levels that are close to, or even above, those in the North. The basic point is that the southern foodstuffs, engineering, wood and furniture industries are quite different from the same industries in the North. Much more than in the North, especially in these industries, southern manufacturing firms are very small, often of an artisan rather than industrial character, and suffering a considerable amount of underemployment. In 1971, for example, the average southern manufacturing establishment had a work force of only 4.3 as against 10.0 in the North, while almost 27 per cent of the southern manufacturing work force was self-employed as against slightly less than 14 per cent in the North.

Small firms are not necessarily inefficient, nor need they have low levels of productivity. On the whole, however, they tend to lack capital and entrepreneurship and to operate with little plant or equipment, much of which is often out of date. Usually, they have substantially lower levels of productivity than larger firms and pay a lower remuneration to labour. A national survey in 1963 found, for example, that manufacturing firms employing 10 persons or less had a value-added per person in employment that was only some 45 per cent of that in firms employing more than 100. Similar conclusions are likely to apply in the South. Although there is little quantitative evidence, we suspect that the large number of small southern manufacturing firms is an important explanation of its low average value-added in manufacturing.

It is unfortunate that there are no data for value-added per person employed by size of firm and by region, since this would allow us to standardise for firm size and thereby to examine the differences between firms of the same size in the same industry between North and South. Our view is that, although differences would exist, with the North having higher productivity, these would not be as great as those between firms of different sizes.

So far this section has been concerned with trying, through an analysis of inter-regional productivity differentials, to explain the relatively low expenditure per head. We have seen that the explanation rests on two basic features of the southern economy. First, it has an economic structure that is heavily weighted with the nationally low-productivity sector of agriculture and is deficient in industry, particularly manufacturing. Secondly, and more important, similar industries and sectors in the South have lower levels of productivity than the North.

But low income or expenditure per head is only one of the facets of the southern problem, and we have already seen that there are others (not unrelated) – in particular, high unemployment and under-employment, high levels of out-migration and low activity rates. All of these reflect a basic feature of the South – slack labour markets – and these, in turn, are principally a consequence of two factors – first, the high rate of population growth, and secondly, the slow expansion of employment opportunities.

The natural increase in the southern population is at a rate well above that of the North. This, and the historical trend, is shown in table 6.6. The birth rates in both regions between 1881 and the First World War were not greatly dissimilar, with the South only some 6 per cent or so above the North. This was generally compensated by a higher southern death rate, with the result that the excess of births over deaths per thousand inhabitants was about the same in both North and South. After the First World War the birth rate fell sharply in the North but much less so in the South. At the same time the death rates fell substantially in both regions. The period after the Second World War saw further considerable falls in the southern death rate;

Table 6.6 Rates of natural population change: North and South
(*per '000 inhabitants*)

Year	Birth rate North	Birth rate South	Death rate North	Death rate South	Excess of births over deaths North	Excess of births over deaths South
1881–1885	36.1	40.5	26.2	28.8	9.9	11.7
1896–1900	33.3	35.8	21.8	25.1	11.5	10.7
1911–1914	30.5	33.6	17.8	21.1	12.7	12.5
1921–1925	27.0	34.5	16.0	18.6	11.0	15.9
1936–1940	20.2	29.1	12.8	15.6	7.4	13.5
1951–1955	14.4	23.5	9.9	9.2	4.5	14.3
1956–1960	14.7	23.1	10.1	8.8	4.6	14.3
1961–1965	16.5	22.5	10.1	8.6	6.4	13.9
1965–1970	15.8	21.0	10.3	8.4	5.5	12.6

Sources: The data to 1955 are taken from Svimez *Un Secolo di Statistiche Italiane: Nord e Sud 1861–1961* (Rome, 1961). The data for 1956 onwards are calculated from Comitato dei Ministri per il Mezzogiorno *Studi Monografici sul Mezzogiorno* (Rome, various issues).

indeed, as table 6.6 shows, the southern death rate is now lower than that for the North. In consequence, the southern excess of births over deaths per thousand inhabitants became far higher than the figure for the North.

An obvious point, though one that deserves to be made, is that the North/South birth and death rate differentials involve quite substantial absolute differences. The excess of southern births over deaths in the 1960s, for example, meant that the natural increase of the southern population was almost 270,000 per annum. If the South had had the northern rates in this period, the annual increase would have been only some 120,000. The difference between this and the actual increase is not substantially different from the southern annual net emigration flow.

Beyond, but associated with, the natural increase in the southern population, a second factor explaining the South's slack labour markets is its economic structure, characterised, as we have seen, by a heavy dependence on agriculture – a sector that is declining rapidly in terms of employment. Table 6.7 shows southern and northern employment in broad employment groups for 1951, 1960 and 1970.

The table illustrates clearly the quite massive employment decline in agriculture in both North and South. In the South agricultural employment, measured in labour units, fell by around 450,000 in the 1950s and by a more substantial 713,000 in the 1960s. Northern agriculture, reflecting the alternative employment opportunities available, has seen even greater falls, both in absolute and percentage terms, with almost 900,000 labour units leaving the sector in the 1950s and an enormous 1.4 million in the 1960s.

In many ways, the use of labour units underestimates the exodus from agriculture, since many of the marginal workers (who, it will be recalled, are considered as being the equivalent of one-third of a full-time worker) are marginal workers by circumstances, and not by inclination. They earn their livelihood, albeit a poor one, from agriculture. If we measure the agricultural employment trends on the basis of total employment, whether marginal or not, the movement from the land is even more spectacular. On this basis, as table 6.7 shows, southern agricultural employment fell by 1.9 million – from 3.7 million in 1951 (after a period of a hundred years when it had remained stuck at the 3–3.7 million mark). In both North and South the percentage falls were more serious in the 1960s than the 1950s, though the absolute movements out of southern agriculture did not differ greatly between the two decades. In the North, on the other hand, and reflecting the tightening labour markets in that region during the 1960s, the numbers leaving agriculture were markedly greater than in the 1950s. Some 1.9 million left northern agriculture during the 1960s as against 1.3 million in the 1950s.

Table 6.7 Employment trends in North and South
('000)

South

	1951					1960					1970				
	Full-time self-employed	Full-time employees	Marginal workers	Total workers	Total labour units	Full-time self-employed	Full-time employees	Marginal workers	Total workers	Total labour units	Full-time self-employed	Full-time employees	Marginal workers	Total workers	Total labour units
Agriculture, forestry and fishing	1589.4	732.5	1357.1	3679.0	2774.3	1324.6	719.3	821.1	2865.0	2317.6	797.4	700.9	320.0	1828.3	1605.0
Industry	364.9	797.8	142.8	1305.5	1210.3	357.4	1125.7	257.3	1740.4	1568.9	331.0	1489.4	164.0	1904.4	1795.1
–manufacturing	319.2	425.6	123.6	868.4	786.0	284.2	513.7	206.6	1005.5	866.7	261.4	688.9	87.8	1030.1	971.6
–construction	40.2	299.9	17.7	357.8	346.0	67.4	532.8	49.1	649.3	616.6	66.0	647.8	73.3	787.1	738.2
Tertiary	412.9	498.9	216.0	1127.8	983.8	527.1	660.6	214.2	1401.9	1259.1	742.8	770.6	88.0	1601.4	1542.7
Public administration	—	378.7	—	378.7	378.7	—	465.0	—	465.0	465.0	—	611.4	—	611.4	611.4
Total	2367.2	2407.9	1715.9	6491.0	5347.0	2209.1	2970.6	1292.6	6372.3	5610.6	1881.2	3492.3	572.0	5945.5	5564.2

North

	1951					1960					1970				
	Full-time self-employed	Full-time employees	Marginal workers	Total workers	Total labour units	Full-time self-employed	Full-time employees	Marginal workers	Total workers	Total labour units	Full-time self-employed	Full-time employees	Marginal workers	Total workers	Total labour units
Agriculture, forestry and fishing	2814.6	556.6	1589.9	4961.1	3901.0	2312.4	463.7	925.9	3702.0	3084.7	1248.6	304.1	302.0	1854.7	1653.6
Industry	716.2	3424.7	356.6	4497.5	4259.7	776.5	4319.0	552.0	5647.5	5279.5	795.3	5207.3	302.0	6304.6	6103.5
–manufacturing	632.7	2638.0	316.8	3587.5	3376.3	658.3	3221.5	467.8	4347.6	4035.7	658.6	4078.1	190.5	4927.2	4800.2
–construction	74.4	639.2	37.3	750.9	726.0	108.7	935.5	81.9	1126.1	1071.5	128.4	953.6	106.9	1188.9	1117.6
Tertiary	1017.9	1505.4	461.1	2984.4	2677.0	1365.1	1928.2	373.8	3667.1	3417.9	1603.1	2391.5	169.0	4163.6	4050.9
Public administration	—	759.0	—	759.0	759.0	—	902.6	—	902.6	902.6	—	1178.6	—	1178.6	1178.6
Total	4548.7	6245.6	2407.6	13,201.9	11,596.8	4454.0	7613.5	1851.8	13,919.3	12,684.8	3647.0	9081.5	773.0	13,501.5	12,986.2

Source: ISTAT *Occupati Presenti in Italia 1951–1970* (Rome, 1971).

It is interesting from table 6.7 to observe the type of worker who left agriculture – primarily, in both North and South, the self-employed and the marginal workers. The decline of 1.2 million labour units in southern agriculture between 1951 and 1970 is accounted for, to the extent of 67.7 per cent, by a reduction of self-employed workers and 29.6 per cent by marginal workers (converted to labour unit equivalents). Full-time employees explain a mere 2.7 per cent. Not very dissimilar proportions obtain also in the North with 69.7 per cent of the fall in labour units between 1951 and 1970 being explained by a reduction in self-employed workers, 19.1 per cent by marginal workers and the remaining 11.2 per cent by full-time employees. Calculated in terms of total employment rather than labour units, 42.6 per cent of the southern fall is explained by the decline in self-employed workers and 55.7 per cent by marginal workers. The figures for the North are 50.4 and 41.4 per cent respectively.

The heavy movement of the self-employed workers out of agriculture could have aided the restructuring of Italian agriculture and provided the necessary conditions for increasing the size of farm unit and reducing the degree of fragmentation. In many instances, however, as we have seen, the farmer leaving his land has not sold it – a result of inadequate government policies to exploit this situation, combined with the peasant instinct to hold on to his land and, for many farmer migrants, the desire to 'retire back' to his plot at some stage in the future.

One final point that deserves to be made in the context of the agricultural employment trends is that agriculture is a sector where occupational change also normally requires residential change. In the South especially, jobs in other sectors are not generally available in the rural areas, and the agricultural worker has to move out of his village or town into the major centres for alternative employment. As mentioned earlier, he generally goes to a southern centre first and then uses this as a stepping-stone to the North or abroad.

While in the North the decline in agriculture, measured in labour units, has been almost offset by the increase in industrial employment, this is far from the case in the South, where industrial labour units increased by only 359,000 in the 1950s and 226,000 in the 1960s. In the face of the agricultural decline, the growth of southern manufacturing employment has been particularly disappointing, the number of manufacturing labour units increasing by a mere 186,000 between 1951 and 1970 as against 1.5 million in the North. The southern construction industry has increased its employment over the period more than manufacturing. The point does, however, need to be made that much of the construction industry is of a low-productivity, low-income character, though, of course, better than agriculture.

Finally, the tertiary sector has grown very rapidly in both North and South, with 559,000 new labour units being created between 1951 and

1970 in the latter region and 1.4 million in the former. The percentage growth in the South, has, however, been greater than in the North. Considering that service employment is generally linked to overall employment and income growth, the rapid percentage growth in the South is on the surface surprising, and without doubt reflects the fact that the sector has operated as a reservoir for people not able to get jobs elsewhere. The extent of service underemployment is generally accepted as being substantial.

Overall southern employment, measured in labour units, increased by 264,000 in the 1950s and fell slightly by 47,000 in the 1960s, though this latter fall probably reflects more the depressed state of the Italian economy in 1970 than any long-run trend. Over the whole period 1951–70 there was a growth of only slightly more than 10,000 labour units per annum, and this well explains the reason why southern activity rates are so low and why unemployment, underemployment and migration are so high. Using total employment (irrespective of whether marginal or not) rather than labour units, the employment plight of the South stands out even more clearly. In 1951 total southern employment was 6.5 million. By 1970 it was 6.0 million – a quite substantial fall of half a million jobs. It is with figures such as these that the various southern labour market indicators, discussed earlier, become more easy to understand.

It is generally accepted that southern agriculture still has to face quite a substantial decline. One authoritative estimate, for example, forecasts that the total number of agricultural jobs will fall to 1.4 million in 1976 and to 1.2 million in 1981,[23] as against the 1970 figure of 1.8 million. This implies absolute falls on an annual basis that are some 15,000 below those experienced in the 1960s, but are none the less serious for all that.

With the anticipated continual decline in agriculture and with the existing slack southern labour markets, it is obvious that a major part of southern policy needs to be based on industrial development. The policies for southern development, both past and present, and especially in respect of industry, are discussed in the next section.

6.3 Southern development policy

For most observers, 1950 and the creation of the Cassa per il Mezzogiorno is the crucial threshold in the evolution of southern policy, representing the start of major and relevant intervention. In this section we want to describe and analyse the general lines and phases of southern development strategy after 1950, but we start with a brief outline of policy between unification and the creation of the Cassa.

At unification the new State was aware of the problem it had inherited in the South, and its conscience continued to be pricked by a succession of eloquent and informed writers on the 'Southern Question' – by such men, for example, as Fortunato, Villari, il Salvadori and Jacini, the first of a continuing stream of *Meridionalisti* right up to the present day.

The prime form of development policy before the turn of the century (and indeed beyond) concerned infrastructure, and particularly communications and water.[24] In this respect, the new State was generous – more than half of its total expenditure on these items went to the South. The results, especially with railways, were impressive. By the mid-1880s the South was as well endowed with railway lines (though often only single-track) as the North. Little was done, however, to change the agricultural holding system or to redistribute land, except for some marginal church and public land. This reluctance to interfere with the agricultural structure, or to plan integrated large-scale land reform and land improvement schemes, remained until after the Second World War. Most agricultural development policies, right up to 1950, were small-scale, lacking in funds, and, very important, 'more appropriate for a northern type agricultural structure where credit facilities and water supplies were the most serious obstruction to growth. In the South there was a need . . . for structural reorganisation and for comprehensive and integrated land improvement programmes stretching from the hills to the sea.'[25]

While weak and inappropriate policies were pursued for agriculture, there were virtually none for industry. The great battery of incentives that now form the basis of current Italian industrial mobility strategy did not exist at all up to the turn of the century, and although fiscal and customs duty concessions were introduced in the first decade of the twentieth century, they were slight, and the funds available small. Fortunato described the policies as 'generous charity and clumsy patching', while another contemporary observer likened them to a 'doctor who limits himself in the administration to a fevered man, to that dose of quinine needed to protect himself, in the event of the patient's death, from an accusation of responsibility'.[26]

One must not, however, be over-critical of this early lack of industrial policy, or indeed the shortcomings of southern development policy in general. The economic framework or analysis needed for relevant regional strategies was not developed until after the Second World War, while the economic doctrines of the period before the First World War were not such as to encourage substantial state intervention.

In the face of inadequate and inappropriate regional policies, and the detrimental Fascist policies discussed earlier, the position of the South deteriorated rapidly relative to the North. By 1950 the disparities between North and South were more serious than they had been at any time during the previous century. In the immediate post-Second World War period the general economic situation in Italy was desperate, as we have seen in chapter 1, with serious inflation and a need to rebuild a shattered country. National crises generally see neglect of sectional interests, and regional problems are no exception. Given the circumstances of the time, it was almost inevitable that economic reconstruction was, for the most part, based on the old structure and the existing industrial centres. Up to 1950 regional policies 'were largely of an emergency character in order to deal with the South's most elementary and serious deficiencies with respect to sewage and water'.[27]

The Cassa per il Mezzogiorno, approved by all parties except the extreme left, 'who belittled the government plan, calling it insufficient',[28] was created in 1950 with the purpose of aiding the South's social and economic development. Its efforts were to be organic in the sense that they were to involve schemes which would otherwise require the intervention of a number of ministries (with the associated operational problems). The Cassa's policies and expenditures were to be co-ordinated with the ordinary administration and were intended to be additive, not substitutive. It was to work on a multi-year plan and was endowed with the substantial sum of 1000 milliard lire (about 570 million pounds) for its first ten years of life – equal to some 10 per cent of 1951 Italian national income.

Given the difficult national economic circumstances just prior to the creation of the Cassa, it represented a laudable innovation. A cautionary first-aid or assistance, rather than radical, strategy was what might have been expected.

The decision to take this apparently radical step was influenced by a number of factors. First, 1949 saw evidence of great discontent in the South with a number of serious, politically engineered strikes and invasions of the land. Purposeful policies and actions were obviously required to counter these pressures. (It might be added that the political gains for the government arising from the southern policies were slight. See appendix.) Secondly, it was recognised very clearly that the major drawback of earlier policies was their *ad hoc* and unco-ordinated character. In both agriculture and infrastructure there had been too few attempts to develop large-scale and integrated schemes. The supra-ministerial or organic character of the Cassa and its anticipated interventions would, it was hoped, avoid these shortcomings. Thirdly, the government was encouraged and pushed by two bodies – Svimez (*Associazione per lo Sviluppo dell'Industria nel Mezzogiorno*) and the World Bank. The latter, at an early stage, had offered financial assistance for comprehensive development plans and this, though not taken as initially proposed, influenced the form of the Cassa. Svimez, a research body created in 1946, has, through careful study and analyses, had a considerable impact on southern development policy and played an important part in setting the early roles of the Cassa. The final factor encouraging more radical policies was the view that southern development would provide markets for northern industry and so encourage its expansion.

The greater part of the Cassa's efforts up to 1957 were non-industrial. About 77 per cent of the original allocation of 1000 milliard lire was intended for agriculture and almost all the remainder for infrastructure. The decision to aid agriculture to such a great extent was based on the belief that the South's problem was largely a result of this sector's poverty. In the context of the period this was understandable, particularly since large-scale industrial development, either in the South or North, was considered unlikely in the short run. The view was therefore taken that the main need was to try to improve conditions in southern agriculture and especially to increase employment. The great land reform schemes, many of which, as we shall see, are now criticised because of the small size of farm involved, reflected this objective of creating more employment opportunities on the land. Moreover, much of the Cassa's agricultural expenditure in the first decade was 'to improve conditions of life in the rural areas' (mainly housing), and only at the start of the second decade 'was it aimed at farm changes with a productive objective'.[29] With respect to infrastructure, it was hoped that improvements would of themselves create conditions for spontaneous industrial development and in addition that the infrastructure expenditure would have large regional multiplier effects, thus giving a further boost to southern development and income. In the event, the multipliers were low, ranging from 1.07 for railway works to 1.35 for road works.[30] The infrastructure was anyway too small-scale and spatially spread to have much effect in developing an appropriate environment for industry, often being of an 'assistance' or 'public works' nature. It was obvious that industrial development would not be secured on any scale without a generous incentive scheme to encourage industrial mobility. In fact, until the major industrialisation schemes of 1957, little industrial development took place.

It may seem surprising that the authorities were tardy in providing industrial incentives. The reasons were first, as mentioned above, the expectation that agricultural and infrastructure developments would encourage spontaneous industrial development. Secondly, there was a reluctance to interfere too much with northern industrial growth for fear that this might endanger the competitiveness of Italian exports. Thirdly, and probably most important, the southern economic structure was dominated by agriculture and it was felt that intervention in this sector would give quick results.

By the mid-1950s, and urged on by a variety of economists and politicians, it was accepted that southern development required a more active industrialisation policy, and a law, which among other things incorporated this objective, was introduced in 1957. Although most observers consider 1950 as being the watershed for southern policy, it is our view that the industrialisation policy originating in 1957 was just as important.

There were three major facets of the 1957 industrial development policy. First, there was the proposal to introduce a great range of industrial mobility incentives. Secondly, the government made a start to an industrial growth area policy. Thirdly, the state holding sector was obliged to increase its investments in the South.

The incentives proposed in 1957 (but because of political problems only finalised in 1959) were for indigenous as well as new firms and included fiscal concessions (of which the most important was a ten-year exemption from profits tax which at that time was between 28 and 36 per cent); grants of up to 25 per cent of building costs and 10 per cent of plant and equipment costs (20 per cent if purchased from southern producers); and loans at subsidised interest rates covering 70 per cent or even more of total investment costs.[31] In addition, facilities for the provision of risk capital were developed. Two points need to be made about these incentives. The first is that the grants and loans were awarded on a selective basis, the proportion paid being dependent on the firm satisfying a number of criteria. These were openly declared in the case of the building grants, and favoured large-scale projects in modern industrial sectors, of low capital intensity, and located in designated growth areas (though with a tendency to favour the more poorly developed ones). Such overt selectivity in respect of incentives (and later policies made them more selective) is very rarely found in other European countries. The second point that needs to be made about the incentives is that funds to finance them were slender – only some 20 million pounds per annum for the period 1957–65 (plus another 14 million pounds in foreign loans). This amount did not allow all applicants to be aided, and consequently the industrial development policy was less strong than it appeared on paper.

The year 1957 also saw the beginnings of Italian growth area policy, involving a purposeful attempt to concentrate development in a few selected areas that had, in the past, shown a potential for rapid growth. The major rationale of the policy was that a major impediment to industrial development in an area like the South is a lack of the external economies present in the North, and especially the benefits of industrial concentration – in particular, a large and diversified industrial labour market and the presence of supplies and services *in situ*. The growth area policy was thus aimed at simulating these external economies. It was left to local authorities to form consortia, draw up development plans and propose themselves to the central authorities. Two types of growth area were involved – Areas of Industrial Development (Aree di Sviluppo Industriale) and Nuclei of Industrialisation (Nuclei di Industralizzazione). The major difference was size, the former being expected to have a population over 200,000. The criteria used in deciding whether or not an area was eligible for designation were complicated but the prime, if vague, requirement was that it should have experienced rapid growth in the past or shown a potential for such growth. In the event, all the applicant areas were accepted even though there were some modifications of their detailed plans by the central authorities. Some twelve Areas and thirty Nuclei were finally designated and every province had one or the other. The result was really a policy of dispersed concentration rather than concentration *per se*. Areas and Nuclei held some 45 per cent of the population and virtually all postwar southern industrial development had taken place within their boundaries. The industrial incentives, as we have seen, favoured the growth areas, and this, together with instructions to the state holding sector to concentrate its development in such areas, meant that the greater part of future industrialisation would be similarly placed.

It may appear cruel to have left a not inconsiderable proportion of the southern population outside the growth areas. Two points, however, need to be kept in mind. First, past industrial development was, as we have said, largely in the growth areas. Thus the policy could be viewed in the more neutral sense of being little more than anticipatory planning. Secondly, and more important, if it is accepted that a policy of this type, by creating external economies, gives rise to a faster rate of overall southern growth than would otherwise be the case, it means that the prospects of the non-growth area population finding employment *within* the South are all the greater. In basic terms the choice is between a spread policy with a slower resolution of the southern problem and a continuing heavy outward migration, or a growth area policy with more jobs within the South and lower levels of outward migration.

The final major aspect of the new industrial policy started in 1957 was the decision to involve the state holding sector to a greater degree in southern development. The 1957 law specified that the sector was to locate in the South 40 per cent of its total investments by 1964–65 as against an actual 20 per cent in 1957, and that at least 60 per cent of investment in new industrial enterprises was similarly to go to the South. In the event, the sector more than fulfilled these targets and has represented a very major force in southern industrialisation. During the period 1958–69 its industrial investments accounted for some 34 per cent of the southern total. The role of the state holding sector in southern development is discussed in detail in chapter 7.

The mandate for the Cassa was due to expire in 1965, and in that year a new law was introduced which prolonged its life until 1980. There were, in addition, a number of policy changes. First, the total funds available to the Cassa for the period 1965–69 were increased quite considerably, being doubled relative to the previous fifteen years if calculated on an annual basis. The monies for industrial development were increased substantially. Between 1950 and 1965 about 7 per cent of the Cassa's funds (excluding loans from abroad which, being repayable, are not comparable with the Cassa's own funds) had been spent on industrial development: of the funds awarded in 1965, 41.3 per cent were destined for this end. Agriculture saw a cut in its proportion, even though in absolute terms the allocation was increased by around 50 per cent – again on an annual basis. The 1965 allocation for industry for the period 1966–69 was some 170 milliard lire (around 100 million pounds) per annum. The point was made earlier that southern industrialisation policy suffered from a lack of funds. Obviously the new allocations eased the situation, though most observers considered that the sums involved were still inadequate, a feeling that was confirmed by the fact that the Cassa had exhausted its industrial budget by 1968. To everybody's surprise, more resources were made available in 1969 – some 900 milliard lire – in order to allow it to fulfil its commitments and to carry it through to the next major southern law in 1971. The second point to be made about the 1965 policy was that the industrial development incentives became more generous and selective. The location, size and industrial sector criteria used in the building grants from 1957, and described above, were extended, with some modifications, to loans and to equipment grants. Thirdly, policy became much more oriented towards the growth area strategy. As well as industrial growth areas, tourist areas were designated and the incentives available for the promotion of tourist activities were largely limited to these areas. Similarly with agriculture – the Cassa's land reform, soil conservation and irrigation schemes (and the associated financial assistance to farmers) had earlier been confined to a few areas where good returns could be expected. This policy of concentration was formalised, and to some degree toughened, in 1965. It is not an exaggeration to say that by 1965 the Cassa ceased to be a southern development agency and became limited instead to specified industrial, agricultural and tourist areas within the South. Those parts of the South outside these areas were left largely to the inefficient ordinary administration. Perhaps as many as two million people living in the *osso* (bone) of the South suffered this fate. The final policy change in 1965 involved an attempt to tie southern policy to the national plan. This plan, a revised version of an earlier plan for 1965–69 which never got through Parliament in time, covered the five years 1966–70. It set specified objectives for the South, but the prime goal, and the one on which most others depended, was that of locating there 40 per cent of the nation's new non-agricultural jobs. This was ambitious, particularly considering that the ratio attained in the period 1959–63 was only some 25 per cent. In the event the plan did not attain its objective, only 27 per cent being secured.[32] In consequence, the other objectives in respect of unemployment and migration also failed to be achieved.

After a prolonged debate the Cassa was allocated new funds for the quinquennium 1971–75 in October 1971, and the law making these provisions gave new directions for policy.[33]

There were six major features of the new law. First, the funds allocated to the Cassa were greatly increased relative to earlier years, being given 3125 milliard lire to spend over the quinquennium – some 625 milliard lire per annum and almost 60 per cent above the 1965 allocation. It is anticipated that 50 per cent of the new funds will be spent on industrial development. Secondly, new guidelines were laid down for the state holding sector, it being obliged to place in the South 80 per cent of its investments in new industrial enterprises as opposed to the 1957 proportion of 60 per cent. In addition, 60 per cent (as against the 1957 figure of 40 per cent) of the sector's total investments must be in the South. Thirdly, southern development policy was placed more firmly within national planning. An earlier committee of ministers for extraordinary intervention in the South was wound up and its responsibilities (the planning and co-ordination of southern development policies) transferred to CIPE. As a result, CIPE now has the responsibility for setting the general strategy and criteria of southern development policy while, as before, the minister for extraordinary intervention in the South has the task of operating these policies through the Cassa and other executive bodies.[34]*

A fourth point about the new law concerns the industrial development incentives. The major changes were in respect of grants and subsidised loans. Under the earlier (1965) system the loan awarded was determined by the location, industrial type and size of the enterprise. As we have seen, firms located in growth areas were favoured as were modern industries and the larger-scale firm. A points system, based on these criteria, was used to calculate the proportion of investment that could be covered by a loan, the minimum being 15 per cent and the maximum some 70 per cent, but lower in all cases for investments above a specified level.[35]* The maximum grant for buildings, plant and equipment was 20 per cent and again, as with loans, was lower for very large investments.[36]* The grants for all groups could be increased by 50 per cent (not percentage points) for that part of the investment which involved machinery and equipment purchased from southern producers. The grant figures given so far are all maxima. The actual grant awarded depended on openly stated criteria similar to those used for loans giving a grant that could run from a minimum of 2 per cent to a maximum of 20 per cent of fixed investments, without taking account of any premium for southern purchases. The new system for grants and loans introduced in 1971 was simpler and somewhat less selective. A prime factor in deciding the element of assistance is the size of the firm and its expansion. Three categories are isolated. First, small firms, defined as those that are making a fixed investment, or end up with total investments, of between 100 million lire and 1.5 milliard lire; secondly, firms that make a fixed investment, or have or reach a total investment level, of between 1.5 milliard lire and 5 milliard lire; and finally, firms that make a fixed investment, or have or reach a total investment level, above 5 milliard lire. Small firms are eligible for grants of 35 per cent of their investment in buildings and plant and equipment (increased to 45 per cent if located in an area where the population is declining)[37]* and are eligible for loans of 35 per cent.[38]* Medium-sized firms can receive grants of between 15 and 20 per cent of their investment expenditure in buildings, plant and equipment and loans of between 35 and 50 per cent. Large firms are eligible for grants of between 7 and 12 per cent and loans of between 30 and 50 per cent. In terms of both grants and loans, those firms are favoured which use or supply key or propulsive plants already in the South, which have high levels of technology, or which produce new products.[39] There is a continuing discrimination in favour of growth area locations though this now only applies to loans. All grants can be increased by a further 10 percentage points for plant and equipment purchased from southern producers and for expenditure on anti-pollution devices. In general, the new incentive system is aimed, more than previously, at encouraging the development of small- and medium-sized firms in the South. The discrimination in favour of the development of small firms in depopulating areas is an interesting change over the earlier growth area policy, and although the growth areas are still favoured, this, as mentioned earlier, is now only through subsidised loans. Overall, the grants are more generous and the loans, in terms of the investment covered, less so.

A fifth major feature of policy introduced in the 1971 law concerns the control of new development, with the introduction of a variant on the British industrial development certificate system. In the mid-1960s the Italians had given active consideration to a control policy but decided against it because of a fear, probably exaggerated, that firms refused permission to expand in the North would move into other EEC countries, and also because it was felt that the administrative problems would be too serious.[40]* In the early 1970s, however, the view seemed to have been taken that these arguments were no longer valid. The system introduced in the 1971 law (it applied to the whole of Italy) requires that quoted companies with equity capital or more than 5 milliard lire must inform the Ministry for the Budget and Economic Planning of their investment plans. In addition, any expansion of plant by companies, whether quoted or not, in excess of 7 milliard lire must be communicated to the Ministry. The decision as to whether the plans are allowed to go ahead is taken by CIPE. In making its decision, which must be within three months of the application, CIPE is obliged to take into consideration the level of congestion in the area involved and the availability of manpower and infrastructure. Expansions coming within the categories above which are not communicated to the Ministry, or which go ahead in spite of a negative decision, will be 'fined' a sum equal to 25 per cent of the investment. It would be unfair to comment in detail on the system at this stage, though a few general points are worth while. First, the firms controlled by the law are fewer than those by the British industrial development certificate system (which covers any industrial expansion over 10,000 or 15,000 square feet). Presumably, the view was taken in Italy that there would be problems of policing a more comprehensive system. Secondly, the criteria for refusal of planning permission are narrower than with the British system, where the decision on whether to allow a development to take place involves the very broad question of whether it is 'consistent with the proper distribution of industry'. The Italian system, with the criteria as currently stated, gives an impression more of a decongestion weapon than of a regional development measure. Thirdly, the penalty for ignoring CIPE is high but should not be exaggerated. Taking investment costs as being some 20 per cent of total production costs, the penalty amounts to around 5 per cent of total production costs, and many firms may be prepared to pay this. In principle, the Italian control system is appealing, since by relying to some degree on the price mechanism it avoids the criticism of uncommercial bureaucracy which has often been levied at the more administrative British system. It remains, however, to be seen how firmly the policy is operated. Evidence to date indicates a lax approach, no firm having paid the penalty by mid-1973.

A final aspect of the 1971 law which we want to mention briefly concerns the decision to set up a finance company for the South. This was to have the task of providing risk capital to southern concerns, especially medium- and small-sized firms. It was to take over the five existing bodies operating in this field[41]* and have a substantial capital base of 200 milliard lire. In the event nothing has come of the proposal since, soon after the 1971 law, the decision was taken to create regional finance companies instead.

We have chosen in our discussion of the new law to consider only those aspects that are new or represent substantial changes over previous arrangements. The various fiscal concessions mentioned earlier are largely unchanged. The well established policy of allocating at least 40 per cent of state investment expenditure to the South has similarly been continued, modified only in that it is now required to be observed by a number of additional bodies, including IMI and GEPI. The long-established system whereby the public administration is obliged to make 30 per cent of its purchases from southern concerns is also continued.

However, a relatively new and very important regional development incentive which deserves note, even though not mentioned in the new law since it is covered by different legislation, concerns social security concessions. A common feature of industrial mobility policy in Europe and elsewhere is its heavy orientation towards capital. Grants, depreciation allowances, loans at subsidised interest and equity finance are fairly standard weapons in the regional development armoury. Few countries give labour subsidies, in spite of the fact that labour is generally the surplus resource in the problem region. Within the EEC, the United Kingdom with its regional employment premium and Italy are the major exceptions. The Italian scheme was introduced in late 1968. It is a scheme whereby southern artisan and industrial firms received a concession on their social security contributions equal to 10 per cent of their earnings payments, net of overtime. In addition, a further supplementary 10 per cent was conceded on the earnings of all employees taken on after the end of September 1968 and which increased the total number of employees relative to that date. These concessions were financed half by the State and half by the INPS-administered obligatory unemployment fund and were to last until the end of 1972. The total cost of the concession was estimated at some 933 milliard lire – nearly 300 milliard lire per annum over the life of the scheme, a substantial sum by any standards and indeed larger than the annual Cassa funds for industrial development.

Further and more generous legislation was introduced in July 1972. This extended the basic 10 per cent allowance to the end of 1980 and raised the supplement (for additional labour taken on after January 1971) from 10 to 20 per cent of earnings. In brief, the current situation is that all industrial and artisan firms get the equivalent of an annual grant of 10 per cent of their wages bill less any overtime payments; new firms get 30 per cent, while expanding firms receive the basic 10 per cent plus 20 per cent for wages paid to additional labour taken on after January 1971. Ten percentage points of all these concessions are guaranteed to 1980 while the supplement for additional workers will remain until the next piece of legislation setting new dates for the calculation of additional workers – probably in 1974. The regional social security concessions have resulted in a substantial improvement in the value of Italian regional development incentives. For many firms they will be more important than all the other incentives put together.

Taking an overall view of southern industrial development policy, one cannot but be impressed. The policy covers measures to pump purchasing power into the South, to ensure that the South gets a reasonable share of public investment and of the activities of national bodies such as IMI and GEPI, while the industrial mobility system ranges from a generous set of fiscal, financial and labour incentives to the newly introduced policy of industrial control. Italy now has the most comprehensive and powerful set of regional development measures in Europe.

In general, the Italians have been more adventurous than most countries in their regional development policies, and one outstanding example of this was the attempt to create an inter-related industry complex at Bari-Taranto,[42] arousing considerable interest both within Italy and on the part of foreign observers. The complex was planned by an Italconsult team led by Professor Tosco and was largely financed by the EEC. The study commenced in 1962 and was completed in the latter half of 1965. Because of its importance, we want to conclude this policy section with a description and analysis of the plan and its outcome.

An inter-related industry complex involves the simultaneous development of a complex of industries which are inter-related in that they make demands upon each other. The prime task of the planner is, first, to select a suitable sector and secondly, within this sector, to isolate a number of prinicipal units producing specific lines or items and to ensure that their demands for inputs will be such as to encourage the development of supplying units in the surrounding area. In essence, this means that the demand from the principal units must give sufficient economies of scale to the supplying units and thereby allow their location in the area. A successful complex of this nature would mean that the principal units would be economically viable in that their own needs would be satisfied, and so too would the supporting units. Such a complex would have two main advantages. First, it would give large multiplier effects. One of the problems of regional development through industrial mobility is that the firms attracted often buy many of their inputs from outside the region, thus giving low multipliers. This is the case even in industrial regions such as Scotland, where recent research indicates that some 80 per cent of material and semi-finished inputs used by new firms came from outside the region.[43] The situation in a poorly industrialised region such as southern Italy is even worse. Secondly, an inter-related industry complex gets round one of the basic problems of industrial promotion in an area like the South. This is that firms are often reluctant to move into an area where local suppliers are not present while these supplying units are unlikely to develop or enter the region as long as the demand for their product does not exist. This gives rise to an obvious vicious circle.[44]*

The planners decided that the Bari-Taranto complex should be based on heavy and medium engineering, on the grounds that this industry, or at least parts of it, had good market prospects and that some engineering already existed in the area. The presence of the steel mill at Taranto also doubtless played a part in their decision. A large number of lines within this broad sector were then examined for their input requirements and an attempt made to calculate the economic size required for units producing these inputs. The planners eventually ended up with eight principal and twenty-three supplying units and considered that the former would be sufficiently favourably placed with respect to supplies and that the supplying units would, largely through the principal units' markets, be of a sufficient size to be economic. Some observers, however, expressed doubts as to whether the principal units were sufficiently narrowly defined to enable a realistic calculation of inputs to be made and therefore whether the conclusions on the economies of scale for the supplying units were realistic.[45].

The plan was finished in 1965 and the intention was that recruitment of suitable companies should begin almost immediately. This task was largely given to IASM (Istituto per l'Assistenza allo Sviluppo del Mezzogiorno) – one of the most dynamic semi-state research/promotional bodies in Italy. It was expected that construction of the complex would start in 1968–69 and production commence in 1970–71.

There is general agreement that the complex *per se* has failed. While there has been engineering development in the Bari-Taranto area, this has not been in line with the plan. This failure has been in spite of the use of IASM for promotion purposes, in spite of the fact that incentives of above-average values were available, and that the Cassa was willing to provide the necessary infrastructure, including training, for the complex. The reasons for the disappointing outcome of the project have recently been documented by an EEC mission. Among the factors mentioned were, first, that the relatively slow growth of the Italian economy after 1966 limited the degree of industrial mobility in general and made for serious difficulties in recruiting firms to the complex. Secondly, the planners failed to anticipate adequately technological change in the industry and in particular changes in economies of scale. Thirdly, the complex was too much tied to the importance of economies of scale and neglected the multitude of other factors that determine the location of industry. Fourthly, the planners exaggerated the likely response of local suppliers, failing to realise that 'the entrepreneur is more important than the firm'. Fifthly, the state holding sector did not involve itself in the complex as much as might have been expected. In its conclusion, the mission was anxious to stress that the area had seen some development in engineering, even though not in accordance with the plan. Seeming, however, to miss completely the whole point of the exercise, they wrote: 'Certainly the results are not completely in line with the plan, but the regional population is more anxious for tangible results than the fact that these conform with the initial hypotheses.'

Looking down this list, the reasons for failure can be grouped into three sets. First, there are those involving developments that could not be accurately forecast – the downturn of the Italian economy is a case in point. Secondly, there are those which could be corrected in future similar plans, or at least some effort made to reduce their importance, e.g. exaggerated hopes for local industry, failure to take adequate account of technological change and perhaps also the lack of interest by the state holding sector. But thirdly, there are more fundamental factors; in particular the excessive importance that these complexes lay on economies of scale, and the problems of selecting principal units of sufficient narrowness to allow meaningful input analyses to be carried out.

Few would doubt that the basic idea behind these complexes is good, but the problems encountered in practice demand some major rethinking. Beyond their costs, and the planning of them is expensive, they can detract attention from alternative systems and methods of development, some of which could perhaps give similar results. One wonders, for example, how far greater selectivity in incentive systems could give some of the major benefits of the complex approach. Our own view is that complexes, and the interest in them, reflect the hope that they will provide a quick and easy solution to regional problems. Moreover, too often they are seen as *the* solution rather than simply as *one* means of resolving the regional problem. There is a great need to place them in perspective and to see them as just one of a range of measures, and certainly to put an end to any feeling that, either through complexes or indeed any other measures, there is any quick, almost magical, solution to regional problems.

6.4 The results of southern policy

It is never an easy task to interpret the results of regional policy, and the Italian case is more difficult than most. There is a plethora of data available for evaluation but the answers are rarely consistent. The use of different indices, different time periods and different assumptions can give a field day for those who want to indulge in polemic.

In a number of ways, however, there are grounds for saying that the southern problem has not diminished in magnitude over the postwar period. The regional problem indicators mentioned at the start of this chapter show disparities, or have values, that are not much different from those in the early 1950s. Indeed, in some ways the problem seems to have worsened. As we have seen, serious unemployment and under-employment remains, male activity rates have actually fallen, while net migration rose during the 1960s relative to the 1950s. Similarly, the vital national account differentials again indicate that the problem has barely ameliorated. This is shown in table 6.8, which provides data on gross regional expenditure over the period 1951–70. In respect of total gross regional expenditure the South now accounts for a slightly larger proportion of national expenditure than in 1951. This same measure on a *per capita* basis shows a similar slight improvement. A very interesting and startling improvement has, however, taken place with respect to gross southern expenditure per labour unit with an increase from some 79 per cent of the northern figures in 1951 to some 91 per cent in 1970 – the difference between this and the *per capita* differential reflects the low and more rapidly declining southern activity rates. But a point that can hardly be overstressed is that all these southern expenditure figures include a high and swiftly growing bill for net imports (from the North and abroad). Net imports into the South, at 456.2 milliard lire in 1951, were some 15 per cent of southern gross expenditure; by 1970 they were 3074 milliard lire, or nearly 19 per cent. During the 1960s net imports were equal to a massive 70 per cent or so of gross southern investment – a good measure of the region's continuing dependence on outside support. Without this support, the southern problem, at least in terms of income differentials, would have been much more serious and, indeed, would have grown substantially.

Table 6.8   Gross regional expenditure*: North and South

	1951 absolute figures	1970 absolute figures	1970 index (1951 = 100)	1951 South as % of North	1970 South as % of North
at current prices (milliard lire)					
North	7988.5	41,592.4	520.7		
South	2908.5	16,243.6	558.5	36.4	39.1
at 1963 prices (milliard lire)					
North	11,653.0	31,795.1	272.8		
South	4292.0	12,450.0	290.1	36.8	39.2
per head, current prices ('000 lire)					
North		268.4	1185.2	441.6	
South		164.8	837.3	508.1	61.4	70.6
per head, 1963 prices ('000 lire)					
North	391.5	906.0	231.4		
South	243.1	641.8	264.0	62.1	70.8
per labour unit, current prices ('000 lire)					
North	688.9	3202.8	464.9		
South	543.9	2919.3	536.7	79.0	91.1
per labour unit, 1963 prices ('000 lire)					
North	1004.8	2448.4	243.7		
South	802.7	2237.7	278.8	79.9	91.4

* Gross regional expenditure is consumption plus gross investment.

Sources: From data in ISTAT *Annuario di Contabilità Nazionale* (Rome, 1971); and ISTAT, *Occupati Presenti in Italia 1951–70* (Rome, 1971).

The fact that regional labour market and income differentials have not markedly diminished, in spite of twenty years of considerable resources and policies being devoted to the South, is not necessarily something to view with despair. It is undoubtedly the case that the situation would have been much worse without policy. Moreover, in many ways, it is perhaps remarkable that the underdeveloped South has been able to keep up with the very rapid growth in the much more advanced and developed North. More important than the North/South differentials is the growth performance of the South *per se* and the extent to which its economic structure and other features of its backwardness have been changed.

In fact, the structural changes in the South have been enormous. The heavy weighting of agriculture and the slight weighting of industry which, as we have seen, have been factors in the South's lack of development, have changed for the better. Agriculture, which accounted for some 34 per cent of southern gross domestic product at factor cost and current prices in 1951, was down to around 18 per cent by 1970, while industry rose from nearly 24 to 39 per cent over the same period. A similar structural revolution has taken place in respect of employment. In 1951 agricultural labour units represented some 52 per cent of the southern total, falling to 29 per cent by 1970. Part of this loss, amounting to 1.8 million labour units, was offset by an increase in industrial employment, and part by a growth in the tertiary sector. Industry employed nearly 23 per cent of total southern labour units in 1951 and some 32 per cent by 1970 – an increase of 792,000 labour units over the period. Overall, however, as we have seen, the industrial and service sectors were only just capable of absorbing the vast overflow from agriculture, with the result that total employment (in terms of labour units) hardly rose at all between 1951 and 1970. Taking 1951 as 100, the index for 1970 is 104. The total employment index has, in fact, hardly increased since 1956 when it was 103.1, and this explains why many of the southern labour market indicators have stubbornly refused to show any significant improvement.

In every sector, southern output and productivity have risen very considerably. In agriculture, gross domestic product at factor cost and constant prices increased by 62 per cent between 1951 and 1970; in industry it increased by 292 per cent and in the tertiary sector (excluding the public administration with a rise of 81 per cent) by 180 per cent. Considering the great outflow of labour from agriculture, and the small additions to the industrial and tertiary sector labour force, it is not surprising that productivity (gross domestic product at factor cost and constant prices per labour unit employed) rose enormously in most sectors. Agriculture tops the list with an increase of 178 per cent between 1951 and 1970; industry comes next at 164 per cent, followed by the tertiary sector with 84 per cent and finally the public administration with 19 per cent.

The changes in economic structure, together with the rapid growth of southern productivity, are not only important of themselves in giving a higher standard of living for the South; they also reflect other changes, many of which are a direct consequence of policy. In agriculture the productivity growth is partly a consequence of the increased size of farm but, more important, it is also a consequence of the greater use of mechanisation and fertilisers, better drainage systems, more plentiful supplies of water, and wider product markets, as well as the presence of non-agricultural jobs for the labour force, encouraging movement out of the overpopulated rural areas. In industry, the productivity advances reflect the entry of new firms and the growth and development of indigenous concerns – in part a consequence of regional incentives, in part a consequence of the greater market opportunities, but also a result of better education, both at the level of management and the labour force.

The results of southern policy have in many ways been impressive. 'The increase in income and change of economic structure in the area have been quantitatively substantial and certainly greater . . . than the southerners expected at the start of the extraordinary programme.'[46] Even so, the problem is nowhere near resolved. The South is a long way from being weaned-off assistance from the North, while its backward economic structure will remain, probably for many decades, incapable of employing the natural population increase.

6.5 Conclusions

The measures taken by the Italian government to improve the situation in the South have been, in general, laudable, often adventurous and have involved quite enormous resources and transfers. This is not to deny that there are aspects that are open to serious criticism. First, the size of farm created under the land reform schemes was often too small to be viable and normally involved poor land, while supplementary policies in the form of irrigation, drainage and afforestation were frequently long delayed.[47]* In consequence, 'almost 40 per cent of those peasants who were awarded land turned to non-agricultural activities and many of the new proprietors became so poverty-ridden that they actually abandoned the previously expropriated land'.[48] Secondly, too much of the early Cassa programme was devoted to agriculture and infrastructure and too little to industrial development. Thirdly, when meaningful industrial mobility incentives were put on offer, in the very late 1950s, the funds available were small relative to other countries and inadequate to implement the industrial development objectives set for the South; while their impact has been reduced both by the relatively frequent changes in their value and form and by the bureaucracy involved in their award.[49]* Moreover, the incentives have been limited largely to manufacturing industry and the service sector has been neglected – in spite of the potential that the latter offers for regional development. Fourthly, in common with other countries, the form and extent of regional policy has been based more on political factors and judgement than economic analysis. Certainly, as we have seen in chapter 1, there has been a growing consciousness of the economic benefits of southern policies, and indeed some quantification; but neither the data nor the analysis exist to evaluate the full transfer and resource costs and benefits of the policy in general or the cost effectiveness of individual measures. Finally, the southern industrial development policy has perhaps been too Anglo-Saxon and too heavily based on incentives. It appears to have been evolved 'as if the South was, as it effectively is, an hour's flight from Piedmont or Lombardy and not really in another continent'.[50] Incentives *per se* are passive and there is a case for saying that southern industrial development needs more positive policies; in particular more effort and resources to give technical and promotional advice to firms and to provide management training. This is especially important for the small firms which, as we have seen, predominate in the South. This is not to say that bodies and schemes do not exist to pursue these goals. They do, in the form of IASM and various Cassa and other management training schemes, but the funds involved are slight. Similarly, with labour training there has been considerable neglect. The general labour training system in Italy is, as we have seen in chapter 1, very poor, and, though some special schemes are operated in the South, the resources available are very small. And yet the need for more and better training facilities is clear. Recent evidence suggests that the major operational difficulty that firms experience in the South is the shortage of qualified labour, followed by insufficient working capital and inadequate skills of the labour employed.[51]

It is important to note that a major part of southern industrialisation has come not through the operation of the standard industrial mobility measures, but rather through the legal obligation of the state holding sector to locate substantial proportions of its investments in the South (though they do receive the same incentives as private firms). We have already seen that between 1958 and 1969 some 34 per cent of southern gross industrial investment was accounted for by the state holding sector. But the use of the sector for this kind of development does have its drawbacks, not least in that it has primarily involved large, capital-intensive units. It is too extreme to call these 'cathedrals in the desert', but at the same time they have often encouraged less ancillary development than was hoped or expected. Their impact could be greater, and southern industrialisation could proceed much faster, if more attention were paid to the promotion of the smaller, especially indigenous, firms. The difficulties of doing this are enormous, and the political benefits in the short run not likely to be as great as those that arise from the location of a big plant; but the effort would be well worth while. The recent moves to give more and better incentives to the small firms are welcome but will have little success if not backed up by more positive and promotional measures.

We have already seen that in many ways the results of southern policy have been impressive. The disparities between North and South still remain, but in absolute terms the growth rate has been extremely high and the economic structure has changed substantially. Even though southern 'prosperity' is still heavily supported by transfers from the North, the South is without doubt in a far stronger economic position than twenty or even ten years ago. These improvements have, however, been gained at great economic and other costs. In this latter context the human and social costs of migration – an inevitable consequence of southern growth and structural change – have been very large. In part, this can be passed off with a shrug and the old proverb that one can't make omelettes without breaking eggs. But this is too fatalistic a view. The point is that appropriate policies could ease some of the problems associated with migration. A very serious criticism of Italian regional policy-makers is that, although they have introduced plans and laudable policies for growth, they have been slow in adopting apt measures to ease its consequences. Governments have fought shy of giving financial assistance to migrants and have spent insignificant sums in non-growth areas. Indeed, as we have seen, policy has tended to be directed at the development of specified growth areas where there exists a distinct potential for the rapid expansion of tourism, agriculture or industry. A not inconsiderable proportion of the population (more than 10 per cent) lives outside these growth areas. The funds spent by the Cassa on the non-growth areas have been slight, while the ordinary administration, overwhelmed by the problems in the big centres and dogged by its own ineptitude, has also tended to neglect them. For many such areas the future is bleak and certainly there are few prospects for growth. This should not, however, mean that they are neglected by planners or policy.[52]* And yet it is interesting that, while policies and plans for growth abound, there are few for decline – aimed, for example, at helping or even encouraging those who want to leave, ensuring a basic minimum of social and infrastructure services for those who remain, and perhaps financially compensating them for the losses involved in living in a declining area. Any such ideas would of course meet with political objections and would provide intriguing economic questions. The political objections would be based on a mixture of emotion and misunderstanding, and in particular on a view that such policies are not humanitarian. But this is far from the case. Few would doubt the great human and social problems which would arise if growth were not planned and controlled, and yet there is no similar recognition in the case of decline.

There is no easy solution to the problem of the South, and certainly no quick one. The creators of the Cassa anticipated that the South could be 'solved' within a short period – perhaps a decade. Few observers now would be thinking in terms of less than a half century. In the meantime, and indeed a necessary precondition for the resolution of the problem, migration will continue (and probably grow), both within the South and to areas outside it. This will add to the urbanisation process and to the problems we have already noted.

An important feature of recent Italian growth is the fact that it seems to be slowing down. In one way this is consoling, since on past experience the income per head differential between North and South has tended to diminish at times of slow growth and increase during periods of rapid growth.[53] But the important point is that these periods of narrowing were also years when the South itself grew slowly and when industrial investment in particular was slack. It is a well-known fact that industrial mobility and expansion takes place predominantly at a time of boom – encouraged by a shortage of capacity. Certainly, southern industrialisation suffered a severe setback during the 1970–73 recession, especially as this coincided with serious cost inflation thus reducing the possibility of self-finance within and outside the South. As we have seen in chapter 5, retained earnings are a major and vital source of industrial capital – a source of 'risk capital which cannot be replaced by bigger credit concessions'.[54] At this stage in the South's development it is its absolute growth rate rather than the differential between North and South that is important. It is far better that the South grows rapidly, even though more slowly than the North, than that it grows slowly even though more rapidly than the North. But beyond this, any slowdown in southern, or indeed Italian, development will carry with it dangers other than those simply of an economic nature. The migratory flow into the northern and southern cities is by no means wholly a consequence of the economic opportunities existing in those cities. It is in part an attempt to escape from rural life and in anticipation of finding a job in the city. If the expansion of jobs does not match the growth of urban population the situation could become critical. There have already been troubles in some cities in protest against the lack of urban infrastructure. If to this shortcoming was added a lack of jobs the position would obviously be much more serious – a point that is increasingly being accepted by the authorities and one which, among other things, must ensure an intensification of southern development policy.

Notes to chapter 6

1.   An excellent source of historical statistics on the South is Svimez *Un Secolo di Statistiche: Nord e Sud 1861–1961* (Rome, 1961). A good anthology of writing on the 'southern question' is A. Carrà *Orientamenti e Testimonianze sulla Questione Meridionale* Trapani: Célèbres (1965). There is a vast number of books and articles on the economic history of the South, but four that we consider to be very useful are C. Rodano *Mezzogiorno e Sviluppo Economico* Bari: Laterza (1954); P. Saraceno *La Mancata Unificazione Economica Italiana a Cento Anni dall'Unificazione Politica* Rome: Svimez (1961); A. Benzoni 'Il Mezzogiorno nello Stato Italiano' *Il Veltro* No. 6 (1962); R. Eckhaus 'The North-South Differential in Italian Economic Development' *The Journal of Economic History* (September 1961).

2.   Eckhaus, op. cit.; and *Un Secolo di Statistiche,* op. cit.

3.   See M. Grindrod *The New Italy* London: Royal Institute of Economic Affairs (1947), p. 67.

4.   For comparisons of the regional problems in the various EEC countries see Commission of the European Communities *Report on the Regional Problems in the Enlarged Community* (Brussels, 1973).

5.   Comitato dei Ministri per il Mezzogiorno *Studi Monografici sul Mezzogiorno* (Rome, 1971), p. 76.

6.   ibid., p. 75.

7.   *Studi Monografici sul Mezzogiorno* (1970), op. cit., p. 67.

8.   *Studi Monografici sul Mezzogiorno* (1971), op. cit., pp. 66–7.

9.   All the information below on southern emigration abroad is taken from *Studi Monografici sul Mezzogiorno* (1970), op. cit.

10.   ibid., pp. 69–70.

11.   *Studi Monografici sul Mezzogiorno* (1972), op. cit.

12.   Unione Italiana delle Camere di Commercio Industria Artigianato e Agricoltura, *I Conti Economici Regionali 1963–1969* (Rome, 1970).

13.   For further details on provincial incomes in the South see G. Tagliacarne 'Che cosa c'e di nuovo nella dinamica economica del Mezzogiorno' *Nuovo Mezzogiorno* Nos 1–2 (1972), reprinted in *Informazioni Svimez* No. 6 (March, 1972).

14.   The figures used below in the discussion of intra-regional migration between 1951 and 1961 are taken from Cafiero, op. cit. They are based on 'present' rather than 'resident' population and are not therefore strictly comparable with earlier figures for the South as a whole.

15.   *Studi Monografici sul Mezzogiorno* (1970), op. cit.

16.   Over the period 1962–68, for example, the communes of Carapelle, Calvisio and Rocca Pia in the province of Aquila; S Maria del Molise and Las Plassas in Cagliari saw net emigration rates of between 64 and 69 per thousand of the population. This meant that some 45 per cent of the population emigrated over the period. But these are not the worst. The commune of Fracavilla Angilola in the province of Catanzaro, for example, saw 60 per cent of its population emigrate. *Studi Monografici sul Mezzogiorno* (1970), op. cit., p. 59.

17.   J. Meynaud *Rapporto sulla Classe Dirigente Italiana* Rome: Giuffrè (1966), p. 137.

18.   For an excellent series of articles on migrants in the northern triangle, see G. Pellicciari (ed.) *L'Immigrazione nel Triangolo Industriale* Rome: Franco/Angeli (1970).

19.   B. Jossa 'Una Politica per le Piccole e le Medie Imprese' *Rassegna Economica* (1971), p. 631.

20.   *Annuario di Contabilità Nazionale 1971,* op. cit.

21.   ISTAT *Occupati Presenti in Italia: 1951–1970* (Rome, 1971).

22.   For a description and critique of shift/share analysis, see D. Mackay 'Industrial Structure and Regional Growth: A Methodological Problem' *Scottish Journal of Political Economy* (June 1968).

23.   G. De Meo *Evoluzione e Prospettive delle Forze di Lavoro in Italia* Rome: ISTAT (1970), p. 132.

24. For a good description of early Southern policy see A. Servidio *Il Nodo Meridionale* Rome: Edizioni Scientifiche Italiane (1972).

25. K. Allen and M. MacLennan *Regional Problems and Policies in Italy and France* London: Allen and Unwin (1971), p. 43.

26. Servidio, op. cit. pp. 46–7.

27. Allen and MacLennan, op. cit., p. 45.

28. G. Mammarella *Italy After Fascism* Indiana: University of Notre Dame Press (1966), p. 231.

29. V. de Falco 'Nuove Occasioni di Sviluppo per l'Agricoltura' *Rassegna Economica* (1972), p. 762

30. F. Pilloton *Effetti Moltiplicativi degli Investimenti della Cassa per il Mezzogiorno*, Rome: Guiffrè (1960).

31. For details of the industrial aspects of the 1957 law (and the later 1965 law), see Allen and MacLennan, op. cit.

32. See Ministero del Bilancio e della Programmazione Economica 'Programma 1966–70: Obiettivi e Resultati' *Programma Economica Nazionale 1971–75*, p. 35.

33. An extremely useful document covering the 1971 law together with the subsequent norms for its implementation is IASM *Direttive e Norme di Applicazione della Legge 853 per il Mezzogiorno* (Rome, 1972). Much of the information below has been taken from this source.

34. The placing of southern planning and policy directly under CIPE is not as dramatic as it might at first seem. Since 1965 the earlier Committee of Ministers had been obliged to submit their southern plans to CIPE.

35. Loans for investments above 12 milliard lire could not exceed 50 per cent of the amount allocated for the first 12 milliard lire. This was changed in 1968 when fixed investments above 12 milliard lire could receive loans to cover up to 50 per cent of total investment if specified conditions, though these were vague, were met.

36. Fixed investments between 6 milliard lire and 12 milliard lire could not receive a grant in excess of 10 per cent. Initially, investments above 12 milliard lire could only receive a grant for the amount above 12 milliard lire equal to a maximum of 50 per cent of the grants given for the first 12 milliard lire. The situation was not therefore dissimilar to that for loans and, as with loans, in 1968 the position was changed so that investments above 12 milliard lire could receive a maximum grant of 12 per cent.

37. In practice, this covers much of the South – some 80 per cent of southern communes, though, since it largely excludes the main urban conurbations, a far lower proportion of the southern population.

38. Small firms, and indeed all the other size categories, are eligible for loans of fifteen years' duration if the plant is new, or ten years if it is an extension or part of a process of modernisation. In July 1972 the rate of interest for loans was fixed at 6 per cent for large firms and 4 per cent for the rest.

39. For details of the industries and areas especially favoured in the fixing of the loans and grants, see *Direttive e Norme*, op. cit.

40. An informal control system was, however, introduced in 1967 whereby large firms were invited to present their investment plans to CIPE and, through a process of 'plan bargaining' were evaluated by CIPE to check how they fitted in with overall government development programmes, including those for the South. For a discussion of early debates on a system of control in the North see M. Barbato 'Lo Sviluppo del Mezzogiorno: Nuova Fase Operativa' *Rassegna Economica* (1971), pp. 145–59.

41. The five bodies are (1) INSUD (Nuovo Initiative per il Sud), financed by the Cassa and EFIM; (2) FINAM (Finanziaria Agricola per il Mezzogiorno), financed by the Cassa; (3) ESPI (Ente Siciliano Promozione Industriale), financed by the region of Sicily; (4) SFIRS (Società Finanziaria Industriale Rinascità Sardegna), financed by Sardinia; (5) SPI (Promozione e Sviluppo Industriale), financed by IRI. See IASM *La Nuova Legge per il Mezzogiorno*, pp. 34–5.

42. A description of the plan and its objectives can be found in IASM *Studio per la Promozione di un Polo Industriale di Sviluppo in Italia Meridionale*, and Allen and MacLennan, op. cit., pp. 318–27.

43. W. Lever 'Manufacturing Linkages and the Search for Suppliers and Markets' in I. Hamilton (ed.) *The Industrial Firm and Location Decisions* London: Wiley (1974).

44. The results of a recent Confindustria survey would, however, suggest that too much stress should not be placed on linkages in the normal firm's location decision. The survey found that only 9.3 per cent of the firms interviewed mentioned the presence of industries using their output as being among the three most important reasons for their choice of zone in the South and a mere 4.3 per cent mentioned the presence of industries producing products used by the firm. Of all the factors analysed, these two were, in fact, the least important. The most important, in order, were: availability of land, proximity of final markets, proximity of raw materials, good infrastructure, industrial water, availability of qualified labour, cheap or free land from the local authority, proximity to energy and the presence of a growth area. A further question, on the difficulties of running the plant, found that only 11.4 per cent mentioned problems in getting intermediate products – the least important of the problems. The most important, again in order of importance, were: shortages of qualified labour, insufficient working capital, inadequate skills of the labour employed, inadequate infrastructure, delays in the award of finance, difficulties in securing raw materials, inadequate markets and poor public services. See Confederazione Generale dell'Industria Italiana *Per un Rilancio della Politica di Industrializzazione del Mezzogiorno,* (Rome, 1971).

45. Allen and MacLennan, op. cit.

46. P. Saraceno 'Il Sud nel Sistema Economico Italiano ed Europeo' *Almanacca del Mezzogiorno* Bari: Fiera del Levante (1972), p. 12.

47. Moreover, the expropriation policy was not as widespread as originally envisaged. 'By law over 8 million hectares of land in the whole country were to be redistributed over the next ten years, but up to 1960 only about 8 per cent had actually been expropriated and not much more had been affected in the following decade – vested interests and practical obstacles had proved too great'. E. Wiskemann *Italy since 1945* London: Macmillan (1971), p. 19.

48. J. La Palombara *Italy: the Politics of Planning* Syracuse, N.Y.: Syracuse University Press (1966), p. 139.

49. Although the Cassa *per se* is freer of the stranglehold of bureaucracy than is the public administration, it is not responsible for all the southern development programme. Most industrialists operating in the South are highly critical of the degree of bureaucracy to which they are subjected. In a recent survey of firms in the South a question concerned with difficulties encountered in setting up or expanding gave the result that delays in the concession of finance was the major problem (mentioned by 48.4 per cent of interviewees). Other difficulties, many reflecting inefficient bureaucracy, were as follows (the percentage mentioning each factor is in brackets): excessive bureaucracy and intransigence (44.6 per cent); delays in conceding grant (41.9 per cent); delays in the payment of finance (34.3 per cent); deficient infrastructure (22.7 per cent); difficulties in obtaining incentives (21.6 per cent); delays in the completion of contracts (19.2 per cent); delays in being connected to services and other infrastructure (16.8 per cent); difficulties in getting land (9.2 per cent); delays in obtaining financial guarantees (8.1 per cent). For more details see *Per un Rilancio della Politica di Industrializzazione del Mezzogiorno,* op. cit.

50. C. Zappulli 'Il Sud nella Valutazione del Mondo Economico' *Almanacco del Mezzogiorno* op. cit., p. 53.

51. *Per un Rilancio della Politica di Industrializzazione del Mezzogiorno,* op. cit.

52. Interest in the so-called areas of particular depression has recently grown but the discussion is still, in our view, too largely oriented towards their growth rather than their decline. For a very good study of these areas see S. Cafiero *Le Zone Particolarmente Depresse nella Politica per il Mezzogiorno* Rome: Svimez (1973).

53. See I. Santore 'Un quadro statistico del Mezzogiorno' *Almanacco del Mezzogiorno,* op. cit.

54. 'Il Sud nel Sistema Economico Italiano ed Europeo', op. cit., p. 15.

CHAPTER 7

The State Holding Sector
and its Role
in Italian Development

The [White] Knight said . . . 'It's my own invention'. (Alice through the Looking Glass)

THE state holding sector is an important part of the Italian economy and has played a major and growing role in its development. Although primarily engaged in the key industries of steel, heavy engineering, ship-building, telephone services, banking, hydrocarbons and heavy chemicals, it has in recent years also developed strongly in other areas – vehicles, motorways, urban infrastructure, supermarkets, electronics, computer software and nuclear engineering. There are now few sectors of the Italian economy in which the state holding companies do not operate. Many well-known products or concerns are within the system – Alfa Romeo cars, Ducati motorcycles, Alitalia, the Autostrada del Sole, AGIP petroleum, RAI television and radio, Cinecittà and the Banco di Roma. There are some 350 state holding firms in total, employing around 510,000 people in Italy (and a further 22,000 abroad). Their total investment in 1972 was around 1915 milliard lire.

In all there are six state holding groups, each organised and run by an *ente autonomo di gestione* (autonomous management agency). In many ways the *enti* can be viewed as holding companies. Four of these six groups or *enti* are of secondary importance: EAGAT (Ente Autonomo di Gestione per le Aziende Termali), involved in managing and developing spas and associated investment; Ente Autonomo di Gestione per il Cinema, operating in the making and distribution of films; EGAM (Ente Gestione Aziende Minerarie), active in mining and the production of ferrous metals, particularly specialised steels; and, finally, EFIM (Ente Partici-pazione e Finanziamento Industrie Manifatturiere). EFIM, the biggest of these second-order groups, operates in a wide range of manufacturing industries and has been particularly active in buying into, and developing, medium-sized firms, especially in the South.

These four second-order groups are nowhere near as large as the two major groups, IRI (Istituto per la Ricostruzione Industriale) and ENI

(Ente Nazionale Idrocarburi). Total employment in the four is only some three-fifths of that in ENI firms and around 12 per cent of IRI's employment. Their annual fixed investments are about two-fifths of ENI's and one-seventh of those made by IRI. IRI and ENI clearly dominate the state holding sector. They operate in a wide range of fields, though are heavily concentrated in specific sectors. IRI's main activities involve steel, engineering, electronics, shipbuilding, telecommunications, shipping, airlines, radio and television, *autostrade* and banking. ENI is more *monosettoriale* and is primarily engaged in oil and gas prospecting, petroleum refining, transport and distribution and heavy chemicals, though with minor interests in nuclear energy, textiles and engineering.

The state holding sector has grown rapidly over the postwar period and particularly during the 1960s and early 1970s. Taking 1953 as 100, employment in the sector was 115 by 1950 and 195 by 1971, while investment (with 1955 as 100) rose to 218 by 1960 and a massive 994 by 1971. In both investment and employment the sector has grown faster than comparable total national figures and is, therefore, now inevitably a more important part of the economy. In 1953 the sector's employment accounted for 3.5 per cent of full-time non-agricultural employees, 6.0 per cent of full-time industrial employees and 8.0 per cent of industrial employment excluding construction. By 1970 these proportions were 4.0, 7.0, and 7.8 per cent respectively.

The organisational and control structure of the state holding system is discussed in detail later, but some prefatory remarks are worth while. In simple terms, the system has a pyramid organisational structure. At the top is the Ministry of State Holdings, which issues general directives to the *enti* and is accountable to Parliament for their activities. Below the Ministry are the six *enti,* each of which has the task of ensuring the implementation of these directives by the firms it controls. At the base of the pyramid are the firms and enterprises themselves in which the *enti,* directly or indirectly, hold a controlling interest. In the case of both IRI and ENI these firms are organised into various sectors (e.g. shipbuilding, telephones and engineering) and operate under a sub-holding company which has responsibility to the *enti* for the activities of the firms within its sector.

As we shall see, the state holding sector is a unique combination of public and private initiative. The *enti* themselves are, from a financial viewpoint, wholly government-controlled in the sense that the government provides all their equity capital, through a so-called endowment fund, although this fund is also meant to cover the sector's social or national interest interventions. The layers below the *enti* can, and do, seek equity capital from the public, though the *enti* maintain a controlling interest. Given the fragmented nature of private shareholding in many firms, such control can be secured with as little as 15 per cent of the equity capital.

The state holding sector differs from the Italian nationalised industries (railways and electricity generation and distribution) in that, first, it has access to a wider range of finance (the nationalised industries are almost wholly government-financed), and secondly, related, it has a greater degree of freedom. Like the British nationalised industries, those in Italy are directly accountable to a minister and subjected to considerable control in their investments and general strategy (though, an interesting difference, not in their pricing policies). This degree of control is not present in the state holding sector.

In relation to the economy, the state holding system is so large that, by its size alone, it has an important impact. The prime aim of this chapter is to look at the major features of the system, how it is controlled and organised, and its contribution to Italian development. Because of the dominant importance of IRI and ENI, we have concentrated largely on these two groups. The chapter is in six parts. The first two sections, which are largely descriptive, trace the origins and developments of IRI and ENI. Section 7.3 examines how the state holding system is organised and controlled. Section 7.4 is concerned with the sector's sources of finance, while section 7.5 looks at a number of ways in which its efficiency can be gauged. Finally, the sixth section examines the sector's rationale and the various roles it has played in Italian development.

7.1   IRI[1]

IRI was created in January 1933, in response to a serious banking crisis, with the prime objective 'of completing the organisation of credit in relation to the technical, economic and financial re-organisation of the country's industrial activity'.[2] It was initially organised in two independent sections, an industrial finance section (Sezione Finanziamenti Industriali) and a holding section (Sezione Smobilizzi Industriali). The former was created to give long-term finance to Italian private firms, while the holding section had the dual role of giving financial assistance to banks in difficulties and managing those stocks and shares which, during earlier banking salvage and *risanamenti* operations, had fallen into the hands of the State. In some ways the holding section of IRI was just another of many institutes 'generated by the banking crises which had afflicted the country after the end of the First World War'.[3]

There can be little doubt that when IRI was created, like its predecessors, it was seen as being of a temporary, though more comprehensive, nature. It was a body having an 'emergency character'.[4] The big deposit banks were in grave financial difficulties; their earlier credits to industry, particularly after 1929, were almost worthless, and they were not in a position to extend their lending. IRI was aimed at disengaging the banks from industry while, at the same time, through the finance section, taking on their earlier roles.

The finance section of IRI did not, however, operate for very long. The greater part of its loans, some 84 per cent, were to companies or groups in which the holding section of IRI was involved. Improved economic conditions in 1934 and 1935 reduced its relevance. In 1936 it was wound up, its role being taken over by the large credit institute, IMI (discussed in detail in chapter 5).

As already noted, the major early task of IRI's holding section was that of disengaging the banks from medium- and long-term investments through the purchase of these assets from the banks. The price paid was not based on market value but was one that would enable the banks to cover their deposits and other liabilities. The greater part of this operation was completed in 1934. Many of the assets involved were in firms that in turn held controlling interests in the banks themselves, and one of the consequences was that IRI found itself in control of the three most important Italian commercial banks – the Banca Commerciale Italiana, Credito Italiano and the Banco di Roma.

It was envisaged that IRI would sell off its newly acquired assets as the capital market improved, and in the period 1933–36 it did in fact dispose of nearly 50 per cent more assets than it purchased. However, in June 1937, IRI, then made up solely of the holding section, was declared a permanent body. Opinions still differ as to why this step was taken. For some observers it was a decision that reflected the personal view of IRI's leaders and their influence on Mussolini. 'It is rumored in Italy that men like Alberto Beneduce, Francesco Giordani and Donato Menichella, who controlled IRI, were able to prevail upon il Duce not to liquidate the state holdings.'[5] For others it stemmed from the autarkistic and military aims of Fascism or, quite differently, 'perhaps the most absent-minded act of nationalization in history'.[6] The well-known Italian economist Saraceno sees the decision as coinciding with a phase of national policy – 'the idea that the state must actively interest itself in the development of those productive sectors which largely determine the rhythm and progress of the country', and that IRI was 'the ideal instrument for the attainment of these new objectives'.[7] The preamble to the legislation setting up IRI as a permanent body talks of more specific, Fascist-inspired roles, particularly in respect of new activities, which it could assume 'when these are inherent to the defence of the country or the fulfilment of the policy of economic autarky or industrial and agricultural improvements in Italian East Africa'. IRI was certainly tied more closely to the regime. It was to run its operations 'according to the political economic directives of the regime', was gradually to rid itself of those 'holdings and activities which the state has no interest in conserving'; while investments and sales 'in excess of the value of ten million lire' had to be approved by the minister of finance. Most of the men involved in running IRI were appointed by the State.

Inevitably, the three-year period 1937–39, following the declaration of permanence, saw a change in strategy relative to IRI's first three years. Asset sales were substantially cut back, though they continued to exceed new investments. It sold off quite considerable amounts of its holdings in the electrical industry, textiles, agriculture and real estate, as well as a number of foreign investments. On the other side of the coin, substantial investments were made in shipping, engineering and steel – all of which were vital to the Fascist interests of the time and had been spelled out in the 1937 declaration of permanence. By 1939 some 21 per cent of IRI holdings were in the steel industry, 14 per cent in engineering (mainly heavy) and 19 per cent in shipping. These represented considerable increases relative to 1934 when the proportions were 13, 7 and 6 per cent respectively.[8]

By the eve of the Second World War, IRI was by any standards a large group, and controlled quite considerable proportions of Italian industry. It accounted for some 77 per cent of national pig iron output, 45 per cent of steel production, 75 per cent of metal tube output, 67 per cent of iron ore mined, 80 per cent of shipbuilding, 22 per cent of aircraft production, 39 per cent of car production, 50 per cent of arms and ammunition output, 23 per cent of engineering output and about 90 per cent of shipping, as well as owning three of the five major Italian telephone companies.[9] That such control should have been secured in a brief six-year period is remarkable.

Largely for administrative reasons, IRI's various interests were grouped under a number of IRI-controlled *finanziarie* or sub-holding companies. STET was created in 1933 for telephones, Finmare in 1936 for shipping and Finsider in 1937 for iron and steel. The number of these *finanziarie* was extended after the war with the creation of Finmeccanica (engineering) in 1948, Finelettrica (electricity) in 1952 and Fincantieri (shipbuilding) in 1959. Previously these sectors were under direct IRI control.

The war was a disaster for IRI, as indeed it was for Italy as a whole. In the early years of the war it extended its activities in war industries, particularly engineering and chemicals, and sold off more of its textile, real estate and agricultural holdings. This increased gearing to war production was to make for serious difficulties in the postwar period. But in more immediate terms, IRI suffered greatly through war damage because of the nature and location of its activities. The damage caused was 'exceptionally grave in consequence of the fact that IRI interests were particularly strong in the sectors of merchant shipping, which emerged decimated from the war; of pig iron whose plants located for the greater part on the Mediterranean, found themselves immediately in the combat zone; of heavy engineering which was a particularly important target for aerial offensives, expropriation, sabotage and destruction; of electrical and telephone industries in the Centre/South, an area which saw the most prolonged war action'.[10] In more specific terms, some 90 per cent of IRI's shipping and iron and steel capacity, 40 per cent of its electricity capacity and 15 per cent of its telephone capacity was destroyed.[11]

IRI, then, ended the war with considerably reduced productive capacity, and with much of what remained being in war products, or not strictly relevant to postwar conditions, while its labour force was well in excess of its needs, partially reflecting the 'humane policy of IRI leaders, employing men to avoid their conscription or deportation to Germany in the years of the Nazi occupation from 1943 to 1945'.[12]

In view of IRI's Fascist origins and its contribution to the war effort, it is perhaps not surprising that discussions on IRI's future commenced almost immediately the war was ended – discussions that centred around the basic questions of whether it should be dismantled, and perhaps returned to private enterprise, or whether it should be maintained, and if the latter, how it should be controlled. The first of many inquiries along these lines took place in 1946–47, conducted by the Economic Commission to the Constituent Assembly. The evidence submitted reflected a great range of views towards IRI, including one that it was 'the greatest immorality that exists because it gets money when it wants at the price it wants'.[13] In general, however, it was recognised that the return of IRI's holdings to private enterprise was quite out of the question. Italy's postwar capital markets could not have absorbed any large-scale disbanding of IRI and many of its companies were anyway so unprofitable that the private sector would not have taken them at any price. In addition it was appreciated that only an IRI could operate without the need to resort to large-scale redundancy and hence avoid adding to the unemployed.

The economic situation in the immediate postwar years was so acute, and the task of replacing IRI fraught with such short-term dangers, that all political parties, including the Liberals, were obliged to accept the *status quo*. In 1948 IRI was given new statutes, preserving for it those activities which it already held and, reflecting a desire for greater control, placing it under the surveillance of an inter-ministerial committee. How much control has actually been exercised over IRI during the postwar years is something to which we return later. For the present we need only note that the 1948 statutes meant an acceptance of the continuation of IRI. Since then, as we shall see, it has expanded its activities and roles, making itself an increasingly invaluable tool of Italian growth and development.

IRI's postwar recovery was made especially difficult by the extent of the wartime damage and the general shortages of materials and equipment, compounded by the lack of organisational and administrative stability within IRI itself – due in no small part to the immediate postwar uncertainty about its future. Between 1945 and 1948 there was 'organisational chaos'.[14] It was operating without statutes and under a variety of leaders and systems. 'Initiative was left entirely to the Directors-General of the financial companies responsible for the various sectors within IRI, and frequently devolved, through lack of authority, to lower levels. There was, in consequence, no overall plan for reconstruction.'[15]

In spite of these difficulties, most of the IRI sectors had, by 1948, recovered their prewar capacity and were set for continuing, rapid and healthy growth. An important exception was engineering (including shipbuilding). Having been intensively engaged in war output, it was for many years to be a heavy millstone. Employment in this sector was not only large (at 100,000 in the immediate postwar years and accounting for a half of IRI's total employment), it was also heavily geographically concentrated, in Genoa, Naples, Trieste and, to a more limited extent, Milan. At this time the best solution from IRI's viewpoint would probably have been a major restructuring of the engineering sector involving a considerable closure programme and, associated, substantial redundancies. IRI's organisational difficulties would have put problems in the way of any such radical change, but beyond this the government had in 1946 directed that plants should not be closed down, but rather that reconversion and reconstruction should take place within the existing units as far as possible.

Converting from swords to ploughshares is never easy. In the case of IRI engineering it was both difficult and slow. In the shipyards the problem of converting to civil shipbuilding was made more intractable by the industry's uncompetitiveness in foreign markets – a consequence of overmanning and subsequent high labour costs (and both largely a result of the no-redundancy directive), combined with high steel costs following from the substantial degree of protection given to Italian (largely IRI) steel production. In the rest of the engineering sector the problems were no less severe. The domestic market was not capable of absorbing great increases in heavy engineering products, and yet this was the direction in which much of the previous military engineering capacity could be most easily converted. Nor could overseas markets offer any great prospects in this area, for reasons that were not dissimilar to those which affected shipbuilding exports.

In the period up to 1948 (and indeed beyond) the engineering sector made enormous losses and absorbed, in an uneconomic fashion, quite considerable proportions of IRI's investments. In the four years 1945–48 it accounted for some 73 per cent of total IRI net investment. However, it should be noted that this so-called investment was 'used for the greater part to maintain the pay to a labour force for which there was not the possibility of economic employment'.[16]

In 1948 the engineering sector, including shipbuilding, was put under the control of a *finanziaria* – Finmeccanica. This was given similar roles to the *finanziarie* already existing in other sectors: to co-ordinate the engineering sector's development and to give financial, technical and commercial help to the companies under its control.

Since then the engineering sector's problems have to some degree been slowly resolved, though the shipyards (now split off under a new *finanziaria,* Fincantieri) never really, except during the 1972–73 ship-building boom, became profitable or competitive – in no small part a result of union and local opposition to rationalisation. The engineering sector *per se* has been more successful, though it moved only slowly into a break-even situation (with the marked exception of Alfa Romeo, which, accounting for 40–45 per cent of Finmeccanica sales, became profitable in 1953 and has paid out dividends since 1966). Again, union pressures have impeded the implementation of radical schemes of reorganisation and the sector still holds a number (some half-dozen) of extremely un-profitable firms. The other twenty-five or so firms are, however, making regular if modest profits.

For IRI as a whole the period following on from the immediate post-war reconstruction has been one of great change and expansion. Between 1948 and 1972 employment rose by 93 per cent from 233,000 to 451,000 while sales grew some thirteenfold, from 348 milliard lire to 4678 milliard lire. Fixed investment increased fifteenfold between 1950 and 1972, from 103 milliard lire to 1527 milliard lire. In all cases, these rates of growth have been faster than in comparable areas of the national economy. But beyond such global indications of IRI's growth there are a number of other important changes which took place after the immediate postwar reconstruction period, and four in particular. First, IRI moved into new fields; secondly, it located a growing proportion of its development in southern Italy; thirdly, it slowly dropped its role as a hospital for sick firms; and fourthly, it lost control of the important electricity sector. These changes are now treated below in a generalised fashion. An analysis in depth of the issues involved is presented later, particularly in section 7.6.

In the post-reconstruction period, IRI took on a number of new sectors and interests – airlines, *autostrade,* urban infrastructure, television and electronics. In addition it gained control of virtually the whole of the telephone sector. We want now to have a brief look at each of these developments in turn.

The foundations of the Italian postwar airline industry were laid in 1946 when the United Kingdom, the United States and Italy co-operated to create two Italian airlines. The first was Alitalia, to operate primarily on international routes, and owned 40 per cent by BEA and 60 per cent by Italy. The great majority of this latter holding was in the hands of the

Italian State with a small proportion held by IRI. Secondly, there was the LAI (Linee Aeree Italiane), flying domestic routes, 40 per cent of which was owned by TWA and the rest, again, by the Italian State. In point of fact IRI managed the State's shares in both companies and these arrangements continued until 1957 when Alitalia and LAI were merged, TWA and BEA's shares bought out, and the resultant company handed over to IRI. In 1964 Alitalia set up a new subsidiary company ATI (Aero. Trasporti Italiana), which, like LAI, was to operate solely on domestic routes, particularly to and from southern Italy. The company has been run at a loss but has made a real contribution to southern development.

IRI's entry into the Italian motorway (*autostrade*) programme did not come until 1955, when the great expansion of road transport in the early 1950s forced the government to give thought to a major programme of motorway construction.[17] There were doubts about whether the government agency for national and major provincial roads, ANAS (Azienda Nazionale Autonoma Strade Statale), with its problems of securing long-term finance, was capable of developing such a network. Toll motorways under private concerns were an alternative. In 1955, therefore, the proposed network was offered on a concessionary basis (for thirty years) to private ventures. IRI fought for and received the great Autostrada del Sole running from Milan to Naples. This, and later concessions, were operated through the IRI company Società Concessioni e Costruzioni Autostrade, set up in 1956. In later allocations, during the 1960s, IRI got further stretches of motorway construction and management allocated to it. For its part, ANAS ended up with only a relatively small portion of the motorway network and much of this involved unprofitable southern stretches. IRI did not, however, only take over profitable sections. In 1968 it took the unprofitable Bari, Taranto, Sibari route. IRI's efforts in the motorway field have been impressive. It has developed its network largely on time and efficiently, and has played an important role as a pace-setter for other groups, including ANAS. By 1971 some 44 per cent of *autostrade* in use was IRI-owned.

IRI's ventures into urban infrastructure are of very recent origin and grew to some extent out of its motorway interests. In 1966 Infrasud was created, to build and manage a tangential relief motorway for Naples, and since then other more minor IRI companies have been set up to operate in town redevelopment and urban transport programmes. In 1967 Italstat (Società Italiana per le Infrastrutture e l'Assetto del Territorio) was created with the task of controlling Infrasud and IRI's other infrastructure companies. It is a cross between a *finanziaria* and a consultancy company. Much of Italstat's efforts are in the South. IRI's potential role in urban development is very great given, as we have already seen, the poverty of Italian local authorities, both in financial and planning terms, and the great urban revolution taking place in Italy with enormous inflows of people into the major towns.

Italian radio broadcasting up to 1952 was operated on a concessionary basis by RAI, which was itself controlled by an IRI electricity company (SIP). In 1952, when the concession came up for renewal, IRI took direct control, holding 75 per cent of the shares, SIP being left with the remainder. This takeover coincided with the development of television services (started on a regular basis in 1954) and the associated great demand for capital. The 1952 concession was due to expire in 1972 but the decision was then postponed to the end of 1973.[18]* In its operations RAI has had the South firmly in mind. Transmission systems in the South have been developed as rapidly as in the North in spite of smaller audiences, while even in programmes the South's needs have not been neglected. For a period during the 1960s, for example, RAI put out a programme called 'Telescuola' which, among other things, was for the teaching of illiterates.

The telephone sector is not a case of a new field for IRI but rather one where in the postwar period it acquired a virtual monopoly position. In 1925 concessions were given to five private companies to run local telephone services. Each operated in a fairly clearly delineated geographical area with trunk inter-urban and international services being run by a state concern, ASST (Azienda di Stato per i Servizi Telefonici). In 1933, through its salvage operations, IRI secured control of three of these five companies and put them under a specially created *finanziaria*, STET. The two remaining companies (TETI and SET) remained under private control until 1957, when the 1925 concessions expired. It was clearly recognised by then that this twofold division was unwieldy and that unified control was required. The government decided therefore that new concessions would not be granted to the two private companies unless they were under IRI control. The result was that IRI took majority shares, which were then transferred to STET in 1958. Further unity was secured when all five companies were merged to form SIP (Società Italiana per l'Esercizio Telefonico) in 1964. ASST still remains outside the state holding system for reasons that are difficult to appreciate. The evidence is, however, that responsibilities are clearly marked and that ASST's role has been diminished. 'The responsibility of . . . ASST is restricted to calls between the named central exchanges. As a matter of hardware these central exchanges are installed and operated by SIP, which then leases certain lines to ASST.'[19]

The movement of IRI into new activities, together with the cementing of its position in others, has been one of the features of its postwar development. We return later to the general rationale of these interventions. A second feature, which we need only treat briefly since it has been covered in detail in chapter 6, has been the considerable intervention in the South, particularly after 1957 when IRI and the other state holding groups were compelled by law to locate in that region specified proportions of their investments – 40 per cent of their overall Italian investments and 60 per cent of their investments in new industrial enterprises, raised to 60 and 80 per cent respectively in 1971. Before 1957 the greater part of IRI's activities was in the industrialised North – inevitable given that it was set up initially as an industrial salvage agency. The postwar reconstruction of the IRI empire saw a consolidation of this position with few new ventures in the South. 'IRI was by 1955, still very much a northern group . . . In 1955, only 13.9 per cent of its manufacturing employment was in the South and about 11.6 per cent of its total employment. It was locating about 25 per cent of its annual investments in the South and about the same proportion of its manufacturing investments.'[20]

IRI adhered to the 1957 law and indeed went beyond it, in that virtually all its investments in new industrial plant have been in the South. These investments have involved a wide range of activities though by far its major development up to the end of the 1960s was in the capital-intensive steel sector, and particularly at Taranto. This explains why IRI's southern employment growth has been slight relative to its investment expansion. Investments in steel over the period 1958–69 accounted for some 80 per cent of IRI's southern manufacturing investments and around 48 per cent of its total southern investments. In many ways the results of these investments have been disappointing in that secondary development has not followed. However, IRI's plans for the first half of the 1970s involve broader and often less capital-intensive fields. The hope is that these, and especially the Alfasud motor plant near Naples, will induce more substantial secondary effects – points to which we return later.

A third feature of IRI in the postwar period has been a cutback in its role as a hospital for sick firms. We have already made the point that during the 1950s it held on to a number of concerns which, on normal commercial criteria, would have been closed down. This was particularly true in respect of the engineering sector. The better labour market conditions of the very late 1950s saw an easing of this policy with some quite large firms being closed, a number of which had been making startling losses. Ansaldo Fossati, for example, in Genoa 'made losses between 1950 and 1958 of 18 milliard lire, equivalent to 4 milliard lire more than the total wages and salaries bill of the period; and that at the end of this time several years' output of tractors was standing unsold on the company's premises'.[21] Major reconstruction and rationalisation programmes were also carried out in other sectors in the early 1960s, particularly in shipbuilding, with subsequent redundancies, though as we have seen, because of union and local pressures, the reorganisation was not as radical as IRI would have wanted. Those made redundant were retrained, employed in other IRI firms or compensated. For most of the

1950s, however, not only did IRI find it difficult to rid itself of its own lame ducks; it took on others. In 1956 it 'found itself back in the textile sector – from which it had previously entirely withdrawn – as the result of a government mandate to give financial aid to, and reorganise, the largest cotton establishment in the South (Manifatture Cotoniere Meridionali), which was on the brink of failure.'[22] In 1959 it took over the Taranto shipyard, 'a shipyard with obsolete facilities, hardly any orders and practically in a state of bankruptcy, which IRI was required by the Government to take over from private enterprise'.[23] However, during the 1960s and early 1970s it took under its wing very few similarly sick companies, and has indeed got rid of some of its marginal (and often unprofitable firms – sometimes to other state holding groups as part of a general attempt to rationalise the state holding system.[24]* The creation of GEPI in 1971, charged with the major objective of rescuing sick firms, could diminish the need for IRI intervention in this respect, though the point should not be exaggerated since GEPI is not intended to involve itself in large concerns.

An important event for IRI in the postwar period was its loss of the electricity industry. IRI had secured control of a number of electricity companies through its salvage operations in the mid-1930s. The main company involved was SIP (Società Idroelettrica Piemonte), though it also had a minority holding in SME (Società Meridionale di Elettricità), which was the other major Italian electricity company, operating, as the name indicates, on the southern mainland. IRI steadily increased its holdings in SME and by 1939 held 18 per cent of its shares. But it was only in 1951 that it can be said to have gained complete financial control, when it increased its holding to 32 per cent. With the addition of SME to the IRI empire, IRI was operating (though not with a monopoly) in electricity generation, transmission and sales in all of the southern mainland, the greater part of central Italy almost as far north as Florence (but excluding the west coast area), and in the North-West, including Turin but excluding Milan and Genoa. Although its main areas of activity were geographically separated, inter-area transfers were technically feasible by the early 1950s, and partly as a consequence, IRI's electricity sector was put under a *finanziaria* (Finelettrica) in 1952. About a quarter of Italian electricity output was provided by Finelettrica and it held this proportion until nationalisation in December 1962.

The nationalisation of the electricity industry was a result of the growing Italian interest in national planning in the very early 1960s, a recognition that the existing system placed the South at a disadvantage with respect to electricity prices[25]* and, probably most important, the attempt by the Christian Democrat prime minister, Fanfani, to court the moderate left-wing parties – the famous 'opening to the left'.[26] Beyond the IRI holdings, the electricity sector was fragmented and in need of rationalisation. It is interesting that there was little discussion of doing this through IRI. Admittedly, it might have been difficult given the large number of companies involved, but political factors doubtless weighed heavy in the decision to nationalise rather than 'IRI-ise'. To use IRI would neither have placated the Christian Democrat conservative wing in their opposition to the takeover of the private firms, nor have gone far enough for the Socialists or the Christian Democrat left wing.

The nationalisation law was passed in December 1962 and much of the electricity industry was put under ENEL (Ente Nazionale di Energia Elettricà). Plants owned by industrial firms producing electricity for their own needs, as well as companies operated by local or regional administrations, were excluded from nationalisation, so that ENEL became responsible for slightly less than 75 per cent of national electricity output.

The old electricity companies were compensated at nationalisation on the basis of their average share prices between 1959 and 1961. However, compensation was paid not to individual shareholders but rather to the companies themselves, 'to give them an opportunity to enter other productive activities . . . thereby providing additional stimulus for growth'.[27] (One might add that these hopes were to some degree frustrated, and some of the old electricity companies, by their intervention in what was for them the relatively unknown sector of manufacturing, did more harm than good. The problems of Montecatini–Edison, for example, are not an entirely unrelated consequence of electricity nationalisation.) Although individual shareholders had the right to withdraw, there is evidence that few did. This was particularly true of the IRI firms. It will be recalled that there were two major IRI companies in the field – SIP and SME. After nationalisation, SIP was merged with the five IRI telephone companies to form a new company under STET, having the initials SIP but a different name (Società Italiana per l'Esercizio Telefonico). The compensation funds were used to a large extent for the modernisation of the telephone sector. SME's compensation was used in a more interesting manner. The company was given a new name (Società Meridionale Finanziaria), though retaining its old initials, and took on completely new activities. It became a holding company under IRI, acquiring shares in a wide range of activities in industry, construction, large-scale retailing and agriculture. Its best known acquisitions have been in the food and confectionery industry, and it now has a controlling interest in the well-known companies of Motta, Surgela, Alemagna, STAR and CIRIO. SME has purposefully made substantial acquisitions in the South and has played a useful role in that area. It might be added that SME's activities in the food and confectionery industries have also deprived the large food multinationals from making substantial takeovers of the Italian confectionery industry. This role of protecting

Italian industry from foreign domination is a very recent one for IRI. Given the degree of foreign ownership of Italian industry (see p. 44 above) and the growing political interest in the issue, it could be an expanding role in the future.

A final feature of IRI's postwar development is that it has generally kept abreast of the latest technological advances, Alitalia was among the first of the world's airlines to make widespread use of jets and has recently made a rapid expansion in jumbo jet operations. The development of a steel industry, based heavily on large modern integrated plants and producing cheap iron and steel in a country with few of the necessary natural resources, has represented a major achievement and removed a considerable impediment to industrial development. The telephone sector is now wholly operating with STD and has made considerable use of advanced satellite transmission systems, while IRI's *autostrade* programme has resulted in roads of the highest standards. The shipbuilding sector, though technologically backward throughout most of the 1950s, saw a considerable development of production systems during the 1960s. In a number of sectors IRI has been only too happy to use sophisticated foreign technology even where this required the formation of joint companies with foreign concerns.

By the 1970s IRI was easily Italy's biggest company, whether measured by asset value, employment or sales. International comparisons are always difficult, but it is certainly among the twenty largest firms in the world. Within Italy its size means that it accounts for a not inconsiderable proportion of economic activity. In 1971 it employed some 407,000 workers, equal to 3.3 per cent of full-time non-agricultural Italian employees. Its manufacturing employment, at 246,000, was equal to 5.1 per cent of full-time manufacturing employees. Its manufacturing fixed investments (in 1970) at 412 milliard lire were 11.1 per cent of the relevant national figure.

In spite of the great postwar changes in the IRI empire noted above, it still remains largely a heavy-industry, key-sector group. In 1970, 84 per cent of its manufacturing sales (and 53 per cent of its total sales) were accounted for by steel, engineering (mainly heavy) and shipbuilding. In 1960 the proportions had been 87 and 57 per cent respectively. During the period 1960–70, 93 per cent of IRI's manufacturing investments and 41 per cent of its total investments were in these sectors. This sectoral concentration of investment has meant that IRI has tended to increase its market share in these sectors. In 1967 it produced 94 per cent of Italy's pig iron as against 60 per cent in 1951, 58 per cent of steel as against 42 per cent in 1951, and held 80 per cent of shipbuilding capacity as against the 1951 level of 62 per cent. Moreover, it has a complete monopoly in the telephone sector as against 59 per cent of telephone business in 1951 and, similarly, an Italian monopoly of air transport.[28]

The predominance of IRI in these key sectors and the lack of national, even if not international, competition inevitably gives rise to risks unless there is some degree of certainty that IRI is working in the national interest. The system of government control over IRI and the other state holding groups is the subject of a later section.

7.2 ENI[29]

In many ways ENI's history is no less interesting and tumultuous than that of IRI. ENI was created by Act of Parliament in February 1953, and given the wide ranging task of 'promoting and developing activities in the national interest within the field of hydrocarbons and natural gases'[30] and, in 1969 with a change in its charter, in chemicals, nuclear fuels and allied fields. On creation it took control of a variety of earlier state and semi-state concerns. The history of these, and the factors and discussions behind the setting-up of ENI itself, are important for an understanding of its later development and performance.

Although indigenous oil and gas had long been known to exist in Italy they were hardly exploited, in spite of generous fiscal incentives. Italian companies operating in this field were more interested in foreign than in domestic exploration and development. In the early 1920s, when the great majority of Italian oil supplies were provided by British or American companies (and some 17 per cent from the USSR), the State decided that the only way to secure greater development of indigenous reserves was by the formation of a state or para-state company. In 1926, therefore, AGIP was created, and given the task of searching for oil (at home and abroad), and of extracting and refining it. The company was owned 60 per cent by the State, 20 per cent by the insurance company INA (Istituto Nazionale delle Assicurazioni) and 20 per cent by the state-run general obligatory insurance fund.

In many ways, until the creation of ENI, AGIP was the centre-pin of a range of state and semi-state companies in the oil, natural gas and allied industries. AGIP's statutes gave it quite wide powers of investment, and these were used. It bought itself a dominant interest in a Dutch-controlled firm, ROMSA (Raffineria Oli Minerali), which operated a refinery at Fiume in northern Italy; AGIP took prime responsibility for the refinery and left ROMSA with the task of selling lubricants and other by-products from the plant. AGIP was also involved in ANIC (Azienda Nazionale Idrogenazione Combustibili), created in 1936 and owned half by Montecatini and half by the state railways and AGIP. ANIC built two refineries (with substantial government aid), which were working by 1938. Beyond ROMSA and ANIC, AGIP also took shares in SNAM

(Società Nazionale Metanodotti), set up in 1941 to build and manage methane pipelines, as well as to distribute and sell methane. SNAM was owned 30 per cent by AGIP, 30 per cent by Regie Terme di Salsomaggiore (a state firm) and 30 per cent by ENM (Ente Nazionale Metano). This latter was a public corporation created in 1940, having the task of methane exploration and extraction in Italy. In many ways ENM, in the methane field, had similar roles to AGIP in oil.

The war spelled disaster for the Italian oil and gas industry, and for the companies involved. The two ANIC refineries were very badly damaged, the Fiume refinery was annexed by Yugoslavia, and AGIP's substantial colonial and wartime East European activities were taken away from it. In addition, the various distribution systems – pipelines, road and sea tankers – that had been set up by AGIP and the other companies were badly damaged by bombing and sabotage.

As with IRI, the postwar period saw fervent activity to reconstruct the companies and make good the war losses. ROMSA, without its refinery, expanded in the distribution and sales of lubricants, building a number of plants for the production of bituminous emulsions and a mixing plant in north-east Italy. ENM extended its methane production and distribution activities while SNAM, by 1948, was laying large-diameter methane pipelines. For its part, ANIC rebuilt its two refineries, in association with the Standard Oil Company. There can be little doubt, however, that AGIP was the leading light in the postwar reconstruction. It exercised financial control over all the companies mentioned above except ENM; and it is interesting that ENM faded in importance in the postwar period, to be disbanded with ENI's creation in 1953. AGIP's own developments in those areas in which it had direct responsibility were impressive. It rapidly rebuilt its road and sea tanker fleet and its retail petrol stations. But the major postwar development for AGIP was in the exploration and exploitation of hydrocarbons in Italy.

During the interwar years, AGIP had made extensive hydrocarbon surveys in Italy, particularly in the Po Valley. Although by the end of the war neither gas nor oil had been found in commercial quantities, there was plentiful evidence that such finds were distinctly possible. Certainly, in 1945 and 1946, a number of foreign companies were expressing enthusiastic interest about prospects in the Po Valley. However, 'less optimistic it appears, in this period, was the attitude of the government authorities and those in charge at AGIP'.[31] In 1945 the government issued a series of instructions to AGIP to operate a holding policy in its search efforts and to suspend new search programmes, rid itself of surplus labour and plant, and limit its activities to those that would give a quick return.

Pessimism or uncertainty about prospects in the Po Valley was not common to the whole of AGIP. During the war AGIP had been divided into two parts, one operating from Rome and the other in the North.

At liberation the northern section was put under the control of an ex-partisan leader named Enrico Mattei, a man of enormous confidence and drive who was later to play a vital role in the development of ENI. In 1945, convinced of the great prospects in the Po Valley, he fought against any halting of AGIP's exploration programme. In this he was successful and his confidence paid off. A large gas find was made at Caviaga in 1946 and at Ripalta in 1947. In 1948 Mettei was made vice-president of AGIP and this gave a renewed fillip to exploration. In the same year oil was found at a small village whose name was to become famous – Cortemaggiore. From then onwards, AGIP expanded its activities enormously both within the areas of its own direct responsibilities and by encouraging the companies in which it held shares. In particular, the production of methane increased from 28 million cubic metres in 1948 to 724 million in 1951, while the pipe distribution system, through SNAM, was expanded to accommodate the growing output and markets.

The various state and semi-state companies discussed above, involved in hydrocarbon exploration, development and distribution, had grown up at different times and were relatively poorly co-ordinated. Their tasks and roles often wastefully overlapped. At the same time, AGIP's oil finds, and the continued growth of methane output, excited public opinion and forced the government actively to consider how the rapidly growing hydrocarbon industry should be organised and its vast needs for capital met. The final outcome, after very lengthy discussion and debate, was the state holding company ENI, created in February 1953. The point deserves to be stressed that the debates leading to the creation of ENI were very protracted, even by Italian standards. The bill was discussed in Parliament for some one and a half years, and three years or so of committee work had preceded its introduction. One of the prime reasons for the long discussions was that there was considerable disagreement about whether ENI should be given a monopoly of exploration and exploitation in the Po Valley. Mattei argued strongly for this, and although the monopoly was finally conceded it was not without considerable misgivings by many members of Parliament.

In many ways ENI was based on the IRI model. The law setting it up declared it as being legally a public corporation and, like IRI, it was to operate through controlled or tied companies. It took over the State's holdings in AGIP, ANIC, ROMSA and SNAM and thus held majority control in all these companies. ENM was disbanded. Mattei was made ENI's first president and under him it expanded rapidly to become one of the largest oil and chemical concerns in the world.

The period up to the death of Mattei in March 1962 (in an aeroplane crash) was one of considerable, and to some degree buccaneering, expansion. Fixed investments, between 1954 and 1962, increased eightfold, sales by 170 per cent, and employment by 250 per cent. The Po Valley natural gas finds were rapidly being exploited and large-scale gas and oil exploration was conducted in other countries, followed by considerable investments aimed at extraction. Large investments were also made in refineries and distribution systems (including major natural gas pipelines within Italy) to process and distribute the oil and gas. Moving forward in the production process the group expanded its petrochemical interests and particularly in fertilisers (thereby breaking what had been a relative monopoly in Italy). ENI considered itself, however, very much an energy group, and in the latter half of the 1950s, to complement its other energy interests, it started to invest heavily in nuclear energy – in research and in the construction and management of nuclear power stations. Much of this activity came to an end in 1962 when electricity was nationalised.

In many ways ENI was more fortunate than IRI. It did not inherit large investments in heavy and declining industries, nor was it used to the same degree in rescue operations. It did not, however, completely escape these burdens, and was encouraged to take over a few ailing engineering firms (of which Pignone was the most important) and some textile concerns, including the large firm Lanerossi. As part of a state holding rationalisation programme, it took over IRI's textile interests in 1970.

The expansion of ENI had, to a large extent, been financed by Po Valley gas. This sold at prices only slightly below those for petroleum and yet both development and exploitation costs were much lower. By securing a monopoly here, ENI had obtained what was not far short of a money printing press. The difficulties that the government experienced in controlling ENI, discussed later, were to a large extent a result of the fact that the group was financially independent of government – quite different from IRI.

After the death of Mattei, ENI went through a very difficult period. In part this was no doubt a consequence of the loss of Mattei and the fact that there was no natural successor. But, probably more important, ENI had made quite enormous investments between 1961 and 1963 including the major petrochemical complex at Gela in Sicily. In these three years the ENI group invested 25 per cent more than in the whole of the previous seven-year period. In many ways ENI was overstretched and needed substantial outside funds, particularly since the Italian depression of 1964–65 resulted in surplus capacity and cutback on the prospects of self-finance. This, combined with difficult capital markets in this period, forced ENI to ask the government for an increase in its endowment fund. (The role of the endowment fund in the state holding system is discussed in detail later.) In 1953, on being created, ENI had been given an endowment fund of 30 milliard lire. Between 1953 and 1963, reflecting Mattei's own views, and the profits from gas, it was increased by only 6.9 milliard lire. In 1964, however, ENI had to seek an increase of 25 milliard lire, and a further 20.5 milliard in 1965. Even so, it had to cut back on investment. Gross fixed investment fell, as a result of the factors above as well as the completion of the Gela project, from 264 milliard and 236 milliard lire in 1962 and 1963 to 167 milliard and 134 milliard lire in 1964 and 1965 respectively.

In the period since 1966 ENI has seen steady growth and consolidation. Investment rose some 280 per cent between 1966 and 1972, sales by 130 per cent and employment by 45 per cent. By 1972 ENI employed nearly 80,000 workers. To a much greater extent than previously, the post-1966 growth has been financed through the endowment fund. Total fixed investments since the mid-1960s have been covered to the extent of around one-quarter by the endowment fund, and it almost seems to have become a rule of thumb that this proportion of ENI's capital requirements should be met in this way. The proportion is higher than with IRI, reflecting the view that ENI, more so than IRI, is involved in activities that demand more research, are in general riskier, and in consequence need a higher proportion of non-fixed interest capital.

As with IRI, ENI has been locating a substantial proportion of its investments in the South. Being generally capital-intensive they have not carried with them any great expansion of employment – at least not in any direct sense. In 1972, ENI's southern employment was around 18,300 (of which 5,000 were in the textile sector) – equal to some 29 per cent of ENI's total Italian employment. The indirect effects of its southern activities are much more difficult to evaluate. In respect of ancillary development, however, there must be disappointment. As with the key IRI projects (with the possible exception of Alfasud), the big ENI refineries and petrochemical plants have directly promoted, i.e. other than any demonstration effects, relatively little ancillary development. This is a point to which we return later.

By 1972 ENI was a major industrial concern. It controlled more than 180 companies (of which a hundred or so were operating exclusively abroad), was the fourteenth biggest petroleum company in the world in terms of turnover, and was a major world producer of petrochemicals. Although its prime functions are, as at inception, the exploration, production and distribution of hydrocarbons, it has, through acquisitions and restructuring, built up other interests though many of these are linked to its activities in the hydrocarbons field. It is not difficult to illustrate this point by looking at the relationships between ENI's nine principal firms, or *capogruppo* (ENI's equivalent of the IRI *finanziarie*). AGIP, the fulcrum of the ENI empire, explores and exploits natural gas and petroleum, with SNAM Progetti and SAIPEM doing the contract drilling and relevant construction and pipeline work. SNAM distributes the AGIP products through SAIPEM-laid pipelines. ANIC refines AGIP oil and produces petrol and petrochemicals in plants constructed by SNAM Progetti, SAIPEM and Nuovo Pignone. Lanerossi uses synthetic fibres produced by ANIC on looms built by Nuovo Pignone, while SOFID searches out funds for the whole group. In many ways it is convenient and not unrealistic to see the ENI empire as a large, vertically-integrated combine even though it would be wrong to overstate the degree of inter-dependence. For example, SNAM Progetti and SAIPEM (operating in similar fields and in competition with each other) do a considerable amount of work for non-ENI firms – refinery construction, pipe-laying operations, petrochemical plant construction and drilling. Some of these plants and activities are in Italy and, indeed, for ENI competitors.

So far we have described the evolution of the two major groups in the state holding sector. We have barely tried to differentiate them from private sector holding companies, nor have we probed, in any depth, behind the reasons for their developments and roles. It is the task of succeeding sections to try, among other things, to correct this, starting with the way in which the sector is organised and controlled – a key aspect considering its importance in the economy as a whole.

7.3   Organisational structure and control

The state holding sector's organisational structure of control is basically quite simple. It is in the form of a pyramid. At the top is the government (in practice the inter-ministerial planning committee, CIPE), which sets the general directives and guidelines. The next level is the Ministry of State Holdings which, since 1956, has had the task of overseeing the sector and guaranteeing that it 'pursues the objectives fixed by the political powers [Parliament and government] within the context of the needs of a market economy'.[32] Below the Ministry are the *enti* such as IRI, 'whose job it is to convert the general directives of economic policy established by the government authorities into investment and production programmes for the enterprises it controls'.[33] Next come the *finanziarie* – 'entrusted with the task of guiding, co-ordinating and controlling firms operating in the same branch of industry, besides performing other tasks of a financial nature similar to those performed by private holding companies'; while at the base of the pyramid are the individual companies with 'operational responsibilities to carry out the group's policy at the production level'.[34]

Although this is a meaningful representation of the sector's organisa-tional structure, in practice it needs some qualification, and in two respects in particular. First, some enterprises are controlled directly by the *enti* without going through an intermediary in the form of a *finanziaria*. For example, IRI itself controls Alitalia and the IRI banks. These cases of direct control generally arise when there are so few operating companies in a sector that the creation of a *finanziaria* would be wasteful. A second complication is that, although the IRI *finanziarie* are simply holding companies, in ENI their equivalent (*capogruppo*) are also producing companies. The reasons for this are fairly obvious. While IRI purposefully created the *finanziarie* solely to carry out co-ordinating, technical and commercial roles for the enterprises in the various sectors, ENI inherited its *capogruppo*, and they were already involved in production. In some ways, ENI itself is the closest approximation to the IRI *finanziarie*, while the companies such as AGIP are similar to a big IRI firm like Italsider, which not only has holdings in other firms but also itself produces goods.

An important question is how the *enti* and *finanziarie* exercise control over the system. The prime form of control is financial. The *enti* have a dominant equity interest in the *finanziarie* (although in the case of ENI it only controls the four main *capogruppo*) which in turn have a controlling interest in the minor *capogruppo*. In contrast, IRI owns the great majority of shares in all its *finanziarie*. In both IRI and ENI the *finanziarie* or *capogruppo* hold controlling proportions of equity in their companies. In many cases this involves more than a 50 per cent holding.

Given that control of a company can often be secured with far less than a 50 per cent holding, because of the fragmentation of other shareholdings, it may seem surprising that both IRI and ENI do not take smaller holdings and use the capital released to expand their empires. There are, however, a number of reasons for this. First, the Italian equity market is so weak that any substantial unloading by the state holding sector just could not be absorbed. Secondly, private investors could be reluctant to take such equity in so far as the attitudes of the private shareholder, who often wants a good return, and the state shareholder, which has as its objective social policies and reinvestment, can be in conflict. One would not however want to overstress this point, particularly since capital gains (especially attractive for tax evaders) and reinvested profits are not necessarily at odds with each other. At the same time, it is necessary to note that in many of the state holding firms it is a case of the sector holding equity not in partnership with small private shareholders, but rather with other large firms, and controlling a particular company to serve their common needs. Thirdly, many of the firms where the *ente* or *finanziaria* has large shareholdings are making either losses or very low profits (even though they may have good future prospects). The private shareholder would generally show little interest in such equity. Finally, there is by no means a large number of private sector companies into which the state holding sector could or would want to buy. The sector has never been successful with small firms and tries to steer clear of any further intervention in that size group. At the same time, a number of the very big private Italian firms (e.g. Fiat) are controlled by family interests or, alternatively, are such that their take-over would be politically unacceptable. For although no major political party has advocated the breakup of the state holding sector, there is no such unanimity on expansion. Although the left-wing parties would applaud such a move (particularly if there was an associated strengthening of government control), the Christian Democrats, particularly the right-wing elements, would be far less sympathetic. There is, in fact, a growing feeling within the Christian Democrat party that private industry, crushed between foreign takeovers and subsidised state holding companies, is having a raw deal. Montecatini–Edison is particularly interesting in this context. In spite of its enormous losses and problems, the state holding sector has been kept clear of any direct takeover, though IRI and ENI do have a 50 per cent interest in the 'committee of control' which runs Montecatini–Edison. The remaining 50 per cent is held by private interests (mainly Fiat and Pirelli) with IMI as chairman. More extensive and overt control by the state holding sector has been deterred, first by the fact that Montecatini–Edison is so large relative to ENI (the obvious candidate for the takeover), secondly because ENI's statutes would need to be changed to allow such a takeover, and thirdly (most important) because of a feeling in the Christian Democrat party that Montecatini is one of the last bastions of private enterprise.

The control exercised by the *enti* and the *finanziarie* over their respective empires is tight, and certainly involves more than merely turning up at company annual meetings and passively listening to the annual report. The board of directors in Italian companies is elected by those who hold a controlling interest in the companies, and both the *enti* and the *finanziarie* exercise this power. Companies that try to go against the wishes of the *enti* or *finanziarie* see changes in their directors. He who owns the piper calls the tune.

More interesting, and much more subtle, than the relationship and system of control between *enti, finanziarie* and operating companies is that between the *enti* and the government. In principle, as we have seen, this is straightforward. In their statutes the *enti* are expected to pursue the various general directives laid down for them by the relevant government body (currently CIPE), and since 1956 the Ministry of State Holdings has existed to ensure, among other things, that such directives are pursued. A variety of statements by both the Ministry and the *enti* might seem to confirm the subservience of the *enti* to the government's wishes. In its annual report of 1968, the Ministry commented that 'the system of state holdings is an organic group of initiatives which operate in a wide range of sectors but which in their efforts are headed by a single centre of policy direction and of active administration which is the Ministry of State Holdings'.[35] Petrilli (the president of IRI), in his fascinating collec-

tion of essays on state industries, sees IRI in a neutral and subservient
position *vis à vis* the government – 'an extremely elastic and ductile
instrument for attaining public objectives with the minimum of resources
on the part of the treasury',[36] and 'an instrument at the service of the
government'.[37] In practice, it is not at all easy to assess the degree of
control over the *enti*, or indeed to decide whether or not the relationship
between government and *ente* is more akin to the tail wagging the dog
rather than vice versa.

There is general agreement that there was little government control
over the *enti* before the creation of the Ministry of State Holdings.
Officially, under the first postwar decree concerning IRI, passed in April
1946, the overall control of IRI was the responsibility of CIR (Comitato
Interministeriale per la Ricostruzione). The 1948 IRI statutes transferred
these powers to the Council of Ministers (the Italian Cabinet) though
much of the control apparently remained with CIR.[38] For both the
Council of Ministers and CIR, the control of IRI would be just one of
many tasks they faced, probably low on their list of priorities and outside their normal scope of activities. We have already seen that it was a
government directive which led to IRI's policy of retaining labour in the
immediate postwar years, but beyond this, by most accounts, the degree
of government influence was slight. Reflecting a concern over this, and
the general uncertainty about what was to be done with IRI, the postwar period up to 1956 saw a number of inquiries and commissions
examining IRI and the state holding sector in general.[39]

> In 1946–47 an investigation by the Economic Commission of
> the Constituent Assembly into attitudes towards nationalisation
> and IRI . . . proposed greater control of IRI's activities by
> Parliament and co-ordination of all institutions financed by the
> State budget, under a single technical committee responsible to
> Parliament. No measures followed upon these proposals, and in
> subsequent years there was little evidence of much co-ordinated
> guidance or utilisation of the public sector. The anachronistic
> position of scattered State holdings, inadequately controlled by
> the Government and often wasteful, occasionally even com-
> peting among themselves, formed the object of continual
> polemic; eventually in 1951 Ugo La Malfa was appointed
> minister to submit a report on the reorganisation of all State
> holdings. So confused was the situation that La Malfa even had
> difficulty in compiling a complete list of State industrial assets.
> His report was followed by the customary official silence.[40]

A few years later there was yet another report following on 'the
appointment of a parliamentary committee [the Giacchi Committee] to
examine IRI's structure and to propose reforms. The report of the

Giacchi committee in 1966 presented a telling indictment of government failure to use its power to lay down policy directives for IRI.[41] Certainly, when ENI was headed by Mattei, there was a flagrant disregard for political pressures, or at least for those that were at odds with Mattei's own views. Right up to his death in 1962 Mattei exerted more political pressure than was placed upon him. He used ENI funds in political activities (in support of the Christian Democrats) and to gain controlling interests in organisations, including newspapers, which would be useful in securing his objectives. 'The legislature itself, it was said, could not [control him], not merely because such control is cumbersome but also because far too many members of Parliament owed their seats to ENI's financial support.'[42] The president of Confindustria said that 'in the field of hydrocarbons, there were committed acts which if committed by us would have been considered felonies'.[43] A more generous view of Mattei is that 'basically he had the same realistic, or pessimistic approach to Italian politics as Giolitti and de Gasperi and, like Giolitti, he was ready to use corruption more or less openly for what he considered a noble and superior end'.[44] However, it would be wrong to think that ENI's independence stemmed solely from the powerful personality of Mattei. As we have seen, ENI was in a much more favourable position than IRI because it was operating in prosperous sectors where there was little need to resort to government or market finance, with its associated controls. After the initial endowment fund paid in 1953 ENI received little more from the government until 1964. Since then it has had an increase in most years. It is generally accepted that ENI now toes the government line, or at least does so much more than before 1963.

One of the characteristics of Italian politics is that the time between recognising and documenting a problem and taking action to resolve it can be extremely long. The various postwar inquiries into IRI and the state holding sector produced no firm results until 1956. Even then, one doubts whether action would have been taken if, in 1953, the left-wing of the Christian Democrat party had not advocated the sector's withdrawal from Confindustria and the setting up of a Ministry of State Holdings.[45] The decision to disengage from Confindustria, a much more powerful body than the British CBI, was important. Confindustria has a substantial influence on Italian economic policy and was, and is, the major body negotiating with the trade unions over pay and conditions. As we have seen in chapter 4, the sector's withdrawal certainly had important implications for Italian collective bargaining.

Opposition to the withdrawal of the sector from Confindustria, and the creation of a controlling ministry, was strong. Confindustria, seeing a loss of power, opposed it, as did the usual extreme groups who wanted the sector either nationalised or returned to private enterprise. It was not until 1956 that the necessary legislation was passed and the Ministry of State Holdings set up. The Ministry had the task of supervising, co-ordinating and controlling the sector. In this respect it took over powers that had previously been exercised by a variety of ministries and other bodies. The Ministry itself was placed under a newly created inter-ministerial committee 'to coordinate the action of the Ministry of State Holdings with that of other ministries concerned in respect of the general policy relating to the various sectors controlled by the Ministry'.[46] The law demanded that within one year the sector should be disengaged from Confindustria, and that future bargaining with the unions should be done by newly formed employers' associations specifically created for the sector. As a result, Intersind was set up as the employers' association for IRI and EFIM companies, and ASAP for ENI companies. The law furthermore laid down that all companies in the sector should be 'organised within self-administered bodies'.[47] However, the majority of the sector was already appropriately organised so that the only change required was to group various real estate and spa concerns under a new holding agency, EAGAT, cinema concerns under the Ente Autonomo di Gestione per il Cinema, and a variety of mineral and metal manu-facturing companies under the newly created EGAM. The idea here, reflecting a fear of excessive bureaucracy if the various companies continued under direct government control, was to provide a buffer between government and the operating companies. The law laid down that the creation of these intermediate bodies should be carried out within a year. The process was, however, only completed in the early 1970s.

The disengagement of the sector from Confindustria, and the creation of holding agencies for the various miscellanea that the Ministry had inherited, were fairly clear-cut tasks. Much more difficult was the ques-tion of how and to what degree the Ministry should exercise control over its new empire. It fully recognised the delicacy of its task. As late as 1968, its director-general was writing of the Ministry that 'instead of waging a long and sterile "war of competences" it has wisely shelved this problem and devoted itself to carrying out the fundamental tasks allotted to it by the law, foremost among which are the detachment of the firms from the employers' unions of private industry controlled by Confindustria and the setting up of autonomous holding corporations'.[48]

It is never easy to reach any firm conclusions on the degree of control exercised by ministries over their areas of competence. Certainly the Ministry of State Holdings possesses a key element of power – the appointment and removal of *enti* directors (except in the case of IRI), though it is not the only body involved in this decision and, anyway, this is too strong for normal control requirements. Some observers have considered the Ministry's control to be minimal and indeed have viewed such bodies as IRI as being 'a machine without a driver'.[49] There are examples of power being exercised by the Ministry – the decision to build the Taranto steel mill apparently originated (though firmly supported by IRI) with the Ministry – but power exercised on an *ad hoc* basis is quite different from control. Control is of a continuing nature. A point that deserves mention in this context is that the Ministry has slender resources and this must limit the degree to which it can appreciate the needs and shortcomings of the sector.[50]*

In 1966 the Ministry was ten years old and the annual report for 1967 contained a number of passages that reflected the nature and weakness of its control. 'The principle facility [of control] remains that of issuing general directives, which carry, however, an obligation more in a political sense than one of law,'[51] and that this lack of precise control gave rise to an anomalous situation in that 'the body which before the country, parliament and government has the responsibility for the development of the State Holdings, is not, in many cases, in a position to declare institutionally the terms of its wishes to the firms which are placed under its control'.[52] The Ministry was at pains to point out that it did not want an 'indiscriminate and irrational'[53] increase in its power, but the desire for some increase was obviously there. Certainly the Ministry had, and has, less control over the *enti* than the *enti* would tolerate over their own empires.

In a number of ways, the problems of the Ministry arose from the fact that it did not know in detail what role it was supposed to be playing. 'Supervision' and 'co-ordination' are broad terms open to a number of interpretations. In practice it was an impotent intermediary. Major decisions on the sector were made by the inter-ministerial committee while the Ministry lacked the resources to make any detailed financial or other examination of the sector such as to give it a more continuing management role. In part, the situation was improved in 1967 when the inter-ministerial committee for the state holding sector was abandoned and its powers transferred to CIPE (of which the Ministry is, of course, a member). CIPE is a powerful body (superficially at least), created to devise and implement Italian national plans. In making the Ministry of State Holdings responsible to CIPE the aim was to insert the sector much more into the planning programme. The Ministry's role now became clearer. It was to represent the sector in the planning process, defend it from excessive demands, and supervise it in the attainment of the objectives set for it. Unfortunately, the waters were muddied again in the early 1970s when the 1971–75 national plan fell into abeyance, largely a result of political uncertainty and confusion; and yet again the question of the Ministry's role was thrown into the open.

Doubts about the Ministry's role have been heightened by recent events, which indicate that the *enti* are not wholly content to leave the Ministry to represent them in parliamentary discussions and decisions –

one of its prime and continuing roles, as we have already seen. The first example of this came in a debate on the Alfasud project by a specially constituted parliamentary commission. Both the commission and IRI wanted the opportunity to debate the issues between themselves, and not through the Ministry. The Ministry resisted this, making the point that it was responsible for the sector. In the end IRI got its way.[54] The second example was in the early 1970s, when IRI was applying for a further increase in its endowment fund, and the case was debated by IRI's president and chairman and a parliamentary commission rather than through the convential intermediary of the Ministry of State Holdings. Again there was Ministry opposition.

It is important to make the point that such quarrels between the *enti* and the Ministry are rare. In general there has not been any conflict on other major issues. In spite of the lack of clarity regarding their respective roles, any 'difficulties have been overcome thanks to the sensibility of the political direction and the attitude of knowledgeable responsibility by the directors of the *enti'.*[55] In other words, commonsense has prevailed.

But it is not only because of commonsense that clashes have been avoided. The various layers of the system generally share a common purpose on most issues and, above all, see the need to secure rapid economic growth tempered by social and national considerations. Sometimes the initiatives to secure these objectives have come from the government authorities, but more often, especially in the service sector, they have come from the *enti*. 'The history of the service sector shows that in many cases the policy of the state was crystallised only by the intervention of IRI – as if IRI wrote its own instructions.'[56]* That the tail should often have wagged the dog raises some fundamental questions of politics and democracy, but in practical terms it should not be condemned outright when the dog and tail have similar objectives, which was generally the case in the 1960s and early 1970s. It is perhaps praiseworthy when the dog, represented by a succession of weak governments and served by a poor civil service, is unable to formulate or execute such objectives and the tail is both willing and able.

Given the lack of Ministry power and the seeming general coincidence of *enti* and government objectives, one naturally wonders whether the Ministry is superfluous. The ex-vice-chairman of IRI recently described the Ministry as 'empty of content and with functions limited to the parliamentary representation of the *enti'.*[57] As we have seen, even this latter role has been diminished since the *enti* have recently taken to representing themselves before Parliament on some major issues. In part, then, there is a case for describing the Ministry as being superfluous, though, as with any ministry, its power and roles are determined more by the strength of the minister than the formal powers of his department. It can be argued, however, that if the Ministry is superfluous it represents a fairly innocuous superfluity. Certainly, there is little evidence that the *enti* would want to see it dissolved altogether, finding it normally to be a useful buffer between themselves and government. On the other hand it is, as we have seen in chapter 1, only one of a number of economics ministries, and its very presence adds to the problem of co-ordinating general economic programmes and policies. In recent years there have been growing demands in Italy for a single economics ministry.[58] Politically this seems unlikely, the present system allowing power in the economics field to be spread among the various parties in the coalitions. But in the event of any headway being made in this direction, the Ministry of State Holdings could be among the first to go.

7.4 Finance

This section is concerned first with the various forms of finance available to the sector and secondly how, in practice, its financial needs have been met.

The sources of finance available to the *enti* are slightly different from those available to the *finanziarie* (a word that is used in this section to include the ENI *capogruppo* as well as the IRI *finanziarie*) and the operating companies. The *enti* have five main sources of finance – bonds, medium- and long-term loans, short-term loans, self-finance and state finance. The *finanziarie* and the companies differ in that they do not enjoy direct access to state finance but, on the other hand, are able to raise money by floating equity. We shall now look at these various forms of finance.

The *enti* are 100 per cent government-owned and are not allowed to float equity; the *finanziarie,* as mentioned above, can and do. Initially, the IRI *finanziarie* had 100 per cent of their equity owned by IRI but this has now changed. All the IRI *finanziarie* have made use of equity issues, and in most cases IRI has been content to see its own holdings diminish in importance. In Finsider and STET, for example, IRI now has only some 55 per cent of the total equity. These were sectors in which the market was content to take the issues. With other *finanziarie,* however, the market has not been so generous and issues have needed to be taken up wholly by the *enti.* One hundred per cent of Fincantieri equity is still owned by IRI, as is 99.9 per cent of Finmeccanica. This virtually complete take-up of equity issues by IRI, and the recognition that the dividends paid will be slight or non-existent, is one way in which IRI subsidises sectors that are either in financial difficulties or undertaking tasks that are not wholly commercial. ENI is a little more complicated. It holds 100 per cent of the equity in two of its nine *capogruppo* (SNAM and AGIP Nucleare) and majority holdings in another two (AGIP, 84 per cent, and ANIC, 70 per cent). The remaining five *capogruppo* are controlled through holdings by these four. (Nuovo Pignone, for example, is controlled one-third by AGIP and two-thirds by SNAM. SNAM Progretti is controlled by AGIP, SNAM and ANIC, each holding a third. Only Lanerossi, out of these five *capogruppo*, has outside equity, 26 per cent, with ANIC holding the rest.)

The operating companies can also issue equity. The *finanziarie* can bid for these'shares in the open market or can take up the whole block, the numbers taken being dependent on a variety of factors. Where a *finanziaria* is at the margin of control and wishes to maintain its controlling interest, it will need at least half the shares issued. It may want more when it considers that the returns will be high and when an increase in cash flow is desirable or, alternatively, when the returns are likely to be low and the firm is operating in line with the public interest or other directives of the *enti* or *finanziaria*. Although from the viewpoint of control and subsidisation, equity is an important aspect of the state holding sector's financial system, viewed simply as a source of finance it is far less important. In the 1960s only some 3.5 per cent of the sector's financial needs were met through equity. This reflects the poorly developed Italian equity market, the well developed medium- and long-term loan market, and the seemingly courageous attitude by Italian industrialists towards high gearing (i.e. a high proportion of fixed interest loans to total capital).

Bonds and medium- and long-term loans are an extremely important source of finance for the state holding sector. In the 1960s, 35.4 per cent of its financial needs came from these sources and were used by all layers, i.e. *enti* and *finanziarie* as well as operating companies. About 45 per cent of this form of finance came from bonds with the rest being medium- and long-term loans. The bonds are put on the market in the same way that any other company would float them. (In the immediate postwar period, and up to 1953, treasury guarantees were given on IRI bonds, but this practice has since become unnecessary and been dropped.) The choice between offering bonds or taking medium- and long-term loans depends on the anticipated ease with which the bonds can be marketed. In practice, any shortfall would be taken by the *ente* or the *finanziaria* (depending who was floating them) or, alternatively, by the various Italian medium- and long-term industrial credit institutes. Securing finance through bonds and medium- and long-term loans gives rise to no questions of control for the sector – this source of finance has no voting rights. It does, however, increase the gearing ratio and this can be a serious problem when business experiences a downturn. To reduce this problem IRI has made use of convertible debentures, i.e. convertible into equity. Even so, the gearing ratio remains high in the state holding sector, as well as in Italian industry in general (see chapter 5). In the case of the state holding sector, however, two factors serve to protect it from some of the more serious consequences. First, financial problems arising from high gearing can be met by reducing dividends on equity and, in as far as much of this is owned by the *enti* or *finanziarie,* without an excessive outcry or the lack of confidence that would follow if large numbers of private shareholders were involved. At the same time, this point should not be overstressed since any such action will impair the possibility of future recourse to outside finance. Secondly, serious financial problems could be met by state finance through the endowment fund – to which we return shortly.

All levels of the state holding sector resort to short-term borrowing. This comes from the banks, and in IRI's case from its own banks, though seemingly on the same terms as would be given to any other customer. ENI, as we have seen, has its own finance company which searches out funds – long and short – for the group. In the sector as a whole, short-term finance is not unimportant. In the 1960s, 13.2 per cent of financial needs were met in this way – well in excess of the amount financed through equity. The importance of short-term finance has, of course, fluctuated considerably from year to year. Short-term borrowing is generally an expensive way to secure finance.[59] It is a source that would be used if there were an expectation that medium- and long-term interest rates were going to fall. For example, in the period 1962–64 Italian interest rates were high, as part of the government's deflationary package, and the sector consequently borrowed short to a quite considerable degree. A further reason for borrowing short would be if there were difficulties in securing medium- and long-term capital. The various credit institutes were squeezed between 1962 and 1964 and this was a further factor giving rise to the heavy short borrowing in those years. The sector would also borrow short if it were expecting an increase in state finance and merely wanted what was tantamount to a bridging loan. Finally, short borrowing may be needed if, for technical or other reasons, an issue of bonds is delayed. Heavy short-term borrowing by IRI in 1966, for example, reflected not only a delay in the award of an increase in the endowment fund but also a delay in the issue of IRI-guaranteed *autostrade* bonds – the issue was scheduled for 1966 but did not take place until 1967.[60]

Self-financing is an important source of funds for all layers of the state holding sector. In the 1960s, 34.3 per cent of the sector's financial needs were met in this way. This, though seeming high, is relatively low by Italian standards. The Bank of Italy's sample of large manufacturing firms indicates that around 55 per cent of Italian industries' capital needs were met through self-finance over the period 1966–70,[61] as against 37 per cent in the state holding sector. That the state holding sector should have a lower level of self-financing is perhaps understandable bearing in mind that the main sources of self-finance are depreciation funds and, to a far lesser degree, retained profits. There are two relevant points here. First, and most important, much of Italian industry will find it more difficult than the state holding sector to raise external finance and will have to rely more on their own resources. Secondly, many of the state holding firms are making only slight profits and would probably be axed by the private sector.

We come finally to the State as a source of finance – primarily through the endowment fund. Increases in the endowment funds are *ad hoc* payments by the government to the *enti*. Considerable awards were made in the late 1940s to help IRI with its recovery programme (which was being carried out in difficult capital market conditions) and to compensate it for its various non-commercial policies, and especially in the shipbuilding and engineering sectors. However, between 1951 and 1959 IRI had no further awards while ENI's endowment fund remained virtually unchanged from its creation until 1964. Increases in endowment funds, which must be voted by Parliament, are made for three reasons. First, they serve to cover the *enti* for uncommercial activities carried out at the government's request or with its encouragement. This appears to have been a prime factor in the early postwar period, particularly with respect to shipbuilding and engineering, and it also played a part in IRI's increased endowment fund at the end of the 1950s soon after it had taken on the ailing Taranto shipyard. Secondly, and not very dissimilar to our first point, increases have been made to compensate the *enti* for government-encouraged developments which, in the short run at least, are likely to give a low rate of return. The Taranto steel mill and the Alfasud plant are examples of this. Both in the maintaining of un-commercial enterprises and the promotion of developments involving a deferred return, the endowment fund is being used to cover *oneri impropri,* or social obligations. But, thirdly, it appears that increases have been sought and paid in recent years to finance that portion of investment which it was considered could not be covered by the capital market or self-finance, or, probably more important, where resort to the capital market (which in Italy generally means fixed interest capital) would result in an undesirable rise in the gearing ratio.

These three basic reasons for increasing the endowment funds of the *enti* are interesting in that they reflect two quite different views about these funds. The first is that they represent a capital grant from the government. This view was particularly pertinent in the immediate post-war period when uncommercial plant was being maintained. The second view, more relevant in the 1960s, is that they are a form of equity investment by the government aimed especially at avoiding excessively high gearing – an equity investment on which it expects a dividend, even if deferred. However, as we shall see later, the financial return has been insignificant.

It is important not to get the endowment fund out of proportion in that it has not represented a very major source of capital. In the 1960s, only some 12.5 per cent of the sector's total capital requirements were met in this way. The proportion has however been rising steadily and the EEC, at least, has become concerned about the element of subsidy involved – in response to which the Ministry of State Holdings takes the quite realistic line that the public sector in all member countries is subsidised to some, unassessed, degree.

We have already given rough estimates of the importance of the various sources of finance to the state holding sector. We now want to look at these in more detail. Table 7.1 shows the various sources of finance for the sector since the creation of the Ministry of State Holdings in 1956. A number of points arise from the table. Some of these, already covered in our earlier discussion, can be treated briefly.

Table 7.1   State holding sector: sources of finance, 1956–1970
(*per cent composition*)

	1956–1970	1956–1960	1961–1965	1966–1970
Self-finance	33.5	34.6	28.1	37.4
State contributions	11.1	5.6	8.8	14.9
Sale of assets	1.3	2.1	0.6	1.6
Equity	3.8	9.0	2.7	2.8
Bonds	14.3	20.7	20.1	7.3
Medium- and long-term loans	19.8	20.7	21.7	18.0
Short-term borrowing ...	16.2	7.2	18.0	18.0
Total	100.0	100.0	100.0	100.0
Absolute total (milliard lire)	11,758.0	1991.0	4319.0	5449.0

Source: Calculated from Ministero delle Participazioni Statali *Relazione Program-matica* (Rome, various years).

Over the whole period 1956–70 the proportion of capital needs covered by self-financing, at about a third, has remained high. The sector's ability to hold the percentage over the years 1966–70 is particularly impressive in view of the disastrous outcome in 1970 when the self-financing ratio fell to 28.7 per cent.[62*] This was a consequence of the great increase in capital needs (some 50 per cent over the 1969 level), falling profits resulting from the wave of strikes in 1969–70, and the sector's difficulties in absorbing the major wage increases subsequently conceded, combined with the sector's high gearing and consequent need to continue paying out interest on its borrowings in spite of its financial performance.

Table 7.1 shows how the State's contribution has been steadily rising. This reflects the sector's rapidly growing capital requirements (some in areas and activities where early high returns cannot be expected) and the difficulties of fully satisfying these by recourse to the market or by self-financing,[63]* together with a government recognition, no doubt encouraged by the *enti,* that more equity-type capital would make life much easier.

Over the whole period 1956–70, equity *per se,* as we have seen, has been a relatively unimportant source of finance – some 3.8 per cent of total capital requirements. This is a result of a number of factors. First, Italian equity markets are poorly developed. Secondly, equity finance is administratively expensive relative to bonds.[64]* Thirdly, the Italian equity market has had years when it has been extremely sluggish and where new issues would not easily have been taken up. The very low proportion of equity financing, for example, in 1964 and 1965 (0.3 per cent and 1.2 per cent respectively), was a consequence of extremely unfavourable equity market conditions – repeated in 1970 and 1971 when it amounted to only 1.0 and 1.5 per cent respectively. Finally, the proportion of the sector's capital requirements financed through equity will depend on the industrial sector requiring the finance. A low proportion in particular years may reflect the fact that the groups that are seeking capital do not make use of equity finance to any great degree. The very low proportion in 1967 (0.7 per cent), for example, was a result of the fact that IRI (which in the 1960s had been responsible for some 60 per cent of the equity raised by the state holding sector) was seeking capital issues for 'companies in which there is no, or virtually no, outside capital'.[65]

Bonds and medium- and long-term loans have been a major source of finance for the sector, and were a fairly stable source until 1966–70 when there was a substantial drop, particularly in bonds. Bond financing was pulled down by two very bad years in this period – 1966, when the proportion was 5 per cent, and 1970, when there was a negative figure of 1.9 per cent. In both years this form of credit (and medium- and long-term credit in general) was expensive and in short supply. The sector was therefore obliged to borrow short.

The proportion of the sector's capital requirements met by borrowing short raises some interesting issues. During the 1960s it had to finance nearly 20 per cent of its financial needs through short borrowing – a much higher proportion than in the 1950s. This high percentage reflects the financial knife-edge on which the sector operates. We have already seen that its financial system is one that is characterised by high gearing and a heavy reliance on self-finance. This works well in a stable economic environment with high profits, but is vulnerable to any departure from these conditions. The years 1968 and 1969 see the system in suitable conditions. Profits were high and money markets easy, with the result that it was able to finance a considerable increase in its capital requirements by self-financing and medium- and long-term borrowing. The year 1970 indicates the sector's vulnerability. Encouraged by the government, it had embarked on a substantial investment programme. Profits, however, for the reasons mentioned earlier, were low, and the self-financing ratio fell from 45.2 per cent in 1969 to 28.7 per cent in 1970. In addition, medium- and long-term money markets were tight and costly (in part a result of deliberate deflationary policy), with the result that these sources of finance only covered some 22 per cent of capital needs as against 52 per cent in 1969. The outcome was that the sector had to borrow some 37.6 per cent of its capital needs on the short-term market. The absolute amount borrowed short was 632 milliard lire – more than the sector's whole annual capital requirements in the 1950s. In 1971 the sector again borrowed a substantial amount of short money (535 milliard lire) – some 22 per cent of its very high financial requirements for that year. The proportion would undoubtedly have been higher had it not been for a massive increase in the endowment fund (covering 23 per cent of capital requirements) and much easier medium- and long-term borrowing conditions, allowing 35 per cent of capital requirements to be covered from this source.

As we have said, the system whereby the sector is financed provides no problems in stable and growing market conditions and when the labour situation allows high levels of self-finance. Chapter 2 above suggests that these conditions (which have been present through most of the postwar period) will not be found in the future, and that the events which gave rise to the sector's difficulties in 1970–71 may become more common. If this is the case then there are strong arguments for changing the system of finance for the sector. The continually growing proportion of the sector's capital needs which is being met by the equity-type endowment fund represents a move in the right direction. At the same time, as more and more of the sector's finance comes from the State, there must surely be introduced clearer financial objectives and a stronger degree of government control – but without dampening entrepreneurial drive.

7.5   Efficiency and performance

A question that is frequently asked of the state holding groups is whether they are efficient, or merely great awkward lumbering giants. The question is difficult to answer for three main reasons. First, there is no simple and obvious measure of efficiency. Secondly, measures that are used need to be compared with the same measures in other industries elsewhere in Italy or abroad, and this is often difficult because we must be sure that we are comparing like with like. Thirdly, the state holding sector has objectives and roles (discussed in detail later) other than simple efficiency. The problem of reaching meaningful conclusions on the sector's activities is one reason why it is such a lush pasture for polemic, giving great scope for observers to reach conclusions that coincide with their own ideological or preferred stance. With these difficulties firmly in mind, this section looks tentatively at two sets of measures of efficiency and the problems involved in their use. The first is a standard measure of productivity using value-added per employee. The second involves financial measures of efficiency and returns on capital.

Table 7.2   Value-added per employee: state holding sector v. Italian manufacturing in general, 1967

('000 lire)

	State holding sector	Italian manufacturing*	Italian manufacturing minus state holding sector
Textiles	1900	1679	1669
Oil, gas and chemicals ...	9350	4374	4082
Iron and steel	4600	3658	3027
Engineering**	2818	2568	2544
Manufacturing	4500	2587	2424

* The general Italian figures only cover units of more than 100 employees except where the industry is characterised by small units, when the lower limit of 50 employees is used. Because of the size of state holding units, this provides few problems, and is in fact advantageous from the viewpoint of comparison.
** Engineering includes shipbuilding.

Sources: Ministero delle Participazioni Statali *Relazione Programmatica* (Rome, 1970), pp. 52–3; and ISTAT *Annuario Statistico Italiano* 1969 (Rome, 1970).

Table 7.2 shows value-added per employee for Italian manufacturing in general and for the state holding sector, together with the same measure for individual manufacturing industries, for the fairly 'average year' of 1967. The table shows that in every industry covered the state holding sector has a higher value-added per employee. Inevitably, the difference increases when the state holding sector data are subtracted from the 'Italian manufacturing in general' data. In those areas where the state holding sector is a major force, e.g. iron and steel, oil, gas and chemicals, the difference changes quite substantially.

The results in table 7.2 need to be interpreted with caution, for a number of reasons. First, the industry groupings are broad – not through preference, but because of the limited amount of disaggregated data available for the state holding sector. This means that often we are not really comparing like with like. For example, the state holding engineering group is primarily involved in heavy engineering and shipbuilding. The non-state holding engineering sector is largely in light, consumer products. Similarly, with iron and steel the state holding sector is mainly in basic iron and steel products while private industry has concentrated on specialist steels. The availability of more industrially disaggregated data would, however, not fully overcome the problems of comparability, and this brings us to our second point. Even within the same narrow industries the state holding sector units are often larger and more capital-intensive. Any strict comparison would therefore require the figures to be further standardised to take account of these two elements. Thirdly, high value-added need not necessarily mean high productivity. It can reflect exploitation of a monopoly or near-monopoly situation. We have already seen that in many industries the state holding sector accounts for a considerable proportion of national output. We would not want to overstress this point, for although the sector in some fields controls a high proportion of national output, it often has to face competition from other countries, and particularly within EEC. Nevertheless the point has some relevance.

Turning to financial performance, we want to examine this from two viewpoints. The first is an analysis of the financial performance of IRI and ENI as *enti, i.e. as holding companies.* Secondly, we want to look at the financial performance of the ENI *group (i.e. enti, capogruppo* and companies) and try to relate this to comparable data for Italian industry in general. We would have liked to have done a similar exercise for the IRI group but unfortunately the relevant data are not available.

Table 7.3 shows a number of financial figures and ratios for IRI and ENI as holding companies in the three years 1968 to 1970, expressed as annual averages. A number of points arise from this table. The prime one is that, viewing IRI and ENI as commercial concerns, they have secured poor returns. IRI's net profits averaged 0.1 per cent of total assets, and ENI did only slightly better at 0.2 per cent. IRI's total income (and this is before subtracting operating expenses) as a percentage of total assets was 4.7 per cent while that for ENI was 3.8 per cent. These returns compared with an average cost of borrowing of some 6.5 per cent.

The State receives 65 per cent of the net profits of both IRI and ENI as a repayment or return on their endowment funds. If we view the endowment fund as simply being equity capital contributed by the government, then the State has had a very poor return for its money – at least in terms of dividend. It can be seen from table 7.3 that the sums

Table 7.3   IRI and ENI: financial position and performance: annual averages, 1968–1970

(*milliard lire*)	IRI	ENI
A. Total assets*	1322.9	1465.6
B. Total endowment fund	596.0	413.1
C. A−B	726.9	1052.5
D. Net profit	1.3	2.5
E. Total income**	62.3	55.5
F. ·D ÷ A (per cent)	0.1	0.2
G. D ÷ C (per cent)	0.2	0.2
H. E ÷ A (per cent)	4.7	3.8
I. E ÷ C (per cent)	8.6	5.3
J. 65 per cent of D	0.8	1.6
K. J ÷ B (per cent)	0.1	0.4

* Total assets exclude contra accounts.
** Total income includes all dividends, interest and other income before operating expenses.

Source: IRI and ENI *Annual Reports* (Rome, various years).

paid to the State under the 65 per cent rule have been equal to 0.8 per cent of the endowment funds paid to IRI and 1.6 per cent in the case of ENI. It can be argued that the State has preferred to take its profits through capital appreciation rather than dividends but it is difficult, if not impossible, to work out a return taking account of this point.

It is, of course, misleading to see the endowment fund as being mere equity capital, in spite of the way it is treated in the accounts. In part, as we have seen, it can be viewed as being the method by which the sector is covered for its social obligations, and in this sense is more of a capital grant than equity. One way, albeit a crude one, of dealing with this point is to deduct the endowment fund from the value of total assets. On this basis, IRI's and ENI's net profits become 0.2 per cent of assets net of endowment funds paid – increases relative to the calculation on the basis of total assets, but still low. Looking at total income, this becomes 8.6 per cent of assets net of the endowment fund in the case of IRI, and 5.3 per cent for ENI; though the point does deserve to be stressed that total income used in these calculations is before charging costs. Also, as already noted, the calculation involves the extreme assumption that the whole of the endowment fund is to cover social obligations and that no return was expected upon it.

The endowment fund, and how to treat it, is a very real problem in the evaluation of the financial performance of the *enti*. It is also present in any attempt to evaluate the financial performance of the *groups* as a whole (i.e. *enti, finanziarie* and companies) – much more important than the evaluation of the *enti* themselves. This is our next task.

Table 7.4　Financial position and performance: ENI group v. other Italian companies

(*milliard lire*)

		ENI group	General company sample	Industrial company sample	Specific industry sample
A.	Amortisation　...　...	161.5	860.5	665.8	192.7
B.	Net trading profit　...	16.3	−37.6	−46.5	− 0.1
C.	Interest and other similar payments　...　...	70.5	738.2	576.3	162.0
D.	Assets in property, plant and equipment　...	2635.8	20,293.9	15,261.9	5701.4
E.	Endowment fund　...	445.9	−	−	−
F.	Total assets　...　...	3711.8	34,071.8	27,674.5	9684.5
G.	Current liabilities　...	707.8	9158.3	8189.3	2438.9
H.	Amortisation fund　...	1158.9	8921.1	7354.2	2637.8
I.	$(A+B+C) \div D$　(per cent)	9.4	7.7	7.8	6.2
J.	$(A+B+C) \div E$　(per cent)	6.7	4.6	4.3	3.7
K.	$(A+B+C) \div (F-G)$　(per cent)　...　...	8.3	6.3	6.1	4.9
L.	$(B+C) \div (F-H)$ (per cent)	3.4	2.8	2.6	2.3
M.	$(B+C) \div (F-G-H)$ (per cent)　...　...　...	44.7	4.4	4.4	3.5
N.	$(A+B+C) \div (F-E)$　(per cent)　...　...　...	7.6	−	−	−
O.	$(A+B+C) \div (D-E)$　(per cent)　...　...　...	11.3	−	−	−

Sources: The ENI figures are taken from ENI *Annual Reports* (Rome, various years). All other figures are from Mediobanca *Dati Cumulativi di 555 Società Italiane* (1968–71).

Table 7.4 shows consolidated account figures relevant to an understanding of the ENI group's financial position and performance. The figures are annual averages for the two years 1969 and 1970, and have been set against three other series from a reasonable sample of Italian companies. The 'general company sample' covers Italian companies operating in industry and services. With the 'industrial company sample' we have tried to compile figures more relevant for a comparison with ENI by excluding economic activities in which ENI has no interests, or where it was felt that the activity was so heterogeneous as to swamp those in which ENI has interests.[66]* The 'specific industry sample' covers those activities in which ENI is strongly represented.[67]* Obviously, the industries included in these various series are slightly arbitrary, but there is no reason to think that the results would have been changed substantially by including or excluding industries that might be the subject of debate.

It is never easy to compare firms, and table 7.4 should be viewed as giving no more than a broad indication of the ENI group's relative financial performance. Nevertheless, the results are fairly clear and most interesting. Using a variety of accounting formulae, ENI does very well relative to the general company sample; even better, with one exception, compared with the more relevant industrial company sample; and better still when set against the very relevant specific industry sample. It will be noted that at the end of the table there are calculations of ENI's financial performance on the basis of assets net of the endowment fund and thereby taking account of the possible view, mentioned above, of the endowment fund as being solely a payment to cover social obligations. On this basis, as one would expect, ENI does even better.

There is certainly little to suggest from these data that ENI is anything other than a group of above-average efficiency. It is a great pity that comparable data are not available for IRI, though one should add that IRI's view is that its heterogeneous nature, relative to the fairly homogeneous ENI, is such as to deprive any consolidated income statements of real meaning. IRI's reply to any criticism that it is inefficient is a simple but telling one – that all but 9.2 per cent (endowment fund) of its assets have been financed by the market. Market rates must, of course, be paid to secure these funds and IRI's performance has been such as to enable it to obtain most of the (growing) funds it requires from the market.[68] Similar points would, however, apply to ENI.

7.6 Southern development and other roles

There are few who would doubt that the state holding sector has played a major part in postwar Italian development. The various activities in which the sector has operated have enjoyed rapid rates of growth, often from a poor base, and are generally as technologically advanced and efficient as units elsewhere in Europe. The efficiency of the sector's operations in such key areas as steel, energy and chemicals has made for lower costs in other industries relying on these products as inputs. Moreover, the state holding sector formula has been a useful means of securing capital in a country with poorly developed capital markets, and it is difficult to imagine that private enterprise could have attained the sector's achievements. But, in addition, the sector has played a number of other major roles in Italian growth and development. During our discussion of the postwar history of IRI and ENI we have already touched on a number of these, but we now want to present them in a more specific manner.

First, it has tinged commerce with social considerations. Particularly in the early postwar period, IRI held on to labour which, on sheer commercial grounds, should have been made redundant. Both IRI and

ENI have taken on firms that were in grave difficulties, injected new capital and management, and often been able to build them up into profitable concerns. Examples of such successes are ENI's intervention with Lanerossi and IRI's with ATES (electronics) and Costruzioni Metalliche Finsider (steel structures). Plant closures, when unavoidable, have often been delayed either until the local labour markets were able to absorb the surplus labour, or until jobs could be found in other parts of the state holding sector. These 'lame duck' interventions tended to diminish in the 1960s, when the relatively tighter labour markets made such a role less important, and the state holding groups themselves were getting increasingly worried about the effects of such interventions on their competitiveness. Although at the end of the 1960s the sector was still to some degree a hospital for sick firms, only two or three rooms, so to speak, were being used for this purpose. The role of assistance, which had largely dominated the sector's origins, had substantially declined. However, in the early 1970s the Italian economy, as we have seen, ran into a serious recession. The number of bankruptcies rose considerably and many firms were in serious financial difficulties. Nevertheless, at a time when the state holding sector was expanding its investments rapidly, and much of this in the South, it was felt unwise to burden it further with any large-scale rescue of these firms. There was also a strong feeling in the *enti* that they did not want, and in the current competitive climate could not revert on any scale to, their earlier hospital role. In the event, an arrangement was worked out which seemed to please everybody. A new finance company (GEPI), to operate under guidelines set by CIPE, was created in March 1971.[69] It had the specific aim of rescuing small- and medium-sized firms in 'transitory difficulties' by taking minority or majority shareholdings (or granting finance on favourable terms) with the basic aim of maintaining or increasing employment. The GEPI's funds were contributed by the large credit institute IMI (30 milliard lire) and the state holding groups, EFIM, ENI and IRI (10 milliard lire each). It may seem that this was just another way of burdening the sector at one remove but this is not the case, for the government agreed to increase the endowment fund of each of the *enti* by 10 milliard lire. The contribution of the sector will therefore be largely in terms of expertise and experience rather than finance.

A second role of the state holding sector has been that of leading the rest of the economy by example. It has been at the forefront in the application of new production techniques, and in management and labour training. By example, competition and poaching this has been transmitted to other sectors of the economy, though it is a slow process, particularly in respect of labour training, where Italian standards, as we have seen in chapter 1, remain abysmal. In the field of industrial relations the sector has definitely been a leader, its employers' associations, Intersind and ASAP, being much more modern-thinking and adventurous than Confindustria (see chapter 4). The sector's wages and conditions of work are among the best in Italy. It is not easy to know, however, whether this is a result of less conservative thinking by the sector, a weaker bargaining stance, or a result of the fact that their labour force is more unionised and holds many members of the radical metalworkers' union. Probably it is a combination of all three.[70] Few would doubt, however, that the sector has forced Confindustria to take a more realistic and reasoned view of industrial relations.

A third role of the sector has been to inject competition into parts of the Italian economy. The point has been made frequently in this book that Italy is a dualistic economy. Its economic structure is characterised by a great number of small, almost artisan, firms and, on the other side of the coin, by a relatively small number of large, near-monopoly, technologically advanced firms. On several occasions the state holding sector has moved into activities characterised by heavy concentration or near monopoly. Clear examples are the entry of IRI into cement manu-facture, thereby breaking a number of local monopolies that were unquestionably abusing their powers; ENI's developments in the fertiliser field, until then dominated by one firm; and the decision by IRI, through Alfasud, to break into popular car production, to the obvious annoyance of Fiat. This competitive role of the sector could be particularly impor-tant in the Italian context, where, in spite of the heavy concentration of output in a few firms, and in spite of numerous attempts to introduce anti-monopoly measures, there currently exists no relevant legislation. It would however be wrong to overstate the importance or value of the sector's interventions in the field of monopolies and restrictive practices. Beyond the examples given above there are, in fact, few others where the sector has played this role. Much of the sector's expansion has been in activities in which it was already strong, and in many industries it is the state holding sector itself that is in the near-monopoly situation. The detrimental effects of national monopolies and restrictive practices are anyway tending to diminish, because of membership of the EEC and the resulting increase in competition. Moreover, one may question whether the state holding sector type of intervention is necessarily the best,[71] particularly since it may encourage further mergers by private enterprise to protect its position. The Montecatini–Edison merger, for example, was in part a response to ENI's moves into the fertiliser market. It may also merely shift the 'monopolist' into other fields or, alternatively, bankrupt him, either of which may be undesirable. Few would doubt that the need for a monopolies and restrictive practices policy in Italy would be better met by legislation rather than by the use of the state holding sector.

Fourthly, and more positive, the state holding sector has moved into activities where private enterprise or the State itself have been unable or unwilling to intervene. The capital requirements of the steel industry, for example, make it inconceivable that private enterprise could have built the industry up to its current levels, while outright nationalisation was not politically acceptable. The system of finance, in particular, made it doubtful whether the State alone could have developed the motorway programme. The growing role of IRI in urban infrastructure is a consequence of the shortcomings of local authorities and the public administration in the execution of those tasks which by rights should be theirs. IRI's takeover of the telephone sector reflected the need for a monopoly combined with a widespread distrust of giving this to private industry, the political unacceptability of nationalisation, as well as misgivings about the efficiency of a nationalised telephone service.

A fifth role of the state holding sector has been in counter-cyclical policy. In this respect its role could be substantial, not only because of its importance in the economy, but also because of the inadequacies of monetary policy for reflationary purposes (and its detrimental side effects in Italy's case when used in a deflationary way), and the difficulties in the way of operating fiscal policy (see chapter 5). However, in the context of this counter-cyclical role, two points need to be made. First, the sector can suffer costs by adapting or rephasing its investments since, though this may be in the national interest, it could be against the sector's commercial interests. This point should, however, not be overstressed, in that a substantial proportion of the sector's investments concern infrastructure and telephones – markets where investment is not excessively influenced by short-term business conditions. Secondly, the sector was not, in fact, used to any great degree as a counter-cyclical weapon until recently. Up to 1963 monetary policy was adequate to control Italy's relatively minor cycles, while during the economic crisis of 1963–65 the sector was certainly not used in a counter-cyclical manner. It will be recalled from earlier chapters that the economy overheated in the early 1960s and that in 1963–64 the government was forced to introduce a deflationary package. This was highly 'successful' – indeed, more so than was envisaged or desired in that the economy virtually stagnated in 1964 and 1965 with the result that the government rapidly had to revise its policies and encourage new investments. How did the state holding sector fit in with these conditions and needs? The sector had already started to cut back on its investments in 1963, when they rose by a mere 6.2 per cent as against some 35 per cent per annum in the previous two years. National fixed investment in industry and in transport and communications rose by nearly 17 per cent in 1963. It would be wrong, however, to think that the sector's 1963 cutback was necessarily a purposeful attempt to comply with the government's deflationary policy of that year. Instead, it is more realistic to see it as coinciding with the completion, or near completion, of the massive ENI Gela project and that of IRI at

Taranto, combined with ENI's financial difficulties, discussed earlier. The sector did not increase its investments during 1964 and 1965 and indeed they fell, by 0.5 per cent and 8.9 per cent respectively. Admittedly, these were below the decline in total Italian fixed investment in comparable activities (industry, communications and transport), with falls of 12.5 per cent and 12.6 per cent, but they were falls for all that, and at a time when the government was striving, with inappropriate monetary policy and inadequate fiscal policy, to revive the economy. The sector's fixed investments fell again in 1966, by 11.1 per cent, while total Italian fixed investment in comparable activities rose by 8.8 per cent. In brief, there is little evidence, in this period, of the sector playing a counter-cyclical role. It is indeed only recently, in the period after 1969, that the sector has been more closely tuned to national economic needs. During the 1970–73 recession, when national investment growth slowed down dramatically, the sector massively expanded its own investments – with the full encouragement of the government. The sector's investments increased, for example, by 42.4 and 33.7 per cent in 1970 and 1971 respectively – against rises in national fixed investment of 14.9 and 1.6 per cent. There is evidence, as we have seen in chapter 2, that the Italian economy is moving now into a phase of greater cyclical instability. One can expect the state holding sector to be used increasingly in an attempt to counter this, particularly in view of the deficiencies of Italian fiscal and monetary policies.

The final major postwar role of the sector has been in southern development. This has been discussed briefly in earlier sections, but as we believe it to be a very major function, it deserves treatment at greater length. As we have seen, as part of a set of measures aimed at more rapid southern industrial development, the state holding groups were, in 1957, obliged by law to locate in the South 60 per cent of their investments in new industrial plant and 40 per cent of their total investments – raised to 80 per cent and 60 per cent respectively in 1971. At the time of the 1957 law the sector, for reasons explained earlier, was largely concentrated in the North, with only some 17 per cent of its total employment and a similar proportion (19.4 per cent) of its manufacturing employment in the South. Over the period 1953–57 a mere 22 per cent of the sector's total investment, and 30 per cent of its manufacturing investment, was in the South.

The state holding groups largely adhered to the law – a point worthy of mention in itself in the Italian context. Virtually all of the sector's Italian investment in new industrial plant has been in the South, and, between 1958 and 1971 some 49.4 per cent of its manufacturing investments and 40.2 per cent of its total investment has been there. The proportion of the sector's investments going to the South has tended to rise since 1957. While in the four years 1958–61, 27.9 per cent of its manufacturing investments and 28 per cent of total investments were in the South, these proportions had risen to 43.3 and 36.2 per cent respectively by 1966–69, and to 57.5 and 49.6 per cent in 1970–71.

These geographic changes in the sector's investments inevitably carried with them similar though less dramatic changes in respect of employment – largely because many of the investments were in capital intensive plants. An indication of this is given by the fact that over the period 1958–69, 52.5 per cent of the sector's southern manufacturing investments were in the iron and steel industry, 25.1 per cent in the oil and gas industry and 9.2 per cent in chemicals and petrochemicals. Even so, while in 1957 only some 19 per cent of the sector's manufacturing employment and 17 per cent of its total employment in Italy was in the South, this had risen to 28 and 26 per cent respectively by 1971.

The point needs to be kept in mind that this spatial restructuring of the sector took place during a period when its investments, and to a lesser extent its employment, were rising rapidly. Viewed in absolute terms the sector's growth of investments in the South is impressive. Its southern manufacturing investments rose nearly ninefold between 1958–61 and 1968–71, from 180 to 1575 milliard lire, while its total southern investments rose nearly sevenfold, from 442 to 2965 milliard lire. The sector's southern manufacturing employment rose from around 27,000 in 1958 to some 68,000 in 1970 (52,000 to 96,000 in respect of total employment).

Considered simply in quantitative terms, the sector's contribution to southern development has been impressive. Over the period 1958–69 its industrial investments represented some 33.7 per cent of total southern industrial investments and were up to 39.7 and 45.9 per cent in 1970 and 1971 respectively. While the sector's manufacturing activities employed nearly 6 per cent of full-time southern manufacturing employees in 1958, this had risen to nearly 10 per cent by 1970.

The figures above, though illustrating well the crucial role that the sector has played in southern development, tend if anything to give only a partial picture of its impact. In manufacturing its plants have provided a demonstration effect, indicating to private enterprise that a southern location is not the disaster which it was often thought to be. Beyond manufacturing, the sector has made other contributions to southern development, particularly in the field of communications – vital in breaking the South from its backwardness. The *autostrade* programme, heavily involving IRI, has been pushed through at remarkable speed; the telephone sector has concentrated much of its investments in the South; while the IRI-controlled ATI, in spite of losses, has provided important air links within the South and to the North. RAI, often an easy target for criticism, has, as we have seen, oriented some of its programmes towards resolving a continuing problem in the South, that of illiteracy.

Keeping to the subject of impact, but on a more negative tack, the

sector's manufacturing investments and projects have generally had disappointing secondary effects beyond the usual (and low) multipliers and
beyond demonstration effects. Ancillary development of new firms, either
supplying the sector's plants or taking their output and processing it yet
further, has not been large. New development around the sector's two
major plants at Taranto and Gela has been slight and has involved other
parts of the state holding sector rather than private industry. The term
'cathedrals in the desert' has become a fashionable way to describe these
plants. Given the lack of industry in the South and the shortage of
entrepreneural talent, combined with a continuing reluctance of northern
firms to go to the South, perhaps it was optimistic to expect any rapid,
large-scale ancillary development. It is a depressing thought that the
state holding sector may need to take on the role of developing ancillary
industry – depressing because this kind of development often involves
small-scale firms and the sector has never been successful in managing
such firms. On the other hand, the ancillary developments around IRI's
Alfasud plant near Naples have been promising. The plant is already in
production and will have an output of 300,000 cars per annum by 1974–75
and will employ 15,000 people. IRI was very conscious of the poor build-
up of ancillary units around the British Development Area car plants
but is more hopeful in the case of Alfasud – not least because its size
(it is much bigger than the United Kingdom plants) makes it more
capable of giving adequate economies of scale to supporting units. The
prospects for economies of scale were improved yet further by Fiat's
decision in the late 1960s to locate a substantial amount of its vehicle-
producing activity in the South. The secondary results of Alfasud and
Fiat have been impressive – it is estimated that in 1971 some 17,500 jobs
had been created in secondary activities associated directly or indirectly
with the new motor plants.[72] This is quite a substantial amount of induced
employment, just about as much again as the employment in the motor
plants *per se,* and it certainly negates any cry of cathedrals in the desert.
As the motor plants build up to full capacity, and as demand for spares
grows, it is reasonable to expect further ancillary development.

So far, we have shown the state holding sector largely in a favourable
light. In such basic industries as steel, engineering and chemicals it has
consolidated and often expanded its position, building them up, often
from a low or non-existent base, to high levels of technology and
efficiency, while at the same time tempering commercial objectives with
social and broader national considerations. In addition, as we have seen,
the sector's development has involved industries and roles beyond those
that it inherited. In some ways it would be possible to depict the sector's
postwar expansion into new fields as being *ad hoc* and simply a case of
empire-building; but this would be misleading. Rather, its new roles and
activities have been in response to demands and problems which, either

for economic or political reasons, could not be resolved satisfactorily in any other way. Its expansion in telephones and television, for example, met a need for a national system when nationalisation was not politically feasible. Its motorway and urban infrastructure developments reflected a pressing need which neither the public administration nor private enterprise could satisfy at an acceptable speed. Its roles in counter-cyclical policy and in monopolies and restrictive practices reflect Italy's political, fiscal and public administration deficiencies. In many ways, indeed, the sector's development can be seen as a response to major Italian economic shortcomings – in particular the poor capital markets which restrict private enterprise, and the low standard of public administration which limits the State from successfully taking on activities and roles which in other countries are its either by right or by convention.

The sector's success in stepping in where others were fearful or impotent, and its tinging of commercial with national considerations, has stimulated great interest in the system on the part of foreign observers and in Italy has protected it from major criticism. But this success has its dangers.

First, there is a risk, in Italy and abroad, of seeing the sector as capable of doing anything and of solving any problem. This is both misleading and perilous. In particular, the sector has never been successful in managing small firms and, associated with this, its possible role in the development of the South must, realistically, be seen as limited.[73] The sector is quite capable of setting up propulsive units, and other reasonably large-scale ancillary units, but it can do little more to secure faster growth of the smaller units that form the major part of the southern industrial structure, and which are the key to the resolution of the southern problem.

Secondly, an obvious but important point is that the sector's various national interest roles have not been without their costs. Regional development, counter-cyclical, anti-monopoly and many of its other interventions involve taking actions that, in the short run at least, may run counter to commercial needs. The growing importance of the endowment fund in the sector's finances reflects in part the heavy cost of these tasks and the desire to avoid too serious an effect on its competitiveness, as well as being a way of injecting more equity-type capital into the system. The endowment fund is one possible measure of the costs of the sector's national interest roles. Whether there are other costs through cross-subsidisation and a lower-than-maximum rate of return is difficult to say. Certainly the system allows an element of cross-subsidisation. Member firms could, for example, be obliged to buy from other parts of the sector. In practice this seems to be almost completely absent. Alternatively, cross-subsidisation could come through the financial system with the sector's firms taking sub-optimal decisions and these being tolerated by the *finanziarie, enti* or, indeed, by the market. Even though strenuously denied by the *enti,* who argue that the only subsidies involved are through the endowment fund, the extent to which such cross-subsidisation does occur remains uncertain.

Our third and final point about the state holding sector is a broad one. It is that there are alternatives to the system. Many of the activities in which the sector operates are nationalised in other countries or run by private enterprise. Moreover, the various national interest roles could be replaced by other measures and systems. The more rapid development of the South, for example, could be pursued by improving regional incentives or imposing more severe development restrictions on private enterprise in the North. The counter-cyclical role could be replaced by stronger and more efficient fiscal policy. Its infrastructure development function could be dropped if the system and finances of the public administration were not so disastrous. The anti-monopoly roles are limited, have dangers, and could be better met by relevant anti-monopoly legislation. The rescuing of sick firms could be achieved by nationalisation or through financial measures. And so on.

In the Italian context it is not difficult to reply to these points. The state holding system already existed, and it would have been almost inconceivable for policy-makers not to use it to attain their objectives. But in addition, in Italy many of the alternatives listed above either are not feasible or could only be introduced at considerable cost and/or with delay. Frequent attempts have been made to introduce monopolies and restrictive practices legislation, but without success. One doubts whether it would be politically acceptable to channel directly large amounts of public money into sick private firms. Attempts to improve the adequacy of Italian capital markets have so far come to little more than nought. The system of public administration seems almost impossible to reform. Because of the industrial structure it is doubtful whether substantially more powerful incentives would appreciably increase the movement of private industry to the South. Given the political structure in Italy, large-scale nationalisation would not be acceptable.

Within the Italian political and economic context then, the state holding system fits well and performs a useful function. It is not altogether obvious that in a different environment or country, allowing greater use of alternatives, the system would be of the same value.

Notes to chapter 7

1. Much of the information in this section on the early history of IRI is taken from Professor Saraceno's excellent survey in Ministero dell'Industria e del Commercio, *Istituto per la Ricostruzione Industriale* Vol. III (Report of Professor

P. Saraceno) (Turin, 1956).
2. Preamble to 1933 decree setting up IRI.
3. Saraceno, op. cit., p. 4.
4. ibid., p. 2.
5. La Palombara *Italy: The Politics of Planning* Syracuse, N.Y.: Syracuse University Press (1966), p. 15.
6. A. Schonfield *Modern Capitalism* Oxford: Oxford University Press (1965), p. 179.
7. Saraceno, op. cit., p. 38.
8. For further details of the changes in IRI's holding structure between 1934 and 1939, see Saraceno, op. cit., p. 132.
9. R. Romeo *Breve Storia della Grande Industria in Italia* Rome: Cappelli (1967) p. 172.
10. Saraceno, op. cit., p. 67.
11. ibid., p. 67 and pp. 375–81.
12. M. Posner and S. Woolf *Italian Public Enterprise* London: Duckworth (1967), p. 26.
13. Quoted in G. Amato (ed.) *Il Governo dell'Industria in Italia* Bologna: Il Mulino (1972) p. 226. This book contains a substantial number of extracts from articles (some of historic importance) on the state holding sector.
14. Posner and Woolf, op. cit., p. 26.
15. ibid., pp. 26–7.
16. Saraceno, op. cit., p. 74.
17. For a good discussion of IRI's role in the Italian motorway programme, see N. Despicht 'Diversification and Expansion: the Creation of Modern Services' in S. Holland (ed.) *The State as Entrepreneur* London: Weidenfeld and Nicolson (1972) pp. 138–46.
18. The decision to extend the concession for another year was taken at a time when there was substantial debate about the freedom of the press and the news media in general, following the takeover of a number of major newspapers by private industrial firms. It was felt that more time was required to consider how, if at all, the radio and television services should be reorganised so as to take account of these developments. It might be added that RAI is one of the least 'happy' sections of the IRI empire. By all accounts IRI exercises relatively little control and RAI is dominated by the political parties.
19. Despicht, op. cit., p. 137.
20. K. Allen 'Regional Intervention' in *The State as Entrepreneur,* op. cit., p. 174.
21. V. Lutz *Italy: a Study in Economic Development* Oxford: Oxford University Press (1962) p. 279.
22. ibid., p. 280.
23. IRI *Annual Report 1959* p. 101.
24. IRI's textile firms passed to ENI in 1970, its railway rolling stock firms and an armament company were transferred to EFIM in 1968, and a textile machinery company to EGAM in 1971. On the other hand IRI took over three heavy electrical equipment companies from EFIM between 1970 and 1973.
25. In 1959 electricity for lighting cost 33.2 lire per kWh in the North, 35.5 lire in the Centre, 40.1 lire on the southern mainland and 42.4 lire in the Islands. Small- and medium-sized industries in the same year were paying 18.7 lire for electricity for power purposes in the North, 19.4 lire in the Centre, 22.2 lire on the southern mainland and 24.0 lire in the Islands. A. Servidio *Il Nodo Meridionale* Naples: Edizioni Scientifiche Italiane (1972) p. 212.
26. For a very good discussion of the political forces leading to the nationalisation of the electricity industry, see La Palombara, op. cit.
27. ibid., p. 74.
28. Figures taken largely from M. Guidi 'State Holdings in the Italian Economy' *Review of Economic Conditions in Italy* Banco di Roma (September 1968).
29. The greater part of the information used for the early history of ENI has been taken from L. Faleschini and G. Kojanec 'Ente Nazionale Idrocarburi' in

Volume IV of *Enciclopidia del Petrolio e del Gas Naturale*.
30. Article 1 of Law N.136 (10 February 1953), which created ENI.
31. Faleschini and Kojanec, op. cit., p. 5.
32. Ministero delle Participazioni Statali *Relazione Programmatica* (Rome, 1972) vol. 1, p. 39.
33. G. Petrilli 'IRI and Planning' *Review of Economic Conditions in Italy* Banco di Roma (March 1965).
34. ibid.
35. Ministero delle Participazioni Statali *Relazione Programmatica* (Rome, 1968) p. 19.
36. G. Petrilli *Lo Stato Imprenditore* Cappelli (1967) p. 101.
37. ibid, p. 84.
38. Saraceno, op. cit., p. 193.
39. For a very good discussion of these inquiries see Amato, op. cit., pp. 223–35; and Posner and Woolf, op. cit.
40. Posner and Woolf, op. cit., pp. 30–1.
41. ibid, pp. 32–3.
42. La Palombara, op. cit., p. 57.
43. ibid., p. 57.
44. N. Jucker *Italy* London: Thames and Hudson (1970) p. 143.
45. For details of these early political manoeuvres, see La Palombara, op. cit., pp. 28–33. It is interesting that a proposal for a Ministry of State Holdings had been put forward in 1951 by La Malfa's report into the state holding sector. See Amato, op. cit., p. 231.
46. Law No. 1589 (December 1956), setting up the Ministry of State Holdings (article 4).
47. ibid., article 3.
48. Guidi, op. cit., p. 345.
49. Posner and Woolf, op. cit., p. 128.
50. The law setting up the Ministry, fearful of the danger of stilting entrepreneurial spirit in the sector by excessive bureaucracy, limited its personnel, permanent and temporary, to 100. Although this was later changed, the Ministry still remains understaffed.
51. Ministero delle Participazioni Statali *Relazione Programmatica* (Rome, 1967) p. 17.
52. ibid., p. 17.
53. ibid., p. 17.
54. For details of this dispute see C. Johnson 'Relations with Government and Parliament' in *The State as Entrepreneur*, op. cit., pp. 212–13.
55. Ministero delle Participazione Statali *Relazione Programmatica* (Rome, 1967) op. cit., p. 18.
56. Despicht, op. cit., p. 154. On the other hand, IRI's proposal in 1967 for the development of colour TV programmes was turned down by the government on the grounds that this was too consumer-oriented.
57. See the article by B. Visentini in *Corriere della Sera* (22 June 1973).
58. See G. Ruffolo *Rapporto sulla Programmazione* Rome: Laterza (1973). Visentini, op. cit., also strongly advocates such a move.
59. See Posner and Woolf, op. cit., pp. 81–3, for a good discussion of the factors encouraging the sector to borrow short.
60. IRI *Annual Report 1966* pp. 61–2.
61. Banca d'Italia *Relazione Annuale 1970* pp. 330–1.
62. The self-financing ratio fell yet further, to 18.7 per cent, in 1971. This was a result of a government-encouraged expansion of investment (nearly 40 per cent above the 1970 level) combined with depressed conditions in the Italian economy. For details of capital sources in 1971 see Ministero delle Participazioni Statali *Relazione Programmatica* vol. 1 (Rome, 1973) p. 65.
63. In 1971 these conditions were encountered in an acute form (see n. 62), and a massive 23 per cent of the sector's financial needs were met by state finance.

64.   'As a rule, it costs a company about 12–14 per cent to ensure its shareholders an annual payout of 6–7 per cent in dividends – which is necessary to compete with the typical yield on bonds – while that incurred in issuing fixed income securities is only 10–11 per cent', *Financial Times* (27 April 1972).

65.   IRI *Annual Report 1967* p. 56.

66.   Excluded were retail trade, public services, *autostrade,* water and gas, rail transport and 'various transport'.

67.   Included are chemicals, artificial and synthetic fibres, petroleum and textiles.

68.   For a clear statement of this view see IRI *Annual Report 1971* pp. 99–102.

69.   Law No. 184 (22 March 1971).

70.   For a discussion of labour relations in IRI, see by W. Kendall 'Labour Relations' in *The State as Entrepreneur,* op. cit., pp. 219–31.

71.   For further discussion of this point see Posner and Woolf, op. cit.

72.   IASM *Situazione del Lavoro Indotto nel Mezzogiorno dalle Iniziative nel Settore delle Auto* (Rome, 1971).

73.   For a further discussion of this point see *Lo Stato Imprenditore,* op. cit., p. 181.

APPENDIX:

Postwar Political Developments*

Will you, won't you, will you, won't you, will you join the dance? (Alice in Wonderland)

THE rapid postwar growth and development of the Italian economy has taken place in spite of frequent changes of government – nearly thirty between 1945 and 1972. Many of these changes have reflected the frustration of successive governments which, through slender margins or internal squabblings, were unable to get their legislation through Parliament. *Immobilismo* has been a key characteristic of Italian politics over much of the postwar period. Essential legislation on education, health, housing, taxation and transport has frequently been long delayed, often lasting through a number of different governments. Most governments have been coalitions of several parties, each having within it a wide spectrum of opinion. The problems of reconciling the differing party views, and the difference within parties, has not been easy. As we have seen in chapter 1, a notable feature of Italy since the war has been the failure to evolve relevant policies to deal with the major socio-economic consequences of rapid economic growth, and much of this is a result of her frequently unstable and impotent coalitions.

To the casual British observer, the Italian political scene can give the impression of complete confusion. The system seems one which, like much that is ludicrous in this world, could either warrant a learned study or be used as a basis for a comedy. In fact, postwar Italian politics have been characterised by quite firm, and often forecastable, trends. It is the aim of this brief appendix to trace the political developments in Italy since the war. It has no pretensions of being comprehensive, but is directed solely at providing some political context for the economic developments and issues discussed in the rest of the book.

During the war, the various anti-Fascist political parties had co-operated well together and formed committees of national liberation (CNLs) in most of the major towns. These committees often provided the base of the resistance movement in the North. There was a hope that the wartime inter-party co-operation would continue to operate, at least

* The authors are grateful to Mr Paul Littlewood of Glasgow University who collaborated in the preparation of this appendix.

267

during the desperate immediate postwar period; and the first government, set up in June 1945, was, like the CNLs, composed of all six anti-Fascist parties (Communists, Christian Democrats, Liberals, Socialists, Democratic Labour and the Action Party, all of which except the last had existed before the war in some form or another). This coalition was led by the respected resistance leader, Parri. However, inter-party strife, present in some degree towards the end of the war, started almost immediately, and within months the government collapsed. 'Parri himself, always an idealist, and a man of action as well, when faced with the emergencies of resistance, had proved less adept when dealing with the intricacies of party disputes'.[1] Although the coalition held together, Parri was replaced in December 1945 by the Christian Democrat, De Gasperi, a courageous anti-Fascist politician of quite enormous resilience. In spite of a number of changes of government, he was to remain prime minister for the next eight years or so.

Until mid-1946 there was no elected parliament, its functions being performed largely by a *consulta,* the 429 members of which were 'nominated by the government on the basis of lists put forward by the political parties and the trade unions'.[2] In June 1946, elections were held for a so-called constituent assembly, whose main task was to draw up a new constitution. The results of these, the first national elections in postwar Italy, mirrored those of the earlier local elections, with the great majority of votes going to the Christian Democrats (35.2 per cent), the Socialists (20.7 per cent) and the Communists (19.0 per cent).[3]

The Christian Democrat party had been formed during the war, replacing the earlier *Partito Populare.*[4]* It was, and remains, basically Catholic, securing most of the votes from rural areas and the middle classes.[5] The party does, however, hold a great range of views across the political spectrum, and many of its members could be confused with the more moderate but reformist Socialists or, on the right, with the Liberals. The diversity of views among the Christian Democrat deputies (MPs), organised into coherent groups or *correnti,* and combined with outside pressure from such powerful Catholic groups as ACI,[6]* provides considerable problems of management for the party's leaders and has often made the party more conservative than it would otherwise have been. Other parties have, of course, not been immune to these sorts of problems[7] but, since the Christian Democrats have been the core of all postwar governments, their intra-party conflicts have to some degree been at the root of Italian governments' inability to make vital reforms.

The Socialist party (PSI) and the Communist party (PCI) were in 1946 strongly linked. The Italian Communist party had been formed in 1921 by disgruntled Socialists but, exiled by Mussolini, the leaders of the two parties had in 1934 signed a Unity of Action pact. This was reaffirmed in October 1946, providing for the 'coordination of joint decisions on all problems and at all levels'.[8] As we shall see, however, this unity was more apparent than real.

Among the other parties in the 1946 elections, and securing 4.4 per cent of the votes, were the Republicans – stable, deliberate, anti-clerical and anti-communist, but with their support heavily concentrated in Romagna, for historical reasons. There were also the Liberals (very much to the right of the British Liberal party and becoming more right-wing later, when the Christian Democrats moved to the left). 'The Italian Liberals claimed political descent from Cavour; to many their liberalism seemed indeed a century out of date. Their enemies said that the only liberty in favour of which they felt strongly was the liberty of the entrepreneur; though not entirely so, they were in effect the party of the less enlightened industrialists and bankers.'[9] In the 1946 elections the Liberals combined with the Labour Democrats (a minor CNL group based in the South)[10]* and secured 6.8 per cent of the votes.

Three other parties in the 1946 elections are worthy of mention. First, the Uomo Qualunque, or Everyman's party, got 5.3 per cent of the votes. This party, led by a journalist named Guglielmo Giannini, who 'wore a monocle and no necktie and professed equally inconsequent policies',[11] was a don't-know or cynics' party laced with a positive distaste for the existing parties and political system. It 'derided all the idealism of the moment and appealed to rank-and-file former Fascists who were frightened of developments',[12] and in particular to sections of the middle classes who had doubts about how far the anti-Fascist purges would go. It died soon after the 1948 elections when it merged with the Liberals, though many of its members were later to join the neo-Fascist party (MSI – Movimento Sociale Italiano). Secondly, there was the Action Party, which pulled only 1.5 per cent of the votes and collapsed soon after. This left-wing resistance party had little in its postwar programme that differed from the other major parties, and 'failed to establish clear lines of policy, although, perhaps because, it included many of the best, the most ingenious minds of Italy. Without the simplicity these people were unable to discover they could never attract sufficient popular support to make the party politically worthwhile.'[13] The azionisti spread themselves among the Socialist, Communist and Republican parties. Thirdly, there was the right-wing Monarchist party, which held, other than Monarchists, many of the ardent ex-Fascists who, the Fascist party being constitutionally illegal, found it a reasonable refuge until the more distinctly neo-Fascist MSI party developed in the very late 1940s. The Monarchists captured 2.8 per cent of the votes.

After the 1946 elections De Gasperi was again asked to form a government and, given that the main role of the constituent assembly was to devise a constitution, he decided on a government encompassing a wide range of views. It held Christian Democrats, Communists, Socialists, and Republicans; and lasted for less than a year. Its problems started in early 1947 when the Socialists split. The more moderate Socialists had for some time been worried by the ties between their party and the Communists. As the cold war built up in Europe and the Italian Communists showed continuing allegiance to Russia, the situation became intolerable for these moderates. In January 1947, led by Saragat, nearly a half of the Socialist deputies left the party and formed the more moderate, Social Democrat, PSLI (Partito Socialista dei Lavoratori Italiani), later (1952) renamed PSDI (Partito Socialista Democratico Italiano). The PSDI was 'a respectable, revisionist Marxist party that appeals to the skilled worker élite, to artisans and clerical workers – even to some employers and managers – who are in search of a dignified and not too virilant leftism'.[14] The veteran leader, Nenni, remained as head of the Socialist party – a man who was *simpatico,* no intellectual, and who stuck with the Communists largely because he was haunted by his strong belief in working class unity, and particularly by the feeling that 'Mussolini had won by dividing the working class and that this must never be allowed to happen again'.[15] As a result of Saragat's moves, the Socialists withdrew from the government, which then resigned, only to be reconstituted along the same lines shortly afterwards. It was obvious, however, that this was a temporary arrangement to see the Constitution agreed and, this done in May 1947, De Gasperi resigned again to clear the way for a government purged of the extreme left.

At the end of May De Gasperi returned to power with a new (minority) government, made up largely of Christian Democrats. The immediate postwar all party co-operation was definitely at an end, and 'was gradually replaced by a political battle conducted with no holds barred'.[16] It is perhaps little short of amazing that this minority government was able to start the successful process of halting the serious inflation which, as we have seen in chapter 1, had plagued Italy since the war. A number of attempts were made to bring the government down, but it survived – a result of right-wing political support and brilliant tactics by De Gasperi. Its victories in this respect doubtless lent credibility to its policies against inflation and encouraged the Social Democrats and Republicans to join it in December 1947.

Parliamentary elections were held in April 1948. In many ways the battle was between the Communists and the anti-Communists, and whether Italy should cement her growing ties with the West or 'ally' with the East. Direct financial aid was given to the two sides by the USA and USSR.[17] At one time it looked as if the struggle would be very close, but this in itself encouraged greater effort by the anti-Communists, and not least by the Church with its enormous influence, which, along with Confindustria, gave substantial financial support to the anti-Communist parties, and particularly the Christian Democrats.[18] 'As far as the Church itself was concerned, the outcome of the Italian elections was a matter too serious for neutrality. The Church, therefore, supported with all available means, the anti-Communist side.'[19] The government's economic success, particularly in curbing inflation, profited the 'democratic' parties while the Communists were not helped by the *coup d'état* in Czechoslovakia, nor by Marshall Aid which had been agreed by early 1948. In the 1948 elections the Communists and Socialists presented joint lists and fought as the 'Democratic Popular Front'. Even so, they secured only 31.2 per cent of the votes for the Chamber of Deputies. (All the voting figures provided in this appendix are for the Chamber of Deputies – by far the most important of the two houses set up by the 1947 Constitution, the other house being the Senate.) This compared unfavourably with the 39.7 per cent of votes secured by the Communists and Socialists fighting separately in 1946. Much, though by no means all, of this fall was undoubtedly a consequence of the Socialist split, since the Social Democrats got 7.1 per cent of the votes. Although, by the time of the election, the Christian Democrats were expected to do well, the extent of their success astounded most observers. They got 48.5 per cent of the votes as against their 1946 proportion of 35.2 per cent – a gain of 4.7 million votes, which gave them 55 per cent of the seats in the Chamber of Deputies. There is little doubt that the Christian Democrats profited from the slump in the fortunes of the right-wing parties. The Liberal party, fighting with the Uomo Qualunque party, got a mere 3.8 per cent of the votes as against a combined vote of 12.1 per cent in the 1946 elections when they fought separately. Some of these lost votes doubtless went to the newly formed MSI, which got 2 per cent of the total, but the Christian Democrat party was the main beneficiary. The Republicans also lost votes, securing only 2.5 per cent in 1948 as against 4.4 per cent in 1946.

The results of the 1948 elections were of vital importance for Italy. They confirmed her position in the West and were to leave the Communists in permanent opposition. This meant that a quarter or so of the electorate was to remain 'in an attitude of systematic and intransigent opposition'.[20] The creation of this state within a state was dangerous, giving rise to a continual 'potential danger of anti-democratic coups as a result of the constant pressures to which the government was subjected from both right and left extremists'.[21]

As already noted, the Christian Democrat vote was such as to give them a majority in the Chamber of Deputies but De Gasperi, called again to form a government, decided on a coalition of the centre parties – a *quadripartito,* made up of Christian Democrats, Social Democrats, Republicans and Liberals. De Gasperi 'attached great importance to this combination of Catholic and secular centrist forces, believing that the presence of the three secular parties would help to counteract the inevitable tendencies towards clericalism in his own party and serve as a counter poise to its conservative wing, strengthened in the recent election'.[22] Moreover, these other parties were 'needed in the staffing of foreign and economic agencies. Small in number, the minor democratic parties were relatively rich in brains'.[23] The coalition held 366 seats in the Chamber of Deputies out of a total of 574.

The Communists, embittered by the election results, harrassed the government in Parliament and also encouraged extra-parliamentary opposition through strikes, go-slows and, in the South, by urging the peasants to occupy land on the big estates. The years 1948 and 1949 were particularly difficult ones for Italy, when many feared a revolution. Such fears were probably unfounded since the extreme left, after the Bakunin-led anarchism of the 1870s, had been schizophrenic. 'Once it abandoned anarchism and entered its Marxist phase, Italian socialism could never make up its mind over the question of legality or illegality, revolution or evolution.'[24]* In July 1948, however, an assassination attempt was made on the life of the Communist leader, Togliatti. A general strike was declared, roadblocks were set up in the principal northern towns, and weapons reappeared, so few years after the wartime resistance when they had last been used. 'One word from the party directorate would have been enough to transform the street demonstrations into an armed insurrection. But the word was not given, the [Communist party] leaders themselves undertook the task of pacifying the masses, and after a few days normal conditions were restablished.'[25] The party was obviously intent on stopping short of revolution.

Nevertheless the extreme Communist moves in 1948 and 1949 were not without repercussions. One consequence was a split in the then united trade union organisation, CGIL, with the moderates and anti-Communists forming their own unions (see chapter 4 above), in part no doubt encouraged by the 'democratic' parties in their attempts to weaken the Communist position. The Communist agitation also encouraged, and some would say obliged, the government to introduce dramatic reforms in 1950, though with the economy virtually recovered from the war and with the underpinning of Marshall Aid, it is arguable that these would have come anyway. The reforms involved the taxation system and new and dramatic policies for the South, where the Communists were finding a good seedbed for their ideas. The Cassa per il Mezzogiorno was created and land reform schemes involving the expropriation and break-up of big estates were initiated (see chapter 6).

The government got few benefits from these policies and, indeed, probably lost out. The right wing, worried by the government's egalitarian and seemingly left-wing moves, was strengthened while the left wing had been seen to effect changes. The Communists persuasively argued that the government, in its southern policy at least, had merely responded to what was tantamount to a *fait accompli*. The coalition collapsed and was restored in some form or another on a number of occasions, at the expense of radical reform. Within the government, and particularly in his dealings with his own party, De Gasperi had to steer a middle course. 'Much of the energy and time of those who then were in power, first of all De Gasperi, were consumed in the attempt to maintain an equilibrium between the demands of the progressives and the intransigent opposition of the conservatives, and when certain measures could not be put off any longer, they were subject to such compromise as to denature their substance.'[26] Slowly, the centre parties lost support, and this was clearly shown in the 1951 and 1952 local elections, with losses for the Christian Democrats and gains by the extremes of left and right, particularly in the South. The government became worried about the likely outcome of the June 1953 general elections.

In desperation, they introduced a bill making changes in the electoral law which was not dissimilar to the Fascist (Rocco) law of 1926. The bill proposed that any party or alliance that secured more than half the seats should be given bonus seats in the Chamber of Deputies in order to make their position stronger. It is, perhaps, unfair to see this proposal simply as one aimed at saving the coalition, for it could, as De Gasperi hoped, have given greater stability to Italian politics. The bill did in fact get through Parliament to become known as the 'trick law', and though repealed soon after, without doubt it lost the government votes in the 1953 elections. In the event, however, the centre parties got slightly less (49.2 per cent) than the 50 per cent of votes required to benefit under the law. The extreme left and right parties increased their votes and seats considerably.

The period 1953–58 saw Italian politics in a very poor state. The centre coalition governments were weak even when united, which was rare. There were six governments in this period. The first three and the last were made up of Christian Democrats alone (*monocolore* governments), while in those years when the centre government was in power there was continual strife within the coalition. The Liberals were moving to the right, financed heavily by Confindustria and big business, while the Social Democrats were beginning to move back towards the Socialists. For their part, the Republicans, though giving support, stayed outside the government. Major reforms in this atmosphere were impossible, particularly as the Christian Democrat leaders, moving slightly left, were in trouble with the right wing of their own party. In general, the governments of this period, 'based on limited majorities, sometimes kept in power through the abstention of extreme right-wing parties, could not undertake broad measures for economic progress and social reform'.[27] The last of the 1953–58 governments was again *monocolore* Christian Democrat, set up in 1957 under the premiership of Adone Zoli.

It secured its vote of confidence only through Monarchist and neo-Fascist support. Even the Christian Democrat party was at pains to point out that it was not really a Christian Democrat government. Being so close to the national elections, due to be held in 1958, and the centre system of government now being in disrepute, no other coalition was possible. Without doubt this was one of the weakest of the postwar governments, and yet also one of the strongest since nobody wanted to see it fall. 'Zoli's major strength lay in the certainty that, in the event of his fall, the President of the Republic would be compelled to dissolve Parliament and call for new elections, an eventuality that all parties feared, in view of their unpreparedness to face the electorate.'[28] In this paradoxical situation a number of major reforms were pushed through including, as we have seen in chapter 6 above, substantial new policies for the South.

It was becoming fairly obvious that the centre coalition had become an unsatisfactory form of government; and, led by Fanfani and Moro, there was a growing view within the Christian Democrat party that the only feasible alternative was a centre–left government, i.e. one including the Socialists. This mood was helped by the new President, Gronchi, elected in 1955 and very sympathetic to a leftish move. At the same time, events in Russia and Hungary were pushing the Socialists away from the Communists. In 1956 there was a meeting between the Socialist and Social Democrat leaders to try to reconcile their differences, and in 1957 the Unity Pact between the Socialists and Communists was rescinded. This removed yet another hurdle for a centre–left government. The general election results of 1958 seemed to give added support to the idea of a centre–left government with the Christian Democrats, Socialists and Social Democrats securing gains and the Communists' vote stagnating. The Liberals also gained – doubtless from the disgruntled right wing of the Christian Democrats. The Monarchists and MSI saw their votes reduced substantially.

In spite of these favourable forces and factors, the road to a centre–left government was not easy. Fanfani, one of its architects, formed a government in 1958 composed of Christian Democrats and Social Democrats, and prepared a programme of reforms which it was hoped would attract the Socialists. The government fell within six months. It was brought down ostensibly by a scandal, but the basic reason was the fear engendered within the Christian Democrat party by these strong left-wing moves, combined with a personal dislike by many deputies for the erratic Fanfani.

It was, perhaps, almost inevitable that the Christian Democrat party should move to the right again after this experiment, and in 1959 and the first half of 1960 there was a succession of governments composed of Christian Democrats with right-wing (including MSI) support, culminating in one led by Tambroni – a right-wing Christian Democrat 'strong' man. The MSI was given new confidence by its seeming importance to government, and in July 1960 held a congress in Genoa which gave rise to serious riots in that and other northern cities (as well as violence in Parliament). These events, combined with the centre–left coalitions being set up in many of the northern cities, both pushed and encouraged the Christian Democrats to reverse direction again and to seek out another centre–left government. At first this took the form of external Socialist support for a basically Christian Democrat government, but in January 1962 the Socialists were formally invited to join the government. By this time the Catholic Church, under Pope John, had become more sympathetic to the left wing. Given its enormous influence, this had an important effect on Christian Democrat attitudes towards the left, and indeed on public opinion in general.[29]* The Socialists themselves, having rescinded the Unity Pact with the Communists, were seeking a re-unification with the Social Democrats and were keen on joining a government composed of Christian Democrats, Social Democrats and Republicans. The Liberals went into opposition.

The Socialists' conditions for their support included stronger economic planning, education reforms, the nationalisation of electricity, and the development of regional government. Against most expectations Fanfani honoured the majority of these commitments, although the point does deserve to be made that the left wing of the Christian Democrat party was in favour of both economic planning and the nationalisation of the electricity industry. Economic planning proposals were being discussed by May 1962, the electricity industry was nationalised by the autumn, and reforms of the school system were quickly introduced, including the raising of the school-leaving age to fourteen and the start of a unified secondary school system. There were, however, no moves on the subject of regional government, the Christian Democrats being fearful that the North and Centre regions would be dominated by Socialist–Communist coalitions. The right-wing Christian Democrats were in any case already worried, arguing that the government had given too much away without getting much in return from the Socialists, in particular a promise of a break with the Communists in the local elections. They were especially concerned at the speed with which the Socialists appeared to have been converted to democracy. 'Many of these people thought that its new attitude concealed a menace, and the [Socialist party] would prove to be a Trojan horse, which would attempt to introduce its former Communist ally into the citadel of the government.'[30] Moreover, at the end of 1962 the Italian boom was ending and the more conservative elements in the Christian Democrat party were blaming the situation on the reforms. In part this was not unfair. The nationalising of electricity had precipitated a great capital outflow from Italy which severely damaged the balance of payments (see chapter 3 above). It was only through powerful and masterful work by the party secretary Moro (and apparently a plea from the Vatican that solidarity should be maintained in the name of Christian unity)[31] that the Christian Democrat party held together.

The electorate, however, was not so easy to marshall, and the Christian Democrats were hard hit in the general elections of April 1963. Their share of votes fell to 38.3 from 42.4 per cent in 1958, losing votes to the right and left. The Liberals profited, increasing their proportion of votes from 3.5 to 7.0 per cent. The Monarchist proportion fell from 2.2 to 1.7 per cent, many of these votes doubtless going to the Liberals and the MSI, the latter seeing their proportion rise from 4.8 to 5.1 per cent. It was the left wing, however, that did best. The continuingly generous attitude by the Church towards the left, including a seemingly insignificant audience in March 1963 given by Pope John to Krushchev's daughter, doubtless allowed more people, and especially women (who accounted for some two-thirds of Christian Democrat support) to vote for the left in good conscience. Although the Socialist vote fell slightly, from 14.2 to 13.8 per cent, the Social Democrats' increased from 4.5 to 6.1 per cent. Both socialist parties picked up votes from the left wing of the Christian Democrats, but they also lost some of their own members who were disconcerted by the move away from the Communists. The Communist vote, doubtless aided by the Church's attitude and by the party's impressive use of television to exploit a politically immature electorate,[32] increased from 22.7 to 25.5 per cent, securing another million votes. The Republicans stagnated at 1.4 per cent of the vote.

A centre–left coalition was now almost a necessity for the Christian Democrats if they were to form a government with adequate strength; and, after a brief caretaker government, a centre–left coalition under Moro (who was to remain prime minister for the next four years or so) was formed in November 1963. This included Christian Democrats, Socialists, Social Democrats and Republicans. Nenni was made deputy prime minister. 'The Catholic–Socialist *connubio* which could have saved Italian democracy in 1919–22 came into being at last.'[33] The Socialists had a strong influence on the government's policies – their proposals for regional government and a five-year economic plan were accepted. They did, however, pay a price. Many of their members thought that the move was a betrayal of working-class unity, and found their party's acceptance of an Italy within NATO particularly distasteful. In January 1964, 25 of the 87 Socialist deputies left the Socialist party and the coalition to form PSIUP (Partito Socialista Italiano di Unità Proletaria) – a party in many respects more left-wing and radical than the Communists. But at the time this did not appear to herald any major crisis for the remaining deputies in the Socialist party. Rather, with the radicals gone, it seemed to facilitate their adoption of a moderate left-wing stance and their acceptance of a firm commitment to participation in government. This seemed to be confirmed in 1966 when, doubtless aided by Saragat's recent promotion to president, the Socialists and the continuingly moderate Social Democrats united to form a single party – PSU (Partito Socialista Unificato).

The centre–left government was not without its problems, not least because it came to power just when the economy had overheated and needed to be deflated and, as part of this, government expenditure was being curbed. These were not ideal conditions for reform. In addition, the terrible floods in 1966 diverted government energy from longer term tasks. Moreover, the right wing of the Christian Democrats was becoming increasingly worried about the left-wing moves and held up a number of reforms. The government collapsed a number of times before the general election of 1968, but was re-formed each time with the old centre–left coalition led by Moro. In spite of initial optimism, over the five years 1963–68 the pressing need for reforms had not been met and there was a growing discontent with the government's failures in this respect and with the return of *immobilismo* to the political scene. Pope Paul, who succeeded Pope John, was a much more cautious leader, and the more open and reforming outlook of the Church that had developed under John was stifled under the new papal leader. The younger generation in particular grew disenchanted with both the Church and politics. 'The young idealists spoke increasingly of a *Repubblica Conciliare, . . .* which should turn Pope John's dream into reality by drawing in all men of goodwill from all parties.'[34] The government did succeed in legislating for regional government, in February 1968, but overall it is fair to say that 'little tangible was achieved'[35] by the centre–left governments of the mid-1960s.

The general election results of May 1968 spelled trouble for the left wing of the coalition. Although the Christian Democrats and Republicans made gains, increasing their votes relative to 1963 from 38.3 to 39.1 per cent and from 1.4 to 2.0 per cent respectively, PSU secured a mere 14.5 per cent as against a combined total of 19.9 per cent in the 1963 elections when the Socialists and Social Democrats fought separately. PSIUP profited from these losses and took 4.5 per cent of the vote. The Communists also gained, their vote rising from 25.3 per cent in 1963 to 26.9 per cent in 1968. The right-wing MSI and Monarchist parties lost votes. The general election brought Moro's long period as premier to a close, and while PSU tried to clarify their own political position, Leone stepped in with a temporary *monocolore* government, performing the same holding operation he had managed before Moro's accession in 1963.

Despite PSU's setback, by the end of 1968 Rumor succeeded in forming a new centre–left government with the same distribution of ministries as in Moro's final government. But, significantly, only ten of the twenty-six ministers of Moro's government served in Rumor's. Differences reappeared between the Saragatiani and Nenniani Socialists, and in July 1969 the former split from the main party, recreated the Social Democrat party, and subsequently resigned from the coalition, leading directly to its collapse. This was to be the start of a period of great political instability and social upheaval in Italy.

Rumor first formed a temporary Christian Democrat government with external Socialist support, and then, in March 1970, succeeded in forming another centre–left coalition (Christian Democrats, Republicans, the recreated Social Democrats and Socialists). In June 1970, the results of the elections for the newly constituted regions (as well as those for some provinces and town councils) seemed to confirm electoral support for the coalition, with the Republicans gaining, the Socialists and Social Democrats recouping some of their lost support and the Christian Democrats losing only slightly. The extreme parties lost ground, except the MSI who improved their position. Then, suddenly and surprisingly, Rumor resigned. The reasons for this are still not clear. One factor was undoubtedly his fear of the violence that had developed in Italy. Since March 1969, Italy had suffered an exceptional wave of strikes, mass demonstrations, bombings and shootings. It is known that Rumor was both depressed and puzzled by these events. But another factor must have been the growing difference of opinion between the Social Democrats and the right wing of the Christian Democrats on the one hand, and the Socialists and left wing factions of the Christian Democrats on the other. The Social Democrats insisted that the Socialists were being, at the least, inconsistent in their continued participation in the government while simultaneously forming ruling coalitions with the Communists in the regional councils in North and Central Italy. Despite the optimism at the start of his premiership, Rumor and his colleagues had failed to push through virtually any of the reforms they had promised. The disturbances of the period were not unassociated with these failures.

After several false starts, a new centre–left government was formed under Colombo in August 1970 to face the task of satisfying the ever-increasing, vociferous and sometimes violent demands for reform in health, housing, transport, education, taxation and divorce. Colombo's cabinet had an almost identical composition to that of his predecessor, not only in political structure but also in personalities. Of the twenty-nine ministers, twenty-seven had served in Rumor's last cabinet and twenty held the same ministry.

The social disorders and rumour (recently confirmed) of attempts to take over power, including a full-scale *coup d'état*,[36]* were widely reported by the mass media and commented upon by politicians. This served to attract more attention to the MSI, and to develop a sustained campaign against the Communist party and the extra-parliamentary left.

In the 1971 elections (for councils in the region of Sicily, two provinces and eighty-eight municipalities), the MSI made unprecedented gains. Some of this increase was at the expense of the Liberals and the Monarchists, but the Christian Democrats also conceded a substantial number of votes to the right. The Socialists, Social Democrats and Republicans all increased their percentage of the vote, the Socialists probably benefiting from Communist and PSIUP losses.

The end of 1971 witnessed an important event, the presidential election, which widened the differences between the factions within the Christian Democrat party. After a farcical period in which parties and factions jockeyed for position, on the twenty-third ballot Leone was elected to succeed Saragat as a result of the declared support of members of the MSI and Monarchist parties. This contributed significantly to the widening rift between, in particular, the Socialists and the other members of the coalition. In January 1972 the Republicans, claiming dissatisfaction with the government's failure to pass and enact reforms in housing, health, education and economic policy, withdrew their support; and although not numerically crucial, their withdrawal indicated the impossibility of the government continuing in office.

Following several attempts to find another centre–left formula, Andreotti became prime minister of a new *monocolore* Christian Democrat government. It was now clear that the general elections due to take place in 1973 would have to be held a year early – not simply so that a contentious referendum on divorce could be shelved or postponed (such an event being certain to increase the cleavages within the Christian Democrat party, and between it and the other members of the coalition) but, more important, so that a new and firmer basis for coalition government might be found.

After a national campaign in which the Christian and Social Democrats seemed far more disposed to attack the left rather than the right, it was no great surprise that the 1972 general elections benefited the right, harmed the left and little affected the centre parties. The MSI gained 2.9 per cent more votes than in 1968 – largely attributable to its assimilation of the now defunct Monarchists and the losses of the Liberals (down by 1.9 per cent). The Christian Democrats' percentage of votes dropped marginally (by 0.3 per cent); the Republicans continued to grow (by 0.9 per cent); and the Socialists and Social Democrats gained slightly (by 0.2 per cent). Finally, although the Communists gained a little ground (up 0.3 per cent), their allies in PSIUP were obliterated, losing all their twenty-three seats. Three new left-wing parties which had emerged before these elections all fared badly, gaining 1.3 per cent of the votes, but no seats.

In spite of these changes, Andreotti was again made prime minister designate, and began negotiations for a five-party coalition government comprising Liberals as well as the Christian and Social Democrats, Republicans and Socialists. This would have been a motley collection, covering the whole ideological spectrum of Italian 'democratic' parties. Success was virtually inconceivable. The Socialists refused to participate in a government that included the Liberals, and the Republicans, partly in sympathy with the Socialists, offered only external support. Andreotti, with the backing of an increasingly anti-Socialist Social Democrat party, therefore turned to a right–centrist formula. In June 1972 the new government, comprising Christian Democrats, Social Democrats and Liberals, was sworn in. It had a majority in the Chamber of Deputies of four (plus external support from the fourteen Republicans).

So ended Italy's first period of centre–left rule. Although it had begun amidst great hopes, by 1972 there was disillusionment all round; great rifts had opened up between the Socialists and Social Democrats and, more crucially perhaps, between the right and left within the Christian Democrats. On balance there was very little to show in the way of social and other reform.

But already in 1972 there were signs that reversion to the old right-centrist formula was to be no happier a solution to Italy's political, not to say economic and social, problems. Criticism of Andreotti's govern-ment was not slow to begin and steadily increased over the next ten months, especially with regard to its inability to cope with inflation and the deteriorating balance of payments. Meanwhile leading politicians, including many in the Christian Democrat party itself, were beginning to talk again of the viability of a centre–left coalition. Months before the eventual fall of Andreotti's government, Fanfani and others were seeking out a new basis of Christian Democrat unity, producing a formula, accepted at the 1973 party congress, that spelled the death of the ruling coalition.

This move was closely associated with a reversal of attitudes by both the Christian Democrats and most of the mass media soon after the 1972 elections, when they began to blame the right rather than the left for the continuing incidence of violence. The responsibility for the Reggio Calabria riots was finally acknowledged to lie at the door of the MSI and former Monarchists rather than the Communists. The left-wing suspects for the 1969 Milan and Rome bombings were released and replaced by right-wing suspects. Parliament decided by a massive majority to proceed with an investigation as to whether Almirante, leader of the MSI, was in fact reconstituting a Fascist party (outlawed in the Italian Constitution). These changes in attitudes were reflected in the local election results of November 1972, which seem to indicate that the gains made by the right in the 1971 and 1972 elections were not an enduring phenomenon.

Thus, by 1973 conditions did not favour the continuation of Andreotti's government, and pressed for a swing back to the left. The final blow to the government came in May, when the Christian Democrat minister of posts and telecommunications sent out an apparently unconstitutional ministerial decree which outlawed private utilisation of cable television, without ever having consulted the other coalition parties. The Republicans withdrew their support from the minister, and when the Christian Democrats refused to dismiss him, withdrew their support from the whole government. In June the government fell, and the Christian Democrats set about reconstituting the centre–left. This task, allotted to Rumor, was not easy. In the Christian Democrat Party, Colombo and his faction were reluctant to co-operate, the Social Democrats split seriously in voting which of their members were to take ministerial positions, and in the PSI an even more serious rift occurred when two factions failed to support the party's decision to negotiate for inclusion in the government.

Nevertheless, a new government was finally formed in July 1973, made up of Christian Democrats, Socialists, Social Democrats and Republicans. Rumor made clear at the outset that the new government would in no way act with the MSI, and would accept support from the Communists – strengthening the increasingly frequent hints of a possible future alliance between the Christian Democrats and Communists. Whether or not this will ever happen is impossible to predict. Certainly it is inconceivable without a major crisis in the Christian Democrat party, possibly resulting in a secession by its right wing. But whatever happens, it is the Christian Democrat–Communist relationship that will be at the centre of political debate for the foreseeable future in Italy – although with the chronic instability of Italian government, the future that *can* be foreseen is very small indeed.

Notes to appendix

1. M. Grindrod *Italy* London: Ernest Benn (1968) pp. 94–5.
2. ibid., p. 96.
3. A comprehensive survey of Italian postwar voting patterns, and used as a source in this appendix, can be found in Presidency of the Council of Ministers *Italy – Documents and Notes* supplement to No. 6 (November–December 1971).
4. After the new Italian state took Rome in 1870, a major split developed between it and the Church, and in 1874 'the Pope pronounced the famous *non expedit* whereby faithful Catholics were instructed not to participate in Italian political affairs either as voters or candidates . . . For the first half-century of its existence the Italian nation was deprived of the active support and participation of many of its most able and talented elements.' D. Germino and S. Passigli *The Government and Parties of Contemporary Italy* New York: Harper and Row (1968) p. 11. The deprivation of Italian political life from this papal injunction should not, however, be exaggerated. 'The natural skepticism of the Italian people, their

tendency to disregard directives of any kind, the sense of remoteness and detachment and often of defiance with which, especially in Southern Italy, the priest is looked upon, contributed to mitigate the consequences of the orders of the Church.' M. Einaudi and F. Goguel *Christian Democracy In Italy and France* Indiana: University of Notre Dame Press (1952) p. 4. It was, however, only in 1919, when the *non expedit* was revoked (pushed by Vatican fears about the growth of Socialism), that a Catholic party could be formed. This was the *Partito Populare,* headed by Sturzo, a Sicilian priest. It performed brilliantly in the 1919 elections, winning over a hundred seats and making it the second-largest party in Italy, the Socialist party being the first. The party was suppressed by the Fascists in 1926, to reappear during the resistance and in the postwar period under its new name of the Christian Democrat party.

5.   For an analysis of Christian Democrat voters (and indeed voters for the other major Italian political parties) see J. La Palombara *Interest Groups in Italian Politics* Princeton: Princeton University Press (1964) pp. 93–6.

6.   Italian Catholic Action (ACI) is a Catholic pressure group with a membership of around three and a half million, cutting across all classes. It is the lay arm of the Church in Italy and, at least until recently, has exercised considerable political influence. For a discussion of ACI and other Italian pressure groups see La Palombara, op. cit.

7.   For a discussion of *fazionismo* in the Socialist party on a local scale see S. Barnes *Party Democracy: Politics in an Italian Socialist Federation* New Haven, Conn.: Yale University Press (1967).

8.   Germino and Passigli, op. cit., p. 106.

9.   E. Wiskemann *Italy Since 1945* London: Macmillan (1971) p. 4.

10.   The policies of the Labour Democrats differed little from the major parties. The alliance with the Liberals was strange considering that it was moderately left-wing and this move 'alienated the working class elements within the party, many of whom withdrew from it'. M. Grindrod *The New Italy* London: Royal Institute of Economic Affairs (1947) p. 39. It died soon after the 1946 elections, its members going into either the Liberal or Republican party.

11.   J. Adams and P. Barile *The Government of Republican Italy* London: Allen & Unwin (1961) p. 156.

12.   Wiskemann, op. cit., p. 4.

13.   ibid., p. 13.

14.   La Palombara, op. cit., p. 96.

15.   Wiskemann, op. cit., p. 6.

16.   G. Mammarella *Italy after Fascism: A Political History 1943–65* Indiana: University of Notre Dame Press, p. 147.

17.   See ibid., p. 192.

18.   See J. Meynaud *Rapporto sulla Classe Dirigente Italiano* Milan: Giuffrè (1966) pp. 128–30 and p. 194.

19.   Einaudi and Goguel, op. cit., p. 54.

20.   Mammarella, op. cit., p. 286.

21.   ibid., p. 286.

22.   Grindrod, op. cit., p. 113.

23.   Einaudi and Goguel, op. cit., p. 57.

24.   Germino and Passigli, op. cit., p. 16. By the late nineteenth century it had agreed to evolution in the short run and revolution in the long run. 'Thus peaceful reforms were to hasten the day of the violent revolution! ' ibid., p. 17.

25.   Mammarella, op. cit., p. 214.

26.   ibid., pp. 242–3.

27.   ibid., p. 261.

28.   ibid., p. 307.

29.   The influence of the Catholic Church in Italy should never be underrated. In the early 1960s, about 50 per cent of Italians went to Mass every week (Meynaud, op. cit., p. 121). The Church has substantial influence on voting patterns, a power it has not hesitated to use. Its interference in Italian politics originated in the

Church's distaste for Italian unification, when it lost much of its property and temporal influence. State and Church remained very much at loggerheads, in spite of the withdrawal of the Papal *non expedit* in 1919, until the Lateran Pacts of 1929 were signed with 'the long-awaited "man sent by providence" (the words are those of Pius XI) . . . who was more than willing "to trample on the putrid carcass of democracy" (the words are those of Benito Mussolini)'. The Pacts, among other things, returned to the Church much of its influence and power. However, the Vatican was not long in recognising its errors, and by the early 1930s 'the Church gradually discovered that between her own moral and political and social doctrine and the doctrines of Fascism there was a substantial incompatability' (Einaudi and Goguel, op. cit., p. 25). It then played a useful role in combating Fascism, though retaining a strong anti-Communist stance. In the postwar period the Church continued to meddle in Italian politics until Pope John came to power, and even early in his reign it was urging that 'every Catholic must follow the political directive of the Church'. These directives were largely in favour of the Christian Democrats, and certainly against the left-wing parties. Even with the changed policy of John, and his view in early 1962 of the left that 'they are all my children, let them be' (Meynaud, op. cit., p. 132), individual Catholic leaders still held strongly to their centre and right-wing views. The Archbishop of Salerno, for example, on the defeat of Fanfani's centre–left government sent a telegram to a member of Parliament: 'Congratulations. Failure of Fanfani's centre–left government is divine work. Italy safe. Rome still holy. I bless you.' The Church continues to dominate the centre–right of the Christian Democrats and, through ACI, exercises a considerable influence on Italian political life. All unallocated quotes from Adams and Barile, op. cit., pp. 225–9.

30. Mammarella, op. cit., p. 321.
31. La Palombara, op. cit., p. 98.
32. For an analysis of political ignorance in Italy relative to other countries, see ibid., pp. 101–2.
33. C. Seton-Watson *Italy from Liberalism to Fascism: 1870–1925* London: Methuen (1967) p. 712.
34. Wiskemann, op. cit., p. 69.
35. ibid, p. 59.
36. This was not the first plan for a *coup d'état* in Italy. Another, and more serious, had been planned in July 1964.

A Postscript

THIS book was largely completed towards the end of 1973, and at that time very few 'hard' data for that year were available. Consequently, the book gives only limited coverage to events in 1973 and 1974. Since early 1973, however, there have been a number of dramatic developments in the Italian economy, of which the impact of the Middle East oil crisis was only one. These developments can be summarised in terms of two basic trends – an accelerating rate of inflation and a rapidly deteriorating balance of payments. The combination and worsening of these connected trends gave rise to problems which, in June 1974, some observers felt to be a prelude to the economic and political collapse of the country. It is the purpose of this brief postscript to outline the main economic events in Italy since 1973, and to assess their possible significance for the future.

Throughout 1973 as a whole, the Italian economy had suffered a marked deterioration in the balance of payments and a considerable acceleration of inflation. Provisional balance of payments figures show an overall deficit of 4907 million dollars, which compounded a current account deficit of 2517 million dollars, and a net capital outflow of 2390 million dollars. Within these figures, the most alarming trend was in respect of visible trade which leapt from a tiny surplus of 2 million dollars in 1972, to a deficit of 3950 million dollars in 1973. (The usual offsetting items of invisibles and unilateral transfers remained in steady surplus, to the tune of 1433 million dollars compared with 1448 million dollars in 1972.) The deterioration in respect of inflation was equally dramatic. Whereas domestic prices rose by a manageable 6 per cent in 1972, this rate had almost doubled, to 10.5 per cent, in the course of 1973.

To some extent, these problems can be seen as an inevitable by-product of another major feature of the Italian economy at this time – a rapid growth of real incomes. The long-awaited recovery from the post-1970 depression arrived at last in 1973. GNP rose in real terms at a creditable 6.0 per cent, a figure reminiscent of the 'miracle' years and well above the 1.6 per cent and 3.1 per cent recorded in 1971 and 1972 respectively. Industrial production increased by 8.7 per cent, and gross investment rose from 20 to 23 per cent of GNP. However, this recovery was secured only after three years of solidly expansionary monetary policy, and its late arrival is evidence of the extreme difficulties faced by a government

285

whose only instrument of reflation is monetary policy – a point discussed in chapter 5. Moreover, the monetary base pumped into the economy in the course of 1972 and 1973 undoubtedly played some part in the aggravation of Italy's inflationary and balance of payments problems. The trade-off between domestically generated recovery and internal and external monetary stability began to emerge clearly in the course of 1973, and was to become the central issue in the political crisis of June 1974, as we shall see.

Monetary policy, then, was broadly expansionary throughout 1973, but particularly in the first nine months. In the year up to September 1973 the supply of monetary base increased by 17 per cent. The main source of this increase was the Treasury deficit, which amounted to 3400 billion lire by September 1973. However, towards the end of 1973, although the general direction was still expansionary, measures were being introduced in recognition of the deteriorating balance of payments and prices situation. In September 1973, the Bank of Italy raised its re-discount rate from 4.0 to 6.5 per cent. Selective quantitative controls of the banks' lending operations had already been introduced. Also, in an attempt to protect the bond market and therefore keep long-term interest rates low, the authorities introduced a new rule whereby the banks were to invest around 4000 milliard lire in bonds (as against 3000 milliard lire freely purchased in 1972). In short, the authorities were now attempting to maintain growth, while taking measures to protect the balance of payments on capital account through the raising of short-term interest rates.

However, it would be an over-simplification to attribute Italy's balance of payments and inflationary problems in 1973 solely to an over-zealous expansionary monetary policy or the revival of the economy. There were other more vital factors at work, over which the Italian authorities had much less control.

The increased rate of inflation which Italy suffered in 1973, was, to a great extent, imported. We have laid great stress throughout this book on Italy's dependence on foreign supplies of food and raw materials. Given this, the dramatic increase in certain key world prices (excluding oil at this time) resulted in a deterioration of Italy's terms of trade – falling from 97.3 in December 1972 to 83.2 in December 1973. Besides the implications for the balance of payments, which we discuss below, this led directly to a substantial increase in the domestic cost of living. Moreover, such imported inflation had potent effects on wages, largely through the 'escalator' clauses in Italian wage agreements. In the twelve months up to October 1973 industrial wages rose by 26.4 per cent. One should quickly add that this increase was not solely 'escalator induced'. It was also partly a consequence of the wage agreements concluded in 1972–73 which, though less inflationary than was anticipated at the time, nevertheless increased real wages by 14.6 per cent over the same period.

The government's initial response to these inflationary trends came in mid-1973, with the introduction of direct price controls (see chapter 5). The early effectiveness of these controls was reflected in a halving of the average monthly rise in the cost of living in the third quarter of 1973 (to 0.5 per cent). There were signs, however, that these controls were breaking down by the end of the year, when inflation regained its earlier pace of one per cent per month.

Parallel with these inflationary problems, the balance of payments was running into progressively greater deficit and, like the inflation, this is only partially explicable in terms of domestic growth. Certainly the most serious aspects of the balance of payments deficit lay in visible trade, and particularly in an expansion of imports (over 40 per cent in 1973); but it has been estimated that only one-third of the growth of the import bill in 1973 was attributable to an increase in the volume of imports,[1] (which would reflect increased domestic demand whether due to domestic inflation or income growth). The remainder of this spectacular import leap was due to price increases; partly attributable to changes in the terms of trade mentioned earlier, and partly to the downward float of the lira, especially in July 1973. More serious balance of payments problems were avoided by the fact that exports continued to grow rapidly – by over 20 per cent in 1973. However, the problems in respect of visible trade were compounded by large-scale speculation – showing itself not only on capital account, but also on current account. There is little doubt that the poor current account performance in 1973 was in part a consequence of speculation in respect of tourist 'expenditures' abroad and the exploitation of leads and lags by importers and exporters. This latter form of speculation was in spite of the fact that the authorities had, very early in 1973, introduced a system whereby the time limit for import payments was cut from 90 to 30 days, and that for exports from 360 to 90 days.

The 1973 balance of payments deficit was financed largely by borrowing on the Eurodollar market by the special credit institutes and the state holding sector, with the result that by December 1973 Italy's gold and foreign exchange reserves had not been significantly reduced.

Thus, by the end of 1973, Italy's economic fortunes were, at best, mixed. The domestic economy had recovered from its long slump and was growing at an impressive rate. Inflation was, however, serious, and both this and the balance of payments were giving cause for concern. Nevertheless, the situation in 1973 had none of the features of desperation which were to characterise 1974 – a condition which was closely linked to the Middle East oil crisis.

Although the temporary cut in Middle East oil supplies in late 1973 had a dramatic initial impact on Italy, the more significant development for the long-run was the subsequent four-fold increase in the price of oil. Although this is a burden which will be borne by all the oil importing countries, it hit Italy particularly hard. Some 85 per cent of Italian energy requirements are met by oil imports, and 87 per cent of these come from the Middle East and North Africa. The impact of the oil price increase was felt both on domestic prices and on the balance of payments. Although it is difficult to establish a date at which the oil price increases began to 'bite', it is certainly the case that in the early months of 1974 inflation accelerated to over 2 per cent a month, while the trade gap widened to a massive 1290 million dollars in the month of April. Apart from measures to conserve fuel supplies, the government was slow to respond to this heightened crisis. It was not until Spring 1974 that the government began to tighten monetary controls, and to take strong measures to protect the balance of payments. In the latter context, April 1974 saw a dramatic departure from the almost religious commitment to free trade which had characterised Italy's postwar development. The government introduced a 50 per cent import deposit scheme whereby importers were obliged to 'invest' 50 per cent of their foreign exchange requirements in a special non-interest bearing account at the Bank of Italy. This measure was as notable for its political impact on the EEC as for its economic implications. In addition, tourists were allowed to take abroad no more than 20,000 lire in banknotes. The other side of Italy's new economic policy in 1974 concerned monetary deflation. The government placed a ceiling on the 1974 Treasury deficit; the re-discount rate was raised again, to 9.0 per cent; bank lending was restricted to an 8 per cent increase between March and September 1974 (and to a ceiling of 15 per cent by March 1975); long-term interest rates were allowed to move up a little more freely. The combination of these measures amounted to a considerable monetary squeeze.

However, by June 1974, the economic crisis was precipitating a political crisis. The Bank of Italy was arguing that monetary stringency was the only course open to Italy, if simply to increase Italy's international credit worthiness at a time when a huge international borrowing operation would have to be mounted to salvage the now critical balance of payments position. The government was divided on this issue and the Socialists in particular were arguing that the recently regained employment growth should not be sacrificed in the interests of the balance of payments – a view most certainly shared by the unions. This split brought down the centre–left coalition which had been set up under Rumor some 2 months earlier, and the country was plunged into what was somewhat extravagantly claimed by some observers to be Italy's most serious political crisis since the war.

The political crisis, at least, was alleviated by the agreement among the finance ministers of the countries collectively known as the 'Group of Ten', that countries in balance of payments difficulties be allowed to back foreign loans with gold valued at the free market price, as opposed to the lower central bankers' price – the former being some 250 per cent higher than the latter. Since a substantial proportion of Italy's reserves were held in gold, this move greatly improved Italy's credit position and made the 'tiding-over' of Italy's immediate balance of payments problem much more manageable. At the same time, it took the heat out of the political crisis, allowing Rumor to stay in office and the coalition to be revived – the Socialists probably being pacified by a promise of less stern deflationary measures, a promise doubtless made possible by the stronger balance of payments situation subsequent to the gold arrangement.

What are the long-term implications of the developments of 1973–74? It seems likely that movements in the terms of trade in the future will continue to be against Italy, and to this extent further strain will be put on her visible trade balance. Coupled with the continuing volatile nature of capital account, this does not augur at all well for the balance of payments as a whole. Moreover, the evidence from a year of floating suggests that the lags involved in using devaluation as an adjustment mechanism are too long for short-run comfort. This leads to the rather pessimistic conclusion that deflationary monetary policy, with all its attendant evils for the Italian economy (see chapter 5), is the best available alternative. As a result, we must regard the growth performance of 1973 to be something less than the beginning of a new 'miracle'.

Rapid inflation, balance of payments difficulties, and slow growth are a dangerous combination, particularly for a country like Italy where, as we have seen in Chapter I, increased social investment is so badly needed – investment which is unlikely to be carried out in a deflated, stagnant economy. Although the potential for long-run growth remains, the latest Italian crisis has pushed these long-term prospects further into the future; and in the short run one can only hope that the painful adjustment which the economy is about to make will lead to nothing worse than periodic changes of government.

Notes to the postscript

1. See Banca Nazionale del Lavoro *Italian Trends* Vol. XV, n. 6 (June, 1974).

Name Index

Adams, J., 45
Allen, K., 141, 142, 215, 264
Amato, G., 45, 264, 265
Ammassari, G., 142
Andreotti, G., 279, 280

Baffi, P., 101, 174, 175
Bain, J., 24, 45
Balloni, V., 173, 174
Barile, P., 45
Barnes, S., 282
Beckerman, W., 71
Beneduce, A., 220
Benzoni, A., 214
Bianchi, G., 141
Bognetti, G., 153, 173, 174
Busca, A., 46, 47, 141

Cafiero, S., 46, 47, 141, 214, 216
Campa, G., 174
Carrà, A., 214
Cavour, C., 269
Chandler, J., 141
Clough, S., 43, 102
Colombo, E., 278, 281

D'Aragona, G., 46
De Falco, V., 46, 215
De Gasperi, A., 208, 209, 240, 270, 271, 273
De Meo, G., 141, 214
Denison, E., 57, 70, 107, 141
De Rosa, L., 43, 44
Despicht, N., 264, 265
Di Magliano, R., 141
Dugo, A., 141

Eckhaus, R., 70, 214
Einaudi, M., 43, 282
Ercolani, P., 3, 9, 43

Faleschini, L., 264, 265
Fanfani, A., 274, 275, 280, 283
Fazio, A., 174
Finoia, M., 44, 46
Flanders, A., 141
Foa, B., 174
Forte, J., 45

Fuà, G., 3, 9, 43, 174

Germino, D., 281, 282
Gerschenkron, A., 4, 43
Giannini, G., 209
Giólitti, G., 240
Giordani, F., 220
Guidi, M., 264, 265
Goguel, F., 43, 282
Gorrieri, G., 45, 46, 126, 142, 143, 144
Graziani, A., 67, 68, 69, 71, 174, 175
Grindrod, M., 214, 281, 282
Gronchi, G., 274
Gross, R., 102, 143
Giugni, G., 143, 144
Guidi, E., 47

Hansen, B., 173, 174
Hildebrand, G., 174
Hirschmann, A., 174
Holland, S., 264
Horowitz, D., 43

Johnson, C., 265
Jossa, B., 214
Jucker, N., 265

Kaldor, N., 71
Keating, M., 102
Kendall, W., 266
Kindleberger, C., 52, 53, 54, 55, 56, 57, 64, 67, 68, 70, 71
Kojanec, G., 264, 265
Krushchev, N., 276

La Malfa, G., 173, 175
La Malfa, U., 38, 103, 141, 239, 265
Lamfalussy, A., 71
La Palombara, J., 45, 143, 215, 264, 265, 282, 283
Leamer, E., 102
Leone, G., 277, 279
Lever, W., 216
Lewis, W., 52, 53, 54, 55, 56, 57, 69
Littlewood, P., 267
Lo Faso, S., 155, 173
Logli, P., 44
Lutz, F., 78, 101, 174, 175

An Introduction to the Italian Economy

Lutz, V., 54, 55, 56, 57, 63, 67, 70, 71, 101, 126, 127, 131, 142, 143, 174, 175, 264

Mackay, D., 214
MacLennan, M., 215
Mammarella, G., 44, 215, 282, 283
Martinelli, U., 141
Marzano, C., 173
Masera, F., 102, 175
Matassi, L., 43
Mattei, E., 233, 234, 240
Menichella, D., 174, 175, 220
Mesalles, V., 103
Meynaud, J., 45, 214, 282, 283
Milne, A., 1
Miurin, P., 102
Modigliani F., 103, 175
Morcaldo, G., 155, 173
Mussolini, B., 220, 268, 270
Myers, R., 141

Napoletano, D., 143
Negro, N., 43
Nenni, P., 270, 276

Parri, F., 268
Parrillo, E., 142
Pasca di Magliano, R.,
Passigli, S., 281, 282
Pellicciari, G., 214
Petrilli, G., 265
Pietranera, G., 102
Pilloton, F., 215
Pontolillo, V., 160, 174
Posner, M., 264, 265
Predetti, A., 142
Preti, L., 44, 46, 47
Prinzi, D., 44

Roccas, M., 102
Rodano, C., 214

Romani, F., 174
Romeo, R., 264
Rosenstein-Rodan, P., 70
Ross, A., 114, 141
Ruffolo, G., 44, 45, 47, 174, 265
Rumor, M., 277, 278, 281, 287, 288

Salviuolo, G., 46
Santore, I., 216
Saraceno, P., 214, 216, 220, 263, 264, 265
Saragat, G., 270, 277, 279
Schonfield, A., 264
Semprini, M., 45
Servidio, A., 44, 215, 264
Seton-Watson, C., 43, 283
Simpson, E., 174
Stern, R., 61, 83, 84, 102

Tagliacarne, G., 214
Tamagna, F., 174, 175
Tambroni, F., 274
Togliatti, P., 272
Tosco, E., 205
Tremelloni, R., 43
Turner, H., 142
Turone, S., 143, 144

Ventriglia, F., 45, 46
Vicarelli, F., 103
Vinci, S., 141
Visentini, B., 265

Welk, W., 43,
Wilson, T., 70, 141
Wiskemann, E., 43, 216, 282, 283
Woolf, S., 264, 265

Zacchia, C., 102
Zagari, E., 143, 144
Zappulli, C., 216
Zoli, A., 273, 274

Subject Index

Absenteeism: in industry, 116; in schools, 11, 20–1.
ACI, 268, 282n., 283n.
Action party, 268, 269.
Activity rates: causes, 112–3; in South, 12, 34, 178, 179–80, 183, 207; international comparison, 29, 112; postwar trends, 112–3.
AGIP, 217, 231, 232, 233, 235, 245; see also ENI.
Agricultural Guidance and Guarantee Fund, 17.
Agriculture: and Fascism, 6, 7; effects of tariff war, 2; employment, 14–5, 30, 56, 111–2, 105–8; immediate postwar conditions, 9; impact of EEC, 17, 31; imports, 87; in South, 12, 17, 34, 176, 177, 186–7, 209, 210; marginal workers, 15, 106–7; output growth, 13, 51, 57; performance during take-off, 3, 4; policy, 17, 31; postwar product switching, 16, 17; pre-take-off conditions, 2, 3; productivity, 11, 13, 15, 16, 31, 117; size of farm, 15, 16, 30, 31, 46n.; strikes, 114; structural change, 15, 16; wartime destruction, 8; wartime performance, 9; see also Land reform.
Aid: to Italy in immediate postwar period, 10, 75–8; to underdeveloped countries, 14, 44n.
Airlines: under IRI, 217, 224–5, 230, 237, 260.
Alfa Romeo, 217, 224.
Alfasud, 227, 243, 247, 261.
Alitalia, see Airlines.
ANAS, 225.
ANIC, 231, 232, 233, 235, 236, 245; see also ENI.
ASAP, 241, 257.
ASST, 226; see also Telephones.
ATES, 256.
Autarky, see Fascism.
ATI, 225; see also Airlines.
Autostrada del Sole, 217.
Autostrade, see Motorways.

Balance of payments: chapter 3; capital account, 14, 40, 61–2, 64, 69, 76–7, 93–8, 99–101, 102–3n.; contribution to growth, 14, 17, 40, 99; current account, 14, 40, 69, 75, 76–7, 78–93; early postwar developments, 72–8; prospects, 40–1, 92–3, 101, 288; under Fascism, 6; 1973 developments, 284, 286; see also: Export led growth; Exports; Gold and foreign exchange reserves; Imports; Invisible.
Banche di credito ordinario, 158.
Banche di interesse nazionale, 158.
Banche popolari cooperative, 158.
Banks: and bond market, 162–3; Banking Act 1936, 158; control of foreign business, 167, 169, 170; during take-off, 2, 3; effects of First World War, 4; interwar developments, 158, 219–20; lending policies, 159, 170; ownership, 159; reserve requirements, 163–6; structure, 158–9; see also IRI.
"Battle of Births", 6.
"Battle for Grain", 6, 177.
Banknote remittances, see Smuggling banknotes.
Birth rate: 190; postwar, 29; under Fascism, 6.

Calabria tax, see Tax system.
Capital account on balance of payments, see Balance of payments.
Capital markets: bonds, 162–3, 266n.; inadequacies, 18–19, 161–3, 172, 237, 245, 249, 258, 266n.; short term, 163; weakness of equity markets, 161–2, 249, 266n.; see also Banks; Special credit institutes; State holding sector.
Cars: ownership, 28.
Cascade-tax, see tax system.
Cassa per il Mezzogiorno, see Southern policy.
Casse di credito di prima categoria, 158.
Casse rurali e artigiani, 158.
Centre-left governments, 146, 228, 276–80, 283n.
Centre-right governments, 280–1, 271–2.
CGIL, 132, 134, 136, 272.
Chemical industry: conditions in early 1950's, 11; during First World War,

4–5; earnings, 120; exports, 60, 61, 80; output, 60, 61; postwar developments, 16; productivity, 188, 251.

Christian Democrat party: 268, 269, 270, 271, 273, 274, 276; and electricity industry, 228–9, 275; and state holding sector, 238, 240; and trade unions, 133; attitude to regional devolution, 26, 275; business ties, 25; interwar activities, 5–7; origins, 281–2n.; range of views, 23, 268; support of Church, 268, 270–1.

Church, Roman Catholic: and Fascism, 282–3n.; and state, 281–2n.; 282–3n.; attitude to Christian Democrat party, 268, 270–1; attitude to right wing, 136, 275, 276, 277, 282; influence, 282–3n.; plea for political unity, 276; *see also* ACI.

Cinecittà, 217.

CIP, 146.

CIPE, 45n., 201, 202, 215n., 236, 238, 242, 256.

CIR, 239.

CIS, 160.

CISL, 133, 134, 138, 139, 143n.

CISNAL, 133.

Civil service and public administration: difficulties of reform, 23, 263; employment, 105–8; inadequacies, 21–3, 24, 38, 45n., 70, 152, 216n.; privileges, 142n.; regional differences, 27.

Clothing and footwear: exports, 60, 80; output, 60; productivity, 60, 188.

Coal, 8, 18.

Collective bargaining, *see* Industrial relations.

Common Market, *see* EEC.

Communist party: 268, 269, 270, 271, 278; and trade unions, 132, 133, 272; immediate postwar attitudes, 272; relations to Socialist party, 26, 268–9, 270, 271, 274, 275; support of USSR, 270.

Confindustria: attitude to trade unions, 134, 139; withdrawal of state holding sector, 240–1.

Constant market share analysis, 61, 83–4, 102n.

Construction industry: employment, 31–2, 56, 105, 108; in South, 187; size of firm, 31–2, 131.

Consumption: distortion of, 21n.; postwar growth, 31, 58.

Cost of living, *see* Inflation

Cottage industry workers, *see* Outworkers.

Court of Accounts, 22.

CREDIOP, 175n.

Current account on balance of payments, *see* Balance of payments.

Death rates, 29, 190.

Delegati, *see* Factory committees.

Demand management techniques, *see* Monetary policy and fiscal policy.

Democratic Labour party, 268, 269, 282n.

Dualism: 39, 42, 46n.; and export led growth, 66–8; changing legal framework, 127–9; extent, 130–1; Graziani thesis, 67–8; Kindleberger thesis, 52–7, 67; labour market, 126–31, 142n.; Lewis model, 52–7; Lutz thesis, 54–7, 67; role of unions, 40, 54–6, 63; *see also*: Industry, size of firm; Outworkers; South.

Ducati, 217.

EAGAT, 217, 241.

Earnings: 119–21; relative to productivity, 124–5; relative to UK, 119–21.

ECA tax, *see* Tax system.

Economic growth: chapter 2; advantage of low technological base, 18; and dualism, 52–7, 67–8; capital market constraints, 18–19, 161–3; contribution of indigenous fuel, 18; demand management constraints, 19–20, 41–2, 69–70, 156–7, 171–3, 262; education and training constraints, 20–1; failure to absorb labour supply, 29–30, 68; false, 65; favourable postwar factors, 17–18; immediate postwar performance, 9; international comparisons, 49–50; political and administrative constraints, 21–5, 157, 171; postwar overview, 13–17, 50–2, 56–7, 61–2, 64, 69; pre-First World War, 1–4; prospects, 39–42, 68–70; role of balance of payments, 14, 17–18, 40, 99; role of investment, 37, 40, 58–9, 64–5; role of labour switching, 14–15, 17, 53–4, 68, 107; social constraints, 35–6; stability, 49–50, 64; the period 1950–63, 52–64, 168; the period 1964–72, 64–70; 1973 recovery, 284; *see also* Export led growth.

Education: schools, 11, 20–1, 25, 36–8; universities, 21, 25; *see also* Industrial training.

EEC: and IVA, 150, 151; and state holding sector, 248; as a source of emigrants' remittances, 92, 112; effects on agriculture, 17; effects on balance of payments, 14; effects on growth, 62–3; effects on exports, 81; effects on imports, 87, 102n.; monetary union, 40–1, 101; share of labour force in

agriculture, 30; size of farm, 30, 31, 46n.; social security contributions, 124.
Efibanca, 160.
EFIM, 215n., 217, 241, 256, 264n.
EFTA: import growth, 102n.; share of Italian exports, 81.
EGAM, 217, 264n.
Electricity industry: under IRI, 221, 222, 224, 226, 228–9, 230, 264n.; *see also* Nationalisation.
Electronics: under IRI, 224.
Emigrants' remittances: postwar trends, 76, 77, 90–2.
Emigration: abroad, 29, 111–2, 182; inter-regional, 34, 108, 178, 180–2, 183–4, 207; limits on, 128.
Employment: agriculture, 11, 12, 14–15, 30, 56, 105–8; by size of firm, 130–1; contribution of switching to growth, 14–15, 17, 53–4, 68, 107; industry, 12, 14, 15, 31–2, 56, 105–8, 130; national plan targets, 30; outworkers, 33, 128, 129, 130, 143n.; services, 105–8; South, 12, 34, 176, 185, 190–4, 209; state holding sector, 217–8, 230, 235; trends, 30, 105–8; *see also* Marginal workers.
Endowment fund, *see* State holding sector.
ENEL, *see* Electricity industry.
Engineering industry: earnings, 120; exports, 60, 61, 80; heterogeneity, 61; output, 60, 61; productivity, 60, 81, 188, 251; under IRI, 221, 223–4, 227, 244, 252; *see also* Southern policy; Alfasud.
ENI: and sick firms, 234; and South, 235; as a vertically integrated concern, 235–6; efficiency and profitability, 252–5; employment, 235; importance, 218, 235–6; investment, 233–5; main activities, 217–8, 231, 236–7; organisation and control, 234, 236–44; origins, 231–3; postwar developments, 232–5; sources of finance, 244, 245; war damage, 232; *see also* State holding sector.
ENM, 232, 233; *see also* ENI.
Equity finance, *see* Capital markets.
Ergo Omnes, 128, 129.
ESPI, 215n.
European Economic Community, *see* EEC.
European Payments Union, 74.
Evasion: and tax reform, 151; earnings declarations, 120; social security, 128, 129–30, 143n.; tax, 44n.; 149–50; wage payments, 128, 143n.
Exchange rates: and monetary union,

40–1, 69; caution in use of, 121; early postwar stabilisation policy, 73–4; floating, 101, 147, 288; note, xii; 1949 adjustments, 102n.
Export-led growth, 40, 59–63.
Exports (visible): and dualism, 67–8, 69; commodity composition, 79–80; competitiveness, 14, 61, 63, 66–7, 68, 74, 81–5; geographic distribution, 81; guarantee facilities, 85; immediate postwar, 9; performance at and before take-off, 3; postwar trends, 13, 51, 58, 63–4, 66, 76, 79–86, 99–101; prospects, 101; role of state, 84–5, 150; share in GDP growth, 59–60; under Fascism, 5; wartime, 9; *see also* Export led growth; individual industries.

Factory committees, 137, 138, 139–41.
Family allowances, 36, 122, 142n.
Fascism: and IRI, 220–1, 222; and land reform, 7; and trade unions, 6, 132; early political developments, 5; effects on economy, 5–8; effects on South, 6–7, 177; *see also* Second World War.
FEOGA, *see* Agricultural Guidance and Guarantee Fund.
FIAT, 96, 140, 261.
Fifty per cent rule, 73.
FIL, 133.
FIM, 174n.
FINAM, 215n.
Fincantieri, 221; *see also* Shipbuilding.
Finelettrica, 221; *see also* Electricity industry.
Finniare, 221; *see also* Shipping.
Finmeccanica, 221; *see also* Engineering.
Finsider, 221; *see also* Iron and steel industry.
First World War: effects on the economy, 4–5.
Fiscal policy: and tax reforms, 151; in the 1950's, 156; in the 1960's, 156–7; in the 1970's, 157; political constraints, 25, 157; shortcomings, 19, 20, 41–2, 147–57, 173; *see also* Social security.
Food consumption: an international comparison, 28.
Food, drink and tobacco industry: earnings, 120; exports, 60, 80; output, 60; productivity, 80.
Foreign exchange reserves, *see* Gold and foreign exchange reserves.
Foreign ownership, *see* industry.
Freight and insurance: in balance of payments, 76–7, 88.

GATT, 85.

GEPI, 203, 204, 228, 256.
GESCAL, 46–7n.
Gold and foreign exchange reserves: 14, 286, 288; postwar accumulation, 75–8, 98, 99.
Government expenditure, *see* Public expenditure.
Gross Domestic Product, *see* Economic growth; Standard of living.
Gross National Product *see* Economic growth; Standard of living.

Health system, 36, 38, 122, 123.
Hot autumn, 100, 114, 136–8, 171.
Housing: conditions in early 1950's, 11–12; inadequacies, 36, 38, 46–7n.; South, 12; uninhabited, 46n.

IASM, 206, 211, 215n.
IGE, *see* Tax system.
Illiteracy: 11, 12; in South, 12, 184, 226, 260, *see also* Dualism.
IMI, 158, 174n., 203, 204, 220, 256.
Immobilismo, 26, 277.
Imports (visible): commodity composition, 86–7; dependence upon, 67, 73, 86, 287; deposit scheme, 287; financed by aid, 10; geographic distribution, 87; immediate postwar 9; performance at and before take-off, 3; postwar trends, 64, 76, 86–7, 99–101, 286; prospects, 101; under fascism, 6; wartime, 9; *see also* Tariffs
Imposta complementare progressiva sul reddito, *see* Tax system.
Imposta esauriale sui redditi delle persone fisiche, *see* Tax system.
Imposta esauriale sui redditi delle persone giuridiche, *see* Tax system.
Imposta di famiglia, *see* Tax system.
Imposta generale sull'entrata (IGE), *see* Tax system.
Imposta locale sui redditi, *see* Tax system.
Imposta sulle società, *see* Tax system.
Imposta sull'incremento di valore degli immobili, *see* Tax system.
Imposta sul reddito dei fabbricati, *see* Tax system.
Imposta sul valore aggiunto (IVA), *see* Tax system.
Imposta sui redditi di richezza mobile, *see* Tax system.
Imposta sui terreni, *see* Tax system.
INA, 231.
INAM, 122; *see also* Health system.
Incompatabilità, *see* Trade unions.
Industrial relations and collective bargaining: and state holding sector, 18, 135, 240–1, 256–7; articulated bargaining, 135; developments, 39–40, 68–9, 131–41; plant bargaining, 129, 133, 134–41; *see also*: Factory committees; Hot autumn; Prices and incomes policy; Strikes; Trade unions; Workers' charter; Workers' council.
Industrial training, 18, 21, 256.
Industry: absenteeism, 116; concentration, 24; conditions in early 1950's, 11, 15–16; effects of German banking system, 3; employment, 11, 12, 14–15, 30, 31, 32, 56; foreign ownership, 44n., 229–30; interwar performance, 6, 7; mergers, 24; postwar output growth, 13, 51, 57, 60, 284; pre-take-off conditions and performance, 2, 3; productivity, 13, 15, 30, 57, 60, 65, 117; size of firm, 11, 12, 31–2, 131, 189, 262; South, 12, 34, 76, 177, 187–9, 209; sources of finance, 161–2; strikes, 114; take-off, 3, 4; wartime destruction, 8, 221–2, 232; wartime performance, 4–5, 9; *see also* Dualism; individual industries; Manufacturing; South; State holding sector.
Infant mortality, 184; in early 1950's, 11.
Inflation: after First World War, 5; after Second World War, 9, 74, 164–5; during Second World War, 7, 9; postwar, 57, 63; policy in immediate postwar period, 74, 164–5; 1973 developments, 284, 286.
Infrasud, 225; *see also* Motorways.
INPS, 122, 123.
INSUD, 215n.
Intersind, 241, 256.
Inter-related industry complex, *see* Southern policy.
Investment: abroad, 93–6; effects of tax reform, 171–2; fictitious foreign, 96–8; importance of self-finance, 14, 39–40, 65–6, 246–7, 265n.; lack of social investment, 35–9, 42, 108, 288; postwar, 13–14, 19–20, 30, 51, 52, 58, 64–5, 70n., 284; role in dualism, 67–8; role in excess labour supply theories, 55, 58, 62; state holding sector, 218, 223, 224, 227, 230, 233–5, 258–9.
Invisibles: freight and insurance, 76–7, 88; income from capital, 76–7, 88; postwar performance, 14, 76–7, 87–93; prospects, 92–3, 101; tourism, 76–7, 78, 88, 89–91, 102, 103n.; transport, 76–7, 88; *see also* Emigrants' remittances.
IRFIS, 160.
IRI: and the banks, 158, 159, 219–20, 237, 246; and the South, 225, 226,

226–7, 228; compensation for public administration inadequacies, 38; defence against foreign ownership, 229–30; effects of war, 221–2; efficiency and profitability, 222, 252–5; employment, 224, 230; immediate postwar problems, 221–4; importance, 217–8, 221, 230–1; investment, 223, 224, 227, 230; main activities, 217–8; organisation and control, 220–1, 222, 223, 236–44; origins, 219–21; rescueing of sick firms, 227–8; sources of finance, 244, 245; technological change, 230; *see also* Airlines; Electricity; Electronics; Engineering; Iron and Steel; Motorways; Shipbuilding; Shipping; State holding sector; Telephones; Television.

Iron and steel industry: condition in early 1950's, 11; exports, 60, 61, 80; output, 60, 61; postwar developments, 16; postwar shortages, 9; productivity, 60, 61, 188, 251; protection and subsidies before take-off, 2, 4; under IRI, 221, 222, 227, 230, 242, 244, 247, 252, 258.

Istituti di credito di diritto pubblico, 158.

ISVEIMER, 160.

Italstat, 225; *see also* Motorways.

IVA, *see* Tax system.

Labour costs: relation to productivity, 124–6; relation to value added, 125; trends, 65–6, 67; *see also* earnings; social security; wages.

Labour units: definition, xii.

LAI, 225; *see also* Airlines.

Land reform and reclamation: failure after First World War, 5; postwar, 16, 17, 197, 210, 216n.; under Fascism, 7.

LCGIL, 133.

Leather, furs, etc: exports, 60, 80; output 60; productivity, 60, 188.

Liberal party: 268, 271, 273, 275, 276, 282n.; and state holding, 222; business ties, 25, 273; political position, 269.

Manufacturing: conditions in early 1950's, 11; earnings, 119–20; employment, 12, 31–2, 105–8; exports, 60, 80; imports, 86–7; marginal workers, 106–7; postwar output and productivity growth, 13, 60, 251; pre-First World War, 3; size of firm, 11, 12, 32, 56, 130–1, 189; South, 12, 187–9; war performance and recovery, 9; *see also* Dualism; individual industries.

Mansholt plan, 31.

Marginal workers: definition, xii; movement out of agriculture, 15, 106–7; trends, 106–7, 191, 192, 193, 194.

Marshall plan, 10, 78, 221, 272.

Maternity allowances, 122.

Mediobanca, 160.

Mediocredito, 160.

Meridionalismo, 35–6, 195.

Metalworkers, 135, 136, 139, 257.

Military expenditure in Italy, 88.

Milliard: definition, xii.

Minculpop, 7.

Monarchist party, 269, 274.

Monetary policy: bank rate, 167, 285, 287; banks' reserve requirements, 163–6; composition and control of monetary base, 165–8, 285; control of foreign borrowing, 167, 169, 170; immediate postwar period, 8, 164–5, 168, 175n.; operation of, 69, 168–72, 285, 287; shortcomings, 19–20, 41–2, 70, 171–2; the 1950's, 168; the 1960's, 169–71.

Monopoly and restrictive practices, 18; policies, 24–5, 257, 262, 263.

Motorways: postwar, 37; under Fascism, 7; under IRI, 224, 225–6, 230, 258, 260, 262, 263.

Montecatini Edison, 96, 229, 238, 257.

MSI, 269, 271, 274, 275, 278, 280.

Nationalisation, 219; of electricity, 99, 171, 219, 228–9, 234, 275.

National plans: 1966–70, 22, 30, 38, 146, 200; 1971–75, 38, 242.

Non-metallic mineral industry: exports, 60, 61, 80; output, 60, 61;·productivity, 60, 61, 188.

Oil and natural gas, 18, 231–6, 251; impact of Middle East crisis, 268–8; *see also* ENI.

Outworkers, 33, 128, 129, 130, 143n.

Overtime: limitations, 120.

"Pact of Rome", 132.

Paper industry: exports, 60, 80; output, 60; productivity, 60, 188.

Partito Popolare, *see* Christian Democrat party.

PCI, *see* Communist party.

Pensions, 36, 122, 123, 140.

Plant bargaining, 129, 133, 134–41.

Political developments: coup d'état, 278, 283n.; effects on postwar economic development, 23–5, 38, 157, 171, 267; inability to make reforms, 267–83; interwar, 5–7, 268; postwar, 267–83;

war and immediate postwar, 10, 267–70; *see also* individual political parties.

Population: postwar trends, 29; present, definition of, xii; resident, definition of, xii; in South, 178, 190–1; trends before First World War, 3; under Fascism, 6–7.

Pressure groups, 24–5, 268, 282n., 283n.

Prices, *see* Inflation.

Prices and incomes policies, 145–6, 286.

Productivity: agriculture, 11, 13, 15, 16, 31, 117; industry, 13, 15, 30, 57, 60, 65, 117; relation to labour costs, 124–6; relation to wages and earnings, 14, 57, 63, 65, 68, 118–9, 124–6, 143n.; South, 12, 17, 34, 186–9, 209–10; state holding sector, 251–2; *see also* individual industries.

Profits: in state holding sector, 252–5, 262–3; trends, 65–6, 67, 68.

PSDI, *see* Social Democrat party.

PSI, *see* Socialist party.

PSIUP, 276, 279.

PSLI, *see* Social Democrat party.

PSU, 277.

Public administration, *see* Civil service.

Public expenditure: and the South, 203; as growth stimulus, 63, 70; composition, 152–3; in fiscal policy, 152–6; postwar growth, 51, 152–3; relation to GNP, 152; the budget, 152–4; time profiles, 155; under Fascism, 6; wartime, 7; *see also* Residui passivi.

Quotas, *see* Tariffs.

RAI, *see* Television.

Railways: pre-take-off development, 2, 4; wartime destruction, 8.

Redundancy pay, 122–8.

Regional devolution, 25–7, 275–6.

Republicans, 269, 270, 271, 273, 275, 281; political position, 269; and trade unions, 133.

Residui attivi, 154.

Residui passivi, 22; causes, 154–6; definition, 154; extent of problem, 154; long run implications, 156.

Retail and wholesale trades, 32; problems of reform, 24.

Rocco law, 273.

ROMSA, 231, 232, 233; *see also* ENI.

Rubber industry: exports, 60, 80; output, 60; productivity, 60, 188.

Second World War: destruction during, 7–8, 232; economic conditions during, 7; effects on South, 8, 177; lack of preparedness for, 7; political developments, 267–8.

Self-finance, *see* Investment.

Services: employment trends, 105–8; postwar output growth, 51; strikes, 114; underemployment, 111.

SET, 226; *see also* Telephones

SFIRS, 215n.

Shift and share analysis, 188.

Shipbuilding: postwar developments, 16; productivity, 251; protection and subsidies of before take-off, 2; under IRI, 221, 223–4, 228, 230, 244, 247.

Shipping: under IRI, 221, 222; wartime destruction, 8.

SIP, 226; *see also* Electricity Telephones.

SAIPEM, 235, 236; *see also* ENI.

SME, 228, 229–30.

Smuggling of banknotes: 88, 89, 96–8, 102–3n.; policy against, 97–8, 102–3n.

SNAM, 231, 232, 233, 235, 236, 245; *see also* ENI.

Social Democrats: 270, 271, 278; and socialists, 270, 273, 274, 275, 277; and trade unions, 100; political position, 278.

Socialist party: 268, 269, 270, 276, 287, 288; and Social Democrats, 270, 273, 274, 275, 277; break-up of PSIUP, 276; relation to Communists, 268–9, 270, 271, 274, 275; role in regional devolution, 25.

Social security: and strikes, 115; benefits, 121–3; contributions and finance, 20, 65, 121, 123–6, 148; coverage, 123, 125, 128, 142n.; fiscalisation, 126, 157, 174n.; in countercyclical policy, 20, 157; in regional development, 203–4; treatment of self-employed, 46n.; *see also* Evasion; Family allowances; Health system; Maternity allowances; Pensions; unemployment pay.

SOFID, 236; *see also* ENI.

Southern policy: agriculture, 195, 197, 200, 210; between 1950 and 1957, 196–8; controls on northern development, 202–3; factors in creation of Cassa, 196–7; finance companies, 203, 215n.; funds, 196, 199–200, 201, 204, 210; growth areas, 198–9, 200; incentives for industry, 198, 200, 201–2, 203–4, 210, 211, 215n.; industry, 195, 197, 198–207, 210–11; infrastructure, 195, 196, 197, 210; inter-related industry complex, 204–7; post-1957, 198–207; pre-1950, 194–6; results, 34–5, 207–9, 213; shortcomings, 210–1, 213; state holding sector, 18, 30, 199, 211–2, 225–6, 226–7, 235, 259–61, 262, 264n; *see also* South.

South: activity rates, 12, 34, 178, 179–80, 183, 207; agriculture, 12, 17, 34, 176, 177, 185, 186–7, 191, 192, 193, 194, 209, 210, 216n.; and Fascism, 6–7, 177; area, 177–8; causes of the problem, 185–94; early history, 2, 176–7; economic structure, 185, 187, 209; employment, 12, 34, 176, 185, 190–4, 209; housing, 12; illiteracy, 12, 184, 226, 260; in early 1950's, 12; income per head, 178, 179, 180, 183, 207–9; industrial location requirements and experience, 216n.; industry, 12, 34, 176–7, 187–90, 191, 192, 193, 209; infant mortality, 184; marginal workers, 191, 192, 193, 194; migration, 34, 108, 178, 180–2, 183–4, 207; population, 178, 190–1; productivity, 12, 186–9; small firms, 189; standard of living, 12, 35, 179; underemployment, 12, 34, 186–7; unemployment, 12, 34, 178, 183, 186, 187, 207; war damage, 8, 177; *see also* Southern policy.

Special credit institutes: borrowing abroad, 100–1, 286; functions and activities, 159–61, 167; government intervention, 160–1, 175n.; interest subsidies and problems, 160–1, 162.

SPI, 215n.

Standard of living: at end of Second World War, 8; at start of 1950's, 11, 12; in South, 12, 35, 179; international comparison, 27–8.

State holding sector: and Confindustria, 240–1; and small firms, 262; areas of activity, 217–9; compensation for public administration inadequacies, 38, 258, 262, 263; compensation for poor capital markets, 18, 255, 258; countercyclical policy, 20, 258–9, 262, 263; efficiency and profitability, 250–5, 262–3; employment, 217–8, 230, 235, 260; endowment fund, 218, 234–5, 240, 243, 246, 247–8, 252–3, 262–3; importance, 217–9, 221, 230–1, 235–6; industrial relations, 18, 135, 241, 256–7; industrial training, 18, 21, 256; in key industries, 18, 255; in monopolies and restrictive practices, 18, 257, 262, 263; in regional development, 18, 30, 199, 211–2, 225–6, 228, 235, 259–61, 262, 263, 264n.; Ministry of state holdings, 218, 236, 238, 240–4, 265n.; organisation and control, 24, 43, 218–9, 220–1, 223, 236–44, 244–5; rescuing sick firms, 18, 227–8, 234, 255–6, 263; roles, 16, 238–9, 255–63; sources of finance, 244–9, 265n.; *see also* IRI; ENI.

STET, *see* Telephones.

Strikes: during take-off, 4; funds, 115; international comparison, 115–6; interwar, 5; postwar features and trends, 113–6, 134.

Svimez, 196.

Take-off, 1–4.

Tariffs and quotas: pre-take-off policy, 2; policy in postwar period, 14, 62–3, 74–5, 146–7; under Fascism, 6, 72–3.

Tax system: Calabria tax, 149; ECA tax, 149; evasion, 44n., 149–50; farming out, 149; general structure, 147–52; IGE, 84, 150, 171; imposta complementare progressiva sul reddito, 149; imposta di famiglia, 149; imposta esauriale sui redditi delle persone fisiche, 151; imposta esauriale sui redditi delle persone giuridiche, 151; imposta locale sui redditi, 151; imposta sui redditi agrari, 148; imposta sui redditi di richezza mobile, 148–9; imposta sui terreni, 148; imposta sulle società, 149; imposta sull incremento di valore degli immobili, 151; imposta sul reddito dei fabbricati, 148; IVA, 84, 150, 151, 171; reforms, 20, 41–2, 150–2, 171–2; regional finance, 26, 27; witholding tax, 96–7, 99, 149; *see also* Fiscal policy.

Telephones: ownership, 28; under IRI, 221, 222, 226, 230, 244, 258.

Television: ownership, 28; under IRI, 217, 224, 226, 260, 264n.

Terms of trade, 75, 101, 285, 288.

TETI, 226; *see also* Telephones.

Textiles: earnings, 120; exports, 60, 75, 80; output, 60; productivity, 60, 188, 251; protection and subsidies before take-off, 2; under ENI, 234; under IRI, 228, 234, 264n.

Theories of economic growth: Denison thesis, 57; export-led growth, 59–63; Graziani thesis, 67–8; Kindleberger thesis, 52–7, 67; Lewis model, 52–7; Lutz thesis, 54–7, 67.

Tourism: Italian holidays, 89, 102n.; policies for, 92; speculation, 286; *see also* Invisibles.

Trade unions: and dualism, 40, 54–6, 68, 126n., 142n.; and inflation, 63, 65, 68; and political parties, 132, 133, 134, 139, 272; attitudes of Confindustria, 134, 139; early developments, 132; effects of agricultural exodus, 15; effects on investment, 14, 39–40; interest in social reform, 37, 140n.,

144n.; membership, 129, 140–1; moves towards unity, 136, 138–9; under Fascism, 6, 132; weaknesses in 1950's, 134, *see also* Industrial relations.

Transport: in balance of payments, 76–7; low investment, 38; postwar quality, 37; pre-take-off development, 2, 4; under Fascism, 7; wartime destruction, 8.

UIL, 133, 138, 139.

Underemployment: definition, 110; in agriculture, 11; in South, 12, 34, 178, 183, 186–7; postwar trends, 56, 110–1.

Unemployment: discouraged unemployed, 110; immediately after First World War, 5; in early 1950's, 11; in South, 12, 34, 178, 183, 207; pay, 36, 122–3; postwar trends, 14, 56, 109–10; registration system, 128, 142–3n.; sources of data, 109–10.

Unification: economic conditions at, 29.

Unity of Action Pact, 268–9.

Universities, *see* Education.

Uomo Qualunque party, 269, 271.

Urbanisation: problems, 35–6, 39, 41, 42, 108, 184, 213; trends, 37, 107–8, 182.

Value-added tax, *see* Tax system.

Vehicle industry: conditions in early 1950's, 11; earnings, 120; exports, 60, 61, 80; output, 60, 61; postwar developments, 16; productivity, 60, 61, 188.

Wages: agriculture, 46n., 117–9; and trade unions, 118–9; drift, 119, 125; *ergo omnes*, 128, 129; industry, 65, 117–9; outworkers, 33; relation to productivity, 14, 57, 63, 65, 68, 118–9, 143n.; 1973 developments, 285–6; *see also* Earnings, individual industries.

War, *see* First World War and Second World War.

Withholding tax on dividends, *see* Tax system.

Wood and furniture industry: exports, 60, 80; output, 60; productivity, 60, 188.

Workers' Charter, 137–8.

Workers' earnings abroad, *see* Emigrants' remittances.

Works councils, 133–4, 135.